Srimad Bhagavad Gita

Om Books International

Reprinted in 2026

Om Books International

Corporate & Editorial Office
A-12, Sector 64, Noida 201 301
Uttar Pradesh, India
Phone: +91 120 477 4100
Email: editorial@ombooks.com
Website: www.ombooksinternational.com

Sales Office
107, Ansari Road, Darya Ganj
New Delhi 110 002, India
Phone: +91 11 4000 9000
Email: sales@ombooks.com

ISBN: 978-81-19750-60-3

Printed in India

10 9 8 7 6 5 4 3 2

Contents

An Introduction to Srimad Bhagavad Gita

The Bhagavad Gita is the dialogue between Lord Krishna and Arjuna on the eve of the battle of Kurukshetra between the Pandavas and the Kauravas when Arjuna is reluctant to fight his near and dear ones and Lord Krishna urges him to fight in this holy war as it is his duty to do so.

The Bhagavad Gita is the sacred book of the Hindus which has passed on its wisdom from generation to generation, initially orally and then, through numerous texts that have been translated into several languages across the world. However, the value of the Bhagavad Gita is not measured by the language in which it has been translated, but in the wisdom of its content.

Bhagavad means 'blessed' and Gita means 'song'. Thus, the Bhagavad Gita means 'The Song of the Blessed One'. The Bhagavad Gita is also described as The Song of the Blessed Lord, in a reference to Lord Krishna, an incarnation of Lord Vishnu on earth and of the Highest Divinity. The Bhagavad Gita is considered a 'smriti', a text which is remembered, in Hindu tradition and culture more than a 'shruti', a text that is revealed. Because the Bhagavad Gita is a part of the great Indian epic, the Mahabharata, it also finds a place in the smriti texts. That is where the Bhagavad Gita differs from the Vedas and the Upanishads as it is not so authoritative and that is where its beauty and universal acceptance lies. However, the Bhagavad Gita is also called the Gitopanishad and the Yogopanishad which also bestows upon it the status of an Upanishad. Also, as the Bhagavad Gita is considered one of the Upanishads, it has also been granted the status of a shruti. The Bhagavad Gita is also known as the Upanishad of the Upanishads. The analogy of the wise and the learned in Indian scriptures is that the Upanishads are the symbolic cow while Lord Krishna is the cowherd who milks the cow in the presence of the third Pandava, Arjuna, who is represented as the calf. The milk that nourishes the calf is the Bhagavad Gita!

The Bhagavad Gita is also called a mokshashastra or the scripture of liberation as it covers the science of the Absolute or the Supreme One and teaches us the way to attain Him. The Bhagavad Gita is a book of rare excellence which is a must-read for all individuals for them to apply the principles and wisdom into their daily lives. One of the most respected and admired Hindu scriptures, the Bhagavad Gita was written in Sanskrit, its 700 verses continuing to inspire great personalities globally with its unparalleled wisdom. The scripture is more of a way of life than just a religious text, having been translated into more than 80 languages and is a constant in religious and philosophical discussions around the world. It is said that anyone who studies the Gita with discipline and good intent is on the right path to reach God. Lord Krishna Himself tells Arjuna that with the devoted study of the scriptures, a person "has worshipped and loved Me with the Yoga of Knowledge."

The very objective of this simplified English translation is that the spiritual light that is the Bhagavad Gita can reach the world at large so that people can benefit from its wisdom. It is rightly said- 'Vasudhaiva Kutumbakam' (The world is my family).

"The Bhagavad Gita is for anyone who wants to succeed, approach any given situation with level-headedness and skill, and find the sparkle within oneself."

— Sri Sri Ravi Shankar

"When I read the Bhagavad Gita and reflect about how God created this universe, everything else seems so superfluous."

— Albert Einstein

CHAPTER 1

ARJUNA VISHAD YOGA

(THE DESPONDENCY OF ARJUNA)

CHAPTER 1

ARJUNA VISHAD YOGA (THE DESPONDENCY OF ARJUNA)

There is little philosophy on offer in Chapter One, but it gives us precious insight into human personality. Srimad Bhagavad Gita is relayed to us by Sanjaya who is the commentator of the Gita with the blind king Dhritarashtra as the audience in the palace of Hastinapur, a distance of approximately 120 km from the battlefield of Kurukshetra. Sanjaya was blessed with divine vision by Veda Vyasa, and narrates the events of the battlefield to Dhritarashtra.

The two armies of the Pandavas and the Kauravas are arrayed on the battlefield in strategic military formations to face each other in battle. The blind king Dhritarashtra, father of the hundred Kauravas and uncle of the Pandavas, asks Sanjaya to describe the scenes of the battlefield to him. Arjuna, the greatest archer of the Pandava army, with Lord Krishna as his charioteer, experiences a crisis just before the commencement of the battle. When he sees his family members, teachers, and friends on the opposite side of his army and he realises that he has to kill them in battle, Arjuna's resolve breaks and he feels dejected when he imagines the consequences of this Great War as well as the sins to be incurred by killing one's loved ones.

Overwhelmed by grief and pity, Arjuna's strength and resolve deserts him and he is bewildered. After presenting several moral and noble reasons to Lord Krishna about why he does not wish to fight, Arjuna lays down his bow and sits down on his chariot. This reluctance to fight his kith and kin indicates Arjuna's kindness and purity of heart. Hence, he is the perfect one to receive the transcendental knowledge from Lord Krishna in the form of the Bhagavad Gita.

1

धृतराष्ट्र उवाच
धर्मक्षेत्रे कुरुक्षेत्रे
समवेता युयुत्सवः।
मामकाः पाण्डवाश्चैव
किमकुर्वत संजय।।

dhṛtarāṣṭra uvāca
dharma-kṣetrekuru-kṣetre
samavetā yuyutsavaḥ
māmakāḥ pāṇḍavāścaiva
kimakurvata sañjaya||

dhṛtarāṣṭraḥ—King Dhṛtarāṣṭra; uvāca—said; dharma-kṣetre—in the place of pilgrimage; kuru-kṣetre—in the place named Kurukṣetra; samavetāḥ— assembled; yuyutsavaḥ—desiring to fight; māmakāḥ—my party (sons); pāṇḍavāḥ—the sons of Pāṇḍu; ca—and; eva-certainly; kim— what; akurvata— did they do; sañjaya—O Sañjaya.

Meaning: Dhritarashtra said: O Sanjaya, after gathering together in the holy land of law of Kurukshetra, what did my sons and the sons of Pandu do, who desired to fight each other?

2

संजय उवाच
दृष्ट्वा तु पाण्डवानीकं
व्यूढं दुर्योधनस्तदा।
आचार्यमुपसंगम्य
राजा वचनमब्रवीत्॥

sañjaya uvāca
dṛṣṭvā tu pāṇḍavānīkaṁ
vyūḍhaṁ duryodhanastadā
ācāryam upasaṅgamya
rājā vacanamabravīt||

sañjayaḥ—Sañjaya; uvāca—said; dṛṣṭvā—after seeing; tu—but; pāṇḍava-anīkam—the soldiers of the Pāṇḍavas; vyūḍham—arranged in military phalanx; duryodhanaḥ—King Duryodhana; tadā—at that time; ācāryam—theteacher; upasaṅgamya—approaching nearby; rājā—the king; vacanam—words; abravīt—spoke.

Meaning: Sanjaya said: When King Duryodhana saw the army of the sons of Pandu assembled in war formation, he approached Guru Dronacharya, and spoke these words.

3

पश्यैतां पाण्डुपुत्राणाम्
आचार्यमहतीं चमूम्।
व्यूढां द्रुपदपुत्रेण
तव शिष्येण धीमता ॥

paśyaitāṁ pāṇḍu-putrāṇām
ācāryamahatīṁcamūm
vyūḍhāṁ drupada-putreṇa
tava śiṣyeṇa dhīmatā ||

paśya—behold; etām—this; pāṇḍu-putrāṇām—of the sons of Pāṇḍu; ācārya—O teacher; mahatīm—great; camūm—military force; vyūḍhām—arranged; drupada-putreṇa—by the son of Drupada; tava—your; śiṣyeṇa—disciple; dhīmatā—very intelligent.

Meaning: O my Guru, O king, I can see this huge army of the sons of Pandu, so expertly arrayed for battle by that intelligent disciple of yours, the son of Drupada, Drishtadyumna.

4

अत्र शूरा महेष्वासा
भीमार्जुनसमा युधि।
युयुधानो विराटश्च
द्रुपदश्च महारथः॥

atra śūrā maheṣvāsā
bhīmārjuna-samā yudhi
yuyudhāno virāṭaśca
drupadaśca mahā-rathaḥ||

atra—here; śūrāḥ—heroes; maheṣvāsāḥ—mighty bowmen; bhīma-arjuna—Bhīma and Arjuna; samāḥ—equal; yudhi—in the fight; yuyudhānaḥ—Yuyudhāna; virāṭaḥ—Virāṭa; ca—also; drupadaḥ—Drupada; ca—also; mahārathaḥ—great fighter.

Meaning: Here in this army, are great heroes and archers who are equals of Bhima and Arjuna in warfare. They are Yuyudhana, Virata, and the great chariot warrior Drupada.

5

धृष्टकेतुश्चेकितानः
काशिराजश्च वीर्यवान् ।
पुरुजित्कुन्तिभोजश्च
शैब्यश्च नरपुङ्गवः॥

dhṛṣṭaketuś cekitānaḥ
kāśirājaś cavīryavān
purujitkuntibhojaśca
śaibyaśca nara-puṅgavaḥ||

dhṛṣṭaketuḥ—Dhṛṣṭaketu; cekitānaḥ—Cekitāna; kāśirājaḥ—Kaśirāja; ca—also; vīryavān—very powerful; purujit—Purujit; kuntibhojaḥ—Kuntibhoja; ca—and; śaibyaḥ—Śaibya; ca—and; nara-puṅgavaḥ—heroes in human society.

Meaning: There is Drishtaketu, Chekitana, the king of Kashi, Purujit, Kuntibhoja, and Shaivya who are all bulls among men.

6

युधामन्युश्च विक्रान्त
उत्तमौजाश्च वीर्यवान् ।
सौभद्रो द्रौपदेयाश्च
सर्व एव महारथाः॥

yudhāmanyuś ca vikrānta
uttamaujāśca vīryavān
saubhadro draupadeyāśca
sarva eva mahā-rathāḥ ||

yudhāmanyuḥ—Yudhāmanyu; ca—and; vikrāntaḥ—mighty; uttamaujāḥ—Uttamaujā; ca—and; vīryavān—very powerful; saubhadraḥ—the son of Subhadrā; draupadeyāḥ—the sons of Draupadī; ca—and; sarve—all; eva—certainly; mahā-rathāḥ—great chariot fighters.

Meaning: There are brave and bold warriors like Yudhyamanyu and Uttamaujas, Abhimanyu, son of Subhadra, and the five sons of Draupadi who are all Maharathis and great chariot warriors.

7

अस्माकं तु विशिष्टा ये
तान्निबोध द्विजोत्तम।
नायका मम सैन्यस्य
सञ्ज्ञार्थं तान्ब्रवीमि ते॥

asmākaṁ tu viśiṣṭā ye
tānnibodha dvijottama
nāyakā mama sainyasya
saṁjñārthaṁ tānbravīmi te||

asmākam—our; tu—but; viśiṣṭāḥ—especially powerful; ye—those; tān—them; nibodha—just take note, be informed; dvijottama—the best of the brāhmaṇas; nāyakāḥ—captains; mama—my; sainyasya—of the soldiers; saṁjñā-artham—for information; tān—them; bravīmi—I am speaking; te—your.

Meaning: O highest of the twice-born, best of the brahmanas, mark as well those distinguished warriors among us, who are the qualified leaders of my army. I describe them for your information.

8

भवान्भीष्मश्च कर्णश्च
कृपश्च समितिंजयः ।
अश्वत्थामा विकर्णश्च
सौमदत्तिस्तथैव च॥

bhavānbhīṣmaśca karṇaśca
kṛpaśca samitiñjayaḥ
aśvatthāmā vikarṇaśca
saumadattis tathaiva ca||

bhavān—yourself; bhīṣmaḥ—Grandfather Bhīṣma; ca—also; karṇaḥ—Karṇa;ca—and; kṛpaḥ—Kṛpa; ca—and; samitiñjayaḥ—always victorious in battle; aśvatthāmā—Aśvatthāmā; vikarṇaḥ—Vikarṇa; ca—as well as; saumadattiḥ—the son of Somadatta; tathā—and as; eva—certainly; ca—and.

Meaning: Personalities like you Dronacharya, Bhishma, Kripacharya, Ashwatthama, Vikarna, and Somadatta's son Jayadratha, who are undefeated in battle.

9

अन्ये च बहवः शूरा
मदर्थे त्यक्तजीविताः।
नानाशस्त्रप्रहरणाः
सर्वे युद्धविशारदाः॥

anyeca bahavaḥ śūrā-
mad-arthetyakta-jīvitāḥ
nānā-śastra-praharaṇāḥ-
sarveyuddha-viśāradāḥ ||

anye—many others; ca—also; bahavaḥ—in great numbers; śūrāḥ-heroes; mad-arthe-for my sake; tyakta-jīvitāḥ—prepared to risk life; nānā—many; śastra-weapons; praharaṇāḥ—equipped with; sarve—all of them; yuddha—battle; viśāradāḥ—experienced in military science.

Meaning: There are also many other heroes who are ready to lay down their lives for my sake. All of them are equipped with various destructive weapons, and are highly skilled and experienced in military science.

10

अपर्याप्तं तदस्माकं
बलं भीष्माभिरक्षितम्।
पर्याप्तं त्विदमेतेषां
बलं भीमाभिरक्षितम् ॥

aparyāptaṁ tad asmākaṁ
balaṁ bhīṣmābhirakṣitam
paryāptaṁ tvidam eteṣāṁ
balaṁ bhīmābhirakṣitam ||

aparyāptam—immeasurable; tat—that; asmākam—of ours; balam—strength; bhīṣma—by Grandfather Bhīṣma; abhirakṣitam—perfectly protected; paryāptam—limited; tu—but; idam—all these; eteṣām—of the Pāṇḍavas; balam—strength; bhīma—by Bhīma; abhirakṣitam—carefully protected.

Meaning: This great force of ours, commanded by Grandfather Bhishma is flawless and their force, protected by Bhima is no match for us.

11

अयनेषु च सर्वेषु
यथाभागमवस्थिताः ।
भीष्ममेवाभिरक्षन्तु
भवन्तः सर्व एव हि ॥

ayaneṣu ca sarveṣu
yathā-bhāgamavasthitāḥ
bhīṣmam evābhirakṣantu
bhavantaḥ sarva eva hi ||

ayaneṣu—in the strategic points; ca—also; sarveṣu—everywhere; yathābhāgam—as they are differently arranged; avasthitāḥ—situated; bhīṣmam—unto Grandfather Bhīṣma; eva—certainly; abhirakṣantu—support may be given; bhavantaḥ—all of you; sarve—respectively; eva- certainly; hi—and exactly.

Meaning: Hence, all of you must extend full support to Grandfather Bhishma, stationed in your respective divisions in the passage of the army, and protect Bhishma alone.

12

तस्य सञ्जनयन्हर्षं
कुरुवृद्धः पितामहः।
सिंहनादं विनद्योच्चैः
शंखं दध्मौ प्रतापवान् ॥

tasya sañjanayan harṣaṁ
kuru-vṛddhaḥ pitāmahaḥ
siṁha-nādaṁ vinadyoccaiḥ
śaṅkhaṁ dadhmau pratāpavān ||

tasya—his; sañjanayan—increasing; harṣam—cheerfulness; kuru- vṛddhaḥ —the grandsire of the Kuru dynasty (Bhīṣma); pitāmahaḥ—the grandfather; siṁha-nādam—roaring sound, like a lion; vinadya—vibrating; uccaiḥ—very loudly; śaṅkham—conchshell; dadhmau—blew; pratāpavān—the valiant.

Meaning: Then Bhishma, the eldest of the Kuru dynasty, the glorious grandsire, blew loudly on his conch-shell like the roar of a lion, giving Duryodhana great joy.

13

तत: शंखाश्च भेर्यश्च
पणवानकगोमुखा:।
सहसैवाभ्यहन्यन्त
स शब्दस्तुमुलोऽभवत् ॥

tataḥ śaṅkhāśca bheryaśca-
paṇavānaka-gomukhāḥ
sahasaivābhyahanyanta
sa śabdastumulo'bhavat ||

tataḥ—thereafter; śaṅkhāḥ—conchshells; ca—also; bheryaḥ—bugles; ca—and; paṇava-ānaka—trumpets and drums; go-mukhāḥ—horns; sahasā—all of a sudden; eva—certainly; abhyahanyanta—being simultaneously sounded; saḥ—that; śabdaḥ—combined sound; tumulaḥ—tumultuous; abhavat—became.

Meaning: This was followed by other conch-shells, bugles, trumpets, drums, and horns that blared suddenly. The combined sound was terrible to hear.

14

ततः श्वेतैर्हयैर्युक्ते
महति स्यन्दने स्थितौ।
माधवः पाण्डवश्चैव
दिव्यौ शंखौ प्रदध्मतुः ॥

tataḥ śvetair hayair yukte
mahati syandane sthitau
mādhavaḥ pāṇḍavaścaiva
divyau śaṅkhau pradadhmatuḥ||

tataḥ—thereafter; śvetaiḥ—by white; hayaiḥ—horses; yukte—being yoked with; mahati—in the great; syandane—chariot; sthitau—so situated; mādhavaḥ—Kṛṣṇa (the husband of the goddess of fortune); pāṇḍavaḥ—Arjuna(the son of Pāṇḍu); ca—also; eva—certainly; divyau—transcendental; śaṅkhau—conchshells; pradadhmatuḥ—sounded.

Meaning: On the other side of the battlefield, seated on their great chariot drawn by white horses, Lord Krishna and Arjuna blew their splendid divine conch-shells.

15

पाञ्चजन्यं हृषीकेशो
देवदत्तं धनंजयः।
पौण्ड्रं दध्मौ महाशंखं
भीमकर्मा वृकोदरः ॥

pāñcajanyaṁ hṛṣīkeśo
devadattaṁ dhanañjayah
pauṇḍraṁ dadhmau mahā-śaṅkhaṁ
bhīma-karmā vṛkodaraḥ||

pāñcajanyam—the conchshell named Pāñcajanya; hṛṣīkeśaḥ—Hṛṣīkeśa (Kṛṣṇa, the Lord who directs the senses of the devotees); devadattam—the conchshell named Devadatta; dhanañjayaḥ—Dhanañjaya (Arjuna, the winner of wealth); pauṇḍram—the conch named Pauṇḍram; dadhmau—blew; mahā-śaṅkham—the terrific conchshell; bhīma-karmā—one who performs Herculean tasks; vṛkodaraḥ—the voracious eater (Bhīma).

Meaning: Lord Krishna blew his conch-shell called the *Panchajanya*, and Arjuna blew the *Devadatta*. Bhima, the terrible and Herculean in action, blew his enormous conch, the *Paundra*.

16-18

अनन्तविजयं राजा
कुन्तीपुत्रो युधिष्ठिरः।
नकुलः सहदेवश्च
सुघोषमणिपुष्पकौ ॥
काश्यश्च परमेश्वासः
शिखण्डी च महारथः।
धृष्टद्युम्नो विराटश्च
सात्यकिश्चापराजितः ॥
द्रुपदो द्रौपदेयाश्च
सर्वशः पृथिवीपते।
सौभद्रश्च महाबाहुः
शंखान्दध्मुः पृथक्पृथक् ॥

anantavijayaṁ rājā
kuntī-putro yudhiṣṭhiraḥ
nakulaḥ sahadevaś ca
sughoṣa-maṇipuṣpakau ||
kāśyaś ca parameṣvāsaḥ
śikhaṇḍīca mahā-rathaḥ
dhṛṣṭadyumno virāṭaś ca
sātyakiścā parājitaḥ ||

drupado draupadeyāśca
sarvaśaḥ pṛthivī-pate
saubhadrascha amahā-bāhuḥ
śaṅkhāndadhmuḥ pṛthakpṛthak ||

anantavijayam—the conch named Anantavijaya; rājā—the king; kuntī- putraḥ—the son of Kuntī; yudhiṣṭhiraḥ—Yudhiṣṭhira; nakulaḥ—Nakula; sahadevaḥ—Sahadeva; ca—and; sughoṣa-maṇipuṣpakau—the conches named Sughoṣa and Maṇipuṣpaka; kāśyaḥ—the King of Kāśī (Vārāṇasī); ca—and; parameṣvāsaḥ—the great archer; śikhaṇḍī—Śikhaṇḍī; ca—also; mahā-rathaḥ—one who can fight alone against thousands; dhṛṣṭadyumnaḥ—Dhṛṣṭadyumna (the son of King Drupada); virāṭaḥ—Virāṭa (the prince who gave shelter to the Pāṇḍavas while they were in disguise); ca—also; sātyakiḥ—Sātyaki (the same as Yuyudhāna, the charioteer of Lord Kṛṣṇa); ca—and; aparājitaḥ—who were never vanquished before; drupadaḥ—Drupada, the King of Pāñcāla; draupadeyāḥ—the sons of Draupadī; ca— also; sarvaśaḥ— all; pṛthivī-pate—O King; saubhadraḥ—the son of Subhadrā (Abhimanyu); ca—also; mahā-bāhuḥ—greatly armed; śaṅkhān— conchshells; dadhmuḥ— blew; pṛthak pṛthak—each separately.

Meaning: King Yudhishthira, eldest son of Kunti, blew his conchshell, the *Anantavijaya*, and the youngest Pandavas, Nakula and Sahadeva blew the *Sughosha* and the *Manipushpaka* respectively.

The great archer, the King of Kashi, the great chariot-warrior Shikhandi, Dhrishtadyumna, Virata, the unvanquished Satyaki all blew their conches.

Drupada, the sons of Draupadi, and Subhadra's mighty-armed son Abhimanyu blew their respective conches from all sides of the battlefield, O King.

19

स घोषो धार्तराष्ट्राणां
हृदयानि व्यदारयत्।
नभश्च पृथिवीं चैव
तुमुलो व्यनुनादयन् ॥

aghoṣo dhārtarāṣṭrāṇāṁ
hṛdayāni vyadārayat
nabhaś ca pṛthivīṁ caiva
tumulo'bhyanunādayan||

saḥ—that; ghoṣaḥ—vibration; dhārtarāṣṭrāṇām—of the sons of Dhṛtarāṣṭra; hṛdayāni—hearts; vyadārayat—shattered; nabhaḥ—the sky; ca—also; pṛthivīm—the surface of the earth; ca—also; eva—certainly; tumulaḥ—uproarious; abhyanunādayan—by resounding.

Meaning: That tumultuous noise of all the conchshells reverberated through earth and sky, piercing the hearts of the sons of Dhritarashtra with fear.

20

अथ व्यवस्थितान्दृष्ट्वा
धार्तराष्ट्रान् कपिध्वजः।
प्रवृत्ते शस्त्रसम्पाते
धनुरुद्यम्य पाण्डवः ॥

atha vyavasthitāndṛṣṭvā
dhārtarāṣṭrān kapi-dhvajaḥ
pravṛtteśastra-sampāte
dhanurudyamya pāṇḍavaḥ ||

atha—thereupon; vyavasthitān—situated; dṛṣṭvā—looking on; dhārtarāṣṭrān—the sons of Dhṛtarāṣṭra; kapi-dhvajaḥ—one whose flag is marked with

Hanumān; pravṛtte—while about to be engaged; śastra- sampāte—the arrows released; dhanuḥ—bow; udyamya—after taking up; pāṇḍavaḥ—the son of Pāṇḍu(Arjuna);

Meaning: Thus, Arjuna, the son of Pandu who was seated on his chariot, his flag marked with the mighty Hanuman, picked up his bow as the battle was about to begin. Beholding the army of the Kauravas, O King, Arjuna addressed Lord Krishna thus:

21-23

अर्जुन उवाच
हृषीकेशं तदा
वाक्यमिदमाह महीपते।
सेनयोरुभयोर्मध्ये
रथं स्थापय मेऽच्युत ॥
यावदेतान्निरीक्षेऽहं
योद्धुकामानवस्थितान्।
कैर्मया सह योद्धव्यमस्मिन्
रणसमुद्यमे ॥

योत्स्यमानानवेक्षेऽहं य
एतेऽत्र समागताः।
धार्तराष्ट्रस्य दुर्बुद्धेर्युद्धे
प्रियचिकीर्षव ॥

arjunauvāca
hṛṣīkeśaṁ tadā
vākyam idamāha mahī-pate
senayor ubhayor madhye
rathaṁ sthāpayame'cyuta||

yāvad etān nirīkṣe 'haṁ
yoddhu-kāmānavasthitān
kairmayā saha yoddhavyam
asminraṇa-samudyame||

yotsyamānānavekṣe'haṁ
ya ete'trasamāgatāḥ
dhārtarāṣṭrasya durbuddher
yuddhepriya-cikīrṣavaḥ||

arjunaḥ—Arjuna; uvāca—said; hṛṣīkeśam—unto Lord Kṛṣṇa; tadā—at that time; vākyam—words; idam—these; āha—said; mahī-pate—O King.

senayoḥ—of the armies; ubhayoḥ—of both the parties; madhye—in between them; ratham—the chariot; sthāpaya—please keep; me—my; acyuta—O infallible one; yāvat—as long as; etān—all these; nirīkṣe—may look; aham—I; yoddhu-kāmān—desiring to fight; avasthitān—arrayed on the battlefield; kaiḥ—with whom; mayā—by me; saha—with; yoddhavyam—to fight with; asmin—in this; raṇa—strife; samudyame—in the attempt.
yotsyamānān—those who will be fighting; avekṣe—let me see; aham—I; ye—who; ete—those; atra—here; samāgatāḥ—assembled; dhārtarāṣṭrasya—the son of Dhṛtarāṣṭra; durbuddheḥ—evil-minded; yuddhe—in the fight; priya—well; cikīrṣavaḥ—wishing.

Meaning: Arjuna said: O unfallen one, please draw my chariot between the two armies so that I may see all that are present here, eager to do battle with me before the beginning of this great war. Let me behold those who have assembled here to fight as the well-wishers of the evil-minded son of Dhritarashtra.

24

संजय उवाच
एवमुक्तो हृषीकेशो
गुडाकेशेन भारत।
सेनयोरुभयोर्मध्ये
स्थापयित्वा रथोत्तमम्॥

sañjaya uvāca
evamukto hṛṣīkeśo
guḍākeśena bhārata
senayo-rubhayor-madhye
sthāpayitvā rathottamam||

sañjayaḥ—Sañjaya; uvāca—said; evam—thus; uktaḥ—addressed; hṛṣīkeśaḥ—Lord Kṛṣṇa; guḍākeśena—by Arjuna; bhārata—O descendant of Bharata;senayoḥ—of armies;ubhayoḥ—of both; madhye—in the midst of; sthāpayitvā—by placing; rathottamam—the finest chariot.

Meaning: Sanjaya said: Thus addressed by Arjuna, O descendant of Bharata, Lord Krishna drew up the best of chariots in the midst of the two armies.

25

भीष्मद्रोणप्रमुखतः
सर्वेषां च महीक्षिताम्।
उवाच पार्थ पश्यैतान्
समवेतान् कुरूनिति।।

bhīṣma-droṇa-pramukhataḥ
sarveṣāṁca mahīkṣitām
uvāca pārtha paśyaitān
samavetān kurūniti ||

bhīṣma—Grandfather Bhīṣma; droṇa—the teacher Droṇa; pramukhataḥ—in the front of; sarveṣām—all; ca—also; mahīkṣitām—chiefs of the world; uvāca—said; pārtha—O Pārtha (son of Pṛthā); paśya—just behold; etān—all of them; samavetān—assembled; kurūn—all the members of the Kuru dynasty; iti—thus.

Meaning: Steering his grand chariot amid the two armies, before Bhishma, Drona, and all the rulers of earth, Lord Krishna said, O Partha, behold all the Kurus assembled here for battle.

26

तत्रापश्यत्स्थितान् पार्थः
पितृनथ पितामहान्।
आचार्यान्मातुलान्भ्रातृन्
पुत्रान्पौत्रान्सखींस्तथा
श्वशुरान् सुहृदश्चैव
सेनयोरुभयोरपि॥

tatrāpaśyatsthitānpārthaḥ
pitṝn atha pitāmahān
ācāryānmātulān bhrātṝn
putrān-pautrānsakhīṁstathā
śvaśurān suhṛdaś caiva
senayorubhayorapi ||

tatra—there; apaśyat—he could see; sthitān—standing; pārthaḥ—Arjuna; pitṝn—fathers; atha—also; pitāmahān—grandfathers; ācāryān— teachers; mātulān—maternal uncles; bhrātṝn—brothers; putrān—sons; pautrān—grandsons; sakhīn—friends; tathā—too; śvaśurān—fathers-in-law; suhṛdaḥ—well wishers; ca—also; eva—certainly; senayoḥ—of the armies; ubhayoḥ—of both parties; api—including.

Meaning: Then in both the armies, Arjuna saw stationed fathers and grandfathers, teachers, maternal uncles, brothers, sons, grandsons, comrades, fathers-in-law, and well-wishers.

27

तान्समीक्ष्य स कौन्तेयः
सर्वान् बन्धूनवस्थितान्
कृपया परयाविष्टो
विषीदन्निदमब्रवीत्।।

tān samīkṣya sa kaunteyaḥ
sarvānbandhūnavasthitān
kṛpayā parayāviṣṭo
viṣīdann idam abravīt||

tān—all of them; samīkṣya—after seeing; saḥ—he; kaunteyaḥ—the son of Kuntī; sarvān—all kinds of; bandhūn—relatives; avasthitān—situated; kṛpayā—by compassion; parayā—of a high grade; āviṣṭaḥ—overwhelmed by; viṣīdan—while lamenting; idam—thus; abravīt—spoke.

Meaning: When he saw all his friends and relatives waiting, Arjuna, the son of Kunti, was overwhelmed with pity and emotion, and spoke with despondency.

28-29

अर्जुन उवाच
दृष्ट्वेमं स्वजनं कृष्ण
युयुत्सुं समुपस्थितम्
सीदन्ति मम गात्राणि
मुखं च परिशुष्यति॥
वेपथुश्च शरीरे मे
रोमहर्षश्च जायते।
गाण्डीवं स्रंसते
हस्तात्त्वक्चैव परिदह्यते॥

arjunauvāca
dṛṣṭvemaṁ svajanaṁ kṛṣṇa
yuyutsuṁ samupasthitam
sīdanti mama gātrāṇi
mukhaṁ ca pariśuṣyati ||
vepathuś ca śarīre me
roma-harṣaścajāyate
gāṇḍīvaṁ sraṁsate
hastāt tvakcaiva paridahyate ||

arjunaḥ—Arjuna; uvāca—said; dṛṣṭvā—after seeing; imam—all these; svajanam—kinsmen; kṛṣṇa—O Kṛṣṇa; yuyutsum—all in fighting spirit; samupasthitam—all present; sīdanti—quivering; mama—my; gātrāṇi—limbs of the body; mukham—mouth; ca—also; pariśuṣyati—drying up; vepathuḥ—trembling of the body; ca—also; śarīre—on the body; me—my; roma-harṣaḥ—standing of hair on end; ca—also; jāyate—is taking place. gāṇḍīvam—the bow of Arjuna; sraṁsate—is slipping; hastāt—from the hands; tvak—skin; ca—also; eva—certainly; paridahyate—burning.

Meaning: Arjuna said: O Krishna, seeing my kinsmen and friends gathered here ready to fight, the limbs of my body fail to move, and my mouth is parched.

My entire body trembles, and my hair stands on end. My bow, the Gandiva slips from my hand, and my skin is enflamed all over.

30

न च शक्नोम्यवस्थातुं
भ्रमतीव च मे मनः
निमित्तानि च पश्यामि
विपरीतानि केशव ॥

na ca śaknomy avasthātuṁ
bhramatīva ca memanaḥ
nimittāni ca paśyāmi
viparītāni keśava ||

na—nor; ca—also; śaknomi—amIable; avasthātum—to stay; bhramati—forgetting; iva—as; ca—and; me—my; manaḥ—mind; nimittāni—causes; ca—also; paśyāmi—I foresee; viparītāni—just the opposite; keśava—O killer of the demon Keśī (Kṛṣṇa).

Meaning: I am not able to stand as my mind is like a whirlwind. O Keshava, I see only evil signs.

31

न च श्रेयोऽनुपश्यामि
हत्वा स्वजनमाहवे।
न काङ्क्षे विजयं कृष्ण
न च राज्यं सुखानि च॥

na ca śreyo 'nupaśyāmi
hatvā svajanamāhave
na kāṅkṣe vijayaṁ kṛṣṇa
na ca rājyaṁ sukhāni ca||

na—nor; ca—also; śreyaḥ—good; anupaśyāmi—do I foresee; hatvā—by killing; svajanam—own kinsmen; āhave—in the fight; na—nor; kāṅkṣe—do Idesire; vijayam—victory; kṛṣṇa—O Kṛṣṇa; na—nor; ca—also; rājyam—kingdom; sukhāni—happiness thereof; ca—also.

Meaning: I do not forsee any good coming after killing my own friends and relatives in battle, O Krishna; I desire neither victory in battle, nor kingdom, and nor worldly pleasures.

32-35

किं नो राज्येन
गोविंद किं भोगैर्जीवितेन वा
येषामर्थे काङ्क्षितं नो
राज्यं भोगाः सुखानि च।।
त इमेऽवस्थिता युद्धे
प्राणांस्त्यक्त्वा धनानि च
आचार्याः पितरः
पुत्रास्तथैव च पितामहाः।।
मातुलाः श्वशुराः पौत्राः
श्यालाः संबंधिनस्तथा
एतान्न हन्तुमिच्छामि
घ्नतोऽपि मधुसूदन।।
अपि त्रैलोक्यराज्यस्य
हेतोः किं नु महीकृते
निहत्य धार्तराष्ट्रान्नः
का प्रीतिः स्याज्जनार्दन।।

kiṁ no rājyena
govinda kiṁ bhogairjīvitena vā
yeṣām arthe kāṅkṣitaṁ no
rājyaṁ bhogāḥ sukhāni ca||

taime'vasthitā yuddhe
prāṇāṁstyaktvādhanānica
ācāryāḥ pitaraḥ
putrās tathaiva ca pitāmahāḥ ||

mātulāḥ śvaśurāḥ pautrāḥ
śyālāḥ sambandhinastathā
etān na hantum icchāmi
ghnato'pimadhusūdana ||

api trailokya-rājyasya
hetoḥkiṁnumahī-kṛte
nihatya dhārtarāṣṭrān naḥ
kā prītiḥ syāj-janārdana ||

kim—what use; naḥ—to us; rājyena—is the kingdom; govinda—OKṛṣṇa; kim—what; bhogaiḥ—enjoyment; jīvitena—by living; vā—either; yeṣām—for whom; arthe—for the matter of; kāṅkṣitam—desired; naḥ—our; rājyam—kingdom; bhogāḥ—material enjoyment; sukhāni—all happiness; ca—also; te—all of them; ime—these; avasthitāḥ—situated; yuddhe—in this battlefield; prāṇān—lives; tyaktvā—giving up; dhanāni—riches; ca—also; ācāryāḥ—teachers; pitaraḥ—fathers; putrāḥ—sons; tathā—as well as;

eva—certainly; ca—also; pitāmahāḥ—grandfathers; mātulāḥ—maternal uncles; śvaśurāḥ—fathers-in-law; pautrāḥ—grandsons; śyālāḥ—brothers-in-law; sambandhinaḥ—relatives;tathā—as well as; etān—all these; na—never; hantum—for killing; icchāmi—do I wish; ghnataḥ—being killed; api—even; madhusūdana—O killer of the demon Madhu (Kṛṣṇa); api—even if; trailokya—of the three worlds; rājyasya—of the kingdoms; hetoḥ—in exchange; kim—what to speak of; nu—only; mahī-kṛte—for the sake of earth; nihatya—by killing; dhārtarāṣṭrān—the sons of Dhṛtarāṣṭra; naḥ—our; kā—what; prītiḥ— pleasure; syāt—will there be; janārdana—O maintainer of all living entities.

Meaning: What use are kingdoms to us, O Govinda? What use is happiness or worldly pleasures? Or even life itself? The ones for whom we desire kingdoms, enjoyments, and pleasures, they stand in battle now, regardless of life or wealth- Gurus, teachers, fathers, sons, and grandfathers.

Maternal uncles, fathers-in-law, grandsons, brothers-in-law, and other relatives are all standing before me, O Madhusudana. I do not wish to kill them even though I might be killed instead or may survive. I shall not fight them even for the sake of ruling over all the three worlds. Why should I fight them then to gain the kingdom of Earth? What satisfaction would we derive by killing the sons of Dhritarashtra?

36

पापमेवाश्रयेदस्मान्
हत्वैतानाततायिनः
तस्मान्नार्हा वयं हन्तुं
धार्तराष्ट्रान्स्वबान्धवान्॥

pāpam evāśrayed asmān
hatvaitānātatāyinaḥ
tasmān nārhā vayaṁ hantuṁ
dhārtarāṣṭrānsv-abāndhavān ||

pāpam—vices; eva—certainly; āśrayet—must take upon; asmān—us; hatvā—by killing; etān—all these; ātatāyinaḥ—aggressors; tasmāt—therefore; na— never; arhāḥ—deserving; vayam—us; hantum—to kill; dhārtarāṣṭrān—the sons of Dhṛtarāṣṭra; svabāndhavān—along with friends.

Meaning: Sin will catch up with us if we kill these aggressors. Therefore, it is not right on our part to kill Dhritarashtra's sons and our friends and relatives. O Madhava, how can we hope to be happy after killing our own kinsmen?

37

यद्यप्येते न पश्यन्ति
लोभोपहतचेतसः।
कुलक्षयकृतं दोषं
मित्रद्रोहे च पातकम्॥

yadyapy ete na paśyanti-
lobhopahata-cetasaḥ
kula-kṣaya-kṛtaṁ doṣaṁ
mitra-drohe ca pātakam ||

yadi—if; api—certainly; ete—they; na—do not; paśyanti—see; lobha—greed; upahata—overpowered; cetasaḥ—the hearts; kula-kṣaya—in killing the family; kṛtam—done; doṣam—fault; mitra-drohe—quarreling with friends; ca—also; pātakam—sinful reactions;

Meaning: O Janardana, even though these men with minds overpowered by greed do not see the evil of killing one's own family members or the sin of causing harm to one's own friends.

38

कथं न ज्ञेयमस्माभिः
पापादस्मान्निवर्तितुम्।
कुलक्षयकृतं दोषं
प्रपश्यद्भिर्जनार्दन॥

kathaṁ na jñeyam asmābhiḥ
pāpād asmān nivartitum
kula-kṣaya-kṛtaṁ doṣaṁ
prapaśyadbhi rjanārdana||

katham—why; na—shall not; jñeyam—know this; asmābhiḥ—by us; pāpāt—from sins; asmāt—ourselves; nivartitum —to cease; kula-kṣaya—the destruction of a dynasty; kṛtam—by so doing; doṣam—crime; prapaśyadbhiḥ—by those who can see; janārdana—O Kṛṣṇa.

Meaning: Should not we, the ones who possess the knowledge of the sin of exterminating our race, avoid such sin, O Janardana?

39

कुलक्षये प्रणश्यन्ति
कुलधर्माः सनातनाः।
धर्मे नष्टे कुलं
कृत्स्नमधर्मोऽभिभवत्युत॥

kula-kṣayepraṇaśyanti
kula-dharmāḥ sanātanāḥ
dharme naṣṭe kulaṁ
kṛtsnam adharmo'bhibhavatyuta||

kula-kṣaye—in destroying the family; praṇaśyanti—becomes vanquished; kula-dharmāḥ—the family traditions; sanātanāḥ—eternal; dharme—inreligion; naṣṭe—being destroyed; kulam—family; kṛtsnam—wholesale; adharmaḥ —irreligious; abhibhavati—transforms; uta—it is said.

Meaning: With the decline of a race, its entire family tradition is wiped out and its ancient morality ends too. With the extinction of ancient morality, the remainder of the family becomes involved in immorality and irreligious practice.

40

अधर्माभिभवात्कृष्ण
प्रदुष्यन्ति कुलस्त्रियः।
स्त्रीषु दुष्टासु वार्ष्णेय
जायते वर्णसंकरः॥

adharm-ābhibhavāt kṛṣṇa
praduṣyanti kula-striyaḥ
strīṣu duṣṭāsu vārṣṇeya
jāyatevarṇa-saṅkaraḥ ||

adharma—irreligion; abhibhavāt—having been predominant; kṛṣṇa— O Kṛṣṇa; praduṣyanti—become polluted; kula-striyaḥ—family ladies; strīṣu— of the womanhood; duṣṭāsu—being so polluted; vārṣṇeya—O descendant of Vṛṣṇi; jāyate—it so becomes; varṇa-saṅkaraḥ—unwanted progeny.

Meaning: When immorality overcomes the family, O Krishna, the women of the family become corrupt. The whole race grows tainted because of the degradation of womanhood.

41

संकरो नरकायैव
कुलघ्नानां कुलस्य च।
पतन्ति पितरो ह्येषां
लुप्तपिण्डोदकक्रियाः॥

saṅkaro narakāyaiva
kula-ghnānāṁ kulasyaca
patanti pitaro hy eṣāṁ
lupta-piṇḍodaka-kriyāḥ||

saṅkaraḥ—such unwanted children; narakāya—for hellish life; eva—certainly; kula-ghnānām—of those who are killers of the family; kulasya—of the family; ca—also; patanti—fall down; pitaraḥ—forefathers; hi—certainly; eṣām—of them; lupta—stopped; piṇḍa—offerings; udaka—water; kriyāḥ— performance.

Meaning: This taint causes an increase of unwanted population and leads the racedestroyers and the entire race to hell. Family tradition is destroyed as no offerings of oblations of food and water are made to the ancestors in such corrupt families and the ancestors are doomed as a result.

42

दोषैरेतैः कुलघ्नानां वर्ण
संकरकारकैः।
उत्साद्यन्ते जातिधर्माः
कुलधर्माश्च शाश्वताः॥

doṣair etaiḥ kula-ghnānāṁvarṇa-
saṅkara-kārakaiḥ
utsādyante jāti-dharmāḥ
kula-dharmāśca śāśvatāḥ ||

doṣaiḥ—by such faults; etaiḥ—all these; kula-ghnānām—of the destroyer of a family; varṇa-saṅkara—unwanted children; kārakaiḥ—by the doers; utsādyante—causes devastation; jāti-dharmāḥ—community project; kula- dharmāḥ—family tradition; ca—also; śāśvatāḥ—eternal.

Meaning: The crimes of these destroyers of race destroy family traditions and the enduring morality of the race and the nation.

43

उत्सन्नकुलधर्माणां
मनुष्याणां जनार्दन।
नरकेऽनियतं वासो
भवतीत्यनुशुश्रुम ॥

utsanna-kula-dharmāṇāṁ-
manuṣyāṇāṁ janārdana
narake niyataṁ vāso
bhavatīty-anuśuśruma ||

utsanna—spoiled; kula-dharmāṇām—of those who have the family traditions; manuṣyāṇām—of such men; janārdana—O Kṛṣṇa; narake—in hell; niyatam—always; vāsaḥ—residence; bhavati—it so becomes; iti—thus; anuśuśruma—I have heard by disciplic succession.

Meaning: The men whose family morality has perished, O Janardana, find a permanent dwelling in their hellish abode. So we have heard.

44

अहो बत महत्पापं
कर्तुं व्यवसिता वयम्।
यद्राज्यसुखलोभेन
हन्तुं स्वजनमुद्यताः॥

aho bata mahat pāpaṁ
kartuṁ vyavasitā vayam
yad rājya-sukha-lobhena
hantuṁ svajanamudyatāḥ ||

ahaḥ—alas; bata—how strange it is; mahat—great; pāpam—sins; kartum—to perform; vyavasitāḥ—decided; vayam—we; yat—sothat; rājya—kingdom; sukha lobhena—driven by greed for royal happiness; hantum—to kill; svajanam—kinsmen; udyatāḥ—trying for.

Meaning: Alas! What a great sin we are resolved to commit when we are getting ready to kill our own kinsmen because of the greed of the pleasures of happiness and the desire for kingdoms.

45

यदि मामप्रतीकारमशस्त्रं
शस्त्रपाणयः।
धार्तराष्ट्रा रणे
हन्युस्तन्मे क्षेमतरं भवेत्॥

yadi mām apratīkāram aśastraṁ-
śastra-pāṇayaḥ
dhārtarāṣṭr āraṇe
hanyus tanme kṣemataraṁbhavet ||

yadi—even if; mām—unto me; apratīkāram—without being resistant; aśastram—without being fully equipped; śastra-pāṇayaḥ—those with weapons in hand; dhārtarāṣṭrāḥ—the sons of Dhṛtarāṣṭra; raṇe—in the battlefield; hanyuḥ—may kill; tat—that; me—mine; kṣemataram—better; bhavet— become.

Meaning: It would be better for me if I was slain by the sons of Dhritarashtra in battle, who are armed with their weapons, while I am unarmed and unresisting, instead of me having to fight with them.

46

संजय उवाच
एवमुक्त्वार्जुनः सङ्ख्ये
रथोपस्थ उपाविशत्।
विसृज्य सशरं चापं
शोकसंविग्नमानसः॥

sañjaya uvāca
evamuktvārjunaḥ saṅkhye
rathopastha upāviśat
visṛjyasa-śaraṁcāpaṁ
śoka-saṁvigna-mānasaḥ||

sañjayaḥ—Sañjaya; uvāca—said; evam—thus; uktvā—saying; arjunaḥ—Arjuna; saṅkhye—in the battlefield; ratha—chariot; upasthaḥ—situated on; upāviśat—sat down again; visṛjya—keeping aside; sa-śaram—along with arrows; cāpam—the bow; śoka—lamentation; saṁvigna—distressed; mānasaḥ—within the mind.

Meaning: Sanjaya said: Having thus spoken on the battlefield, Arjuna, casting aside his bow and arrow in a mind overwhelmed with grief, sat down on his chariot-seat.

ॐ तत्सदिति श्रीमद्भगवद्गीतासूपनिषत्सु ब्रह्मविद्यायां
योगशास्त्रे श्रीकृष्णार्जुनसंवादेऽर्जुनविषादयोगो नाम प्रथमोऽध्यायः।

Thus in the Upanishad of the Glorious Divine Lay, the Science of Brahma, the Ordinance of Yoga, the Discourse between the Glorious Lord Krishna and Arjuna, the First chapter titled 'Arjun Vishad Yoga' (The Despondency of Arjuna).

CHAPTER 2
SANKHYA YOGA
(THE YOGA OF KNOWLEDGE)

CHAPTER 2
SANKHYA YOGA
(THE YOGA OF KNOWLEDGE)

Chapter Two is considered to be the summary of the Bhagavad Gita. It mainly explains the immortal nature of the soul that resides in the bodies of all living beings, and has been described in extensive detail by Lord Krishna to Arjuna.

When Arjuna refuses to fight the Kaurava army, and presents his moral grounds to justify his action, Lord Krishna does not agree or sympathise with Arjuna's grief and despondency. Instead, he reminds Arjuna that it his duty as a kshatriya to fight for the sake of justice, and tells him to overcome his weakness and sense of delusion. Caught between the predicament of having to kill his own enemies and friends and following Krishna's orders that he should fight them in battle, Arjuna is confused and agitated. He asks Lord Krishna for his guidance, submits to him, and becomes his disciple.

Assuming the role of Arjuna's Spiritual Guru, Lord Krishna teaches him with his discourse that even though the body perishes after death, the soul can never be killed as it is eternal. So, he asks Arjuna not to lament as there is nothing to grieve about. When a kshatriya falls in battle while performing his duty, he attains the Heavens. Hence, Arjuna should be happy that the warriors he is about to kill on the battlefield will achieve births in superior stations in their next lives.

Lord Krishna rationalises Arjuna's decision not to fight because of his desire to enjoy life with his friends and relatives, sacrificing wisdom and sense of duty in the process. Lord Krishna explains the Eternal Reality of the Immortality of the Soul through selfless service to the Supreme One. He also reveals the characteristics of the self-realised one to Arjuna. Lord Krishna advises Arjuna to engage in Sankhya-Yoga, and perform action without forming an attachment to the results of those actions. He urges Arjuna to fight, as in doing so, he will be liberated from the cycle of birth and death to be aligned with the Supreme One by entering his abode.

1

संजय उवाच
तं तथा कृपयाविष्टमश्रु
पूर्णाकुलेक्षणम्।
विषीदन्तमिदं
वाक्यमुवाच मधुसूदनः॥

sañjaya uvāca
taṁ tathā kṛpayāviṣṭamaśru-
pūrṇākulekṣaṇam
viṣīdantam idaṁ
vākyam uvāca madhusūdanaḥ||

sañjayaḥuvāca—Sañjaya said; tam—unto Arjuna; tathā—thus; kṛpayā—by compassion; āviṣṭam—overwhelmed; aśru-pūrṇa—full of tears; ākula—depressed; īkṣaṇam—eyes; viṣīdantam—lamenting; idam—this; vākyam—words; uvāca—said; madhusūdanaḥ—the killer of Madhu.

Meaning: Sanjaya said: Seeing Arjuna overcome with pity and despondency, with eyes that were troubled and tearful, Madhusudana spoke the following words:

2

श्रीभगवानुवाच
कुतस्त्वा कश्मलमिदं
विषमे समुपस्थितम्।
अनार्यजुष्टमस्वर्ग्यम
कीर्तिकरमर्जुन।।

śrī-bhagavān uvāca
kutas tva kasmalam idam
viṣame samupasthitam
anārya-juṣṭam asvargyam
akīrti-karamarjuna||

śrī bhagavān uvāca—the Supreme Personality of Godhead said; kutaḥ—wherefrom; tvā—unto you; kaśmalam—dirtiness; idam—this lamentation; viṣame—this hour of crisis; samupasthitam—arrived; anārya—persons who do not know the value of life; juṣṭam—practised by; asvargyam—that which does not lead to higher planets; akīrti—infamy; karam—the cause of; arjuna—O Arjuna.

Meaning: The Glorious Lord said: O Arjuna, in this hour of crisis, how has this dejection come into you? This kind of behaviour is displayed only by non-Aryans, who are disreputable and for whom the doors of heaven are closed.

3

क्लैब्यं मा स्म गमः पार्थ
नैतत्त्वय्युपपद्यते।
क्षुद्रं हृदयदौर्बल्यं
त्यक्त्वोत्तिष्ठ परन्तप॥

klaibyaṁ mā sma gamaḥ pārtha
naitat tvayy upapadyate
kṣudraṁ hṛdaya-daurbalyaṁ
tyaktvottiṣṭha parantapa ||

klaibyam—impotence; mā—do not; sma—take it; gamaḥ—go in; pārtha—O son of Pṛthā; na—never; etat—like this; tvayi—unto you; upapadyate—is befitting; kṣudram—very little; hṛdaya—heart; daurbalyam—weakness; tyaktvā—giving up; uttiṣṭha—get up; parantapa—O chastiser of the enemies.

Meaning: O Partha, do not yield to impotence. That is not becoming of you. Stand up and abandon this paltry weakness of heart, O slayer of foes!

4

अर्जुन उवाच
कथं भीष्ममहं सङ्ख्ये
द्रोणं च मधुसूदन।
इषुभिः प्रति योत्स्यामि
पूजार्हावरिसूदन।।

arjunauvāca
kathaṁbhīṣmamahaṁsaṅkhye
droṇaṁ ca madhusūdana
iṣubhiḥ prati yotsyāmi
pujarhav ari-sudana ||

arjunaḥ uvāca—Arjuna said; katham—how; bhīṣmam—unto Bhīṣma; aham—I; saṅkhye—in the fight; droṇam—unto Droṇa; ca—also, madhusūdana—O killer of Madhu; iṣubhiḥ—with arrows; pratiyotsyāmi—shall counter attack; pūjā-arhau—those who are worshipable; arisūdana—O killer of the enemies.

Meaning: Arjuna said: O Madhusudana, how can I fight venerable men like Bhishma and Drona with my arrows in battle who are deserving of my reverence instead?

5

गुरूनहत्वा हि महानुभावान्
श्रेयो भोक्तुं भैक्ष्यमपीह लोके।
हत्वार्थकामांस्तु गुरूनिहैव
भुंजीय भोगान्रुधिरप्रदिग्धान्॥

gurūnahatvā hi mahānubhāvān
śreyo bhoktuṁ bhaikṣyamapīha loke
hatvārtha-kāmāṁs tu gurūn ihaiva
bhuñjīya bhogānrudhira-pradigdhān ||

gurūn—the superiors; ahatvā—by killing; hi—certainly; mahā- anubhāvān— great souls; śreyaḥ—it is better; bhoktum—to enjoy life; bhaikṣyam—begging; api—even; iha—in this life; loke—in this world; hatvā—killing; artha—gain; kāmān—so desiring; tu—but; gurūn—superiors; iha—in this world; eva—certainly; bhuñjīya—has to enjoy; bhogān—enjoyable things; rudhira—blood; pradigdhān—tainted with.

Meaning: It is better to live by begging for alms in this world rather than killing elders of high character who are also my Gurus. By killing such superior elders, our enjoyments of wealth and luxury will be stained with blood and won't be worthy of pleasure.

6

न चैतद्विद्मः कतरन्नो गरीयो
यद्वा जयेम यदि वा नो जयेयुः ।
यानेव हत्वा न जिजीविषाम-
स्तेऽवस्थिताः प्रमुखे धार्तराष्ट्राः॥

na caitad vidmaḥ kataran no garīyo
yadvā jayema yadi vāno jayeyuḥ
yāneva hatvā naji jīviṣāmas
te'vasthitāḥ pramukhe dhārtarāṣṭrāḥ||

na—nor; ca—also; etat—this; vidmaḥ—do know; katarat—which; naḥ—us; garīyaḥ—better; yat—what; vā—either; jayema—conquer us; yadi—if; vā—or; naḥ—us; jayeyuḥ—conquer; yān—those; eva—certainly; hatvā—by killing;na—never; jijīviṣāmaḥ—want to live; te—all of them; avasthitāḥ—are situated; pramukhe—in the front; dhārtarāṣṭrāḥ—the sons of Dhṛtarāṣṭra.

Meaning: Nor do I know which is better for us- 'we conquer them' or 'they conquer us'. If we kill the sons of Dhritarashtra, we should not desire to live as well even though they stand opposed to us in the battlefield now.

7

कार्पण्यदोषोपहतस्वभावः
पृच्छामि त्वां धर्मसम्मूढचेताः ।
यच्छ्रेयः स्यान्निश्चितं ब्रूहि तन्मे
शिष्यस्तेऽहं शाधि मां त्वां प्रपन्नम्।।

kārpaṇya-doṣopahata-svabhāvaḥ
pṛcchāmi tvāṁdharma-saṁmūḍha-cetāḥ
yac chreyaḥ syān niścitaṁ brūhi tan me
śiṣyaste›haṁ śādhimāṁ tvāṁ prapannam||

kārpaṇya—miserly; doṣa—weakness; upahata—being inflicted by; svabhāvaḥ—characteristics; pṛcchāmi—I am asking; tvām—unto You; dharma— religion; saṁmūḍha—bewildered; cetāḥ—in heart; yat—what; śreyaḥ—all-good; syāt—maybe; niścitam—confidently; brūhi—tell; tat—that; me—unto me; śiṣyaḥ—disciple; te—Your; aham—I am; śādhi—just instruct; mām—me; tvām—unto You; prapannam—surrendered.

Meaning: My very nature is overcome because of this weakness and my mind is bewildered about righteousness. I ask You to tell me what is good for me. I am Your disciple who has fallen at Your feet with the total surrender of my soul. Please guide me.

8

न हि प्रपश्यामि ममापनुद्याद्
यच्छोकमुच्छोषणमिन्द्रियाणाम्।
अवाप्य भूमावसपत्रमृद्धं
राज्यं सुराणामपि चाधिपत्यम्।।

na hi prapaśyāmi mamāpanudyād
yacchokam ucchoṣaṇam indriyāṇām
avāpya bhūmāv asapatnam ṛddhaṁ
rājyaṁ surāṇāmapi cādhipatyam||

na—do not; hi—certainly; prapaśyāmi—I see; mama—my; apanudyāt—they can drive away; yat—that; śokam—lamentation; ucchoṣaṇam—drying up; indriyāṇām—of the senses; avāpya—achieving; bhūmau—on the earth; asapatnam—without rival; ṛddham—prosperous; rājyam—kingdom; surāṇām—of the demigods; api—even; ca—also; ādhipatyam—supremacy.

Meaning: I cannot find anything that can dispel this grief that is withering away all my senses. I shall be unable to destroy it even if I attained an unrivalled and prosperous kingdom on earth or even sovereignty over the gods in heaven.

9

संजय उवाच
एवमुक्त्वा हृषीकेशं
गुडाकेशः परन्तप।
न योत्स्य इतिगोविन्दमु
उक्त्वा तूष्णीं बभूव ह॥

sañjaya uvāca
evam uktvā hṛṣīkeśaṁ
guḍākeśaḥparantapaḥ
nayotsyaiti govindam
uktvā tūṣṇīṁ babhūvaha ||

sañjayaḥuvāca—Sañjaya said; evam—thus; uktvā—speaking; hṛṣīkeśam— unto Kṛṣṇa, the master of the senses; guḍākeśaḥ—Arjuna, the master at curbing ignorance; parantapaḥ—the chastiser of the enemies; na yotsye—I shall not fight; iti—thus; govindam—unto Kṛṣṇa,the giver of pleasure; uktvā—saying; tūṣṇīm—silent; babhūva—became; ha—certainly.

Meaning: Sanjaya said: Having addressed Hrishikesha thus, Arjuna the destroyer of enemies, said to Lord Krishna: Govinda, I shall not fight, and kept quiet.

10

तमुवाच हृषीकेशः
प्रहसन्निव भारत।
सेनयोरुभयोर्मध्ये
विषीदंतमिदं वचः।।

tam uvāca hṛṣīkeśaḥ
prahasanniva bhārata
senayor ubhayor madhye
viṣīdantamidaṁ vacaḥ||

tam—untohim; uvāca—said; hṛṣīkeśaḥ—the master of the senses, Kṛṣṇa; prahasan—smiling; iva—like that; bhārata—O Dhṛtarāṣṭra, descendant of Bharata; senayoḥ—of the armies; ubhayoḥ—of both parties; madhye—between; viṣīdantam—unto the lamenting one; idam—the following; vacaḥ—words.

Meaning: To Arjuna, despondent in the middle of the two armies, O descendant of Bharata, Lord Krishna spoke these words smilingly:

11

श्रीभगवानुवाच
अशोच्यानन्वशोचस्त्वं
प्रज्ञावादांश्च भाषसे।
गतासूनगतासूंश्च
नानुशोचन्ति पण्डिताः॥

śrī-bhagavān uvāca
aśocyān anvaśocas tvaṁ
prajñā-vādāṁścabhāṣase
gatāsūn agatāsūṁś ca
nānuśocanti paṇḍitāḥ||

śrībhagavānuvāca—the Supreme Personality of Godhead said; aśocyān—that which is not worthy of lamentation; anvaśocaḥ—you are lamenting; tvam—you; prajñā-vādāḥ—learned talks; ca—also; bhāṣase—speaking; gata— lost; asūn—life; agata—not past; asūn—life; ca—also; na—never; anuśocanti— lament; paṇḍitāḥ—the learned.

Meaning: The Glorious Lord said: While speaking words of wisdom, you mourn for those who are unworthy of your grief. Wise men do not grieve either for the dead or for the living.

12

न त्वेवाहं जातु नासं
न त्वं नेमे जनाधिपाः।
न चैव न भविष्यामः
सर्वे वयमतः परम्॥

na tvevāhaṁ jātu nāsaṁ
na tvaṁneme janādhipāḥ
na caiva na bhaviṣyāmaḥ
sarve vayamataḥ param||

na—never; tu—but; eva—certainly; aham—I; jātu—become; na—never; āsam—existed; na—it is not so; tvam—yourself; na—not; ime—all these; janādhipāḥ—kings; na—never; ca—also; eva—certainly; na—not like that; bhaviṣyāmaḥ—shall exist; sarve—all of us; vayam—we; ataḥ param—hereafter.

Meaning: Indeed, there was never a time when I did not exist, nor you, nor all these chiefs of men. Neither in the hereafter shall we all ever cease to exist.

13

देहिनोऽस्मिन्यथा देहे
कौमारं यौवनं जरा।
तथा देहान्तरप्राप्ति
र्धीरस्तत्र न मुह्यति।।

dehino 'smin yathā dehe
kaumāraṁ yauvanaṁ jarā
tathā dehāntara-prāptir
dhīrastatra namuhyati ||

dehinaḥ—of the embodied; asmin—in this; yathā—as; dehe—in the body; kaumāram—boyhood; yauvanam—youth; jarā—old age; tathā—similarly; dehāntara—transference of the body; prāptiḥ—achievement; dhīraḥ—the sober; tatra—thereupon; na—never; muhyati—deluded.

Meaning: As the soul enters the stages of childhood, youth, and old age in this body, it leaves behind the body after death and passes into another body. The self-realised man is not perturbed by such changes.

14

मात्रास्पर्शास्तु कौन्तेय
शीतोष्णसुखदुःखदाः।
आगमापायिनोऽनित्यास्तां
स्तितिक्षस्व भारत॥

mātrā-sparśās tu kaunteya
śītoṣṇa-sukha-duḥkha-dāḥ
āgamāpāyino'nityāstam
stitikṣasva bhārata||

mātrā—sensuous; sparśāḥ—perception; tu—only; kaunteya—O son of Kuntī; śīta—winter; uṣṇa—summer; sukha—happiness; duḥkha-dāḥ—giving pain; āgama—appearing; apāyinaḥ—disappearing; anityāḥ—non permanent; tān—all of them; titikṣasva—just try to tolerate; bhārata—O descendant of the Bhārata dynasty.

Meaning: O son of Kunti, the contact of sense and object which provides happiness, is not permanent. They are like the seasons of heat and cold, and feelings of pleasure and pain. They are born from the sense of perception. Patiently bear them, O Arjuna, without being disturbed.

15

यं हि न व्यथयन्त्येते
पुरुषं पुरुषर्षभ।
समदुःखसुखं धीरं
सोऽमृतत्त्वाय कल्पते॥

yaṁ hi na vyathayanty ete
puruṣaṁ puruṣarṣabha
sama-duḥkha-sukhaṁ dhīraṁ
so 'mṛtatvāya kalpate||

yam—one who; hi—certainly; na—never; vyathayanti—are distressing; ete— all these; puruṣam—to a person; puruṣarṣabha—is best among men; sama—unaltered; duḥkha—distress; sukham—happiness; dhīram—patient; saḥ—he; amṛtatvāya—for liberation; kalpate—is considered eligible.

Meaning: The one who reacts equally in both pleasure and pain and whom these cannot affect is eligible for immortality, O mighty Arjuna.

16

नासतो विद्यते भावो
नाभावो विद्यते सतः।
उभयोरपि दृष्टोऽ
न्तस्त्वनयोस्तत्त्वदर्शिभिः।।

nāsato vidyate bhāvo
nābhāvo vidyate sataḥ
ubhayorapi dṛṣṭo'ntas
tvanayostattva-darśibhiḥ||

na—never; asataḥ—of the non existent; vidyate—there is; bhāvaḥ—endurance; na—never; abhāvaḥ—changing quality; vidyate—there is; sataḥ—of the eternal; ubhayoḥ—of the two; api—verily; dṛṣṭaḥ—observed; antaḥ—conclusion; tu—but; anayoḥ—of them; tattva—truth; darśibhiḥ—by the seers.

Meaning: The discerners of the truth have concluded after studying the nature of both that there is no certainty of the real just like there cannot be uncertainty of the Unreal.

17

अविनाशि तु तद्विद्धि
येन सर्वमिदं ततम्।
विनाशमव्ययस्यास्य
न कश्चित्कर्तुमर्हति॥

avināśi tu tadviddhi
yena sarvamidaṁ tatam
vināśam avyayasyāsya
na kaścitkartumarhati ||

avināśi—imperishable; tu—but; tat—that; viddhi—know it; yena—by whom; sarvam—all of the body; idam—this; tatam—widespread; vināśam—destruction; avyayasya—of the imperishable; asya—of it; na kaścit—no one; kartum—to do; arhati—able.

Meaning: Now, know that all that pervades the entire body cannot be destroyed. No one can cause the destruction of this Imperishable Soul.

18

अन्तवन्त इमे देहा
नित्यस्योक्ताः शरीरिणः।
अनाशिनोऽप्रमेयस्य
तस्माद्युध्यस्व भारत॥

antavanta ime dehā
nityasyoktāḥ śarīriṇaḥ
anāśino'prameyasya
tasmādyudhyasva bhārata||

antavantaḥ—perishable; ime—all these; dehāḥ—material bodies; nityasya— eternal in existence; uktāḥ—it is so said; śarīriṇaḥ—the embodied souls; anāśinaḥ—never to be destroyed; aprameyasya—immeasurable; tasmāt— therefore; yudhyasva—fight; bhārata—O descendant of Bharata.

Meaning: All the bodies within the imperishable soul are perishable. Therefore, Arjuna, fight.

19

य एनं वेत्ति हन्तारं
यश्चैनं मन्यते हतम्।
उभौ तौ न विजानीतो
नायं हन्ति न हन्यते।।

ya enaṁ vettihantāraṁ
yaścaina ṁmanyate hatam
ubhau tau na vijānīto
nāyaṁ hanti na hanyate ||

yaḥ—anyone; enam—this; vetti—knows; hantāram—the killer; yaḥ—anyone; ca—also; enam—this; manyate—thinks; hatam—killed; ubhau —both of them; tau—they; na—never; vijānītaḥ—in knowledge; na—never; ayam—this; hanti—kills; na—nor; hanyate—be killed.

Meaning: He who thinks that it is the soul that kills, and he who thinks it is the soul that is killed, are both ill-informed. This neither kills nor is killed.

20

न जायते म्रियते वा कदाचि-
न्नायं भूत्वा भविता वा न भूयः।
अजो नित्यः शाश्वतोऽयं पुराणो
न हन्यते हन्यमाने शरीरे॥

na jāyate mriyatevā kadācin
nāyaṁ bhūtvā bhavitā vā nabhūyaḥ
ajo nityaḥ śāśvato 'yaṁ purāṇo
na hanyate hanyamāne śarīre||

na—never; jāyate—takes birth; mriyate—never dies; vā—either; kadācit —at any time (past, present or future); na—never; ayam—this; bhūtvā —came into being; bhavitā—will come to be; vā—or; na—not; bhūyaḥ—or has come to be; ajaḥ—unborn; nityaḥ—eternal; śāśvataḥ—permanent; ayam—this; purāṇaḥ—the oldest; na—never; hanyate—is killed; hanyamāne—being killed; śarīre—by the body.

Meaning: The Soul is not born and neither does it die. Nor, having once been, does it ever cease to exist. The Soul is unborn, permanent, everlasting, ancient, and yet fresh. This is not killed even after the body is slaughtered.

21

वेदाविनाशिनं नित्यं
य एनमजमव्ययम्।
कथं स पुरुषः पार्थ कं
घातयति हन्ति कम्।।

vedāvināśinaṁ nityaṁ
ya enam ajam avyayam
kathaṁ sa puruṣaḥ pārthakaṁ
ghātayati hanti kam||

veda—in knowledge; avināśinam—indestructible; nityam—always; yaḥ—one who; enam—this(soul); ajam—unborn; avyayam—immutable; katham—how; saḥ—he; puruṣaḥ—person; pārtha—O Pārtha (Arjuna); kam—whom; ghātayati—hurts; hanti—kills; kam—whom.

Meaning: O Partha, how can the man who knows the Soul as indestructible, permanent, unborn, and eternal, kill anyone or cause anyone to be killed?

22

वासांसि जीर्णानि यथा विहाय
नवानि गृह्णाति नरोऽपराणि।
तथा शरीराणि विहाय जीर्णा-
न्यन्यानि संयाति नवानि देही।।

vāsāṁsi jīrṇāni yathā vihāya
navāni gṛhṇāti naro'parāṇi
tathā śarīrāṇi vihāya jīrṇāny
anyāni saṁyāti navāni dehī||

vāsāṁsi—garments; jīrṇāni—old and worn out; yathā—as it is; vihāya—giving up; navāni—new garments; gṛhṇāti—does accept; naraḥ—a man; aparāṇi—other; tathā—in the same way; śarīrāṇi—bodies; vihāya—giving up; jīrṇāni—old and useless; anyāni—different; saṁyāti—verily accepts; navāni—new sets; dehī—the embodied.

Meaning: Just as a man wears new garments after casting off his old ones, so does the soul cast off old and worn-out material bodies to enter new ones.

23

नैनं छिन्दन्ति शस्त्राणि
नैनं दहति पावकः।
न चैनं क्लेदयन्त्यापो
न शोषयति मारुतः॥

nainaṁ chindanti śastrāṇi
nainaṁ dahati pāvakaḥ
na cainaṁ kledayantyāpo
na śoṣayati mārutaḥ||

na—never; enam—unto this soul; chindanti—can cut into pieces; śastrāṇi—all weapons; na—never; enam—unto this soul; dahati—burns; pāvakaḥ—fire; na—never; ca—also; enam—unto this soul; kledayanti—moistens; āpaḥ—water; na—never; śoṣayati—dries; mārutaḥ—wind.

Meaning: Neither weapons can cleave the soul, nor fire burn it, nor water moisten it, nor can the wind wither it.

24

अच्छेद्योऽयमदाह्योऽयमक्लेद्योऽ
शोष्य एव च।
नित्यः सर्वगतः
स्थाणुरचलोऽयं सनातनः॥

acchedyo'yamadāhyo'yam akledyo
'śoṣya eva ca
nityaḥ sarva-gataḥ
sthāṇur acalo 'yaṁ sanātanaḥ||

acchedyaḥ—unbreakable; ayam—this soul; adāhyaḥ—cannot be burned; ayam—this soul; akledyaḥ—insoluble; aśoṣyaḥ—cannot be dried; eva—certainly; ca—and; nityaḥ—everlasting; sarva-gataḥ—all-pervading; sthāṇuḥ—unchangeable; acalaḥ—immovable; ayam—this soul; sanātanaḥ — eternally the same.

Meaning: The soul is uncleavable and incombustible. This cannot be burned, wetted, or dried. The soul is perpetual, all-pervading, immovable, unchangeable and immemorial.

25

अव्यक्तोऽयमचिन्त्योऽ
यमविकार्योऽयमुच्यते।
तस्मादेवं विदित्वैनं
नानुशोचितुमर्हसि।।

avyakto'yamacintyo
'yam avikāryo 'yam ucyate
tasmād evaṁ viditvainaṁ
nānuśocitum arhasi||

avyaktaḥ—invisible; ayam—this soul; acintyaḥ—inconceivable; ayam—this soul; avikāryaḥ—unchangeable; ayam—this soul; ucyate—is said; tasmāt —therefore; evam—like this; viditvā—knowing it well; enam—this soul; na— do not; anuśocitum—may lament over; arhasi—you deserve.

Meaning: It cannot be perceived, imagined, and is said to be immutable. Therefore, knowing this to be so, you should not grieve for the loss of the body.

26

अथ चैनं नित्यजातं
नित्यं वा मन्यसे मृतम्।
तथापि त्वं महाबाहो
नैवं शोचितुमर्हसि॥

atha cainaṁ nitya-jātaṁ
nityaṁ vā manyase mṛtam
tathāpi tvaṁ mahā-bāho
nainaṁ śocitumarhasi ||

atha—if, however; ca—also; enam—this soul; nitya-jātam—always born; nityam—forever; vā—either; manyase—so think; mṛtam—dead; tathāpi—still; tvam—you; mahā-bāho—O mighty-armed one; na—never; enam—about the soul; śocitum—to lament; arhasi—deserve.

Meaning: If, however, you think that the soul is perpetually born or is perpetually dying, even then you should not grieve like this, O mighty-armed.

27

जातस्य हि ध्रुवो
मृत्युर्ध्रुवं जन्म मृतस्य च।
तस्मादपरिहार्येऽर्थे
न त्वं शोचितुमर्हसि।।

jātasya hi dhruvo
mṛtyur dhruvaṁ janma mṛtasyaca
tasmād aparihārye'rthe
natvaṁ śocitumarhasi ||

jātasya—one who has taken his birth; hi—certainly; dhruvaḥ—a fact; mṛtyuḥ—death; dhruvam—it is also a fact; janma—birth; mṛtasya—of the dead; ca—also; tasmāt—therefore; aparihārye—for that which is unavoidable; arthe—in the matter of; na—do not; tvam—you; śocitum—to lament; arhasi—deserve.

Meaning: If you are sure about the death of what is born and the birth of what is dead, you should not grieve over the inevitable result.

28

अव्यक्तादीनि भूतानि
व्यक्तमध्यानि भारत।
अव्यक्तनिधनान्येव
तत्र का परिदेवना॥

avyaktādīni bhūtāni
vyakta-madhyāni bhārata
avyakta-nidhanāny eva
tatra kā paridevanā||

avyaktādīni—in the beginning unmanifested; bhūtāni—all that are created; vyakta—manifested;madhyāni—in the middle; bhārata—O descendant of Bharata; avyakta—non manifested; nidhanāni—all that are vanquished; eva—it is all like that; tatra—therefore; kā-what; paridevanā—lamentation.

Meaning: All creatures have an unknown origin, manifest in their middle state, and they also have an unknown future. O Bharata, why should you lament then?

29

आश्चर्यवत्पश्यति कश्चिदेन-
माश्चर्यवद्वदति तथैव चान्यः।
आश्चर्यवच्चैनमन्यः शृणोति
श्रुत्वाप्येनं वेद न चैव कश्चित्॥

āścaryavat paśyati kaścid enam
āścaryavadvadati tathaiva cānyaḥ
āścaryavac cainam anyaḥ śṛṇoti
śrutvāpyenaṁ veda na caiva kaścit||

āścaryavat—amazing; paśyati—see; kaścit—some; enam—this soul; āścaryavat—amazing; vadati—speak; tathā—there; eva—certainly; ca—also; anyaḥ—others; āścaryavat—similarly amazing; ca—also; enam—this soul; anyaḥ— others; śṛṇoti—hear; śrutvā—having heard; api—even; enam—this soul; veda—do know; na—never; ca—and; eva—certainly; kaścit—anyone.

Meaning: Some view the soul as marvellous and some describe it as amazing, while none, even after hearing the Shruti, can understand the soul at all.

30

देही नित्यमवध्योऽयं
देहे सर्वस्य भारत।
तस्मात्सर्वाणि भूतानि
न त्वं शोचितुमर्हसि॥

dehī nityam avadhyo 'yaṁ
dehe sarvasya bhārata
tasmātsarvāṇi bhūtāni
na tvaṁ śocitumarhasi ||

dehī—the owner of the material body; nityam—eternally; avadhyaḥ—cannot be killed; ayam—this soul; dehe—in the body; sarvasya—of everyone; bhārata—O descendant of Bharata; tasmāt—therefore; sarvāṇi—all; bhūtāni—living entities (that are born); na—never; tvam—yourself; śocitum —to lament; arhasi- deserve.

Meaning: The Embodied who dwells in everyone's body is eternal and can never be killed, O descendant of Bharata,. Therefore, you should not grieve for anyone.

31

स्वधर्ममपि चावेक्ष्य
न विकम्पितुमर्हसि।
धर्म्याद्धि युद्धाच्छ्रेयोऽ
न्यत्क्षत्रियस्य न विद्यते।।

svadharmamapi cāvekṣya
na vikampitumarhasi
dharmyāddhi yuddhācchreyo'
nyat kṣatriyasya na vidyate ||

svadharmam—one's own religious principles; api—also; ca—indeed; avekṣya—considering; na—never; vikampitum—to hesitate; arhasi—you deserve; dharmyāt—from religious principles; hi—indeed; yuddhāt—of fighting; śreyaḥ—better engagements; anyat—anything else; kṣatriyasya—of the kṣatriya; na—does not; vidyate—exist.

Meaning: Concerning your own duty as a Kshatriya, you should not falter or hesitate; for, to a Kshatriya, there is nothing better than to fight a righteous war.

32

यदृच्छया चोपपन्नां
स्वर्गद्वारमपावृतम्।
सुखिनः क्षत्रियाः पार्थ
लभन्ते युद्धमीदृशम्॥

yadṛcchayā copapannaṁ
svarga-dvāramapāvṛtam
sukhinaḥ kṣatriyāḥ pārtha
labhante yuddhamīdṛśam ||

yadṛcchayā—by its own accord; ca—also; upapannam—arrived at; svarga—heavenly planet; dvāram—door; apāvṛtam—wide open; sukhinaḥ—very happy; kṣatriyāḥ—the members of the royal order; pārtha—O son of Pṛthā; labhante—do achieve; yuddham—war; īdṛśam—like this.

Meaning: Happy are the Kshatriyas, O Partha, who gain the opportunity for such a war unsought, as it is like the gates of heaven opening up for them.

33

अथ चेत्त्वमिमं धर्म्यं
सङ्ग्रामं न करिष्यसि।
ततः स्वधर्मं कीर्तिं च
हित्वा पापमवाप्स्यसि।।

athacettvamimaṁdharmyaṁ
saṅgrāmaṁ na kariṣyasi
tataḥ svadharmam kīrtiṁca
hitvā pāpam avāpsyasi ||

atha—therefore; cet—if; tvam—you; imam—this; dharmyam—religious duty; saṅgrāmam—fighting; na—do not; kariṣyasi—perform; tataḥ—then; svadharmam—your religious duty; kīrtim—reputation; ca—also; hitvā—losing; pāpam—sinful reaction; avāpsyasi—do gain.

Meaning: If, however, you choose not to take part in this righteous war, you will descend from your position of honour and fame, lose your reputation as a great fighter, and incur sin for the neglect of duty.

34

अकीर्तिं चापि भूतानि
कथयिष्यन्ति तेऽव्ययाम्।
सम्भावितस्य
चाकीर्तिर्मरणादतिरिच्यते॥

akīrtiṁ cāpi bhūtāni
kathayiṣyantite'vyayām
sambhāvitasya
cākīrtir maraṇād atiricyate||

akīrtim—infamy; ca—also; api—over and above; bhūtāni—all people; kathayiṣyanti—will speak; te-of you; avyayām—forever; sambhāvitasya—for a respectable man; ca—also; akīrtiḥ—ill fame; maraṇāt—than death; atiricyate—becomes more than.

Meaning: Moreover, people will always proclaim your undying infamy; and infamy to an honourable man is a fate that is worse than death.

35

भयाद्रणादुपरतं
मंस्यन्ते त्वां महारथाः।
येषां च त्वं बहुमतो
भूत्वा यास्यसि लाघवम्॥

bhayād raṇād uparataṁ
maṁsyante tvāṁ mahā-rathāḥ
yeṣāṁ ca tvaṁ bahu-mato
bhūtvā yāsyasi lāghavam||

bhayāt—out of fear; raṇāt—from the battlefield; uparatam—ceased; maṁsyante—will consider; tvām—unto you; mahā-rathāḥ—the great generals; yeṣām—of those who; ca—also; tvam—you; bahu-mataḥ—in great estimation; bhūtvā—will become; yāsyasi—will go; lāghavam—decreased in value.

Meaning: The great warriors who have held your name and fame in high esteem will form opinions that you have abandoned the battlefield only out of fear, and will think of you as a coward.

36

अवाच्यवादांश्च बहून्
वदिष्यन्ति तवाहिताः।
निन्दन्तस्तव सामर्थ्यं
ततो दुःखतरं नु किम्॥

avācya-vādāṁśca bahūn
vadiṣyanti tavāhitāḥ
nindantastava sāmarthyaṁ
tato duḥkhataraṁ nu kim||

avācya—unkind; vādān—fabricated words; ca—also; bahūn—many; vadiṣyanti—will say; tava—your; ahitāḥ—enemies; nindantaḥ—while vilifying; tava—your; sāmarthyam—ability; tataḥ—thereafter; duḥkhataram—more painful; nu—of course; kim—what is there.

Meaning: Your enemies will use reproachful words against you, and will scorn your prowess. What could be more painful for you than that?

37

हतो वा प्राप्स्यसि स्वर्गं
जित्वा वा भोक्ष्यसे महीम्।
तस्मादुत्तिष्ठ कौन्तेय
युद्धाय कृतनिश्चयः।।

hato vā prāpsyasi svargaṁ
jit vā vābhokṣyase mahīm
tasmād uttiṣṭha kaunteya
yuddhāyakṛta-niścayaḥ ||

hataḥ—being killed; vā—either; prāpsyasi—you gain; svargam—the heavenly kingdom; jitvā—by conquering; vā—or; bhokṣyase—you enjoy; mahīm—the world; tasmāt—therefore; uttiṣṭha—get up; kaunteya—O son of Kuntī; yuddhāya—to fight; kṛta—determination; niścayaḥ—uncertainty.

Meaning: Either you will be killed and obtain heaven, or enjoy the earthly kingdom after being victorious. Therefore, stand up, O son of Kunti, and fight this war with determination.

38

सुखदुःखे समे कृत्वा
लाभालाभौ जयाजयौ।
ततो युद्धाय युज्यस्व
नैवं पापमवाप्स्यसि॥

sukha-duḥkhe same kṛtvā
lābhā lābhau jayājayau
tato yuddhāya yujyasva
naivaṁ pāpamavāpsyasi ||

sukha—happiness; duḥkhe—in distress; same—in equanimity; kṛtvā—doing so; lābhālābhau—both in loss and profit; jayājayau—both in defeat and victory; tataḥ—thereafter; yuddhāya—for the sake of fighting; yujyasva—do fight; na—never; evam—in this way; pāpam—sinful reaction; avāpsyasi—you will gain.

Meaning: Prepare yourself to fight only for the sake of fighting, being equally prepared for pleasure and pain, loss or gain, and victory or defeat. By doing so, you shall not incur sin.

39

एषा तेऽभिहिता साङ्ख्ये
बुद्धिर्योगे त्विमां शृणु।
बुद्ध्या युक्तो यया पार्थ
कर्मबन्धं प्रहास्यसि॥

eṣāte'bhihitā sāṅkhye
buddhiryoge tvimāṁ śṛṇu
buddhyā yukto yayā pārtha
karma-bandhaṁ prahāsyasi ||

eṣā—all these; te—unto you; abhihitā—described; sāṅkhye—by analytical study; buddhiḥ—intelligence; yoge—work without fruitive result; tu—but; imām-this; śṛṇu—just hear; buddhyā—by intelligence; yuktaḥ—dove tailed; yayā—by which; pārtha—O son of Pṛthā; karma-bandham—bondage of reaction; prahāsyasi—you can be released from.

Meaning: This, explained to you, is the wisdom and knowledge according to the Sankhya method. Now, hear the knowledge according to the Yoga, and with the help of its wisdom, you can cast off the shackles of Karma, O Partha.

40

नेहाभिक्रमनाशोऽस्ति
प्रत्यवायो न विद्यते।
स्वल्पमप्यस्य धर्मस्य
त्रायते महतो भयात्॥

nehābhikrama-nāśo 'sti
pratyavāyo na vidyate
svalpamapyasya dharmasya
trāyate mahato bhayāt||

na—there is not; iha—in this world; abhikrama—endeavoring; nāśaḥ—loss; asti—there is; pratyavāyaḥ—diminution; na—never; vidyate—there is; svalpam—little; api—although; asya—of this; dharmasya—of this occupation; trāyate—releases; mahataḥ—of very great; bhayāt—from danger.

Meaning: This endeavor does not have any loss of progress, nor is there any retrogression. Even a little travel on this path of righteousness rescues one from the most dangerous fear of birth and death.

41

व्यवसायात्मिका
बुद्धिरेकेह कुरुनन्दन।
बहुशाखा ह्यनन्ताश्च
बुद्धयोऽव्यवसायिनाम्॥

vyavasāyātmikā
buddhir ekehakuru-nandana
bahu-śākhā hy anantāś ca
buddhayo'vyavasāyinām ||

vyavasāyātmikā—resolute Kṛṣṇa consciousness; buddhiḥ—intelligence; ekā—only one; iha—in this world; kuru-nandana—O beloved child of the Kurus; bahu-śākhāḥ—various branches; hi—indeed; anantāḥ—unlimited; ca—also; buddhayaḥ—intelligence; avyavasāyinām—of those who are not in Kṛṣṇa consciousness.

Meaning: Those who walk on this path are resolute in purpose with a common aim and understanding that is right and deliberate. O son of the Kurus, the intelligence of the irresolute are many-branched and endless.

42-43

यामिमां पुष्पितां वाचं
प्रवदन्त्यविपश्चितः।
वेदवादरताः पार्थ
नान्यदस्तीति वादिनः॥

कामात्मानः स्वर्गपरा
जन्मकर्मफलप्रदाम्।
क्रियाविशेषबहुलां
भोगैश्वर्यगतिं प्रति॥

yām imāṁ puṣpitāṁ vācaṁ
pravadanty-avipaścitaḥ
veda-vāda-ratāḥ pārtha
nānyadastīti vādinaḥ||

kāmātmānaḥ svarga-parā
janma-karma-phala-pradām
kriyā-viśeṣa-bahulāṁ
bhogaiśvarya-gatiṁprati||

yām imām—all these; puṣpitām—flowery; vācam—words; pravadanti—say; avipaścitaḥ—men with a poor fund of knowledge; veda-vāda-ratāḥ—supposed followers of the Vedas; pārtha—O son of Pṛtha; na—

never; anyat—anything else; asti—there is; iti—this; vādinaḥ—advocates; kāma- ātmānaḥ—desirous of sense gratification; svarga-parāḥ—aiming to achieve heavenly planets; janma-karma-phala-pradām—resulting in fruitive action, good birth, etc.; kriyā-viśeṣa—pompous ceremonies; bahulām—various; bhoga—sense enjoyment; aiśvarya—opulence; gatim—progress; prati—towards.

Meaning: Men who are not reflective, O Partha, are fond of the flowery words of the Vedas, and say that there is nothing more beyond this under the influence of this flowery speech.

The words of the Vedas recommend many fruitive activities towards attaining heaven, resulting good birth, gratification, power, and so on. Being desirious of selfish gratification and opulent life, they esteem these wrongly as the highest goal of heaven.

44

भोगैश्वर्यप्रसक्तानां
तयापहृतचेतसाम्।
व्यवसायात्मिका बुद्धिः
समाधौ न विधीयते।।

bhogaiśvarya-prasaktānāṁ
tayāpahṛta-cetasām
vyavasāyātmikā buddhiḥ
samādhau na vidhīyate||

bhoga—material enjoyment; aiśvarya—opulence; prasaktānām—those who are so attached; tayā—by such things; apahṛta-cetasām—bewildered in mind; vyavasāyātmikā—fixed determination; buddhiḥ—devotional service of the Lord; samādhau—in the controlled mind; na—never; vidhīyate—does take place.

Meaning: For those who are fond of such selfish gratification and endless power are robbed of the resolute determination needed for the devotional service to the Supreme Lord.

45

त्रैगुण्यविषया वेदा
निस्त्रैगुण्यो भवार्जुन।
निर्द्वन्द्वो नित्यसत्वस्थो
निर्योगक्षेम आत्मवान्।।

traiguṇya-viṣayā vedā
nistraiguṇyo bhavārjuna
nirdvandvo nitya-sattva-stho
niryoga-kṣema ātmavān||

traiguṇya—pertaining to the three modes of material nature; viṣayāḥ—on the subject matter; vedāḥ—Vedic literatures; nistraiguṇyaḥ—in a pure state of spiritual existence; bhava—be; arjuna-O Arjuna; nirdvandvaḥ—free from the pains of opposites; nitya-sattva-sthaḥ—ever remaining in sattva(goodness); niryoga-kṣemaḥ—free from (the thought of) acquisition and preservation; ātmavān—established in the Self.

Meaning: The Vedas deal with the subject of the three modes of material nature. O Arjuna, do not be influenced by this attribute-triad and rise above these modes. Be free from the dualities to settle in permanent goodness. Be self-possessed and unmindful of acquisition and preservation. Be established in the Self.

46

यावानर्थ उदपाने
सर्वतः सम्प्लुतोदके।
तावान्सर्वेषु वेदेषु
ब्राह्मणस्य विजानतः॥

yāvān artha udapāne
sarvataḥ samplutodake
tāvān sarveṣu vedeṣu
brāhmaṇasya vijānataḥ||

yāvān—all that; arthaḥ—is meant; udapāne—in a well of water; sarvataḥ—in all respects; sampluta-udake—in a great reservoir of water; tāvān—similarly; sarveṣu—in all; vedeṣu—Vedic literatures; brāhmaṇasya—of the man who knows the Supreme Brahman; vijānataḥ—of one who is in complete knowledge.

Meaning: What is the use of an all-flooding water source for drinking? The small pond does great service that even great reservoirs of water cannot render. Similarly, of the Vedas are of no use to one whose self is enightened.

47

कर्मण्येवाधिकारस्ते
मा फलेषु कदाचन।
मा कर्मफल
हेतुर्भूर्मा ते संगोऽस्त्वकर्मणि।।

karmaṇy evādhikāras te
mā phaleṣu kadācana
mā karma-phala-
hetur bhūr mā te saṅgo'stvakarmaṇi ||

karmaṇi—prescribed duties; eva—certainly; adhikāraḥ—right; te—of you; mā—never; phaleṣu—in the fruits; kadācana—at any time; mā—never; karma-phala—in the result of the work; hetuḥ—cause; bhūḥ—become; mā—never; te—of you; saṅgaḥ—attachment; astu—be there; akarmaṇi—in not doing.

Meaning: Your power of action extends to the act and never to its fruit. You are not entitled to the fruits of your action so do not seek it. Do not think you are the cause of the results of your action. Have no attachment to inaction.

48

योगस्थः कुरु कर्माणि
संग त्यक्त्वा धनंजय।
सिद्ध्यसिद्ध्योः समो भूत्वा
समत्वं योग उच्यते।।

yoga-sthaḥ kuru karmāṇi
saṅgaṁ tyaktvā dhanañjaya
siddhy-asiddhyoḥ samobhūtvā
samatvaṁ yoga ucyate||

yoga-sthaḥ—steadfast in yoga; kuru—perform; karmāṇi—your duty; saṅgam—attachment; tyaktvā—having abandoned; dhanañjaya—O Dhanañjaya; siddhi-asiddhyoḥ—in success and failure; samaḥ—the same; bhūtvā—having become; samatvam—evenness of mind; yogaḥ-yoga; ucyate—is called.

Meaning: Be settled in Yoga and perform your action, O Dhananjaya, renouncing attachment and being equally prepared for success and failure. Such a state of mind in equipoise is called Yoga.

49

दूरेण ह्यवरं कर्म
बुद्धियोगाद्धनंजय।
बुद्धौ शरणमन्विच्छ
कृपणाः फलहेतवः॥

dūreṇa hy avaraṁ karma
buddhi-yogād dhanañjaya
buddhau śaraṇamanviccha
kṛpaṇāḥphala-hetavaḥ ||

dūreṇa—by discarding it at a long distance; hi—certainly; avaram—abominable; karma—activities; buddhi-yogāt—on the strength of Kṛṣṇa consciousness; dhanañjaya—O conqueror of wealth; buddhau—in such consciousness; śaraṇam—full surrender; anviccha—desire; kṛpaṇāḥ—the misers; phala-hetavaḥ—those desiring fruitive action.

Meaning: O Dhananjaya, action is way inferior to this Yoga of the understanding. Seek shelter in this understanding as the ones who seek the fruits of action have to be pitied.

50

बुद्धियुक्तो जहातीह
उभे सुकृतदुष्कृते।
तस्माद्योगाय युज्यस्व
योगः कर्मसु कौशलम्॥

buddhi-yukto jahātīha
ubhe sukṛta-duṣkṛte
tasmād yogāya yujyasva
yogaḥ karmasu kauśalam||

buddhi-yuktaḥ—one who is engaged in devotional service; jahāti—can get rid of; iha—in this life; ubhe—in both; sukṛta-duṣkṛte—in good and bad results; tasmāt—therefore; yogāya—for the sake of devotional service; yujyasva—be so engaged; yogaḥ—Kṛṣṇa consciousness; karmasu—in all activities; kauśalam—art.

Meaning: The one who is aided by this understanding is not affected by both the good or bad actions even in this life. Therefore, cling on to Yoga which is the supreme joy of all action.

51

कर्मजं बुद्धियुक्ता हि
फलं त्यक्त्वा मनीषिणः।
जन्मबन्धविनिर्मुक्ताः
पदं गच्छन्त्यनामयम्॥

karma-jaṁ buddhi-yuktā hi
phalaṁ tyaktvā manīṣiṇaḥ
janma-bandha-vinirmuktāḥ-
padaṁ gacchantyanāmayam||

karma-jam—because of fruitive activities; buddhi-yuktāḥ—being done in devotional service; hi—certainly; phalam—results; tyaktvā—giving up; manīṣiṇaḥ—devotees who are great sages; janma-bandha—the bondage of birth and death; vinirmuktāḥ—liberated souls; padam—position; gacchanti—reach; anāmayam—without miseries.

Meaning: Renouncing the fruits of action and engaged in devotional service by taking refuge in the Lord, one can be liberated from the cycle of birth and death. One can attain this state free of all miseries in this way.

52

यदा ते मोहकलिलं
बुद्धिर्व्यतितरिष्यति।
तदा गन्तासि निर्वेदं
श्रोतव्यस्य श्रुतस्य च॥

yadā te moha-kalilaṁ
buddhir vyatitariṣyati
tadā gantāsi nirvedaṁ
śrotavyasya śrutasyaca ||

yadā—when; te—your; moha—illusory; kalilam—dense forest; buddhiḥ—transcendental service with intelligence; vyatitariṣyati—surpasses; tadā—at that time; gantāsi—you shall go; nirvedam—callousness; śrotavyasya—all that is to be heard; śrutasya—all that is already heard; ca—also.

Meaning: When your understanding has been cleared from the mazes of delusion, you shall become indifferent to all that you will hear or have heard after gaining a clear knowledge.

53

श्रुतिविप्रतिपन्ना ते
यदा स्थास्यति निश्चला।
समाधावचला बुद्धिस्तदा
योगमवाप्स्यसि॥

śruti-vipratipannā te
yadā sthāsyati niścalā
samādhāv acalā buddhis tadā-
yogam avāpsyasi ||

śruti—Vedic revelation; vipratipannā—without being influenced by the fruitive results of the Vedas; te—your; yadā—when; sthāsyati—remains; niścalā—unmoved; samādhau—in transcendental consciousness, or Kṛṣṇa consciousness; acalā—unflinching; buddhiḥ—intelligence; tadā—at that time; yogam—self-realisation; avāpsyasi—you will achieve.

Meaning: When you are well-informed by hearing and your mind is no longer affected by the conflicting language of the Vedas, your understanding will be firm and perfect. Then, you shall turn to Yoga and will attain the Divine consciousness in the trance of self-realisation.

54

अर्जुन उवाच
स्थितप्रज्ञस्य का भाषा
समाधिस्थस्य केशव।
स्थितधीः किं प्रभाषेत
किमासीत व्रजेत किम्॥

arjunauvāca
sthita-prajñasya kā bhāṣā
samādhi-sthasya keśava
sthita-dhīḥ kiṁ prabhāṣeta
kim āsīta vrajeta kiṁ ||

arjunaḥuvāca—Arjuna said; sthita-prajñasya—of one who is situated in fixed Kṛṣṇa consciousness; kā—what; bhāṣā—language;samādhi-sthasya—of one situated in trance; keśava—O Kṛṣṇa; sthita-dhīḥ—one fixed in Kṛṣṇa consciousness; kim—what; prabhāṣeta—speak; kim—how; āsīta—does remain; vrajeta—walk; kim—how.

Meaning: Arjuna said: O Keshava, what is meant by 'a man of stable understanding whose consciousness is merged in Transcendence'? How does this man of stable understanding talk? How is this man seated and how does he walk?

55

श्रीभगवानुवाच

प्रजहाति यदा कामान्
सर्वान्पार्थ मनोगतान्।
आत्मयेवात्मना
तुष्टः स्थितप्रज्ञस्तदोच्यते।।

śrī-bhagavān uvāca
prajahāti yadā kāmān
sarvānpārtha mano-gatān
ātmany evātmanā
tuṣṭaḥ sthita-prajñastadocyate||

śrī bhagavān uvāca—the Supreme Personality of Godhead said; prajahāti—gives up; yadā—when; kāmān—desires for sense gratification; sarvān—of all varieties; pārtha—O son of Pṛthā; manaḥ-gatān—of mental concoction; ātmani—in the pure state of the soul; eva—certainly;ātmanā —by the purified mind; tuṣṭaḥ—satisfied; sthita-prajñaḥ—transcendentally situated; tadā—at that time; ucyate—is said.

Meaning: The Glorious Lord said: When, O Partha, one rejects all the wordly desires of the mind, and is satisfied by the self in the self alone, he is said to be a man of stable understanding in a state of pure transcendental consciousness.

56

दुःखेष्वनुद्विग्नमनाः
सुखेषु विगतस्पृहः।
वीतरागभयक्रोधः स्थित
धीर्मुनिरुच्यते॥

duḥkheṣvanudvigna-manāḥ
sukheṣu vigata-spṛhaḥ
vīta-rāga-bhaya-krodhaḥ sthita-
dhīrmunir ucyate ||

duḥkheṣu—in the threefold miseries; anudvigna-manāḥ—without being agitated in mind; sukheṣu—in happiness; vigata-spṛhaḥ—without being too interested; vīta—freefrom; rāga—attachment; bhaya—fear; krodhaḥ—anger; sthita-dhīḥ—one who is steady; muniḥ—sage; ucyate—is called.

Meaning: One whose mind is not agitated amidst the threefold miseries, who is not elated in happiness, and who is free from attachment, fear, and anger is of stable understanding and is called a Muni.

57

यः सर्वत्रानभिस्नेहस्त
त्तत्प्राप्य शुभाशुभम्।
नाभिनंदति न द्वेष्टि
तस्य प्रज्ञा प्रतिष्ठिता।।

yaḥ sarvatrān abhisnehas
tattatprāpya śubhāśubham
nābhinandati na dveṣṭi
tasya prajñā pratiṣṭhitā||

yaḥ—one who; sarvatra—everywhere; anabhisnehaḥ—without affection; tat—that; tat—that; prāpya—achieving; śubha—good; aśubham—evil; na—never; abhinandati—prays; na—never; dveṣṭi—envies; tasya—his; prajñā—perfect knowledge; pratiṣṭhita—fixed.

Meaning: He who is without any attachment to anything, who does not rejoice in good times nor grieve during evil times, who neither loves nor hates, is a man who is fixed in perfect understanding.

58

यदा संहरते चायं
कूर्मोऽङ्गानीव सर्वशः।
इन्द्रियाणीन्द्रियार्थेभ्यस्तस्य
प्रज्ञा प्रतिष्ठिता।।

yadā saṁharate cāyaṁ
kūrmo'ṅgānīvasarvaśaḥ
indriyāṇīndriyārthe bhyastasya
prajñā pratiṣṭhitā ||

yadā—when; saṁharate—winds up; ca—also; ayam—all these; kūrmaḥ—tortoise; aṅgāni—limbs; iva—like; sarvaśaḥ—altogether; indriyāni—senses; indriya-arthebhyaḥ—from the sense objects; tasya—his; prajñā—consciousness; pratiṣṭhitā—fixed up.

Meaning: One who is capable of withdrawing his senses from sense-objects on all sides just like the tortoise withdraws his limbs fully within his shell, he has his understanding truly and he is one with God.

59

विषया विनिवर्तन्ते
निराहारस्य देहिनः।
रसवर्ज रसोऽप्यस्य
परं दृष्ट्वा निवर्तते॥

viṣayā vinivartante
nirāhārasya dehinaḥ
rasa-varjaṁ raso 'py asya
paraṁ dṛṣṭvā nivartate ||

viṣayāḥ—objects for sense enjoyment; vinivartante—are practised to be refrained from; nirāhārasya—by negative restrictions; dehinaḥ—for the embodied; rasa-varjam—giving up the taste; rasaḥ—sense of enjoyment; api—although there is; asya—his; param—far superior things; dṛṣṭvā—by experiencing; nivartate—ceases from.

Meaning: The Embodied One may turn away from sense enjoyment through abstinence, but the taste for sense objects remains. But, by experiencing the Supreme One, this taste also disappears as he is fixed in divine consciousness.

60

यततो ह्यपि कौन्तेय
पुरुषस्य विपश्चितः।
इन्द्रियाणि प्रमाथीनि
हरन्ति प्रसभं मनः॥

yatato hy api kaunteya
puruṣasya vipaścitaḥ
indriyāṇi pramāthīni
haranti prasabhaṁ manaḥ||

yatataḥ—while endeavouring; hi—certainly; api—inspite of; kaunteya—O son of Kuntī; puruṣasya—of the man; vipaścitaḥ—full of discriminating knowledge; indriyāṇi—the senses; pramāthīni—stimulated; haranti—throws forcefully; prasabhaṁ—by force; manaḥ—the mind.

Meaning: O son of Kunti, the powerful and tyrannical senses forcibly carry away even the will of a cautious and reflective man who is trying to control these senses.

61

तानि सर्वाणि संयम्य
युक्त आसीत मत्परः।
वशे हि यस्येन्द्रियाणि
तस्य प्रज्ञा प्रतिष्ठिता॥

tāni sarvāṇi saṁyamya
yuktaāsīta mat-paraḥ
vaśe hi yasyendriyāṇi
tasya prajñā pratiṣṭhitā ||

tāni—those senses; sarvāṇi—all; saṁyamya—keeping under control; yuktaḥ—being engaged; āsīta—being so situated; mat-paraḥ—in relationship with Me; vaśe—in full subjugation; hi—certainly; yasya—one whose; indriyāṇi—senses; tasya—his; prajñā—consciousness; pratiṣṭhitā—fixed.

Meaning: The one who restrains all his senses and is settled in Yoga fixes his consciousness upon Me as the highest goal and is a man of steady understanding.

62

ध्यायतो विषयान्पुंसः
संगस्तेषूपजायते।
संगात्संजायते कामः
कामात्क्रोधोऽभिजायते॥

dhyāyatoviṣayānpuṁsaḥ
saṅgas teṣūpajāyate
saṅgāt sañjāyate kāmaḥ
kāmātkrodho'bhijāyate||

dhyāyataḥ—while contemplating; viṣayān—sense objects; puṁsaḥ—of the person; saṅgaḥ—attachment; teṣu—in the sense objects; upajāyate—develops; saṅgāt—attachment; sañjāyate—develops; kāmaḥ—desire; kāmāt—from desire; krodhaḥ—anger; abhijāyate—becomes manifest.

Meaning: When a man muses on the objects of the senses, he develops an attachment for them. Desire springs from attachment, and from desire anger rises.

63

क्रोधाद्भवति सम्मोहः
सम्मोहात्स्मृतिविभ्रमः।
स्मृतिभ्रंशाद् बुद्धिनाशो
बुद्धिनाशात्प्रणश्यति॥

krodhād bhavati saṁmohaḥ
saṁmohātsmṛti-vibhramaḥ
smṛti-bhraṁśād buddhi-nāśo
buddhi-nāśāt praṇaśyati ||

krodhāt—from anger; bhavati—takes place; saṁmohaḥ—perfect illusion; saṁmohāt—from illusion; smṛti—of memory; vibhramaḥ—bewilderment; smṛti-bhraṁśāt—after bewilderment of memory; buddhi-nāśaḥ—loss of intelligence; buddhi-nāśāt—and from loss of intelligence; praṇaśyati—falls down.

Meaning: Anger gives rise to utter delusion, which causes loss of memory. When memory is bewildered, understanding is lost; and from loss of understanding one perishes in the material pool.

64

रागद्वेषवियुक्तैस्तु
विषयानिन्द्रियैश्चरन्।
आत्मवश्यैर्विधेयात्मा
प्रसादमधिगच्छति॥

rāga-dveṣa-vimuktais tu
viṣayān indriyaiścaran
ātma-vaśyair vidheyātmā
prasādam adhigacchati ||

rāga—attachment; dveṣa—detachment; vimuktaiḥ—by one who has been free from such things; tu—but; viṣayān—sense objects; indriyaiḥ—by the senses; caran—acting; ātma-vaśyaiḥ—one who has control over; vidheyātmā—one who follows regulated freedom; prasādam—the mercy of the Lord; adhigacchati—attains.

Meaning: But the one who can control his senses, is deprived of affection and antipathy, and is subversient to the self, obtains the total mercy of the Lord and thus becomes free from attachment and hate.

65

प्रसादे सर्वदुःखानां
हानिरस्योपजायते।
प्रसन्नचेतसो ह्याशु
बुद्धिः पर्यवतिष्ठते।।

prasāde sarva-duḥkhānāṁ
hānir asyopajāyate
prasanna-cetaso hy āśu
buddhiḥ paryavatiṣṭhate ||

prasāde—on achievement of the causeless mercy of the Lord; sarva—all; duḥkhānām—material miseries; hāniḥ—destruction; asya—his; upajāyate—takes place; prasanna-cetasaḥ—of the happy-minded; hi—certainly; āśu—very soon; buddhiḥ—intelligence; pari—sufficiently; avatiṣṭhate—established.

Meaning: The one who is seated in the Divine consciousness is rid of the threefold miseries of material existence. He is in such a happy state that his understanding is thoroughly settled and he is one with God.

66

नास्ति बुद्धिरयुक्तस्य
न चायुक्तस्य भावना।
न चाभावयतः शान्तिर
शान्तस्य कुतः सुखम्॥

nāstibuddhir ayuktasya
na cāyuktasya bhāvanā
na cābhāvayataḥ śāntir
aśāntasya kutaḥ sukham||

na asti—there cannot be; buddhiḥ—transcendental intelligence; ayuktasya—of one who is not connected (with Kṛṣṇa consciousness); na —neither; ca—and; ayuktasya—of one devoid of Kṛṣṇa consciousness; bhāvanā—mind fixed in happiness; na—neither; ca—and; abhāvayataḥ—one who is not fixed; śāntiḥ—peace; aśāntasya—of the unpeaceful; kutaḥ—whereis; sukham—happiness.

Meaning: The one who is not settled in Yoga does not have this understanding, a tranquil mind, and steady intelligence. Without peace of mind, how can there be any happiness?

67

इन्द्रियाणां हि चरतां
यन्मनोऽनु विधीयते।
तदस्य हरति प्रज्ञां
वायुर्नाविमिवाम्भसि।।

indriyāṇāṁ hi caratāṁ-
yanmano'nuvidhīyate
tad asya harati prajñāṁ
vāyur nāvam ivāmbhasi ||

indriyāṇām—of the senses; hi—certainly; caratām—while herding over; yat—that; manaḥ—mind; anuvidhīyate—becomes constantly engaged; tat—that; asya—his; harati—takes away; prajñām—intelligence; vāyuḥ—wind; nāvam—a boat; iva—like; ambhasi—on the water.

Meaning: Just as a gale sweeps away a boat on water, the mind which follows the dictates of the roving senses is drained of its understanding.

68

तस्माद्यस्य महाबाहो
निगृहीतानि सर्वशः।
इन्द्रियाणीन्द्रियार्थेभ्यस
तस्य प्रज्ञा प्रतिष्ठिता॥

tasmādyasyamahā-bāho
nigṛh-itāni sarvaśaḥ
indriyāṇīndriyārthebhyas
tasya prajñā pratiṣṭhitā||

tasmāt—therefore; yasya—of one's; mahā-bāho—O mighty-armed one; nigṛhītāni—so curbed down; sarvaśaḥ—all around; indriyāṇi—the senses; indriya-arthebhyaḥ—for the sake of sense objects; tasya—his; prajñā—intelligence; pratiṣṭhitā—fixed.

Meaning: Therefore, O mighty-armed, his understanding remains steady whose senses are withdrawn from the objects all around him.

69

या निशा सर्वभूतानां
तस्यां जागर्ति संयमी।
यस्यां जाग्रति भूतानि
सा निशा पश्यतो मुनेः

yā niśā sarva-bhūtānāṁ
tasyāṁ jāgarti saṁyamī
yasyāṁ jāgrati bhūtāni
sā niśā paśyato muneḥ||

yā—what; niśā—is night; sarva—all; bhūtānām—of living entities; tasyām—in that; jāgarti—wakeful; saṁyamī—the self-controlled; yasyām —in which; jāgrati—awake; bhūtāni—all beings; sā—that is; niśā—night; paśyataḥ—for the introspective; muneḥ—sage.

Meaning: What is night for all creatures is the time of awakening for the God-realised Yogi. When all other creatures wake up, that is the night for the introspective Muni.

70

आपूर्यमाणमचलप्रतिष्ठं
समुद्रमापः प्रविशन्ति यद्वत्।
तद्वत्कामा यं प्रविशन्ति सर्वे
स शान्तिमाप्नोति न कामकामी॥

āpūryamāṇam acala-pratiṣṭhaṁ
samudramāpaḥ praviśanti yadvat
tadvat kāmā yaṁ praviśanti sarve
sa śāntimāpnoti nakāma-kāmī||

āpūryamāṇam—always filled; acala-pratiṣṭham—steadily situated; samudram—the ocean; āpaḥ—water; praviśanti—enter; yadvat—as; tadvat—so; kāmāḥ—desires; yam—unto one; praviśanti—enter; sarve—all; saḥ—that person; śāntim—peace; āpnoti—achieves; na—not; kāma-kāmī—one who desires to fulfill desires.

Meaning: One gains peace when not disturbed by the flow of desires just as rivers flowing into the ocean which is ever-filling but unchangeable and still. A seeker of desires never attains peace.

71

विहाय कामान्यः
सर्वान्पुमांश्चरति निःस्पृहः।
निर्ममो निरहंकारः
स शान्तिमधिगच्छति।।

vihāya kāmān yaḥ
sarvān pumāṁścarati niḥspṛhaḥ
nirmamo nirahaṅkāraḥ
sa śāntim adhigacchati ||

vihāya—after giving up; kāmān—all material desires for sense gratification; yaḥ—the person; sarvān—all; pumān—a person; carati—lives; nihṣpṛhaḥ—desireless; nirmamaḥ—without a sense of proprietorship; nirahaṅkāraḥ— without false ego; saḥ—all; śāntim—perfect peace; adhigacchati—attains.

Meaning: The man who shakes off all desires for the gratification of the senses goes on to live a life free from desire, considering nothing as his own. Without false ego, he is the one who attains real peace.

72

एषा ब्राह्मी स्थितिः पार्थ
नैनां प्राप्य विमुह्यति।
स्थित्वास्यामन्तकालेऽपि
ब्रह्मनिर्वाणमृच्छति॥

eṣā brāhmī sthitiḥ pārtha
naināṁ prāpya vimuhyati
sthitvāsyām anta-kāle 'pi
brahma-nirvāṇam ṛcchati ||

eṣā—this; brāhmī—spiritual; sthitiḥ—situation; pārtha—O son of Pṛthā; na—never; enām—this;prāpya—achieving;vimuhyati—bewilders; sthitvā—being so situated; asyām—being so; anta-kāle—at the end of life; api—also; brahma-nirvāṇam—spiritual (kingdom of God); ṛcchati—attains.

Meaning: O Partha, the state of being established in Brahma is this. After attaining this state, a man is no longer bewildered. Being in such a state even at the last moment at the hour of death, one can enter the kingdom of the Lord to find repose in Brahma.

ॐ तत्सदिति श्रीमद्भगवद्गीतासूपनिषत्सु ब्रह्मविद्यायां योगशास्त्रे

श्रीकृष्णार्जुनसंवादेसांख्ययोगो नाम द्वितीयोऽध्यायः।

Thus in the Upanishad of the Glorious Divine Lay,
the Science of Brahma, the Ordinance of Yoga,
the Discourse between the Glorious Lord Krishna
and Arjuna, the Second Chapter titled
'Sankhya Yoga' (The Yoga of Knowledge).

CHAPTER 3

KARMA YOGA

(THE YOGA OF ACTION)

CHAPTER 3

KARMA YOGA
(THE YOGA OF ACTION)

Despite Lord Krishna's assurance, Arjuna is still in a state of confusion. He is of the opinion that one should retire from all spheres of active life to practice penance and austerities in the forest. But, Lord Krishna urges him to act. He tells him to fight and perform the duty that has been prescribed as a warrior for Arjuna in this life. Lord Krishna reveals that the performance of prescribed duties is essential for everyone. Each and every member of society is under the obligation of performing the job that is assigned to them in their respective stages of life, according to the norms of that society where they live. That is the Eternal Duty of human beings on earth.

Lord Krishna asks Arjuna to fight in the battle of Kurukshetra without being worried about the results. He asks Arjuna to fight, armed with a spirit of renunciation, and offer all the results or the outcome of the battle to the Supreme One. This, Lord Krishna says, will be the best purification for Arjuna as by performing actions without any attachment to the fruits of action, one attains the Supreme Lord.

Lord Krishna also explains to Arjuna in Chapter Three why such prescribed duties must be followed, the benefit that is gained by such performance, and the harm that is caused by the non-performance of such prescribed duties. Performing sacrifices to please the Lord brings about material prosperity for some and freedom from sins for others. Even a person who is self-realised never abandons his duty as his very actions are for the sake of educating others.

Arjuna then asks Lord Krishna what causes one to participate in sinful acts. Lord Krishna replies that it is lust that causes one to walk on the path of sin. This lust is the reason for the bewilderment of people, causing them to be trapped in the material world and the cycle of birth and death. Lord Krishna reveals that lust springs forth in the senses, mind, as well as understanding, but one can counteract its ill-effects with self control.

1

अर्जुन उवाच
ज्यायसी चेत्कर्मणस्ते मता
बुद्धिर्जनार्दन।
तत्किं कर्मणि घोरे मां
नियोजयसि केशव॥

arjunauvāca
jyāyasī cet karmaṇas tematā
buddhirjanārdana
tatkiṁkarmaṇighoremāṁ
niyojayasi keśava||

arjunaḥ—Arjuna; uvāca—said; jyāyasī—speaking very highly; cet—although; karmaṇaḥ—than fruitive action; te—your; matā—opinion; buddhiḥ —intelligence; janārdana—O Kṛṣṇa; tat—therefore; kim—why; karmaṇi—in action; ghore—ghastly; mām—me; niyojayasi—engaging me; keśava—O Kṛṣṇa.

Meaning: Arjuna said: O Janardana, if You think that knowledge is greater than action, then why do You urge me to engage in this battle with dreadful action, O Kesava?

2

व्यामिश्रेणेव वाक्येन
बुद्धिं मोहयसीव मे।
तदेकं वद निश्चित्य
येन श्रेयोऽहमाप्नुयाम्॥

vyāmiśreṇeva vākyena
buddhiṁmohayasīvame
tadekaṁvadaniścitya
yenaśreyo'hamāpnuyām||

vyāmiśreṇa—by equivocal; iva—as; vākyena—words; buddhim—intelligence; mohayasi—bewildering; iva—as; me—my; tat—therefore; ekam—only one; vada—please tell; niścitya—ascertaining; yena—by which; śreyaḥ—real benefit; aham—I; āpnuyām—may have it.

Meaning: My understanding is bewildered by your intermingled instructions. Please declare decisively what will be the most beneficial for me to obtain goodness.

3

श्रीभगवानुवाच
लोकेऽस्मिन्द्विविधा निष्ठा
पुरा प्रोक्ता मयानघ।
ज्ञानयोगेन साङ्ख्यानां
कर्मयोगेन योगिनाम्॥

śrī-bhagavān uvāca
loke›smindvi-vidhāniṣṭhā
purāproktāmayānagha
jñāna-yogena sāṅkhyānāṁ
karma-yogenayoginām||

śrībhagavānuvāca—the Supreme Personality of Godhead said; loke—in the world; asmin—this; dvi-vidhā—two kinds of; niṣṭhā—faith; purā—formerly; proktā—was said; mayā—by Me; anagha—O sinless one; jñāna- yogena—by the linking process of knowledge; sāṅkhyānām—of the empiric philosophers; karma-yogena—by the linking process of devotion; yoginām—of the devotees.

Meaning: The Glorious Lord said: O sinless one, I have already declared the two-fold path that exists in this world. The two classes of men who realise the Self are the Sankhyas by the Yoga of knowledge and the Yogis by the Yoga of action.

4

न कर्मणामनारंभान
नैष्कर्म्यपुरुषोऽश्नुते।
न च सन्न्यसनादेव
सिद्धिं समधिगच्छति।।

na karmaṇām anārambhān
naiṣkarmyaṁ puruṣo'śnute
na ca sannyasanād eva
siddhiṁsamadhigacchati ||

na—without; karmaṇām—of the prescribed duties; anārambhāt—non- performance; naiṣkarmyam—freedom from reaction; puruṣah—man; aśnute—achieve; na—nor; ca—also; sannyasanāt—by renunciation; eva—simply; siddhim—success; samadhigacchati—attain.

Meaning: Man cannot achieve freedom from activity by non-performance of actions, nor can he attain perfection only by renunciation.

5

न हि कश्चित्क्षणमपि
जातु तिष्ठत्यकर्मकृत्।
कार्यते ह्यवशः कर्म
सर्वः प्रकृतिजैर्गुणैः॥

na hi kaścit kṣaṇam api
jātutiṣṭhatyakarmakṛt
kāryate hy avaśaḥ karma
sarvaḥprakṛti-jairguṇaiḥ||

na—nor; hi—certainly; kaścit—anyone; kṣaṇam—even a moment; api— also; jātu—even; tiṣṭhati—stands; akarma-kṛt—without doing something; kāryate—forced to work; hi—certainly; avaśaḥ—helplessly; karma—work; sarvaḥ—everything; prakṛti-jaiḥ—out of the modes of material nature; guṇaiḥ—by the qualities.

Meaning: No one can remain inactive even for a moment as the material impulses force them to act.

6

कर्मेन्द्रियाणि संयम्य
य आस्ते मनसा स्मरन्।
इन्द्रियार्थान्विमूढात्मा
मिथ्याचारः स उच्यते॥

karmendriyāṇi saṁyamya
yaāstemanasāsmaran
indriyārthān vimūḍhātmā
mithyācāraḥsaucyate ||

karma-indriyāṇi—the five working sense organs; saṁyamya—controlling; yaḥ—anyone who; āste—remains; manasā—by mind; smaran—thinking; indriya-arthān—sense objects; vimūḍha—foolish; ātmā—soul; mithyā-ācāraḥ —pretender; saḥ—he; ucyate—is called.

Meaning: He, who has managed to control the organs of action and the senses, but still has his mind on the objects of the senses, is called a hypocrite who deludes himself.

7

यस्त्विन्द्रियाणि मनसा
नियम्यारभतेऽर्जुन।
कर्मेन्द्रियैः कर्मयोगमसक्तः
स विशिष्यते॥

yas tv indriyāṇi manasā
niyamyārabhate'rjuna
karmendriyaiḥkarma-yogam asaktaḥ
sa viśiṣyate||

yaḥ—one who; tu—but; indriyāṇi—senses; manasā—by the mind; niyamya —regulating; ārabhate—begins; arjuna—O Arjuna; karma-indriyaiḥ—by the active sense organs; karma-yogam—devotion;asaktaḥ—without attachment; saḥ—he; viśiṣyate—by far the better.

Meaning: But, the one who regulates his senses by the mind, O Arjuna, and commences the Yoga of action with the organs of action, he becomes unattached because of his supreme devotion to become a far superior man.

8

नियतं कुरु कर्म त्वं
कर्म ज्यायो ह्यकर्मणः।
शरीरयात्रापि च ते
न प्रसिद्ध्येदकर्मण॥

niyataṁ kuru karma tvaṁ
karmajyāyohyakarmaṇaḥ
śarīra-yātrāpicate
naprasiddhyedakarmaṇaḥ ||

niyatam—prescribed; kuru—do; karma—duties; tvam—you; karma—work; jyāyaḥ—better; hi—than; akarmaṇaḥ—without work; śarīra—bodily; yātrā— maintenance; api—even; ca—also; te—your; na—never; prasiddhyet— effected; akarmaṇaḥ—without work.

Meaning: Perform the action that has been ordained by nature for you, for action is greater than inaction. Even the journey in this physical body of yours is impossible with inaction.

9

यज्ञार्थात्कर्मणोऽन्यत्र
लोकोऽयं कर्मबंधनः।
तदर्थं कर्म कौन्तेय
मुक्तसंगः समाचर॥

yajñārthātkarmaṇo'nyatra
loko'yaṁkarma-bandhanaḥ
tad-arthaṁ karma kaunteya
mukta-saṅgaḥsamācara||

yajña-arthāt—only for the sake of Yajña, or Viṣṇu; karmaṇaḥ—work done; anyatra—otherwise; lokaḥ—this world; ayam—this; karma-bandhanaḥ—bondage by work; tat—Him; artham—for the sake of ;karma—work; kaunteya—O son of Kuntī; mukta-saṅgaḥ—liberated from association; samācara—do it perfectly.

Meaning: All actions other than those selflessly offered to Shri Viṣhṇu cause bondage. Therefore, O son of Kunti, perform your actions free from attachment and for My satisfaction.

10

सहयज्ञाः प्रजाः सृष्टा
पुरोवाचप्रजापतिः।
अनेन प्रसविष्यध्वमेष
वोऽस्त्विष्टकामधुक्॥

saha-yajñāḥprajāḥsṛṣṭvā
purovāca prajāpatiḥ
anenaprasaviṣyadhvam eṣa-
vo'stviṣṭa-kāma-dhuk||

saha—along with; yajñāḥ—sacrifices; prajāḥ—generations; sṛṣṭvā—by creating; purā—anciently; uvāca—said; prajā-patiḥ—the Lord of creatures; anena—by this; prasaviṣyadhvam—be more and more prosperous; eṣaḥ—certainly; vaḥ—your; astu—let it be; iṣṭa—all desirable; kāma-dhuk—bestower.

Meaning: In the beginning of creation, the Lord of offspring created generations of men and demigods with sacrifice, and said: Hereby grow. Let this sacrifice bestow upon you all your cherished desires.

11

देवान्भावयतानेन
ते देवा भावयन्तु वः।
परस्परं भावयन्तः
श्रेयः परमवाप्स्यथ।।

devān bhāvayatānena
tedevābhāvayantuvaḥ
parasparaṁ bhāvayantaḥ
śreyaḥparamavāpsyatha ||

devān—demigods; bhāvayata—having been pleased; anena—by this sacrifice; te—those; devāḥ—the demigods; bhāvayantu—will please; vaḥ—you; parasparam—mutual; bhāvayantaḥ—pleasing one another; sreyaḥ—benediction; param—the supreme; avāpsyatha—do you achieve.

Meaning: Hereby support the gods by sacrifices, and they will support you in return. In this general nourishment all will attain prosperity and Supreme welfare.

12

इष्टान्भोगान्हि वो देवा
दास्यन्ते यज्ञभाविताः।
तैर्दत्तानप्रदायैभ्यो
यो भुंक्ते स्तेन एव सः॥

iṣṭān bhogān hi vo devā
dāsyanteyajña-bhāvitāḥ
tairdattān apradāyaibhyo
yobhuṅktestenaevasaḥ||

iṣṭān—desired; bhogān—necessities of life; hi—certainly; vaḥ—unto you; devāḥ—the demi gods; dāsyante—award; yajña-bhāvitāḥ—being satisfied by the performance of sacrifices; taiḥ—by them; dattān—things given; apradāya—without offering; ebhyaḥ—to the demigods; yaḥ—he who; bhuṅkte—enjoys; stenaḥ—thief; eva—certainly; saḥ—is he.

Meaning: The gods, supported and pleased with your sacrifices will bestow on you all the cherished enjoyments and necessities needed by Man. But the one who enjoys these gifts, without offering them in return to the gods, is indeed a thief.

13

यज्ञशिष्टाशिनः सन्तो
मुच्यन्ते सर्वकिल्बिषैः।
भुञ्जते ते त्वघं पापा
ये पचन्त्यात्मकारणात्॥

yajña-śiṣṭāśinaḥ santo
mucyantesarva-kilbiṣaiḥ
bhuñjatetetvaghampāpā
yepacantyātma-kāraṇāt||

yajña-śiṣṭa—food taken after performance of yajña; aśinaḥ—eaters; santaḥ—the devotees; mucyante—get relief from; sarva—all kinds of; kilbiṣaiḥ—sins; bhuñjate—enjoy; te—they; tu—but; agham—grievous sins; pāpāḥ—sinners; ye—those; pacanti—prepare food; ātma-kāraṇāt—for sense enjoyment.

Meaning: The righteous devotees who offer food first in sacrifice, and eat it only after the sacrifice is completed are released from all sins. Others, who cook food only for their own sake and enjoyment, are the sinful ones who taste only sin.

14

अन्नाद्भवन्ति भूतानि
पर्जन्यादन्नसम्भवः।
यज्ञाद्भवति पर्जन्यो यज्ञः
कर्मसमुद्भवः॥

annād bhavanti bhūtāni
parjanyādanna-sambhavaḥ
yajñādbhavati parjanyo yajñaḥ
karma-samudbhavaḥ||

annāt—from grains; bhavanti—grow; bhūtāni—the material bodies; parjanyāt—from rains; anna—food grains; sambhavaḥ—are made possible; yajñāt—from the performance of sacrifice; bhavati—becomes possible; parjanyaḥ—rains; yajñaḥ—performance of yajña; karma—prescribed duties; samudbhavaḥ—born of.

Meaning: All living creatures exist on food grains, which are produced by rain. Rains spring from sacrifice, and sacrifice is produced by the action of prescribed duties.

15

कर्म ब्रह्मोद्भवं
विद्धि ब्रह्माक्षरसमुद्भवम्।
तस्मात्सर्वगतं ब्रह्म
नित्यं यज्ञे प्रतिष्ठितम्।।

karma brahmodbhavaṁ
viddhibrahmākṣara-samudbhavam
tasmāt sarva-gataṁ brahma
nityaṁyajñepratiṣṭhitam||

karma—work; brahma-Vedas; udbhavam—produced from; viddhi—one should know; brahma—the Vedas; akṣara—the Supreme Brahman (Personality of Godhead); samudbhavam; directly manifested; tasmāt—therefore; sarva-gatam—all-pervading; brahma—Transcendence; nityam—eternally; yajñe—in sacrifice; pratiṣṭhitam—situated.

Meaning: The Vedas prescribe the regulated activities, the action of which is manifested from Brahma who arises from the Imperishable. Hence, the all-pervading Brahma eternally abides in sacrifice.

16

एवं प्रवर्तितं चक्रं
नानुवर्तयतीह यः।
अघायुरिन्द्रियारामो
मोघं पार्थ स जीवति॥

evaṁ pravartitaṁ cakraṁ
nānuvartayatīha yaḥ
aghāyur indriyārāmo
moghaṁpārthasajīvati ||

evam—thus prescribed; pravartitam—established by the Vedas; cakram— cycle; na—does not; anuvartayati—adopt; iha—in this life; yaḥ—one who; aghāyuḥ—life full of sins; indriya-ārāmaḥ—satisfied in sense gratification; mogham—useless; pārtha—O son of Pṛthā (Arjuna); saḥ—one who does so; jīvati—lives.

Meaning: O Partha, a man who does not follow the wheel that is set rolling by the prescribed Vedic system of sacrifice leads a sinful life. This person delights only in the senses, and lives in vain.

17

यस्त्वात्मरतिरेव
स्यादात्मतृप्तश्च मानवः।
आत्मन्येव च सन्तुष्टस्तस्य
कार्यं न विद्यते॥

yas tv ātma-ratir eva
syād ātma-tṛptaśca mānavaḥ
ātmany eva ca santuṣṭas tasya
kāryaṁ na vidyate||

yaḥ—one who; tu—but; ātma-ratiḥ—takes pleasure; eva—certainly; syāt— remains; ātma-tṛptaḥ—self-illuminated; ca—and; mānavaḥ—a man; ātmani— in himself; eva—only; ca—and; santuṣṭaḥ—perfectly satiated; tasya—his; kāryam—duty; na—does not; vidyate—exist.

Meaning: On the other hand, a man who is really devoted to the self and is satisfied with the self, and rejoices in the self- for him there is no obligation of duty.

18

संजय उवाच
नैव तस्य कृतेनार्थो
नाकृतेनेह कश्चन।
न चास्य सर्वभूतेषु
कश्चिदर्थव्यपाश्रय।।

sañjaya uvāca
naiva tasya kṛtenārtho
nākṛteneha kaścana
na cāsya sarva-bhūteṣu
kaścidartha-vyapāśrayaḥ ||

sañjayaḥ—Sañjaya; uvāca—said; na—never; eva—certainly; tasya—his; kṛtena—by discharge of duty; arthaḥ—purpose; na—nor; akṛtena—without discharge of duty; iha—in this world; kaścana—whatever; na—never; ca—and; asya—of him; sarva- bhūteṣu—in all living beings; kaścit—any; artha—purpose; vyapa-āśrayaḥ—taking shelter of.

Meaning: For a self-realised man there lies no interest in what is done and what is not done. He has no interest or reason to perform such work. Nor is there a need for his dependence on any other creature.

19

तस्मादसक्तः सततं
कार्यं कर्म समाचर।
असक्तो ह्याचरन्कर्म
परमाप्नोति पूरुषः।।

tasmād asaktaḥ satataṁ
kāryaṁ karma samācara
asakto hyācarankarma
paramāpnoti pūruṣaḥ||

tasmāt—therefore; asaktaḥ—without attachment; satatam—constantly; kāryam—as duty; karma—work; samācara—perform; asaktaḥ—nonattachment; hi—certainly; ācaran—performing; karma—work; param—the Supreme; āpnoti—achieves; pūruṣaḥ—aman.

Meaning: Therfore, always perform action that needs to be done being unattached. That leads one to attain the Supreme.

20

कर्मणैव हि
संसिद्धिमास्थिता जनकादयः।
लोकसंग्रहमेवापि
सम्पश्यन्कर्तुमर्हसि।।

karmaṇaivahi
saṁsiddhim āsthitā janakādayaḥ
loka-saṅgraham evāpi
sampaśyankartumarhasi ||

karmaṇā—by work; eva—even; hi—certainly; saṁsiddhim—perfection; āsthitāḥ—situated; janaka-ādayaḥ—kings like Janaka and others; loka- saṅgraham—educating the people in general; eva—also; api—for the sake of; sampaśyan—by considering; kartum—to act; arhasi—deserve.

Meaning: Even kings like Janaka and others achieved success by action. Therefore, to educate the popular community, you should also perform action.

21

यद्यदाचरति
श्रेष्ठस्तत्तदेवेतरो जनः।
स यत्प्रमाणं कुरुते
लोकस्तदनुवर्तते॥

yad yad ācarati
śreṣṭhas tattadevetaro janaḥ
sa yat pramāṇaṁ kurute
lokastadanuvartate||

yat—whatever; yat—and whichever; ācarati—does he act; śreṣṭhaḥ—respectable leader; tat—that; tat—and that alone; eva—certainly; itaraḥ—common; janaḥ—person; saḥ—he; yat—whichever; pramāṇam—evidence; kurute—does perform; lokaḥ—all the world; tat—that; anuvartate—followin the footsteps.

Meaning: Whatever a great or superior man does, common or inferior men follow in his footsteps by performing the same action. A great man sets the standards for inferior men all over the world with his exemplary acts.

22

न मे पार्थास्ति कर्तव्यं
त्रिषु लोकेषु किंचन।
नानवाप्तमवाप्तव्यं
वर्त एव च कर्मणि॥

na me pārthāsti kartavyaṁ
triṣu lokeṣu kiñcana
nānavāptam avāptavyaṁ
vartaeva cakarmaṇi||

na—none; me—Mine; pārtha—O son of Pṛthā; asti—there is; kartavyam— any prescribed duty; triṣu—in the three; lokeṣu—planetary systems; kiñcana —anything; na—no; anavāptam—in want; avāptavyam—to be gained; varte—engaged; eva—certainly; ca—also; karmaṇi—in one's prescribed duty.

Meaning: O Partha, there is no work that is prescribed for Me to do, nor is there anything in the three worlds for Me to attain. I am not in want of anything, nor do I need to obtain anything. Yet, I always move amid action.

23

यदि ह्यहं न वर्तेयं
जातु कर्मण्यतन्द्रितः।
मम वर्त्मानुवर्तन्ते
मनुष्याः पार्थ सर्वशः।।

yadi hy ahaṁ na varteyaṁ
jātu karmaṇyatandritaḥ
mama vartmānuvartante
manuṣyāḥ pārtha sarvaśaḥ||

yadi—if; hi—certainly; aham—I; na—do not; varteyam—thus engage; jātu—ever; karmaṇi—in the performance of prescribed duties; atandritaḥ—with great care; mama—My; vartma—path; anuvartante—would follow; manuṣyāḥ—all men; pārtha—O son of Pṛthā; sarvaśaḥ—in all respects.

Meaning: For, if I did not move watchfully amid action, O Partha, all men would follow my path from all sides.

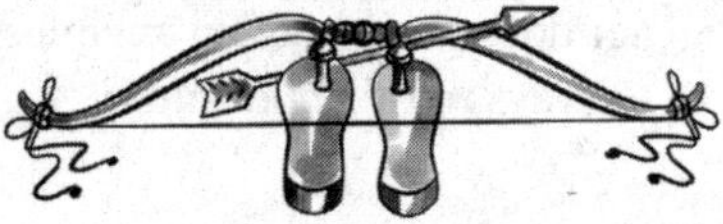

24

यदि उत्सीदेयुरिमे लोका
न कुर्यां कर्म चेदहम्।
संकरस्य च कर्ता
स्यामुपहन्यामिमाः प्रजाः॥

yadi utsīdeyurime lokā
na kuryāṁ karma cedaham
saṅkarasya ca kartā
syām upahanyāmimāḥprajāḥ ||

yadi—if; utsīdeyuḥ—put into ruin; ime—all these; lokāḥ—worlds; na—do not; kuryām—perform; karma—prescribed duties; cet—if; aham—I; saṅkarasya —o unwanted population; ca—and; kartā—creator; syām—shall be; upahanyām—destroy; imāḥ—all these; prajāḥ—living entities.

Meaning: If I did not perform action, all these worlds would fall into ruination. I would also become an author of an unwanted people, and I would destroy the peace of all these creatures.

25

सक्ताः कर्मण्यविद्वांसो
यथा कुर्वन्ति भारत।
कुर्याद्विद्वांस्तथा
सक्तश्चिकीर्षुर्लोकसंग्रहम्।।

saktāḥ karmaṇy avidvāṁso
yathā kurvanti bhārata
kuryādvidvāṁstath
āsaktaścikīrṣurloka-saṅgraham||

saktāḥ—being attached; karmaṇi—prescribed duties; avidvāṁsaḥ—the ignorant; yathā—as much as; kurvanti—do it; bhārata—O descendant of Bharata; kuryāt—must do; vidvān—the learned; tathā—thus; asaktaḥ—without attachment; cikīrṣuḥ—desiring to; loka-saṅgraham—leading the people in general.

Meaning: As the unwise perform their duties attached to action, O Bharata, the wise should act without attachment so that they can lead the masses on the right path.

26

न बुद्धिभेदं जनयेदज्ञानां
कर्मसङ्गिनाम्।
जोषयेत्सर्वकर्माणि
विद्वान्युक्तः समाचरन्॥

na buddhi-bhedaṁ janayed ajñānāṁ
karma-saṅginām
joṣayetsarva-karmāṇi
vidvānyuktaḥ samācaran||

na—do not; buddhi-bhedam—disrupt the intelligence; janayet—do; ajñānām—of the foolish; karma-saṅginām—attached to fruitive work; joṣayet—dove tailed; sarva—all; karmāṇi—work; vidvān—learned; yuktaḥ—all engaged; samācaran—practicing.

Meaning: The wise should not unsettle the minds of the ignorant who are attached to fruitive action. The wise man who is settled in Yoga should create inducement to all actions and especially the action in the spirit of devotion.

27

प्रकृतेः क्रियमाणानि
गुणैः कर्माणि सर्वशः।
अहंकारविमूढात्मा
कर्ताहमिति मन्यते॥

prakṛteḥ kriyamāṇāni
guṇaiḥ karmāṇisarvaś
aḥahaṅkāra-vimūḍhātmā
kartāhamiti manyate||

prakṛteḥ—of material nature; kriyamāṇāni—all being done; guṇaiḥ—by the modes; karmāṇi—activities; sarvaśaḥ—all kinds of; ahaṅkāra-vimūḍha—bewildered by false ego; ātmā—the spirit soul; kartā—doer; aham—I; iti— thus; manyate—thinks.

Meaning: Acts are wholly performed by the attributes of nature. The one whose self is bewildered by egoism in the material world thinks that he is the performer of such activities.

28

तत्त्ववित्तु महाबाहो
गुणकर्मविभागयोः।
गुणा गुणेषु वर्तन्त
इति मत्वा न सज्जते॥

tattvavittumahā-bāho
guṇa-karma-vibhāga
yoḥguṇā guṇeṣu vartanta
itimatvā na sajjate||

tattvavit—the knower of the Absolute Truth; tu—but; mahā-bāho—O mighty-armed one; guṇa-karma—works under material influence; vibhāgayoḥ—differences; guṇāḥ—senses; guṇeṣu—in sense gratification; vartante—being engaged; iti—thus; matvā—thinking; na—never; sajjate—becomes attached.

Meaning: But, O mighty-armed, the knower of the Absolute Truth concerning the attribute-group and the function-group does not engage himself in the senses and their gratification, remaining unattached as he is well aware of the differences between work for fruitive results and work done in devotion.

29

प्रकृतेर्गुणसम्मूढाः
सज्जन्ते गुणकर्मसु।
तानकृत्स्नविदो मन्दान्कृत्स्नविन्न
विचालयेत्॥

prakṛter guṇa-sammūḍhāḥ
sajjanteguṇa-karmasu
tān akṛtsna-vido mandān kṛtsna-
vinnavicālayet||

prakṛteḥ—impelled by the material modes; guṇa-sammūḍhāḥ—be fooled by material identification; sajjante—become engaged; guṇa-karmasu—in material activities; tān—all those; akṛtsna-vidaḥ—persons with a poor fund of knowledge; mandān—lazy to understand self-realisation; kṛtsna-vit—one who is in factual knowledge; na—may not; vicālayet—try to agitate.

Meaning: The ignorant ones who are deluded by the attributes of material nature become attached to the functions of these attributes of the material activities that they pursue. But the perfect knower should not unsettle these dull performers even though these duties are inferior because their knowledge lacks perfection.

30

मयि सर्वाणि कर्माणि
सन्नयस्याध्यात्मचेतसा।
निराशीर्निर्ममो भूत्वा
युध्यस्व विगतज्वरः॥

mayi sarvāṇi karmāṇi
sannyasyādhyātma-cetasā
nirāśīr nirmamo bhūtvā
yudhyasvavigata-jvaraḥ ||

mayi—unto Me; sarvāṇi—all sorts of; karmāṇi—activities; sannyasya—giving up completely; adhyātma—with full knowledge of the self; cetasā—consciousness; nirāśīḥ—without desire for profit; nirmamaḥ—without ownership; bhūtvā—so being; yudhyasva—fight; vigata-jvaraḥ—without being lethargic.

Meaning: Therefore, O Arjuna, surrender all action unto Me, with the mind fixed on the Ruling Self, without desire for gain and thinking nothing as your own, shed your egoism and lethargy, and fight.

31

ये मे मतमिदं
नित्यमनुतिष्ठन्ति मानवाः।
श्रद्धावन्तोऽनसूयन्तो
मुच्यन्ते तेऽपि कर्मभिः॥

ye me matamidaṁ
nityam anutiṣṭhanti mānavāḥ
śraddhāvanto ‹nasūyanto
mucyantete›pi karmabhiḥ ||

ye—those; me—My; matam—injunctions; idam—this; nityam—eternal function; anutiṣṭhanti—execute regularly; mānavāḥ—humankind; śraddhāvantaḥ—with faith and devotion; anasūyantaḥ—without envy; mucyante— become free; te—all of them; api—even; karmabhiḥ—from the bondage of the law of fruitive action.

Meaning: The men who perform their duties according to My injunction, full of faith and without envy, find liberation from the bondage of fruitive actions.

32

ये त्वेतदभ्यसूयन्तो
नानुतिष्ठन्ति मे मतम्।
सर्वज्ञानविमूढांस्तान्विद्धि
नष्टानचेतसः।।

ye tv etad abhyasūyanto
nānutiṣṭhanti me matam
sarva-jñāna-vimūḍhāṁstān viddhi
naṣṭān acetasaḥ||

ye—those; tu—however; etat—this; abhyasūyantaḥ—out of envy; na—do not; anutiṣṭhanti—regularly perform; me—My; matam—injunction; sarva- jñāna—all sorts of knowledge; vimūḍhān—perfectly befooled; tān—they are; viddhi—know it well; naṣṭān—all ruined; acetasaḥ—without Kṛṣṇa consciousness.

Meaning: But those who dislike My teachings and do not abide by them are fools robbed of all knowledge and ruined due to ignorance and bondage.

33

सदृशं चेष्टते स्वस्याः
प्रकृतेर्ज्ञानवानपि।
प्रकृतिं यान्ति भूतानि
निग्रहः किं करिष्यति।।

sadṛśaṁ ceṣṭate svasyāḥ
prakṛter jñānavānapi
prakṛtiṁ yānti bhūtāni
nigrahah kiṁ kariṣyati||

sadṛśam—accordingly; ceṣṭate—tries; svasyāḥ—in one's own nature; prakṛteḥ—modes; jñānavān—the learned; api—although; prakṛtim—nature; yānti—undergo; bhūtāni—all living entities; nigrahaḥ—suppression; kim—what; kariṣyati—can do.

Meaning: Even the wise man of knowledge acts according to his nature. All creatures must follow nature. What shall restraint accomplish?

34

इन्द्रियस्येन्द्रियस्यार्थे
रागद्वेषौ व्यवस्थितौ।
तयोर्न वशमागच्छेत्तौ
ह्यस्य परिपन्थिनौ॥

indriyasye‹ndriyasyārthe
rāga-dveṣau vyavasthitau
tayor na vaśam āgacchet tau
hyasya paripanthinau||

indriyasya—of the senses; indriyasyaarthe—in the sense objects; rāga—attachment; dveṣau—also in detachment; vyavasthitau—put under regulations; tayoḥ—of them; na—never; vaśam—control; āgacchet—one should come; tau—those; hi—certainly are; asya—his; paripanthinau—stumbling blocks.

Meaning: The like and dislike for sense objects are experienced by embodied beings, but one should not fall under the power of the senses and sense objects as they are hurdles on the way to self-realisation.

35

श्रेयान्स्वधर्मो विगुणः
परधर्मात्स्वनुष्ठितात्।
स्वधर्मे निधनं श्रेयः
परधर्मो भयावहः॥

śreyān sva-dharmo viguṇaḥ
para-dharmātsv-anuṣṭhitāt
sva-dharme nidhanaṁ śreyaḥ
para-dharmo bhayāvahaḥ||

śreyān—farbetter; sva-dharmaḥ—one's prescribed duties; viguṇaḥ—even faulty; para-dharmāt—from duties mentioned for others; svanuṣṭhitāt—than perfectly done; sva-dharme—in one's prescribed duties; nidhanam— destruction; śreyaḥ—better; para-dharmaḥ—duties prescribed for others; bhaya-āvahaḥ—dangerous.

Meaning: It is better to perform the duties prescribed for you even though it may lack merit rather than performing another man's duties to perfection. It is preferable to encounter death while performing one's own duty rather than to perform someone else's duty which is full of risk and danger.

36

अर्जुन उवाच
अथ केन प्रयुक्तोऽयं
पापं चरति पूरुषः।
अनिच्छन्नपि वार्ष्णेय
बलादिव नियोजितः॥

arjunauvāca
atha kena prayukto 'yaṁ
pāpaṁ carati pūruṣaḥ
anicchannapi vārṣṇeya
balād iva niyojitaḥ||

arjunaḥuvāca—Arjunasaid; atha—hereafter; kena—by what; prayuktaḥ—impelled; ayam—one; pāpam—sins; carati—acts; pūruṣaḥ—a man; anicchan—without desiring; api—although; vārṣṇeya—O descendant of Vṛṣṇi; balāt—by force; iva—as if; niyojitaḥ—engaged.

Meaning: Arjuna said: O Varshneya, by what is one impelled to commit sin, even against his will as if he is guided by force?

37

श्रीभगवानुवाच
काम एष क्रोध एष
रजोगुणसमुद्भवः।
महाशनो महापाप्मा
विद्धयेनमिह वैरिणम्॥

śrī-bhagavān uvāca
kāma-eṣa krodha-eṣa
rajoguṇa-samudbhavaḥ
mahā-śano mahā-pāpmā
viddhyenamiha vairiṇam||

śrībhagavānuvāca—the Personality of Godhead said; kāmaḥ—lust; eṣaḥ —all these; krodhaḥ—wrath; eṣaḥ—all these; rajo-guṇa—the mode of passion; samudbhavaḥ—born of; mahā-śanaḥ—all-devouring; mahā-pāpmā—greatly sinful; viddhi—know; enam—this; iha—in the material world; vairiṇam—greatest enemy.

Meaning: The Glorious Lord said: It is desire, it is wrath, the offspring of the material modes of passion, which is all-devouring, and know this to be the most sinful enemy of this world.

38

धूमेनाव्रियते वह्निर्यथादर्शो
मलेन च।
यथोल्बेनावृतो गर्भस्तथा
तेनेदमावृतम्॥

dhūmenāvriyate vahnir yathādarśo
malenaca
yatholbenāvṛto garbhas
tathātenedam āvṛtam||

dhūmena—by smoke; āvriyate—covered; vahniḥ—fire; yathā—just as; ādarśaḥ—mirror; malena—by dust; ca—also; yathā—just as; ulbena—by the womb; āvṛtaḥ—is covered; garbhaḥ—embryo; tathā-so; tena—by that lust; idam—this; āvṛtam—is covered.

Meaning: Just as a flame is enveloped in smoke, a mirror covered by dust, an embryo by the womb, so is wisdom enveloped by this lust and desire.

39

आवृतं ज्ञानमेतेन
ज्ञानिनो नित्यवैरिणा।
कामरूपेण कौन्तेय
दुष्पूरेणानलेन च।।

āvṛtaṁ jñānam etena
jñāninonitya-vairiṇā
kāma-rūpeṇa kaunteya
duṣpūreṇānalena ca ||

āvṛtam—covered; jñānam—pure consciousness; etena—by this; jñāninaḥ— of the knower; nitya-vairiṇā—eternal enemy; kāma-rūpeṇa—in the form of lust; kaunteya—O son of Kuntī; duṣpūreṇa—never to be satisfied; analena— by the fire; ca—also.

Meaning: The reason of a rational man is obscured by this eternal enemy, O son of Kunti, in the form of covetousness, burning like an insatiable fire that refuses to be extinguished.

40

इन्द्रियाणि मनो
बुद्धिरस्याधिष्ठानमुच्यते।
एतैर्विमोहयत्येष
ज्ञानमावृत्य देहिनम्॥

indriyāṇi mano
buddhir asyādhiṣṭhāna mucyate
etair vimohayaty eṣa
jñānamāvṛtya dehinam||

indriyāṇi—the senses; manaḥ—the mind; buddhiḥ—the intelligence; asya—of the lust; adhiṣṭhānam—sitting place; ucyate—called; etaiḥ—by all these; vimohayati—bewilders; eṣaḥ—of this; jñānam—knowledge; āvṛtya—covering; dehinam—the embodied.

Meaning: The senses, the mind, and the understanding are the seats of this lust, which envelops the reason of the Embodied One and confounds him.

41

तस्मात्त्वमिन्द्रियाण्यादौ
नियम्य भरतर्षभ।
पाप्मानं प्रजहि ह्येनं
ज्ञानविज्ञाननाशनम्॥

tasmāt tvam indriyāṇy ādau
niyamya bharatarṣabha
pāpmānaṁ prajahi hy enaṁ
jñāna-vijñāna-nāśanam||

tasmāt—therefore; tvam-you; indriyāṇi—senses; ādau—in the beginning; niyamya—by regulating; bharatarṣabha—O chief amongst the descendants of Bharata; pāpmānam—the great symbol of sin; prajahi—curb; hi—certainly; enam—this; jñāna—knowledge; vijñāna—scientific knowledge of the pure soul; nāśanam—destroyer.

Meaning: Therefore, O mighty Bharata, regulate the senses first and bring them under your control. Cast off this cause of sin that is indeed, the destroyer of perception, knowledge, and reason.

42

इन्द्रियाणि पराण्याह-
रिन्द्रियेभ्यः परं मनः।
मनसस्तु परा बुद्धिर्यो
बुद्धेः परतस्तु सः॥

indriyāṇi parāṇy āhur
indriyebhyaḥ paraṁ manaḥ
manasastu parā buddhir yo
buddheḥ paratastu saḥ||

indriyāṇī—senses; parāṇi—superior; āhuḥ—is said; indriyebhyaḥ—more than the senses; param—superior; manaḥ—the mind; manasaḥ—more than the mind; tu—also; parā—superior; buddhiḥ—intelligence; yaḥ—one which; buddheḥ—more than the intelligence; parataḥ—superior; tu—but; saḥ—he.

Meaning: The senses are said to be superior to dull matter, the mind is superior to the senses, and the understanding is superior to the will. But what is even superior to understanding, is the soul.

43

एवं बुद्धेः परं बुद्ध्वा
संस्तभ्यात्मानमात्मना।
जहि शत्रुं महाबाहो
कामरूपं दुरासदम्।।

evaṁ buddheḥ paraṁ buddhvā
saṁstabhy-ātmānamātmanā
jahi śatruṁ mahā-bāho
kāma-rūpaṁdurāsadam ||

evam—thus; buddheḥ—of intelligence; param—superior; buddhvā—so knowing; saṁstabhya—by steadying; ātmānam—the mind; ātmanā—by deliberate intelligence; jahi—conquer; śatrum—the enemy; mahā-bāho—O mighty-armed one; kāma-rūpam—the form of lust; durāsadam—formidable.

Meaning: Having thus understood what is superior to the understanding, knowing oneself to transcend the material senses, the mind, and understanding, and controlling the lower self by the higher self, O mighty-armed, cast off by spiritual strength this eternal enemy named lust.

ॐ तत्सदिति श्रीमद्भगवद्गीतासूपनिषत्सु ब्रह्मविद्यायां योगशास्त्रे

श्रीकृष्णार्जुनसंवादे कर्मयोगो नाम तृतीयोऽध्यायः।

Thus in the Upanishad of the Glorious Divine Lay, the Science of Brahma, the Ordinance of Yoga, the Discourse between the Glorious Lord Krishna and Arjuna, the Third Chapter titled 'Karma Yoga' (The Yoga of Action).

CHAPTER 4

JNANA KARMA SANNYAS YOGA (THE YOGA OF KNOWLEDGE, ACTION, RENUNCIATION)

CHAPTER 4

JNANA KARMA SANNYAS YOGA (THE YOGA OF KNOWLEDGE, ACTION, RENUNCIATION)

Chapter Four of the Bhagavad Gita is about approaching the Ultimate Truth. Lord Krishna reveals to Arjuna the importance of listening to knowledge being imparted, and how spiritual knowledge has been received in the oral tradition over the years by disciples, and the importance of approaching a realised teacher like the Guru. Lord Krishna explains the system of transmission of knowledge through disciplinic succession. He reveals to Arjuna how he had first taught the science of the Bhagavad Gita to the Sun-God, who in turn, imparted this knowledge to his descendants, who passed it on to the first descendants of the human race.

Arjuna is confused because the Sun-God is much older than Lord Krishna, who then explains to Arjuna that the Lord appears on earth in his human incarnation whenever and wherever there is a decline in religion and morality. The one who comprehends this transcendental nature of the Lord attains His Heavenly abode at the time of his death. Everyone surrenders to Krishna, either directly or indirectly, and the Lord reciprocates according to how one surrenders.

Lord Krishna explains to Arjuna how the paths of action, knowledge, and wisdom regarding the Supreme knowledge results in the culmination of the two different paths as the goal to reach the Supreme One is the same. He also explains that every act can be an act of devotion.

Lord Krishna explains to Arjuna how He has created the social system named 'Varnasrama', which created divisions of social and spiritual life with the objective of engaging people in work according to their respective natures. Lord Krishna reveals that by sacrificing the fruitive results of work to the Supreme, people rise to the surface of transcendental knowledge. But, the faithless and ignorant who doubt the knowledge revealed in the scriptures, sink to the depths as they can never be happy or attain God.

1

श्री भगवानुवाच
इमं विवस्वते योगं
प्रोक्तवानहमव्ययम्।
विवस्वान्मनवे प्राह
मनुरिक्ष्वाकवेऽब्रवीत्॥

śrī bhagavān uvāca
imaṁ vivasvate yogaṁ
proktavān-ahamavyayam
vivasvān manave prāha
manurikṣvākave'bravīt ||

śrībhagavānuvāca—the Supreme Personality of Godhead said; imam—this science; vivasvate—unto the sun-god; yogam—the science of one's relationship to the Supreme; proktavān—instructed; aham—I; avyayam—imperishable; vivasvān—Vivasvān (the sun-god's name); manave—unto the father of mankind (of the name Vaivasvata); prāha—told; manuḥ—the father of mankind; ikṣvākave—unto King Ikṣvāku; abravīt—said.

Meaning: The Glorious Lord said: I have explained this imperishable science of yoga to Vivaswan, the Sun-god. He, in turn, instructed it to Manu, who then explained it to Ikshvaku.

2

एवं परम्पराप्राप्तमिमं
राजर्षयो विदुः।
स कालेनेह महता
योगो नष्टः परन्तप॥

evaṁ paramparā-prāptam imaṁ
rājarṣayo viduḥ
sa kāleneha mahatā
yogonaṣṭaḥ parantapa||

evam—thus; paramparā—disciplic succession; prāptam—received; imam—this science; rājarṣayaḥ—the saintly kings; viduḥ—understood; saḥ—that knowledge; kālena—in the course of time; iha—in this world; mahatā—by great; yogaḥ—the science of one's relationship with the Supreme; naṣṭaḥ—scattered; parantapa—O Arjuna, subduer of the enemies.

Meaning: The king-sages were aware of this supreme science received through succession of disciples. But, after the great lapse of time this chain of succession was broken and the Yoga has decayed here, O destroyer of foes.

3

स एवायं मया तेऽद्य
योगः प्रोक्तः पुरातनः।
भक्तोऽसि मे सखा चेति
रहस्यं ह्येतदुत्तमम्॥

sa evāyaṁ mayā te 'dya
yogaḥ proktaḥ purātanaḥ
bhakto 'si me sakhā ceti
rahasyaṁ hyetaduttamam||

saḥ—the same ancient; eva—certainly; ayam—this science; mayā—by Me; te—unto you; adya—today; yogaḥ—the science of yoga; proktaḥ—spoken; purātanaḥ—very old; bhaktaḥ—devotee; asi—you are; me—My; sakhā—friend; ca—also; iti—therefore; rahasyam—mystery; hi—certainly; etat—this; uttamam—transcendental.

Meaning: I have today declared that same ancient science to you, the secret of the relationship with the Supreme, which is the highest secret. That's because you are My devotee as well My friend, and can understand the transcendental mystery of this Yoga.

4

अर्जुन उवाच
अपरं भवतो जन्म
परं जन्म विवस्वतः।
कथमेतद्विजानीयां
त्वमादौ प्रोक्तवानिति।।

arjunauvāca
aparaṁ bhavato janma
paraṁjanma vivasvataḥ
kathametadvijānīyāṁ
tvamādau proktavāniti

arjunaḥuvāca—Arjuna said; aparam—junior; bhavataḥ—Your; janma—birth; param—superior; janma—birth; vivasvataḥ—of the sun-god; katham—how; etat—this; vijānīyām—shall I understand; tvam—You; ādau—in the beginning; proktavān—instructed; iti—thus.

Meaning: Arjuna said: The Sun-god Vivaswan was born much earlier than You. How am I to understand that You have instructed him in this science first?

5

श्रीभगवानुवाच
बहूनि मे व्यतीतानि
जन्मानि तव चार्जुन।
तान्यहं वेद सर्वाणि
न त्वं वेत्थ परन्तप॥

śrībhagavānuvāca
bahūni me vyatītāni
janmāni tava cārjuna
tāny ahaṁ veda sarvāṇi
na tvaṁ vettha parantapa||

śrībhagavānuvāca—the Personality of Godhead said; bahūni—many; me—of Mine; vyatītāni—have passed; janmāni—births;tava—ofyours; ca— and also; arjuna—O Arjuna; tāni—all those; aham—I; veda—do know; sarvāṇi—all; na—not; tvam—yourself; vettha—know; parantapa—O subduer of the enemy.

Meaning: The Glorious Lord said: Many, many births of both you and I have passed, O Arjuna. I know them all but you do not, O destroyer of enemies.

6

अजोऽपि सन्नव्ययात्मा
भूतानामीश्वरोऽपि सन्।
प्रकृतिं स्वामधिष्ठाय
सम्भवाम्यात्ममायया॥

ajo ‘pi sann avyayātmā
bhūtānām-īśvaro’pisan
prakṛtiṁ svām adhiṣṭhāya
sambhav-āmyātma-māyayā||

ajaḥ—unborn; api—although; san—being so; avyaya—without deterioration; ātmā—body; bhūtānām—all those who are born; īśvaraḥ—the Supreme Lord; api—although; san—being so; prakṛtim—transcendental form; svām— of Myself; adhiṣṭhāya—being so situated; sambhavāmi—I do incarnate; ātma-māyayā—by My internal energy.

Meaning: Although I am unborn, and although I am the immutable Lord of all creatures, My transcendental body never dies, and I can take birth in every millennium in My Original Form by My Creative Power.

7

यदा यदा हि धर्मस्य
ग्लानिर्भवति भारत।
अभ्युत्थानमधर्मस्य
तदात्मानं सृजाम्यहम्।।

yadā yadā hi dharmasya
glānirbhavatibhārata
abhyutthānam adharmasya
tadātmānaṁsṛjāmyaham||

yadā—whenever; yadā—wherever; hi—certainly; dharmasya—of religion; glāniḥ—discrepancies; bhavati—manifested, becomes; bhārata—O descendant of Bharata; abhyutthānam—predominance; adharmasya—of irreligion; tadā—at that time; ātmānam—self; sṛjāmi—manifest; aham—I.

Meaning: Whenever there is a deterioration of virtue, decline in religious practices, and the predominance of vice, O Bharata, then I bring forth Myself.

8

परित्राणाय साधूनां
विनाशाय च दुष्कृताम्।
धर्मसंस्थापनार्थाय सम्भवामि
युगे युगे॥

paritrāṇāya sādhūnāṁ
vināśāyacaduṣkṛtām
dharma-saṁsthāpanārthāyasambhavāmi
yuge yuge

paritrāṇāya—for the deliverance; sādhūnām—of the devotees; vināśāya—for the annihilation; ca—also; duṣkṛtām—of the miscreants; dharma—principles of religion; saṁsthāpana-arthāya—to reestablish; sambhavāmi—I do appear; yuge—millennium; yuge—after millennium.

Meaning: For the salvation of the pious, for the destruction of evil-doers, and to establish the principles of virtue, I take birth millennium after millennium.

9

जन्म कर्म च मे
दिव्यमेवं यो वेत्ति तत्त्वतः।
त्यक्त्वा देहं पुनर्जन्म
नैति मामेति सोऽर्जुन॥

janma karma ca me
divyam evaṁ yo vetti tattvataḥ
tyaktvā dehaṁ punarjanma
naiti māmeti so'rjuna||

janma—birth; karma—work; ca—also; me—of Mine; divyam—transcendental; evam—like this; yaḥ—anyone who; vetti—knows; tattvataḥ—in reality; tyaktvā—leaving aside; deham—this body; punaḥ—again; janma—birth; na—never; eti—does attain; mām—unto Me; eti —does attain; saḥ—he; arjuna—O Arjuna.

Meaning: One who really understands my birth and divine activities, he upon leaving the body does not take birth again in the material world but enters My eternal abode, and comes to Me, O Arjuna.

10

वीतरागभयक्रोधा
मन्मया मामुपाश्रिताः।
बहवो ज्ञानतपसा
पूता मद्भावमागताः॥

vīta-rāga-bhaya-krodhā
man-mayāmāmupāśritāḥ
bahavo jñāna-tapasā
pūtāmad-bhāvam āgatāḥ||

vīta—freed from; rāga—attachment; bhaya—fear; krodhāḥ—anger; mat- mayā—fully in Me; mām—unto Me; upāśritāḥ—being fully situated; bahavaḥ—many; jñāna—knowledge; tapasā—by penance; pūtāḥ—being purified; mat-bhāvam—transcendental love for Me; āgatāḥ—attained.

Meaning: Freed from desire, fear, and anger, fully absorbed in Me and sheltered in Me, many persons have been purified by austerity and knowledge of Me to attain to My transcendental nature.

11

ये यथा मां प्रपद्यन्ते
तांस्तथैव भजाम्यहम्।
मम वर्त्मानुवर्तन्ते मनुष्याः
पार्थ सर्वशः॥

yeyathāmāṁ prapadyante
tāṁstathaivabhajāmyaham
mama vartmānuvartante manuṣyāḥ
pārthasarvaśaḥ ||

ye—all of them; yathā—as; mām—unto Me; prapadyante—surrender; tān—unto them; tathā—so; eva—certainly; bhajāmi—do I reward; aham—I; mama—My; vartma—path; anuvartante—do follow; manuṣyāḥ—all men; pārtha—O son of Pṛthā; sarvaśaḥ—in all respects.

Meaning: However men may surrender to Me, I serve and reward them accordingly. From all sides, O Partha, men walk the path that ultimately leads to Me.

12

काङ्क्षन्तः कर्मणां
सिद्धिं यजन्त इह देवताः।
क्षिप्रं हि मानुषे लोके
सिद्धिर्भवति कर्मजा॥

kāṅkṣantaḥkarmaṇāṁ
siddhiṁ yajanta iha devatāḥ
kṣipraṁ hi mānuṣe loke
siddhirbhavatikarmajā ||

kāṅkṣantaḥ—desiring; karmaṇām—of fruitive activities; siddhim—perfection; yajante—worship by sacrifices; iha—in the material world; devatāḥ—the demigods; kṣipram—very quickly; hi—certainly; mānuṣe—in human society; loke—within this world; siddhiḥ bhavati—becomes successful; karmajā—the fruitive worker.

Meaning: Men who seek direct success in fruitive actions in the world perform sacrifice to the gods. In the world of men, success born from action fetches quick results.

13

चातुर्वर्ण्यं मया सृष्टं
गुणकर्मविभागशः।
तस्य कर्तारमपि मां
विद्ध्यकर्तारमव्ययम्॥

cātur-varṇyaṁ mayā sṛṣṭaṁ
guṇa-karma-vibhāgaśaḥ
tasyakartāramapi māṁ
viddhyakartāramavyaya||

cātur-varṇyam—the four divisions of human society; mayā—by Me; sṛṣṭam—created; guṇa—quality; karma—work; vibhāgaśaḥ—in terms of division; tasya—of that; kartāram—the father; api—although; mām—Me; viddhi—you may know; akartāram—as the non-doer; avyayam—being unchangeable.

Meaning: The four divisions of society were created by Me according to the three modes of material nature through their attributes and functions and the work assigned to them. Though I am the Creator of this system, yet know Me as the non-doer and non-actor, being unchangeable.

14

न मां कर्माणि लिम्पन्ति
न मे कर्मफले स्पृहा।
इति मां योऽभिजानाति
कर्मभिर्न स बध्यते॥

na māṁ karmāṇi limpanti
na me karma-phale spṛhā
iti māṁ yo 'bhijānāti
karmabhirnasa badhyate||

na—never; mām—unto Me; karmāṇi—all kinds of work; limpanti—do affect; na—nor; me—My; karma-phale—in fruitive action; spṛhā—aspiration; iti—thus; mām—unto Me; yaḥ—one who; abhijānāti—does know; karmabhiḥ—by the reaction of such work; na—never does; saḥ—he; badhyate—become entangled.

Meaning: There is no action that affects Me as there is no desire in Me for the fruits of action. The one who knows Me thus, does not become a slave to the fruitive actions of work.

15

एवं ज्ञात्वा कृतं कर्म
पूर्वैरपि मुमुक्षुभिः।
कुरु कर्मैव तस्मात्त्वं पूर्वैः
पूर्वतरं कृतम्॥

evaṁ jñātvā kṛtaṁ karma
pūrvairapi mumukṣubhiḥ
kuru karmaiva tasmāt tvaṁ
pūrvaiḥpūrvataraṁkṛtam||

evam—thus; jñātvā—knowing well; kṛtam—performed; karma—work; pūrvaiḥ—by past authorities; api—although; mumukṣubhiḥ—who attained liberation; kuru—just perform; karma—prescribed duty; eva—certainly; tasmāt—therefore; tvam—you; pūrvaiḥ—by the predecessors; pūrvataram—ancient predecessors; kṛtam—as performed.

Meaning: Action was performed with this understanding by the ancient souls who sought and attained liberation. Therefore, you should also perform your duty just like the ancients.

16

किं कर्म किमकर्मेति
कवयोऽप्यत्र मोहिताः।
तत्ते कर्म प्रवक्ष्यामि
यज्ज्ञात्वा मोक्ष्यसेऽशुभात्॥

kiṁ karma kim akarmeti
kavayo'pyatramohitāḥ
tattekarmapravakṣyāmi
yajjñātvāmokṣyase'śubhāt||

kim—what is; karma—action; kim—what is; akarma—inaction; iti—thus; kavayaḥ—the intelligent; api—also; atra—in this matter; mohitāḥ—bewildered; tat—that; te—unto you; karma—work; pravakṣyāmi—I shall explain; yat—which; jñātvā—knowing; mokṣyase—beliberated; aśubhāt—from ill fortune.

Meaning: Even the learned are perplexed about what action is and what can be termed as inaction. I will explain to you the meaning of that action, the knowledge of which will liberate you of all your sins.

17

कर्मणो ह्यपि बोद्धव्यं
बोद्धव्यं च विकर्मणः।
अकर्मणश्च बोद्धव्यं गहना
कर्मणो गतिः॥17॥

karmaṇo hyapi boddhavyaṁ
boddhavyaṁ ca vikarmaṇaḥ
akarmaṇaśca boddhavyaṁ gahanā
karmaṇo gatiḥ||

karmaṇaḥ—workingorder; hi—certainly; api—also; boddhavyam—should be understood; boddhavyam—to be understood; ca—also; vikarmaṇaḥ—forbidden work; akarmaṇaḥ—inaction; ca—also; boddhavyam—should be understood; gahanā—verydifficult; karmaṇaḥ—working order; gatiḥ—to enter into.

Meaning: But, the intricacies of action are difficult to understand because of the course of action. Therefore, one must properly know what action, inaction, and forbidden action are.

18

कर्मण्यकर्म यः
पश्येदकर्मणि च कर्म यः।
स बुद्धिमान्मनुष्येषु स युक्तः
कृत्स्नकर्मकृत्॥

karmaṇyakarma yaḥ
paśyed akarmaṇi ca karma yaḥ
sa buddhimān manuṣyeṣu sa yuktaḥ
kṛtsna-karma-kṛt||

karmaṇi—in action; akarma—inaction; yaḥ—one who; paśyet—observes; akarmaṇi—in inaction; ca—also; karma—fruitive action; yaḥ—one who; saḥ—he; buddhimān—is intelligent; manuṣyeṣu—in human society; saḥ—he; yuktaḥ—is in the transcendental position; kṛtsna-karma-kṛt—although engaged in all activities.

Meaning: One who sees inaction in action and action in inaction is intelligent among men. He is a perfect actor who is settled in Yoga, although engaged in various activities.

19

यस्य सर्वे समारम्भाः
कामसंकल्पवर्जिताः।
ज्ञानाग्निदग्धकर्माणं तमाहुः
पंडितं बुधाः॥19॥

yasya sarve samārambhāḥ
kāma-saṅkalpa-varjitāḥ
jñānāgni-dagdha-karmāṇaṁ tamāhuḥ
paṇḍitaṁ budhāḥ||

yasya—one whose; sarve—all sorts of; samārambhāḥ—in all attempts; kāma desire for sense gratification; saṅkalpa—determination; varjitāḥ— are devoid of ; jñāna—of perfect knowledge; āgni—fire; dagdha—being burnt by; karmāṇam—the performer; tam—him; āhuḥ—declare; paṇḍitam —learned; budhāḥ—those who know.

Meaning: One whose acts are all detached from the fancies of desire and whose actions are led and consumed by the fire of wisdom, the sages call him a *pandita.*

20

त्यक्त्वा कर्मफलासङ्गं
नित्यतृप्तो निराश्रयः।
कर्मण्यभिप्रवृत्तोऽपि
नैव किंचित्करोति सः।।

tyaktvākarma-phalāsaṅgaṁ
nitya-tṛpto nirāśrayaḥ
karmaṇy abhipravṛtto 'pi
naiva kiñcitkaroti saḥ ||

tyaktvā—having given up; karma-phala-āsaṅgam—attachment for fruitive results; nitya—always; tṛptaḥ—being satisfied; nirāśrayaḥ—without any center; karmaṇi—inactivity; abhipravṛttaḥ—being fully engaged; api—in spite of; na—does not; eva—certainly; kiñcit—anything; karoti—do; saḥ—he.

Meaning: Renouncing all attachment to action and the fruits of action, ever satisfied and dependent on nothing, he performs no fruitive action even when impelled to action.

21

निराशीर्यतचित्तात्मा
त्यक्तसर्वपरिग्रहः।
शारीरं केवलं कर्म
कुर्वन्नाप्नोति किल्बिषम्॥

nirāśīryata-cittātmā
tyakta-sarva-parigrahaḥ
śārīraṁ kevalaṁ karma
kurvannāpnoti kilbiṣam||

nirāśīḥ—without desire for the results; yata—controlled; citta-ātmā—mind and intelligence; tyakta—giving up; sarva—all; parigrahaḥ—sense of proprietorship over all possessions; śārīram—in keeping body and soul together; kevalam—only; karma—work; kurvan—doing so; na—never; āpnoti—does not acquire; kilbiṣam—sinful reactions.

Meaning: Such a man has no expectations, is averse to gains, is subdued in mind and body, and gives up all his material possessions except for the basic necessities. Thus performing only bodily acts, he is unaffected by sin.

22

यदृच्छालाभसंतुष्टो
द्वंद्वातीतो विमत्सरः।
समः सिद्धावसिद्धौ च कृत्वापि
न निबध्यते॥

yadṛcchā-lābha-santuṣṭo
dvandvātītovimatsaraḥ
samaḥ siddhāvasiddhau ca kṛtvāpi
na nibadhyate ||

yadṛcchā—out of its own accord; lābha—gain; santuṣṭaḥ—satisfied; dvandva—duality; atītaḥ—surpassed; vimatsaraḥ—free from envy; samaḥ—steady; siddhau—in success; asiddhau—failure; ca—also; kṛtvā—doing; api—although; na—never; nibadhyate—is affected.

Meaning: He who is satisfied with unsought gain, free from duality, is not envious, who is steady in both success and failure is never entangled in the material world even though he is performing actions.

23

गतसङ्गस्य मुक्तस्य
ज्ञानावस्थितचेतसः।
यज्ञायाचरतः कर्म
समग्रं प्रविलीयते॥

gata-saṅgasya muktasya
jñānāvasthita-cetasaḥ
yajñāyācarataḥ karma
samagraṁpravilīyate ||

gata-saṅgasya—unattached to the modes of material nature; muktasya—of the liberated; jñāna-avasthita—situated in transcendence; cetasaḥ—of such wisdom; yajñāya—for the sake of Yajña (Kṛṣṇa); ācarataḥ—soacting; karma—work; samagram—in total; pravilīyate—merges entirely.

Meaning: The one whose attachment is gone, and who is thus free, his mind resting in transcendental knowledge, merges totally with the Supreme.

24

ब्रह्मार्पणं ब्रह्म हविर्ब्रह्माग्नौ
ब्रह्मणा हुतम्।
ब्रह्मैव तेन गन्तव्यं
ब्रह्मकर्मसमाधिना॥

brahmārpaṇaṁ brahma havir-brahmāgnau
brahmaṇā hutam
brahmaiva tena gantavyaṁ
brahma-karma-samādhinā ||

brahma—spiritual nature; arpaṇam—contribution; brahma—the Supreme; haviḥ—butter; brahma—spiritual; agnau—in the fire of consummation; brahmaṇā—by the spirit soul; hutam—offered; brahma—spiritual kingdom; eva—certainly; tena—by him; gantavyam—to be reached; brahma—spiritual; karma—activities; samādhinā—by complete absorption.

Meaning: The act of offering is Brahma, and it is Brahma who offers Brahma-oblation into the Brahma-fire. Brahma is therefore, the goal of one engaged with the mind fixed firmly on Brahma-action.

25

दैवमेवापरे यज्ञं योगिनः
पर्युपासते।
ब्रह्माग्नावपरे यज्ञं
यज्ञेनैवोपजुह्वति।।

daivam evāpare yajñaṁ yoginaḥ
paryupāsate
brahmāgnāvapare yajñaṁ
yajñenaivopajuhvati||

daivam—in worshiping the demigods; eva—like this; apare—some; yajñam—sacrifices; yoginaḥ—the mystics; paryupāsate—worship perfectly; brahma—the Absolute Truth; agnau—in the fire of; apare—others; yajñam—sacrifice; yajñena—by sacrifice; eva—thus; upajuhvati—worship.

Meaning: Some yogis worship God perfectly by offering sacrifice to them. Some offer these sacrifices into the Brahma-fire itself.

26

श्रोत्रादीनीन्द्रियाण्यन्ये
संयमाग्निषु जुह्वति।
शब्दादीन्विषयानन्य
इन्द्रियाग्निषु जुह्वति।।

śrotrādīnīndriyāṇyanye
saṁyamāgniṣu juhvati
śabdādīn viṣayān anya
indriyāgniṣujuhvati ||

śrotra-ādīni—hearing process; indriyāṇi—senses; anye—others; saṁyama—of restraint; agniṣu—in the fire; juhvati—offers; śabda-ādīn—sound vibration, etc.; viṣayān—objects of sense gratification; anye —others: indriya—of sense organs; agniṣu—in the fire; juhvati—sacrifice.

Meaning: Some of them pour the senses into the fire of restraint as sacrifice, beginning with the sense of hearing. Others sacrifice the objects of the senses, beginning with sound.

27

सर्वाणीन्द्रियकर्माणि
प्राणकर्माणि चापरे।
आत्मसंयमयोगाग्नौ
जुह्वति ज्ञानदीपिते॥

sarvāṇīndriya-karmāṇi
prāṇa-karmāṇicāpare
ātma-saṁyama-yogāgnau
juhvati jñāna-dīpite||

sarvāṇi—all; indriya—senses; karmāṇi—functions; prāṇa-karmāṇi—functions of the life breath; ca—also; apare—others; ātma-saṁyama—controlling the mind; yoga—linking process; agnau—in the fire of; juhvati—offers; jñāna-dīpite—because of the urge for self-realisation.

Meaning: Some pour all the sense-functions and vital functions like breath as oblations into the sacrificial fire of self-control.

28

द्रव्ययज्ञास्तपोयज्ञा
योगयज्ञास्तथापरे।
स्वाध्यायज्ञानयज्ञाश्च
यतयः संशितव्रताः॥

dravya-yajñās tapo-yajñā
yoga-yajñāstathāpare
svādhyāya-jñāna-yajñāś ca
yatayaḥsaṁśita-vratāḥ||

dravya-yajñāḥ—sacrificing one's possessions; tapo-yajñāḥ—sacrifice in austerities; yoga-yajñāḥ—sacrifice in eightfold mysticism; tathā—thus; apare—others; svādhyāya—sacrifice in the study of the Vedas; jñāna- yajñāḥ—sacrifice in advancement of transcendental knowledge; ca—also; yatayaḥ—enlightened; saṁśita—taken to strict; vratāḥ-vows.

Meaning: Some ascetics sacrifice all their wealth and material possessions in severe austerities with steadfast vows, some sacrifice with Yoga, and others with the knowledge from reading holy books like the Vedas.

29

अपाने जुह्वति प्राणं
प्राणेऽपानं तथापरे।
प्राणापानगती रुद्ध्वा
प्राणायामपरायणाः॥

apānejuhvati prāṇaṁ
prāṇe'pānaṁ tathāpare
prāṇāpāna-gatī ruddhvā
prāṇāyāma-parāyaṇāḥ||

apāne—air which acts downward; juhvati—offers; prāṇam—air which acts outward; prāṇe—in the air going outward; apānam—air going downward; tathā—as also; apare—others; prāṇa—air going outward; apāna—air going downward; gatī—movement; ruddhvā—checking; prāṇāyāma—trance induced by stopping all breathing; parāyaṇāḥ—so inclined.

Meaning: Some possess the highest aim to regulate the vital currents like the restraint of breath to remain in trance. They practise the stopping of breathing by restraining the course of the incoming breath into the outgoing, and outgoing breath into the incoming.

30

अपरे नियताहाराः
प्राणान्प्राणेषु जुह्वति।
सर्वेऽप्येते यज्ञविदो
यज्ञक्षपितकल्मषाः॥

apare niyatāhārāḥ
prāṇān prāṇeṣhu juhvati
sarve 'py ete yajña-vido
yajña-kṣapita-kalmaṣāḥ||

apare—others; niyata—controlled; āhārāḥ—eating; prāṇān—outgoing air; prāṇeṣu—in the outgoing air; juhvati—sacrifices;sarve—all; api—although apparently different; ete—all these; yajña-vidaḥ —conversant with the purpose of performing; yajña—sacrifices; kṣapita—being cleansed of the result of such performances; kalmaṣāḥ—sinful reactions.

Meaning: Some of them stop the eating process, being regulated in food, and pour the outgoing breath into itself, as a sacrifice. These knowledgeable performers of sacrifice destroy sinful reaction by sacrifice.

31

यज्ञशिष्टामृतभुजो
यान्ति ब्रह्म सनातनम्।
नायं लोकोऽस्त्ययज्ञस्य
कुतोऽन्यः कुरुसत्तम॥

yajña-śiṣṭāmṛta-bhujo
yāntibrahmasanātanam
āyaṁ loko ‘sty ayajñasya
kuto’nyaḥkuru-sattama ||

yajña-sista—as a result of such performances of yajña; amra-bhuja.—those who have tasted such nectar; y.nti—do approach; brahma—the supreme; san.tanam—eternal atmosphere. na—never; ayam—this; lokaḥ—planet; asti—there is; ayajñasya—of the foolish; kutaḥ—where is; anyaḥ—the other; kuru-sattama—O best amongst the Kurus.

Meaning: Tasting the nectar of immortality at the end of such sacrifice, they travel to the abode of Brahma Eternal. One cannot live happily in this world without sacrifice, O best of the Kurus. How can he hope to do so in the other world then?

32

एवं बहुविधा यज्ञा
वितता ब्रह्मणो मुखे।
कर्मजान्विद्धि तान्सर्वानेवं
ज्ञात्वा विमोक्ष्यसे॥

evaṁ bahu-vidhā yajñā
vitatā brahmaṇo mukhe
karma-jānviddhi tānsarvān evaṁ
jñātvā vimokṣyase||

evam—thus; bahu-vidhāḥ—various kinds of; yajñāḥ—sacrifices; vitatāḥ— widespread; brahmaṇaḥ—of the Vedas; mukhe—in the face of; karma- jān— born of work; viddhi—you should know; tān—them; sarvān—all; evam—thus; jñātvā—knowing; vimokṣyase—be liberated.

Meaning: Sacrifices of different types are thus approved by the Vedas, each born from different types of action and spread out at the mouth of Brahma. Knowing them like this, you will attain liberation.

33

श्रेयान्द्रव्यमयाद्यज्ञाज्ज्ञान
यज्ञः परन्तप।
सर्वं कर्माखिलं पार्थ
ज्ञाने परिसमाप्यते।।

śreyān dravyamayād yajñāj
jñāna-yajñaḥparantapa
sarv aṁ karmākhilaṁ pārtha
jñāne parisamāpyate ||

śreyān—greater; dravyamayāt—than the sacrifice of material possessions; yajñāt—knowledge; jñāna-yajñaḥ—sacrifice in knowledge; parantapa—O chastiser of the enemy; sarvam—all; karma—activities; akhilam—in totality; pārtha—O son of Pṛthā; jñāne—in knowledge; parisamāpyate—ends in.

Meaning: The sacrifice of wisdom is greater than the sacrifice of wealth, O destroyer of enemies. Every perfect action, O Partha, culminates in wisdom.

34

तद्विद्धि प्रणिपातेन
परिप्रश्नेन सेवया।
उपदेक्ष्यन्ति ते ज्ञानं
ज्ञानिनस्तत्त्वदर्शिनः।।

tad viddhi praṇipātena
paripraśnena sevayā
upadekṣyanti te jñānaṁ
jñāninastattva-darśinaḥ||

tat—that knowledge of different sacrifices; viddhi—try to understand; praṇipātena—by approaching a spiritual master; paripraśnena—by submissive inquiries; sevayā—by the rendering of service; upadekṣyanti—initiate; te—unto you; jñānam—knowledge; jñāninaḥ—the self-realised; tattva—truth; darśinaḥ—the seers.

Meaning: You learn the truth by homage, by questioning, and by service, A spiritual master will teach you this wisdom. Ask of him submissively and render service upon him. The self-realised soul can share the knowledge with you having seen the truth.

35

यज्ज्ञात्वा न पुनर्मोहमेवं
यास्यसि पाण्डव।
येन भूतान्यशेषेण
द्रक्ष्यस्यात्मन्यथो मयि।।

yajjñātvā na punarmoham evaṁ
yāsyasi pāṇḍava
yena bhūtāny aśeṣāṇi
drakṣyasyātmanyatho mayi||

yat—which; jñātvā—knowing; na—never; punaḥ—again; moham—illusion; evam—like this; yāsyasi—you shall go; pāṇḍava—O son of Pāṇḍu; yena—by which; bhūtāni—all living entities; aśesāṇi—totally; drakṣyasi—you will see; ātmani—in the Supreme Soul; atho—or in other words; mayi—in Me.

Meaning: When you have knowledge of the truth, you will never again be confused, O Pandava. You will know that all living beings are but a part of Me-they are in Me, and are Mine. You will see them all without exception first in the self, and then in Me.

36

अपि चेदसि पापेभ्यः
सर्वेभ्यः पापकृत्तमः।
सर्वं ज्ञानप्लवेनैव
वृजिनं सन्तरिष्यसि॥

api ced asi pāpebhyaḥ
sarvebhyaḥ pāpa-kṛttamaḥ
sarvaṁ jñāna-plavenaiva
vṛjinaṁ santariṣyasi||

api—even; cet—if; asi—you are; pāpebhyaḥ—of sinners; sarvebhyaḥ—of all; pāpa-kṛttamaḥ—the greatest sinner; sarvam—all such sinful actions; jñāna-plavena—by the boat of transcendental knowledge; eva—certainly; vṛjinam—the ocean of miseries; santariṣyasi—you will cross completely.

Meaning: Even if you are the greatest of all sinners, you shall pass across all your sins in the ocean of miseries seated in the raft of this transcendental wisdom alone.

37

यथैधांसि समिद्धोऽग्नि
र्भस्मसात्कुरुतेऽर्जुन।
ज्ञानाग्निः सर्वकर्माणि
भस्मसात्कुरुते तथा।।

yathaidhāṁsisamiddho'gnir
bhasmasātkurute'rjuna
jñānāgniḥ sarva-karmāṇi
bhasmasātkurutetathā ||

yathā—just as; edhāṁsi—firewood; samiddhaḥ—blazing; agniḥ—fire; bhasmasāt—turns into ashes; kurute—so does; arjuna—O Arjuna; jñāna- agniḥ—the fire of knowledge; sarva-karmāṇi—all reactions to material activities; bhasmasāt—to ashes; kurute—it so does; tathā—similarly.

Meaning: Just as a blazing fire reduces firewood to ashes, O Arjuna, the fire of wisdom burns to ashes all reaction to material action.

38

न हि ज्ञानेन सदृशं
पवित्रमिह विद्यते।
तत्स्वयं योगसंसिद्धः
कालेनात्मनि विन्दति।।

na hi jñānena sadṛśaṁ
pavitramihavidyate
tatsvayaṁyoga-saṁsiddhaḥ
kālenātmani vindati ||

na—never; hi—certainly; jñānena—with knowledge; sadṛśam—in comparison; pavitram—sanctified; iha—in this world; vidyate—exists; tat—that; svayam—itself; yoga—devotion; saṁsiddhaḥ—matured; kālena—in course of time; ātmani—in himself; vindati—enjoys.

Meaning: There is no purifier in this world like transcendental knowledge which is the ripened fruit of all mysticism. The Yoga-perfected one finds it in the self in the due course of time without anyone's help.

39

श्रद्धावाँल्लभते ज्ञानं
तत्परः संयतेन्द्रियः।
ज्ञानं लब्ध्वा परां
शान्तिमचिरेणाधिगच्छति॥

śraddhāvāl labhate jñānaṁ
tat-paraḥsaṁyatendriyaḥ
jñānaṁ labdhvā parāṁ
śāntimacireṇ-ādhigacchati ||

śraddhāvān—a faithful man; labhate—achieves; jñānam—knowledge; tat-paraḥ—very much attached to it; saṁyata—controlled; indriyaḥ—senses; jñānam—knowledge; labdhvā—having achieved; parām—transcendental; śāntim—peace; acireṇa—very soon; adhigacchati—attains.

Meaning: A faithful man who controls his senses diligently acquires transcendental knowledge and obtains supreme spiritual peace without anyone's help.

40

अज्ञश्चाश्रद्दधानश्च
संशयात्मा विनश्यति।
नायं लोकोऽस्ति न परो
न सुखं संशयात्मनः।।

ajñaś cāśraddadhānaś ca
saṁśayātmāvinaśyati
nāyaṁloko'stinaparo
nasukhaṁ saṁśayātmanaḥ||

ajñaḥ—fools who have no knowledge in standard scriptures; ca—and; aśraddadhānaḥ—without faith in revealed scriptures; ca—also; saṁśaya—doubts; ātmā—person; vinaśyati—falls back; na—never; ayam—this; lokaḥ—world; asti—there is; na—neither; paraḥ—next life; na—not; sukham—happiness; saṁśaya—doubtful; ātmanaḥ—of the person.

Meaning: But the faithless and ignorant people who are lacking in faith and who doubt the scriptures fail to attain God. There is no happiness prescribed for the doubting soul in this life or the next.

41

योगसन्नयस्तकर्माणं
ज्ञानसञ्छिन्नसंशयम्।
आत्मवन्तं न कर्माणि
निबध्नन्ति धनंजय॥

yoga-sannyasta-karmāṇaṁ
jñāna-sañchinna-saṁśayam
ātma-vantaṁ na karmāṇi
nibadhnantidhanañjaya||

yoga—devotional service in karma-yoga; sannyasta—renounced; karmāṇam—of the performers; jñāna—knowledge; sañchinna—cut by the advancement of knowledge; saṁśayam—doubts; ātma-vantam—situated in theself; na—never; karmāṇi—work; nibadhnanti—do bind up; dhanañjaya—O conquerer of riches.

Meaning: Actions do not bind the one who has renounced the fruits of his action and whose actions are surrendered to Yoga, O Dhananjaya. His doubts are addressed by transcendental knowledge and he is seated firmly in the self and is self-possessed.

42

तस्मादज्ञानसम्भूतं
हृत्स्थं ज्ञानासिनात्मनः।
छित्वैनं संशयं
योगमातिष्ठोत्तिष्ठ भारत॥

tasmādajñāna-sambhūtaṁ
hṛt-sthaṁjñānāsinātmanaḥ
chittvainaṁ saṁśayaṁ
yogamātiṣṭhottiṣṭhabhārata ||

tasmāt—therefore; ajñāna-sambhūtam—outcome of ignorance; hṛt-stham—situated in the heart; jñāna—knowledge; asinā—by the weapon of; ātmanaḥ—of the self; chittvā—cutting off; enam—this; saṁśayam—doubt; yogam—inyoga; ātiṣṭha—be situated; uttiṣṭha—stand up to fight; bhārata—O descendant of Bharata.

Meaning: Therefore, cut all the doubts that have risen in your heart due to ignorance with the sword of knowledge. Armed with the power of Yoga and settled in it, O Bharata, stand up and fight.

ॐ तत्सदिति श्रीमद्भगवद्गीतासूपनिषत्सु ब्रह्मविद्यायां योगशास्त्रे

श्रीकृष्णार्जुनसंवादे ज्ञानकर्मसंन्यासयोगो नाम चतुर्थोऽध्यायः।

Thus in the Upanishad of the Glorious Divine Lay, the Science of Brahma, the Ordinance of Yoga, the Discourse between the Glorious Lord Krishna and Arjuna, the Fourth Chapter titled 'Jnana Karma Sannyas Yoga'(The Yoga of Knowledge, Action, Renunciation).

CHAPTER 5

KARMA SANNYAS YOGA (THE YOGA OF ACTION AND RENUNCIATION)

CHAPTER 5

KARMA SANNYAS YOGA (THE YOGA OF ACTION AND RENUNCIATION)

In Chapter Five, Lord Krishna reveals about material and spiritual knowledge to Arjuna. When Arjuna is still in a state of confusion about which is better among renunciation of work or work done in devotion, Lord Krishna informs him that devotional service is the better path among the two. Lord Krishna says that we can choose either of the two paths as both of them lead us to the same destination. However, the renunciation of actions can prove to be challenging for all men and can only be performed without flaws by someone with total purification of the mind. This desired purification of the mind is only achievable by working in total devotion. Hence, Karma Yoga is a more suitable path for the majority of mankind to achieve the desired goal.

Lord Krishna explains that detachment and renunciation are both means to achieve the same goal. He tells Arjuna that one can attain salvation by pursuing any of these paths. But, as everything belongs to Krishna, there is nothing that is one's own to renounce after all. Hence, whatever one possesses should be used in the

Lord's service by working with total devotion and by controlling the mind and senses to reach a state of divine consciousness.

Such action and renunciation in Krishna consciousness leads to the salvation of the soul by non-attachment to fruitive actions, and this process is called Karma Yoga or the Yoga of Action which helps one escape the tedious cycle of birth and death to be united with the Supreme One. Lord Krishna instructs Arjuna to renounce the ego of individuality and rejoice in the bliss of infinity to reach the Lord.

1

अर्जुन उवाच
सन्न्यासं कर्मणां कृष्ण
पुनर्योगं च शंससि।
यच्छ्रेय एतयोरेकं
तन्मे ब्रू हि सुनिश्चितम्॥

arjunauvāca
sannyāsaṁ karmaṇāṁ kṛṣṇa
punaryogaṁcaśaṁsasi
yacchreyaetayorekaṁ
tanmebrūhisuniścitam ||

arjunaḥ uvāca—Arjuna said; sannyāsam—renunciation; karmaṇām—of all activities; kṛṣṇa—O Kṛṣṇa; punaḥ—again; yogam—devotional service; ca—also; śaṁsasi—You are praising; yat—which; śreyaḥ—is beneficial; etayoḥ—of these two; ekam—one; tat—that; me—unto me; brūhi—please tell; suniścitam—definitely.

Meaning: Arjuna said: O Krishna, first You ask me to renounce work by recommending Sannyasa of actions, and then You ask me to work with devotion by recommending Yoga. Can You please tell me decisively which one is the better of the two?

2

श्रीभगवानुवाच
सन्न्यासः कर्मयोगश्च
निःश्रेयसकरावुभौ।
तयोस्तु कर्मसन्न्यासात्
कर्मयोगो विशिष्यते॥

śrī-bhagavān uvāca
sannyāsaḥkarma-yogaśca
niḥśreyasa-karāvubhau
tayos tu karma-sannyāsāt
karma-yogo viśiṣyate||

śrī bhagavān uvāca—the Personality of Godhead said; sannyāsaḥ—renunciation of work; karma-yogaḥ—work in devotion; ca—also; niḥśreyasa-karau—all leading to the path of liberation; ubhau—both; tayoḥ —of the two; tu—but; karma-sannyāsāt—in comparison to the renunciation of fruitive work; karma-yogaḥ—work in devotion; viśiṣyate—is better.

Meaning: The Glorious Lord said: The renunciation of work or Sannyasa and work done with devotion or Action-Yoga are both producers of the good and perfect for the attainment of liberation. But, of the two, work done in devotional service is preferable to the Sannyasa of action.

3

ज्ञेयः स नित्यसन्न्यासी
यो न द्वेष्टि न काङ्क्षति।
निर्द्वन्द्वो हि महाबाहो
सुखं बन्धात्प्रमुच्यते।।

jñeyaḥsanitya-sannyāsī
yo na dveṣṭi na kāṅkṣati
nirdvandvo hi mahā-bāho
sukhaṁbandhāt pramucyate ||

jñeyaḥ—should be known; saḥ—he; nitya—always; sannyāsī renouncer; yaḥ—who; na—never; dveṣṭi—abhors; na—nor; kāṅkṣati—desires; nirdvandvaḥ—free from all dualities; hi—certainly; mahā-bāho—O mighty-armed one; sukham—happily; bandhāt—from bondage; pramucyate—completely liberated.

Meaning: Let it be known that one who neither dislikes nor desires the fruits of his actions is a constant Sannyasi or Yogi. Such a person is unaffected by all dualities, overcomes material bondage easily, and is totally liberated, O mighty-armed.

4

साङ्ख्ययोगौ पृथग्बालाः
प्रवदन्ति न पण्डिताः।
एकमप्यास्थितः
सम्यगुभयोर्विन्दते फलम्॥

sāṅkhya-yogaupṛthagbālāḥ
pravadanti na paṇḍitāḥ
ekam apy āsthitaḥ
samyag ubhayorvindatephalam||

sāṅkhya—analytical study of the material world; yogau—work in devotional service; pṛthak—different; bālāḥ—less intelligent; pravadanti—do talk; na—never; paṇḍitāḥ—the learned; ekam—in one; api—even though; āsthitaḥ—being situated; samyak—complete; ubhayoḥ—of both; vindate—enjoys; phalam—result.

Meaning: It is the ignorant who say that Yoga is different from Sankhya. The one who is really learned applies himself well to one of the paths to achieve the results in the common fruits of both the practises.

5

यत्साङ्ख्यैः प्राप्यते
स्थानं तद्योगैरपि गम्यते।
एकं साङ्ख्यं च योगं च यः
पश्यति स पश्यति॥

yatsāṅkhyaiḥ prāpyate
sthānaṁ tad yogair api gamyate
ekaṁsāṅkhyaṁcayogaṁca yaḥ
paśyati sa paśyati||

yat—what; sāṅkhyaiḥ—by means of sāṅkhya philosophy; prāpyate—is achieved; sthānam—place; tat—that; yogaiḥ—by devotional service; api—also; gamyate—one can attain; ekam—one; sāṅkhyam—analytical study; ca—and; yogam—action in devotion; ca—and; yaḥ—one who; paśyati—sees; saḥ—he; paśyati—actually sees.

Meaning: The position which is attained by the Sankhyas through devotional service is attained by the Yogi through renunciation as well. The one who sees Yoga and Sankhya as one sees things as they really are.

6

सन्न्यासस्तु महाबाहो
दुःखमाप्तुमयोगतः।
योगयुक्तो मुनिर्ब्रह्म
नचिरेणाधिगच्छति।।

sannyāsas tu mahā-bāho
duḥkhamāptumayogataḥ
yoga-yuktomunirbrahma
na cireṇādhigacchati ||

sannyāsaḥ—the renounced order of life; tu—but; mahā-bāho—O mighty- armed one; duḥkham—distress; āptum—to be afflicted with; ayogataḥ—without devotional service; yoga-yuktaḥ—one engaged in devotional service; muniḥ—thinker; brahma—Supreme; na—without; cireṇa—delay; adhigacchati—attains.

Meaning: But, O mighty-armed, keep in mind that Yogaless Sannyasa is useless and mere renunciation without engaging in the devotional service of the Lord only brings about misery. The sages who are thoroughly purified with their actions of devotion, achieve the Supreme One quickly.

7

योगयुक्तो विशुद्धात्मा
विजितात्मा जितेन्द्रियः।
सर्वभूतात्मभूतात्मा
कुर्वन्नपि न लिप्यते॥7॥

yoga-yukto viśuddhātmā
vijitātmā jitendriyaḥ
sarvabhūtātmabhūtātmā
kurvannapina lipyate

yoga-yuktaḥ—engaged in devotional service; viśuddha-ātmā—a purified soul; vijita-ātmā—self-controlled; jita-indriyaḥ—having conquered the senses; sarvabhuta-ātmabhūta-ātmā—compassionate to all living entities; kurvan api—although engaged in work; na—never; lipyate—is entangled.

Meaning: He who is Yoga-endued, purified of soul, whose self is fully controlled and purified, who is dear to all creatures, and who are all dear to him, he although always involved in action, remains untainted.

8-9

नैव किंचित्करोमीति
युक्तो मन्येत तत्त्ववित्।
पश्यञ्शृण्वन्स्पृशञ्जिघ्रन्न
श्नन्गच्छन्स्वपंश्वसन्॥

प्रलपन्विसृजन्गृह्णन
नुन्मिषन्निमिषन्नपि।
इन्द्रियाणीन्द्रियार्थेषु वर्तन्त
इति धारयन्॥

naivakiñcitkaromīti
yukto manyeta tattva-vit
paśyañśṛṇvanspṛśañjighrann
aśnangacchansvapanśvasan ||

pralapan visṛjan gṛhṇann
unmiṣannimiṣannapi
indriyāṇīndriyārtheṣu vartanta
itidhārayan||

na—never; eva—certainly; kiñcit—anything; karomi—do I do; iti—thus; yuktaḥ—engaged in the divine consciousness; manyeta—thinks; tattvavit—one who knows the truth; paśyan—by seeing; śṛṇvan—by hearing; spṛśan—by touching; jighran—by smelling; aśnan—by eating; gacchan—by going; svapan—by dreaming; śvasan—by breathing; pralapan—by talking; visṛjan— by giving up; gṛhṇan—by accepting; unmiṣan—opening; nimiṣan—closing; api—in spite of; indriyāṇi—the senses; indriya-artheṣu—in sense gratification; vartante—let them be so engaged; iti—thus; dhārayan—considering.

Meaning: A person in the divine consciousness, although seeing, hearing, touching, smelling, eating, walking, sleeping, breathing, speaking, discharging, and opening or closing his eyes always knows that he actually does nothing at all. It is only the material senses that are moving being engaged with their sense-objects, and he is aloof from them all.

10

ब्रह्मण्याधाय कर्माणि
सङ्गं त्यक्त्वा करोति यः।
लिप्यते न स पापेन
पद्मपत्रमिवाम्भसा।।

brahmaṇy ādhāya karmāṇi
saṅgaṁtyaktvākarotiyaḥ
lipyatenasapāpena
padma-patramivāmbhasā ||

brahmaṇi—the Supreme Personality of Godhead; ādhāya—resigning unto; karmāṇi—all works; saṅgam—attachment; tyaktvā—giving up; karoti—performs; yaḥ—who; lipyate—is affected; na—never; saḥ—he; pāpena—bysin; padma-patram—lotus leaf; iva—like; ambhasā—in the water.

Meaning: One who performs actions without attachment, surrendering the results to the Supreme, is unaffected by sinful action just as the lotus leaf remains untouched by water.

11

कायेन मनसा
बुद्ध्या केवलैरिन्द्रियैरपि।
योगिनः कर्म कुर्वन्ति
संगं त्यक्त्वात्मशुद्धये॥

kāyena manasā
buddhyā kevalairindriyairapi
yoginaḥkarmakurvanti
saṅgaṁtyaktvātma-śuddhaye ||

kāyena—with the body; manasā—with the mind; buddhyā—with the intelligence; kevalaiḥ—purified; indriyaiḥ—with the senses; api—even with; yoginaḥ—the Kṛṣṇa conscious persons; karma—actions; kurvanti—they act; saṅgam—attachment; tyaktvā—giving up; ātma—self; śuddhaye—for the purpose of purification.

Meaning: The Yogis who have renounced all attachment, use the body, mind, understanding, and also the senses to perform action for self-purification.

12

युक्तः कर्मफलं त्यक्त्वा
शान्तिमाप्नोति नैष्ठिकीम्।
अयुक्तः कामकारेण
फले सक्तो निबध्यते॥12॥

yuktaḥkarma-phalaṁtyaktvā
śāntim āpnoti naiṣṭhikīm
ayuktaḥ kāma-kāreṇa
phalesaktonibadhyate

yuktaḥ—one who is engaged in devotional service; karma-phalam—the results of all activities; tyaktvā—giving up; śāntim—perfect peace; āpnoti—achieves; naiṣṭhikīm—unflinching; ayuktaḥ—one who is not in Kṛṣṇa consciousness; kāma-kāreṇa—for enjoying the result of work; phale—in the result; saktaḥ—attached; nibadhyate—becomes entangled.

Meaning: The one fixed on Yoga with steadfast devotion attains peace because he offers all the fruits of his actions to Me; whereas a person not united with the Divine, being attached to the fruit by the action of desire becomes entangled.

13

सर्वकर्माणि मनसा
संन्यस्यास्ते सुखं वशी।
नवद्वारे पुरे देही
नैव कुर्वन्न कारयन्॥

sarva-karmāṇi manasā
sannyasyāstesukhaṁvaśī
nava-dvārepuredehī
naiva kurvanna kārayan||

sarva—all; karmāṇi—activities; manasā—by the mind; sannyasya—giving up; āste—remains; sukham—in happiness; vaśī—one who is controlled; nava-dvāre—in the place where there are nine gates; pure—inthecity; dehī—the embodied soul; na—never; eva—certainly; kurvan—doing anything; na—not; kārayan—causing to be done.

Meaning: The Embodied One who controls all his actions by the will by mental renunciation of all actions is the real winner. So, he lives happily in the nine-gated house that is the material body, neither acting nor causing work to be done.

14

न कर्तृत्वं न कर्माणि
लोकस्य सृजति प्रभुः।
न कर्मफलसंयोगं
स्वभावस्तु प्रवर्तते॥

na kartṛtvaṁ na karmāṇi
lokasya sṛjati prabhuḥ
na karma-phala-saṁyogaṁ
svabhāvastu pravartate||

na—never; kartṛtvam—proprietorship; na—nor; karmāṇi—activities; lokasya—of the people; sṛjati—creates; prabhuḥ—the master of the city of the body; na—nor; karma-phala—results of activities; saṁyogam—connection; svabhāvaḥ—modes of material nature; tu—but; pravartate—acts.

Meaning: The Lord does not create the actions of men or the union of action and fruit. All this is exerted by the modes of material nature.

15

नादत्ते कस्यचित्पापं
न चैव सुकृतं विभुः।
अज्ञानेनावृतं ज्ञानं
तेन मुह्यन्ति जन्तवः॥

nādattekasyacitpāpaṁ
nacaivasukṛtaṁvibhuḥ
ajñānenāvṛtaṁ jñānaṁ
tenamuhyanti jantavaḥ||

na—never; ādatte—accepts; kasyacit—anyone's; pāpam—sin; na—nor; ca— also; eva—certainly; sukṛtam—pious activities; vibhuḥ—the Supreme Lord; ajñānena—by ignorance; āvṛtam—covered; jñānam—knowledge; tena—by that; muhyanti—bewildered; jantavaḥ—the living entities.

Meaning: The Supreme Spirit does not receive the sin of any person nor the good done by him. Wisdom is clouded by ignorance of wisdom, which causes people to be bewildered when they come into birth.

16

ज्ञानेन तु तदज्ञानं
येषां नाशितमात्मनः।
तेषामादित्यवज्ज्ञानं
प्रकाशयति तत्परम्॥

jñānena tu tad ajñānaṁ
yeṣāṁnāśitamātmanaḥ
teṣām ādityavaj jñānaṁ
prakāśayatitatparam||

jñānena—by knowledge; tu—but; tat—that; ajñānam—nescience; yeṣām—of those; nāśitam—is destroyed; ātmanaḥ—of the living entity; teṣām—of their; ādityavat—like the rising sun; jñānam—knowledge; prakāśayati—discloses; tatparam—in Kṛṣṇa consciousness.

Meaning: But when the wisdom destroys the non-wisdom of the self, one is enlightened with the knowledge like the sun that lights up and reveals the discovery of the Supreme.

17

तद्बुद्धयस्तदात्मानस्
तन्निष्ठास्तत्परायणाः।
गच्छन्त्यपुनरावृत्तिं
ज्ञाननिर्धूतकल्मषाः॥

tad-buddhayas tad-ātmānas
tan-niṣṭhāstat-parāyaṇāḥ
gacchanty apunar-āvṛttiṁ
jñāna-nirdhūta-kalmaṣāḥ ||

tad-buddhayaḥ—one whose intelligence is always in the Supreme; tad- ātmānaḥ—one whose mind is always in the Supreme; tat-niṣṭhāḥ—whose mind is only meant for the Supreme; tat-parāyaṇāḥ—who has completely taken shelter of Him; gacchanti—goes; apunaḥ-āvṛttim—liberation; jñāna—knowledge; nirdhūta—cleanses; kalmaṣāḥ—misgivings.

Meaning: When one fixes that understanding of the Self so that the mind, understanding, faith, and refuge are all fixed in the Supreme, one is fully cleansed of their sins through complete wisdom to reach the path of liberation.

18

विद्याविनयसम्पन्ने
ब्राह्मणे गवि हस्तिनि।
शुनि चैव श्वपाके
च पण्डिताः समदर्शिनः॥

vidyā-vinaya-sampanne
brāhmaṇegavihastini
śuni caiva śvapāke
ca paṇḍitāḥsama-darśinaḥ||

vidyā—education; vinaya—gentleness; sampanne—fully equipped; brāhmaṇe—in the brāhmaṇa; gavi—in the cow; hastini—in the elephant; śuni—in the dog; ca—and; eva—certainly; śvapāke—in the dog-eater (the outcaste);ca—respectively; paṇḍitāḥ-those who are so wise; sama-darśinaḥ—do see with equal vision.

Meaning: The humble sage is the one who sees with equal vision a learned Brahmana, a cow, an elephant, a dog, and even an outcaste like a dog-eater.

19

इहैव तैर्जितः सर्गो
येषां साम्ये स्थितं मनः।
निर्दोषं हि समं ब्रह्म तस्माद्
ब्रह्मणि ते स्थिताः॥

ihaivatairjitaḥ sargo
yeṣāṁsāmyesthitaṁmanaḥ
nirdoṣaṁ hi samaṁ brahma tasmād-
brahmaṇi te sthitāḥ||

iha—in this life; eva—certainly; taiḥ—by them; jitaḥ—conquered; sargaḥ—birth and death; yeṣām—of those; sāmye—inequanimity; sthitam—so situated; manaḥ—mind; nirdoṣam—flawless; hi—certainly; samam—in equanimity; brahma—the Supreme; tasmāt—therefore; brahmaṇi—in the Supreme; te—they; sthitāḥ—are situated.

Meaning: The ones whose minds are grounded in equality have already conquered the cycle of birth and death. They are flawless like the spotless Brahman and in that Brahma they are fixed.

20

न प्रहृष्येत्प्रियं प्राप्य
नोद्विजेत्प्राप्य चाप्रियम्।
स्थिरबुद्धिरसम्मूढो
ब्रह्मविद् ब्रह्मणि स्थितः॥

na prahṛṣyet priyaṁ prāpya
nodvijetprāpyacāpriyam
sthira-buddhir asammūḍho
brahma-vidbrahmaṇi sthitaḥ ||

na—never; prahṛṣyet—rejoice; priyam—pleasant; prāpya—achieving; na—does not; udvijet—agitated; prāpya—obtaining; ca—also; apriyam —unpleasant; sthira-buddhiḥ—self-intelligent; asammūḍhaḥ—unbewildered; brahmavit—one who knows the Supreme perfectly; brahmaṇi—in the Transcendence; sthitaḥ situated.

Meaning: One should not rejoice on achieving something agreeable nor lament on receiving the disagreeable. The knower of Brahma should be of settled mind and one who should know the science of God to be established in Brahma.

— 21 —

बाह्यस्पर्शेष्वसक्तात्मा
विन्दत्यात्मनि यत्सुखम्।
स ब्रह्मयोगयुक्तात्मा
सुखमक्षयमश्नुते॥

bāhya-sparśeṣv asaktātmā
vindatyātmaniyatsukham
sa brahma-yoga-yuktātmā
sukhamakṣayamaśnute ||

bāhya-sparśeṣu—in external sense pleasure; asakta-ātmā—one who is not so attached; vindati—enjoys; ātmani—in the self; yat—that which; sukham —happiness; saḥ—that; brahma-yoga—concentrated in Brahman; yukta- ātmā—self-connected; sukham—happiness; akṣayam—unlimited; aśnute— enjoys.

Meaning: A liberated person is unattached to external contacts or material sense pleasure, but instead discovers the joy in the self. Settled in eternal communion with the Supreme, he experiences unlimited and eternal joy.

22

ये हि संस्पर्शजा भोगा
दुःखयोनय एव ते।
आद्यन्तवन्तः कौन्तेय
न तेषु रमते बुधः।।

ye hi saṁsparśajā bhogā
duḥkha-yonayaevate
ādy-antavantaḥ kaunteya
na teṣu ramate budhaḥ ||

ye—those; hi—certainly; saṁsparśajāḥ—by contact with the material senses; bhogāḥ—enjoyment; duḥkha—distress; yonayaḥ—sources of; eva—certainly; te—they are; ādi—in the beginning; antavantaḥ—subject to; kaunteya—O son of Kuntī; na—never; teṣu—in those; ramate—take delight; budhaḥ—the intelligent.

Meaning: The wise one does not participate in the sources of misery, caused because of contact with the material senses. O son of Kunti, he does not delight in these pleasures as they have a beginning and an end.

23

शक्नोतीहैव यः सोढुं
प्राक्शरीरविमोक्षणात्।
कामक्रोधोद्भवं वेगं
स युक्तः स सुखी नरः।।

śaknotīhaiva yaḥ soḍhuṁ
prākśarīra-vimokṣaṇāt
kāma-krodhodbhavaṁvegaṁ
sayuktaḥsasukhī naraḥ ||

śaknoti—able to do; iha eva—in the present body; yaḥ—one who; soḍhum—to tolerate; prāk—before; śarīra—body; vimokṣaṇāt—giving up; kāma—desire; krodha—anger; udbhavam—generated from; vegam—urge; saḥ—he; yuktaḥ—in trance; saḥ—he; sukhī—happy; naraḥ—human being.

Meaning: He, who before being released from the body, can withstand the urges of the material senses to check the waves of desire and anger, that man is fixed on Yoga and is a happy man.

24

योऽन्तःसुखोऽन्तराराम
स्तथान्तर्ज्योतिरेव यः।
स योगी ब्रह्मनिर्वाणं
ब्रह्मभूतोऽधिगच्छति॥

yo'ntaḥ-sukho'ntarārāmas
tathāntar-jyotirevayaḥ
sa yogī brahma-nirvāṇaṁ
brahma-bhūto'dhigacchati||

yaḥ—one who; antaḥ-sukhaḥ—happy from within; antaḥ-ārāmah—active within; tathā—as well as; antaḥ-jyotiḥ—aiming within; eva—certainly; yaḥ anyone; saḥ—he; yogī—mystic; brahma-nirvāṇam—liberated in the Supreme; brahma bhūtaḥ self-realised; adhigacchati —attains.

Meaning: The one who is happy within, who is at ease within, who rejoices within, and who is radiant within is the perfect mystic. That Yogi is liberated in the Supreme, and ultimately attains Brahma.

25

लभन्ते ब्रह्मनिर्वाणमृषयः
क्षीणकल्मषाः।
छिन्नद्वैधा यतात्मानः
सर्वभूतहिते रताः॥

labhante brahma-nirvāṇam ṛṣayaḥ
kṣīṇa-kalmaṣāḥ
chinna-dvaidhā yatātmānaḥ
sarva-bhūta-hite ratāḥ||

labhante—achieve; brahma-nirvāṇam—liberation in the Supreme; ṛṣayaḥ —those who are active within; kṣīṇa-kalmaṣāḥ—who are devoid of all sins; chinna—torn off; dvaidhāḥ—duality; yata-ātmānaḥ—engaged in self-realisation; sarva-bhūta—in all living entities; hite—in welfare work; ratāḥ—engaged.

Meaning: The one whose duality and doubts are removed, whose self is controlled, who has always worked for the welfare of all creatures, and whose sins are destroyed, finds refuge in the Supreme.

26

कामक्रोधवियुक्तानां
यतीनां यतचेतसाम्।
अभितो ब्रह्मनिर्वाणं
वर्तते विदितात्मनाम्॥

kāma-krodha-vimuktānāṁ
yatīnāṁyata-cetasām
abhito brahma-nirvāṇaṁ
vartate viditātmanām ||

kāma—desires; krodha—anger; vimuktānām—of those who are so liberated; yatīnām—of the saintly persons; yata-cetasām—of persons who have full control over the mind; abhitaḥ—assured in the near future; brahma-nirvāṇam—liberation in the Supreme; vartate—is there; vidita- ātmanām—of those who are self-realised.

Meaning: The self-knowers, the ones freed from anger and desire, who are self-realised and self-disciplined in conduct, and are always striving for perfection, are sure of finding liberation in the Supreme in the near future.

27-28

स्पर्शान्कृत्वा बहिर्बाह्यां
श्चक्षुश्चैवान्तरे भ्रुवोः।
प्राणापानौ समौ कृत्वा
नासाभ्यन्तरचारिणौ॥

यतेन्द्रियमनोबुद्धि
र्मुनिर्मोक्षपरायणः।
विगतेच्छाभयक्रोधो यः
सदा मुक्त एवं सः॥

sparśān kṛtvā bahir bāhyāṁś
cakṣuścaivāntare bhruvoḥ
prāṇāpānau samau kṛtvā
nāsābhyantara-cāriṇau
yatendriya-mano-buddhir
munirmokṣa-parāyaṇaḥ
vigatecchā-bhaya-krodhoyaḥ
sadā mukta eva saḥ||

sparśān—external sense objects, such as sound, etc.; kṛtvā—doingso; bahiḥ external; bāhyān—unnecessary; cakṣuḥ—eyes;ca—also; eva—certainly; antare—within; bhruvoḥ—of the eyebrows; prāṇaapānau—up and down-moving air; samau—in suspension; kṛtvā—doing so; nāsā- abhyantara —within the nostrils; cāriṇau—blowing; yata—controlled; indriya—senses; manaḥ—mind; buddhiḥ intelligence; muniḥ—the transcendentalist; mokṣa—liberation; parāyaṇaḥ—being so destined; vigata—discarded; icchā—wishes; bhaya—fear; krodhaḥ—anger; yaḥ—one who; sadā—always; muktaḥ—liberated; eva—certainly; saḥ—he is.

Meaning: Banishing all external sense-objects, focusing the eyes and vision between the two eyebrows, equalising the incoming and outgoing breaths within the nostrils, thus controlling the senses, the mind, and the understanding, the meditator becomes free from desire, fear, and anger. The one who is in this perpetual state is certainly liberated.

29

भोक्तारं यज्ञतपसां
सर्वलोकमहेश्वरम्।
सुहृदं सर्वभूतानां
ज्ञात्वा मां शान्तिमृच्छति॥

bhoktāraṁ yajña-tapasāṁ
sarva-loka-maheśvaram
suhṛdaṁ sarva-bhūtānāṁ
jñātvā māṁ śāntimṛcchati ||

bhoktāram—beneficiary; yajña—sacrifices; tapasām—of penances and austerities; sarva-loka—all planets and the demigods thereof; maheśvaram—the Supreme Lord; suhṛdam—benefactor; sarva—all; bhūtānām—of the living entities; jñātvā—thus knowing; mām—Me (Lord Kṛṣṇa); śāntim—relief from material pangs; ṛcchati—achieves.

Meaning: The sages, knowing Me as the final purpose of all austerities and sacrifices, as the Supreme Lord of all the worlds, as the lover of all living beings, attain relief from the pangs of material miseries and find peace.

ॐ तत्सदिति श्रीमद्भगवद्गीतासूपनिषत्सु ब्रह्मविद्यायां योगशास्त्रे

श्रीकृष्णार्जुनसंवादे कर्मसंन्यासयोगो नाम पंचमोऽध्यायः।

Thus in the Upanishad of the Glorious Divine Lay, the Science of Brahma, the Ordinance of Yoga, the Discourse between the Glorious Lord Krishna and Arjuna, the Fifth Chapter titled 'Karma Sannyas Yoga' (The Yoga of Action and Renunciation)

CHAPTER 6

DHYANA YOGA

(THE YOGA OF MEDITATION)

CHAPTER 6

DHYANA YOGA
(THE YOGA OF MEDITATION)

In Chapter Six of the Bhagavad Gita, Lord Krishna passes on the knowledge of meditation, connecting with the Higher Consciousness. Lord Krishna reveals 'Dhyana Yoga' or the Yoga of meditation, and explains the process of this mystic form of Yoga.

While the process of the Yoga of meditation requires one to stop performing material activities, Lord Krishna explains to Arjuna that a true Yogi is not someone who does not perform any duty or action. A real Yogi works according to his duty, but does not desire for the gratification of the senses or longs for the fruits of his actions. The very goal of real Yoga is the union with the Supreme Soul and following His instructions. But, only the one with a controlled mind can achieve this state.

The dualities of material existence like heat and cold, honour and dishonour do not affect the one who is basking in the light of knowledge and self-realisation. The Yogi assumes control over his mind and body by the regulation of activities like eating, sleeping, action, and renunciation to become steady in his meditation process on the transcendent Self to achieve mastery of the mind through the practice of Yoga. Eventually, the Yogi reaches the trance-like state of Samadhi where he experiences Supreme pleasure through the transcendental sense. The highest Yogi is one who always has the Supreme Soul on his mind, and no one else.

1

श्रीभगवानुवाच
अनाश्रितः कर्मफलं
कार्यं कर्म करोति यः।
स सन्न्यासी च योगी च
न निरग्निर्न चाक्रियः॥

śrī-bhagavān uvāca
anāśritaḥkarma-phalaṁ
kāryaṁ karma karoti yaḥ
sa sannyāsī ca yogī ca
na niragnirna cākriyaḥ||

śrībhagavānuvāca—the Lord said; anāśritaḥ—without shelter; karma-phalam—the result of work; kāryam—obligatory; karma—work; karoti—performs; yaḥ—one who; saḥ—he; sannyāsī—in the renounced order; ca—also; yogī—mystic; ca—also; na—not; nir—without; agniḥ—fire; na—nor; ca —also; akriyaḥ—without duty.

Meaning: The Glorious Lord said: One who is unattached to the fruit of action, performs action which should be done, he is a Sanyasi and he is a Yogi, not one who merely engages in the renuncification of action or renounces the sacrificial fire.

2

यं सन्न्यासमिति प्राहुर्योगं
तं विद्धि पाण्डव।
न ह्यसन्न्यस्तसङ्कल्पो
योगी भवति कश्चन॥

yaṁ sannyāsam iti prāhur yogaṁ
taṁ viddhi pāṇḍava
na hyasannyasta-saṅkalpo
yogī bhavati kaścana ||

yam—what; sannyāsam—renunciation; iti—thus; prāhuḥ—they say; yogam—linking with the Supreme; tam—that; viddhi—you must know; pāṇḍava—O son of Pāṇḍu; na—never; hi—certainly; asannyasta—without giving up; saṅkalpaḥ—self-satisfaction; yogī—a mystic transcendentalist; bhavati—becomes; kaścana—anyone.

Meaning: What is called renunciation or Sanyasa, know that to be Yoga, O Pandava; for without renouncing the desire for sense gratification, one can never be a Yogi.

3

आरुरुक्षोर्मुनेर्योगं
कर्म कारणमुच्यते।
योगारूढस्य तस्यैव
शमः कारणमुच्यते॥

āruruksor muner yogaṁ
karma kāraṇamucyate
yogārūḍhasya tasyaiva
śamaḥ kāraṇamucyate ||

āruruksoḥ—of one who has just begun yoga; muneḥ—of the sage; yogam—the eightfold yoga system; karma—work; kāraṇam—the cause; ucyate—is said to be; yoga—eightfold yoga; ārūḍhasya—one who has attained; tasya—his; eva—certainly; śamaḥ—cessation of all material activities; kāraṇam—the cause; ucyate—is said to be.

Meaning: For a sage working his way up the eightfold yoga system, action is said to be the means; and for the one who is already Yoga-mounted, stopping all material activities or pacification is said to be the means.

4

यदा हि नेन्द्रियार्थेषु
न कर्मस्वनुषज्जते।
सर्वसङ्कल्पसन्न्यासी
योगारूढस्तदोच्यते।।

yadāhinendriyārtheṣu
na karmasvanuṣajjate
sarva-saṅkalpa-sannyāsī
yogārūḍhas-tadocyate ||

yadā—when; hi—certainly; na—not; indriya-artheṣu—in sense gratification; na—never; karmasu—in fruitive activities; anuṣajjate—does necessarily engage; sarva-saṅkalpa—all material desires; sannyāsī—renouncer; yoga-ārūḍhaḥ—elevated in yoga; tadā—at that time; ucyate—is said to be.

Meaning: One attains to Yoga when he has no attachment to any material desires, he does not perform action for sense gratification nor fruitive activities.

5

उद्धरेदात्मनाऽत्मानं
नात्मानमवसादयेत्।
आत्मैव ह्यात्मनो
बन्धुरात्मैव रिपुरात्मनः।।

uddhared ātmanātmānaṁ
nātmānamava-sādayet
ātmaivahyātmano
bandhur ātmaiva ripur ātmanaḥ ||

uddharet—one must deliver; ātmanā—by the mind; ātmānam—the conditioned soul; na—never; ātmānam—the conditioned soul; avasādayet—put into degradation; ātmā—mind; eva—certainly; hi—indeed; ātmanaḥ—of the conditioned soul; bandhuḥ—friend; ātmā—mind; eva—certainly; ripuḥ— enemy; ātmanaḥ—of the conditioned soul.

Meaning: One must elevate himself by raising the self, instead of degrading himself by lowering the self. The self is the friend of the self or the conditioned soul, and is also the enemy of the self.

6

बन्धुरात्मात्मनस्तस्य
येनात्मैवात्मना जितः।
अनात्मनस्तु शत्रुत्वे
वर्तेतात्मैव शत्रुवत्॥

bandhur ātmātmanas tasya
yenātmaivātmanā jitaḥ
anātmanas tu śatrutve
vartetātmaiva śatruvat||

bandhuḥ—friend; ātmā—mind; ātmanaḥ—of the living entity; tasya—of him; yena—by whom; ātmā—mind; eva—certainly; ātmanā—by the living entity; jitaḥ—conquered; anātmanaḥ—of one who has failed to control the mind; tu—but; śatrutve—because of enmity; varteta—remains; ātmāeva—the very mind; śatruvat—as an enemy.

Meaning: For one who has conquered the self, the self is the best friend. But for the one who has failed to do so and is conquered by the non-self, the self is the worst enemy.

7

जितात्मनः प्रशान्तस्य
परमात्मा समाहितः।
शीतोष्णसुखदुःखेषु
तथा मानापमानयोः॥

jitātmanaḥ praśāntasya
paramātmā samāhitaḥ
śītoṣṇa-sukha-duḥkheṣu
tathā mānāpamānayoḥ ||

jita-ātmanaḥ—of one who has conquered his mind; praśāntasya—of one who has attained tranquility by such control over the mind; paramātmā—the Supersoul; samāhitaḥ—approached completely; śīta—cold; uṣṇa—heat; sukha—in happiness; duḥkheṣu—in distress; tathā—also; māna—honor; apamānayoḥ—in dishonor.

Meaning: The self of the one who has conquered the self has already attained tranquillity and is settled in the Supreme. For such a man, heat and cold, pleasure and pain, and honour and dishonour are all the same.

8

ज्ञानविज्ञानतृप्तात्मा
कूटस्थो विजितेन्द्रियः।
युक्त इत्युच्यते योगी
समलोष्टाश्मकांचनः॥

jñāna-vijñāna-tṛptātmā
kūṭastho vijitendriyaḥ
yuktaityucyateyogī
sama-loṣṭrāśma-kāñcanaḥ||

jñāna—acquired knowledge; vijñāna—realised knowledge; tṛpta—satisfied; ātmā—living entity; kūṭasthaḥ—spiritually situated; vijita-indriyaḥ—sensually controlled; yuktaḥ—competent for self-realisation; iti— thus; ucyate—is said; yogī—the mystic; sama—equiposed; loṣṭra—pebbles; aśma—stone; kāñcanaḥ—gold.

Meaning: The Yogi who is settled in self-realisation is called so when he is fully satisfied with acquired knowledge and when his senses are completely subdued. For him, a lump of earth, a stone, and gold are the same thing.

9

सुहृन्मित्रार्युदासीन
मध्यस्थद्वेष्यबन्धुषु।
साधुष्वपि च पापेषु
समबुद्धिर्विशिष्यते॥

suhṛn-mitrāry-udāsīna-
madhyastha-dveṣya-bandhuṣu
sādhuṣv api ca pāpeṣu
sama-buddhirviśiṣyate||

suhṛt—by nature a well-wisher; mitra—benefactor with affection; ari—enemy; udāsīna—neutral between the belligerents; madhyastha—mediator between the belligerents; dveṣya—envious; bandhuṣu—among the relatives or well-wishers; sādhuṣu—unto the pious; api—as well as; ca—and; pāpeṣu— unto the sinners; sama-buddhiḥ—having equal intelligence; viśiṣyate—is far advanced.

Meaning: One is said to excel further when he regards everyone—friend, enemy, well-wisher, the envious, the virtuous, the sinner, and the vicious with an equal mind.

10

योगी युञ्जीत सततमात्मानं
रहसि स्थितः।
एकाकी यतचित्तात्मा
निराशीरपरिग्रहः॥

yogī yuñjīta satatam ātmānaṁ
rahasi sthitaḥ
ekākī yata-cittātmā
nirāśīraparigrahaḥ ||

yogī—a transcendentalist; yuñjīta—must concentrate in Kṛṣṇa consciousness; satatam—constantly; ātmānam—himself(by the body, mind and self); rahasi—in a secluded place; sthitaḥ—being so situated; ekākī—alone; yata-cittātmā—always careful in mind; nirāśīḥ—without being attracted by anything else; aparigrahaḥ—free from the feeling of possessiveness.

Meaning: The Yogi should always try to focus his mind on the Supreme Self, living alone in harmony in an isolated place in retirement, keeping the mind and the self under control. He should be free from desire and possessiveness.

11-12

शुचौ देशे प्रतिष्ठाप्य
स्थिरमासनमात्मनः।
नात्युच्छ्रितं नातिनीचं
चैलाजिनकुशोत्तरम्।।
तत्रैकाग्रं मनः कृत्वा
यतचित्तेन्द्रियक्रियः।
उपविश्यासने
युञ्ज्याद्योगमात्मविशुद्धये।।

śucau deśe pratiṣṭhāpya
sthiramāsan-amātmanaḥ
nāty-ucchritaṁ nātinīcaṁ
cailājina-kuśottaram||
tatraikāgraṁmanaḥ kṛtvā
yata-cittendriya-kriya-
ḥupaviśyāsane
yuñjyād yogamātma-viśuddhaye||

śucau—insanctified; deśe—in the land; pratiṣṭhāpya—placing; sthiram—firm; āsanam—seat; ātmanaḥ—self-dependant; na—not; ati—too; ucchritam—high; na—nor; ati—too; nīcam—low; caila-ajna—soft cloth and deer skin; kuśottaram-kuśagrass; tatra—there upon; ekāgram—one attention; manaḥ—mind; kṛtvā—doing so; yata-citta—controlling the mind; indriya—senses; kriyaḥ—activities; upaviśya—sitting on; āsane—on the seat; yuñjyāt—execute; yogam—yoga practise; ātma—heart; viśuddhaye—for clarifying.

Meaning: One should find a seat and fix it in a clean and secluded spot to practice Yoga. This seat should not be too high or low, and should be made up of kusa grass, deer skin, and soft cloth placed one over the other. The yogi should sit on this seat to practice Yoga by controlling the mind and making it single-pointed and also control the senses for the purification of the self.

13-14

समं कायशिरोग्रीवं
धारयन्नचलं स्थिरः।
सम्प्रेक्ष्य नासिकाग्रं स्वं
दिशश्चानवलोकयन्।।
प्रशान्तात्मा विगतभी
र्ब्रह्मचारिव्रते स्थितः।
मनः संयम्य मच्चित्तो
युक्त आसीत मत्परः।।

samaṁ kāya-śiro-grīvaṁ
dhārayannacalaṁ sthiraḥ
samprekṣya nāsikāgraṁsvaṁ
diśaś cānavalokayan||
praśāntātmā vigata-bhīr
brahmacāri-vratesthitaḥ
manaḥ saṁyamya mac-citto
yukta āsīta mat-paraḥ||

samam—straight; kāya-śiraḥ—body and head; grīvam—neck; dhārayan—holding; acalam—unmoved; sthiraḥ—still; samprekṣya—looking; nāsikā—nose; agram—tip ;svam—own; diśaḥ—all sides; ca—also; anavalokayan—not seeing; praśānta—unagitated; ātmā—mind; vigata-bhīḥ—devoid of fear; brahmacāri-vrate—in the vow of celibacy; sthitaḥ—situated; manaḥ—mind; saṁyamya—completely subdued; mat—unto Me (Kṛṣṇa); cittaḥ—concentrated; yuktaḥ—actual yogī; āsīta—being so; mat—unto Me; paraḥ—ultimate goal.

Meaning: One should hold the body, neck, and head evenly in an erect posture with the discipline of a Vedic student while practicing Yoga, and stare steadily at the tip of the nose without looking in other directions. With a subdued, unagitated mind that is without fear and practicing celibacy, one should meditate upon Me making Me the ultimate goal of life.

15

युञ्जन्नेवं सदात्मानं
योगी नियतमानसः।
शान्तिं निर्वाणपरमां
मत्संस्थामधिगच्छति॥15॥

yuñjannevaṁ sadātmānaṁ
yogī niyata-mānasaḥ
śāntiṁ nirvāṇa-paramām
mat-saṁsthāmadhigacchati||

yuñjan—practicing like this; evam—as mentioned above; sadā—constantly; ātmānam—body, mind and soul; yogī—the mystic transcendentalist; niyata-mānasaḥ—regulated mind; śāntim—peace; nirvāṇa-paramām—cessation of material existence; mat-saṁsthām—in the spiritual sky (the kingdom of God); adhigacchati—does attain.

Meaning: Thus regulating the control of the mind, body, and activities, the Yogi obtains the Supreme after the end of material existence when he abides in Me.

16

नात्यश्नतस्तु योगोऽस्ति
न चैकान्तमनश्नतः।
न चाति स्वप्नशीलस्य
जाग्रतो नैव चार्जुन॥

nātyaśnatastu yogo'sti
nacaikāntamanaśnataḥ
na cāti-svapna-śīlasya
jāgrato naiva cārjuna||

na—never; ati—too much; aśnataḥ—of one who eats so; tu—but; yogaḥ—linking with the Supreme; asti—there is; na—nor; ca—also; ekāntam—very low; anaśnataḥ—abstaining from eating; na—nor; ca—also; ati—too much; svapna-śīlasya—of one who sleeps too much; jāgrataḥ—or one who keeps night watch too much; na—not; eva—ever; ca—and; arjuna—O Arjuna.

Meaning: But Yoga is not for someone who eats too much, O Arjuna, or for someone who eats too little, sleeps too much, or does not sleep enough.

17

युक्ताहारविहारस्य
युक्तचेष्टस्य कर्मसु।
युक्तस्वप्नावबोधस्य
योगो भवति दुःखहा।।

yuktāhāra-vihārasya
yukta-ceṣṭasya karmasu
yukta-svapnāvabodhasya
yogo bhavati duḥkha-hā

yukta—regulated; āhāra—eating; vihārasya—recreation; yukta—regulated; ceṣṭasya—of one who works for maintenance; karmasu—in discharging duties; yukta—regulated; svapna-avabodhasya—regulated sleep and wakefulness; yogaḥ—practice of yoga; bhavati—becomes; duḥkha-hā—diminishing pains.

Meaning: The one who is regular in eating and sleeping habits and regular in action and recreation can remove all material misery by the practice of Yoga.

18

यदा विनियतं
चित्तमात्मन्येवावतिष्ठते ।
निःस्पृहः सर्वकामेभ्यो
युक्त इत्युच्यते तदा॥

yadā viniyataṁ
cittam ātmanyevāvatiṣṭhate
nispṛhaḥsarva-kāmebhyo
yukta ity ucyate tadā

yadā—when; viniyatam—particularly disciplined; cittam—the mind and its activities; ātmani—in the Transcendence; eva—certainly; avatiṣṭhate—becomes situated; nispṛhaḥ—devoid of; sarva—all kinds of; kāmebhyaḥ—material desires; yuktaḥ—well situated in yoga; iti—thus; ucyate—is said to be; tadā—at that time.

Meaning: When one regulates his mind totally through Yoga so that it rests only on the self and he is freed from all material desires, he is said to have attained Yoga or becomes a perfected Yogi.

19

यथा दीपो निवातस्थो
नेंगते सोपमा स्मृता।
योगिनो यतचित्तस्य
युञ्जतो योगमात्मनः॥

yathā dīpo nivātastho
neṅgate sopamā smṛtā
yoginoyata-cittasya
yuñjato yogamātmanaḥ||

yathā—as; dīpaḥ—a lamp; nivātasthaḥ—in a place without wind; na— does not; iṅgate—waver; sā upamā—compared to that; smṛtā—likened; yoginaḥ—of the yogī; yata-cittasya—whose mind is controlled; yuñjataḥ— constantly engaged in; yogam—meditation; ātmanaḥ—on Transcendence.

Meaning: Just as a lamp in a windless place does not waver, such is expected of the Yogi of controlled mind who is absorded in meditation with the transcendent Self.

20-23

यत्रोपरमते चित्तं
निरुद्धं योगसेवया।
यत्र चैवात्मनात्मानं
पश्यन्नात्मनि तुष्यति॥
सुखमात्यन्तिकं
यत्तद्बुद्धिग्राह्यमतीन्द्रियम्।
वेत्ति यत्र न चैवायं
स्थितश्चलति तत्त्वतः॥
यं लब्ध्वा चापरं लाभं
मन्यते नाधिकं ततः।
यस्मिन्स्थितो न दुःखेन
गुरुणापि विचाल्यते॥
तं विद्याद् दुःखसंयोगवियोगं
योगसंज्ञितम्।
स निश्चयेन योक्तव्यो
योगोऽनिर्विण्णचेतसा॥

yatroparamate cittaṁ
niruddhaṁyoga-sevayā
yatra caivātmanātmānaṁ
paśyannātmani tuṣyati ||

sukham ātyantikaṁ
yattad buddhi-grāhyamatīndriyam
vetti yatra na caivāyaṁ
sthitaścalati tattvataḥ ||

yaṁlabdhvā cāparaṁ lābhaṁ
manyate nādhikaṁ tataḥ
yasminsthito na duḥkhena
guruṇāpi vicālyate ||

taṁ vidyād duḥkha-saṁyoga- viyogaṁ
yoga-saṁjñitam
sa niścayena yoktavyo
yogo'nirviṇṇa-cetasā ||

yatra—in that state of affairs; uparamate—when one feels transcendental happiness; cittam—mental activities; niruddham—restrained from matter; yoga-sevayā—by performance of yoga; yatra—in that; ca—also; eva—certainly; ātmanā—by the pure mind; ātmānam—self; paśyan—realising the position; ātmani—in the self; tuṣyati—becomes satisfied; sukham—happiness; ātyantikam—supreme; yat—in which; tat—that; buddhi—intelligence; grāhyam—acceptable; atīndriyam—transcendental; vetti—knows; yatra—wherein; na—never; ca—also;

eva—certainly; ayam—in this; sthitaḥ—situated; calati—moves; tattvataḥ—from the truth; yam—that which; labdhvā—by attainment; ca—also; aparam—anyother; lābham—gain; manyate—does not mind; na—never; adhikam—more than that; tataḥ—from that; yasmin—in which; sthitaḥ—being situated; na—never; duḥkhena—by miseries; guruṇāpi—even though very difficult; vicālyate—becomes shaken; tam—that; vidyāt—you must know; duḥkha-saṁyoga—miseries of material contact; viyogam—extermination; yoga-samjñitam—trance in yoga; saḥ—that yoga system; niścayena—with firm determination; yoktavyaḥ—must be practiced; yogaḥ—in such practice; anirviṇṇa-cetasā—without deviation.

Meaning: This stage of attaining perfection is called trance or Samadhi when one's mind is completely unattached from the material mental activities because of the practice of Yoga. This heightens the ability to see the self by the tranquil mind and to rejoice in the self. That joyous state brings one boundless transcendental pleasure and established thus, one never strays away from the truth, and upon gaining this there can be no greater gain. One is never ruffled, even in the greatest difficulty. This leads to immunity from all pain and miseries that rise from material contact.

24

सङ्कल्पप्रभवान्कामां
स्त्यक्त्वा सर्वानशेषतः।
मनसैवेन्द्रियग्रामं
विनियम्य समन्ततः॥

saṅkalpa-prabhavānkāmāṁs
tyaktvā sarvān aśeṣataḥ
manasaivendriya-grāmaṁ
viniyamya samantataḥ ||

saṅkalpa—material desires; prabhavān—born of; kāmān—sense gratification; tyaktvā—giving up; sarvān—all; aśeṣatah—completely; manasā—by the mind; eva—certainly; indriya-grāmam—the full set of senses; viniyamya—regulating; samantataḥ—from all sides.

Meaning: The practice of yoga should be engaged in with firm faith and determination. One should reject all desires born of fancy and control all the senses by the mind.

25

शनैः शनैरुपरमेद्
बुद्ध्या धृतिगृहीतया।
आत्मसंस्थं मनः कृत्वा
न किंचिदपि चिन्तयेत्।।

śanaiḥ śanair uparamed
buddhyādhṛti-gṛhītayā
ātma-saṁsthaṁ manaḥ kṛtvā
na kiñcid api cintayet||

śanaiḥ—gradually; śanaiḥ—stepbystep; uparamet—hesitated; buddhyā—by intelligence; dhṛti-gṛhītayā—carrying the conviction; ātma-saṁstham—placed in transcendence; manaḥ—mind; kṛtvā—doing so; na—nothing; kiñcit—anything else; api—even; cintayet—be thinking of.

Meaning: One should abstain, step by step, fixing the mind on the self by cultivating intelligence, and thus the mind should be fixed on nothing else but the self.

26

यतो यतो निश्चरति
मनश्चंचलमस्थिरम्।
ततस्ततो नियम्यैतदात्मन्येव
वशं नयेत्॥

yatoyato niścalati
manaścañcalamasthiram
tatas tato niyamyaitad ātmanyeva
vaśaṁnayet||

yataḥ—whatever; yataḥ—wherever; niścalati—verily agitated; manaḥ— the mind; cañcalam—flickering; asthiram—unsteady; tataḥ—from there; tataḥ—and thereafter; niyamya—regulating; etat—this; ātmani—in the self; eva— certainly; vaśam—control; nayet—must bring in.

Meaning: From whatever and wherever the mind may wander forth because of its volatile and unsteady nature, one must rule it and restore it to the control of the self.

27

प्रशान्तमनसं ह्येनं
योगिनं सुखमुत्तमम्।
उपैति शांतरजसं
ब्रह्मभूतमकल्मषम्॥

praśānta-manasaṁ hy enaṁ
yoginaṁ sukhamuttamam
upaitiśānta-rajasaṁ
brahma-bhūtamakalmaṣam

praśānta—mind fixed on the lotus feet of Kṛṣṇa; manasam—of one whose mind is so fixed; hi—certainly; enam—this; yoginam—the yogī; sukham—happiness; uttamam—the highest; upaiti—attains; śānta-rajasam—pacified passion; brahma-bhūtam—liberated by identification with the Absolute; akalmaṣam—freed from all past sinful reaction.

Meaning: The yogi, who is so tranquil-minded, liberated, free from passions, Brahma-natured and sinless, attains the highest bliss.

28

यञ्जन्नेवं सदात्मानं
योगी विगतकल्मषः।
सुखेन ब्रह्मसंस्पर्श
मत्यन्तं सुखमश्नुते॥

yuñjannevaṁ sadātmānaṁ
yogī vigata-kalmaṣaḥ
sukhenabrahma-saṁsparśam
atyantaṁ sukhamaśnute||

yuñjan—thus being engaged in yoga practice; evam—thus; sadā—always; ātmānam—self; yogī—one who is in touch with the Supreme Self; vigata—is freed from; kalmaṣaḥ—all material contamination; sukhena—in transcendental happiness; brahma-saṁsparśam—being in constant touch with the Supreme; atyantam—highest; sukham—happiness; aśnute—attains.

Meaning: By constant engagement of the self, the Yogi is freed from sin and material contamination, and easily reaches the highest form of happiness after coming into contact with the Supreme.

29

सर्वभूतस्थमात्मानं
सर्वभूतानि चात्मनि।
ईक्षते योगयुक्तात्मा
सर्वत्र समदर्शनः।।

sarva-bhūta-sthamātmānaṁ
sarva-bhūtāni cātmani
īkṣate yoga-yukta-ātmā
sarvatrasama-darśanaḥ ||

sarva-bhūta-stham—situated in all beings; ātmānam—the Supersoul; sarva—all; bhūtāni—entities; ca—also; ātmani—in the Self; īkṣate—does see; yoga-yukta-ātmā—one who is dovetailed in Kṛṣṇa consciousness; sarvatra— everywhere; sama-darśanaḥ—seeing equally.

Meaning: One who is a true Yogi settled in Yoga sees Me in all creatures, and sees all creatures in Me. The self-realised man has an equal eye and sees Me everywhere.

30

यो मां पश्यति सर्वत्र
सर्वं च मयि पश्यति।
तस्याहं न प्रणश्यामि
स च मे न प्रणश्यति॥

yo māṁ paśyati sarvatra
sarvaṁ ca mayi paśyati ||
tasyāhaṁ na praṇaśyāmi
sa ca me napraṇaśyati ||

yaḥ—whoever; mām—Me; paśyati—sees; sarvatra—everywhere; sarvam—everything; ca—and; mayi—in Me; paśyati—he sees; tasya—his; aham—I; na—not; praṇaśyāmi—am lost; saḥ—he; ca—also; me—to Me; na—nor; praṇaśyati—is lost.

Meaning: The one who sees Me in all, and sees all in Me, is never lost to Me and I am never lost to him.

31

सर्वभूतस्थितं यो मां
भजत्येकत्वमास्थितः।
सर्वथा वर्तमानोऽपि
स योगी मयि वर्तते।।

sarva-bhūta-sthitaṁ yo māṁ
bhajatyekatvamāsthitaḥ
sarvathā vartamāno 'pi
sa yogī mayi vartate ||

sarva-bhūta-sthitam—situated in everyone's heart; yaḥ—he who; mām—unto Me; bhajati—serves in devotional service; ekatvam—oneness; āsthitaḥ—thus situated; sarvathā—in all respects; vartamānaḥ—being situated; api—in spite of; saḥ—he; yogī—transcendentalist; mayi—unto Me; vartate—remains.

Meaning: The Yogi is the one settled on the Oneness and serves me as the Supersoul who exists within all beings and always remains in Me through all circumstances.

32

आत्मौपम्येन सर्वत्र
समं पश्यति योऽर्जुन।
सुखं वा यदि वा दुःखं
स योगी परमो मतः॥

ātmaupamyena sarvatra
samaṁ paśyati yo›rjuna
sukhaṁ vā yadi vā duḥkhaṁ
sa yogī paramo mataḥ ||

ātma—self; aupamyena—by comparison; sarvatra—everywhere; samam—equality; paśyati—sees; yaḥ—he who; arjuna—O Arjuna; sukham—happiness; vā—or; yadi—if; vā—or; duḥkham—distress; saḥ—such; yogī transcendentalist; paramaḥ—perfect; mataḥ—considered.

Meaning: The one who sees the pleasure and pain in every creature as compared to his own self is the perfect Yogi, O Arjuna.

33

अर्जुन उवाच
योऽयं योगस्त्वया प्रोक्तः
साम्येन मधुसूदन।
एतस्याहं न पश्यामि
चंचलत्वात्स्थितिं स्थिराम्॥

arjunauvāca
yo'yaṁ yogastvayāproktaḥ
sāmyena madhusūdana
etasyāhaṁ na paśyāmi
cañcalatvātsthitiṁ sthirām||

arjunaḥuvāca—Arjuna said; yaḥ—the system; ayam—this; yogaḥ—mysticism; tvayā—by You; proktaḥ—described; sāmyena—generally; madhusūdana—O killer of the demon Madhu; etasya—of this; aham—I; na—do not; paśyāmi see; cañcalatvāt—due to being restless; sthitim—situation; sthirām—stable.

Meaning: Arjuna said: O Madhusudana, the system of yoga which you have declared appears impractical and without stability to me as the mind is fickle and restless.

34

चंचलं हि मनः कृष्ण
प्रमाथि बलवद्दृढम्।
तस्याहं निग्रहं मन्ये
वायोरिव सुदुष्करम्॥

cañcalaṁ hi manaḥ kṛṣṇa
pramāthi balavaddṛḍham
tasyāhaṁ nigrahaṁ manye
vāyor iva suduṣkaram||

cañcalam—flickering; hi—certainly; manaḥ—mind; kṛṣṇa—O Kṛṣṇa; pramāthi—agitating; balavat—strong; dṛḍham—obstinate; tasya—its; aham—I; nigraham—subduing; manye—think; vāyoḥ—of the wind; iva—like; suduṣkaram—difficult.

Meaning: For, the mind is restless, violent, stubborn, and powerful, O Krishna. Controlling the mind appears to me to be more difficult than controlling the wind.

35

श्रीभगवानुवाच
असंशयं महाबाहो
मनो दुर्निग्रहं चलम्।
अभ्यासेन तु कौन्तेय
वैराग्येण च गृह्यते॥

śrī bhagavān uvāca
asaṁśayaṁmahā-bāho
mano durnigrahaṁ calam
abhyāsena tu kaunteya
vairāgyeṇa ca gṛhyate||

śrī bhagavān uvāca—the Personality of Godhead said; asaṁśayam— undoubtedly; mahā-bāho—O mighty-armed one; manaḥ—mind; durnigraham—difficult to curb; calam—flickering; abhyāsena—by practice; tu—but; kaunteya—O son of Kuntī; vairāgyeṇa—by detachment; ca—also; gṛhyate—can be so controlled.

Meaning: The Glorious Lord said: O mighty-armed, there is no doubt that the mind is restless and difficult to control. But, practice and detachment serve to control the mind, O son of Kunti.

36

असंयतात्मना योगो
दुष्प्राप इति मे मतिः।
वश्यात्मना तु यतता
शक्योऽवाप्तुमुपायतः॥

asaṁyatātmanā yogo
duṣprāpaitimematiḥ
vaśyātmanātu yatatā
śakyo›vāptumupāyataḥ ||

asaṁyata—unbridled; ātmanā—by the mind; yogaḥ—self-realisation; duṣprāpaḥ—difficult to obtain; iti—thus; me—My; matiḥ—opinion; vaśya—controlled; ātmanā—by the mind; tu—but; yatatā—while endeavoring; śakyaḥ—practical; avāptum—to achieve; upāyataḥ—appropriate means.

Meaning: Yoga can hardly be attained by one whose self is uncontrolled. But, the one whose mind is controlled and he who works hard using the right means and methods is sure to succeed.

37

अर्जुन उवाच

अयतिः श्रद्धयोपेतो
योगाच्चलितमानसः।
अप्राप्य योगसंसिद्धिं
कां गतिं कृष्ण गच्छति॥

arjunauvāca

ayatiḥ śraddhayopeto
yogāccalita-mānasaḥ
aprāpya yoga-saṁsiddhiṁ
kāṁgatiṁkṛṣṇagacchati ||

arjunaḥ uvāca—Arjuna said; ayatiḥ—unsuccessful transcendentalist; śraddhayā—with faith; upetaḥ—engaged; yogāt—from the mystic link; calita—deviated; mānasaḥ—of one who has such a mind; aprāpya—failing; yoga-saṁsiddhim—highest perfection in mysticism; kām—which; gatim—destination; kṛṣṇa—O Kṛṣṇa; gacchati—achieves.

Meaning: Arjuna said: What should be the course of a man with faith who has not controlled himself, and his mind has wandered away from Yoga to not attain the perfection he desired, O Krishna?

38

कच्चिन्नोभयविभ्रष्टश्छिन्ना
भ्रमिव नश्यति।
अप्रतिष्ठो महाबाहो
विमूढो ब्रह्मणः पथि।।

kaccin nobhaya-vibhraṣṭaś chinnā
bhramivanaśyati
apratiṣṭho mahā-bāho
vimūḍhobrahmaṇaḥpathi ||

kaccit—whether; na—not; ubhaya—both; vibhraṣṭaḥ—deviated from; chinna—fallen; abhram—cloud; iva—likened; naśyati—perishes; apratiṣṭhaḥ—without any position; mahā-bāho—O mighty-armed Kṛṣṇa; vimūḍhaḥ—bewildered; brahmaṇaḥ—of Transcendence; pathi—on the path.

Meaning: O mighty-armed, does not such a man who deviates from the path of Transcendence, perish like a rent cloud, bewildered and without any support in the path of Brahma?

39

एतन्मे संशयं कृष्ण
छेत्तुमर्हस्यशेषतः।
त्वदन्यः संशयस्यास्य
छेत्ता न ह्युपपद्यते॥

etanmesaṁśayaṁ kṛṣṇa
chettumarhasyaśeṣataḥ
tvad-anyaḥ saṁśayasyāsya
chettā na hy-upapadyate||

etat—this is; me—my; saṁśayam—doubt; kṛṣṇa—O Kṛṣṇa; chettum—to dispel; arhasi—requested to do; aśeṣataḥ—completely; tvat—Yourself; anyaḥ—without; saṁśayāsya—of the doubt; asya—of this; chettā—remover; na—never; hi—certainly; upapadyate—to be found.

Meaning: O Krishna, I ask you to dispel my doubt completely. Any other than Yourself to remove this doubt cannot be found.

40

श्रीभगवानुवाच
पार्थ नैवेह नामुत्र
विनाशस्तस्य विद्यते।
न हि कल्याणकृत्कश्चिद्दुर्गतिं
तात गच्छति॥

śrī bhagavān uvāca
pārtha naiveha nāmutra
vināśastasya vidyate
na hi kalyāṇa-kṛt kaściddurgatiṁ
tāta gacchati ||

śrībhagavānuvāca—the Supreme Personality of Godhead said; pārtha—O son of Pṛthā; naeva—never is it so; iha—in this material world; na—never;amutra—in the next life; vināśaḥ—destruction; tasya—his; vidyate—exists; na—never; hi—certainly; kalyāṇa-kṛt—one who is engaged in auspicious activities; kaścit—anyone; durgatim—degradation; tāta— thereafter; gacchati—going.

Meaning: The Glorious Lord said: A doer of good never walks in the path of misery. Destruction is not for him, O Partha, either in this life or herafter. One who does good is never overcome by evil.

41

प्राप्य पुण्यकृतां लोकानुषित्वा
शाश्वतीः समाः।
शुचीनां श्रीमतां गेहे
योगभ्रष्टोऽभिजायते॥

prāpyapuṇya-kṛtāṁ lokān uṣitvā
śāśvatīḥ samāḥ
śucīnāṁ śrīmatāṁ gehe
yoga-bhraṣṭo›bhijāyate ||

prāpya—after achieving; puṇya-kṛtām—of those who performed pious activities; lokān—planets; uṣitvā—after dwelling; śāśvatīḥ—many; samāḥ—years; śucīnām—of the pious; śrīmatām—of the prosperous; gehe—in the house of; yoga-bhraṣṭaḥ—one who is fallen from the path of self- realisation; abhijāyate—takes his birth.

Meaning: One who falls from Yoga, after countless years on a life of enjoyment in the world of meritious workers is born in the house of the pure and glorious.

42

अथवा योगिनामेव
कुले भवति धीमताम्।
एतद्धि दुर्लभतरं
लोके जन्म यदीदृशम्।।

athavāyogināmeva
kulebhavatidhīmatām
etaddhi durlabhataraṁ
lokejanmayadīdṛśam

athavā—or; yoginām—of learned transcendentalists; eva—certainly; kule—in the family of; bhavati—takes birth; dhīmatām—of those who are endowed with great wisdom; etat—this; hi—certainly; durlabhataram—very rare; loke—in this world; janma—birth; yat—that which; īdṛśam—like this.

Meaning: Or he may find birth in a family of intelligent Yogis in the house of the pure and glorious who are unparalleled in wisdom. But such births are hard to achieve in this world and are extremely rare.

43

तत्र तं बुद्धिसंयोगं
लभते पौर्वदेहिकम्।
यतते च ततो भूयः
संसिद्धौ कुरुनन्दन॥

tatra taṁ buddhi-saṁyogaṁ
labhatepaurva-dehikam
yatate ca tato bhūyaḥ
saṁsiddhaukuru-nandana||

tatra—thereupon; tam—that; buddhi-saṁyogam—revival of such consciousness; labhate—regains; paurva—previous; dehikam—bodily consciousness; yatate—endeavors; ca—also; tataḥ—thereafter;bhūyaḥ—again; saṁsiddhau—for perfection; kuru-nandana—O son of Kuru.

Meaning: After taking such a birth, he regains the divine consciousness of his earlier life, and strives diligently to make progress again for complete success, O son of the Kurus.

44

पूर्वाभ्यासेन तेनैव
ह्रियते ह्यवशोऽपि सः।
जिज्ञासुरपि योगस्य
शब्दब्रह्मातिवर्तते।।

pūrvābhyāsena tenaiva
hriyatehyavaśo'pisaḥ
jijñāsurapiyogasya
śabda-brahmātivartate||

pūrva—previous; abhyāsena—practice; tena—by the influence of that; eva—certainly; hriyate—is attracted; hi—surely; avaśaḥ—helpless; api—also; saḥ—he; jijñāsuḥ—willing to know; api—so; yogasya—of yoga; śabda-brahma— ritualistic principles of scripture; ativartate—transcends.

Meaning: Because of the virtue of the divine consciousness in his previous life, he is driven to the yogic principles automatically, without even seeking them. Such an enquirer about Yoga transcends the ritualistic principles of the scriptures.

45

प्रयत्नाद्यतमानस्तु योगी
संशुद्धकिल्बिषः।
अनेकजन्मसंसिद्धस्
ततो यात परां गतिम्।।

prayatnādyatamānas tu yogī
saṁśuddha-kilbiṣ
aḥaneka-janma-saṁsiddhas
tatoyātiparāṁgatim||

prayatnāt—by rigid practice; yatamānaḥ—one who endeavors; tu—but; yogī—suchatranscendentalist; saṁśuddha—washed off; kilbiṣaḥ—all kinds of sins; aneka—many, many; janma—births; saṁsiddhaḥ—so achieved perfection; tataḥ—thereafter; yāti—attains; parām—highest; gatim— destination.

Meaning: But, when the Yogi strives to make greater progress being washed off all sins and fully protected after several births, he then attains the highest goal after many years of practice.

46

तपस्विभ्याऽधिको योगी
ज्ञानिभ्योऽपि मतोऽधिकः।
कर्मिभ्यश्चाधिको योगी
तस्माद्योगी भवार्जुन।।

tapasvibhyo 'dhiko yogī
jñānibhyo'pimato'dhikaḥ
karmibhyaś cādhiko yogī
tasmādyogībhavārjuna

tapasvibhyaḥ—than the ascetic; adhikaḥ—greater; yogī—the yogī; jñānibhyaḥ—than the wise; api—also; mataḥ—considered; adhikaḥ— greater than; karmibhyaḥ—than the fruitive worker; ca—also; adhikaḥ—greater than; yogī—the yogī; tasmāt—therefore; yogī—a transcendentalist; bhava—just become; arjuna—O Arjuna.

Meaning: The Yogi is greater than the ascetics and is perceived to be greater than even the men of knowledge. The Yogi is also greater than the men of action. Therfore, O Arjuna, be a Yogi.

47

योगिनामपि सर्वेषां
मद्गतेनान्तरात्मना।
श्रद्धावान्भजते यो मां स मे
युक्ततमो मतः॥

yogināmapisarveṣāṁ
mad-gatenāntarātman
āśraddhāvānbhajateyomāṁ sa me
yuktatamo mataḥ||

yoginām—of all yogīs; api—also; sarveṣām—all types of; mat-gatena—abiding in Me; antaḥ-ātmanā—always thinking of Me within; śraddhāvān—in full faith; bhajate—renders transcendental loving service; yaḥ—one who; mām—Me (the Supreme Lord); saḥ—he; me—Mine; yuktatamaḥ—the greatest yogī; mataḥ—is considered.

Meaning: Of all Yogis, he who serves Me with great faith with the inner self abiding in Me, is most intimately settled with Me in Yoga and is the highest of all men.

ॐ तत्सदिति श्रीमद्भगवद्गीतासूपनिषत्सु ब्रह्मविद्यायां योगशास्त्रे

श्रीकृष्णार्जुनसंवादे ध्यानयोगो नाम षष्ठोऽध्यायः।

Thus in the Upanishad of the Glorious Divine Lay, the Science of Brahma, the Ordinance of Yoga, the Discourse between the Glorious Lord Krishna and Arjuna, the Sixth Chapter titled 'Dhyana Yoga' (The Yoga of Meditation).

CHAPTER 7

JNYANA VIJNYANA YOGA (THE YOGA OF KNOWLEDGE AND REALISATION)

CHAPTER 7

JNYANA VIJNYANA YOGA (THE YOGA OF KNOWLEDGE AND REALISATION)

In Chapter Seven, Lord Krishna offers the knowledge of the absolute reality and shares the opulence of divinity by revealing Himself as the origin of all the material and spiritual energies. Lord Krishna begins by describing the material and spiritual dimensions of God's energies. He reveals that just like beads are strung on a single thread, all these energies originate from Him alone and rest in Him alone. The entire creation begins with Him and dissolves into Him. It is very difficult to overcome this material energy of the Lord, which is called Maya, but those who surrender to Him fully can easily cross over the sea of Maya blessed with His grace.

Lord Krishna explains that even though His power leads to the manifestation of material nature in the creation of the three material states of goodness, passion, and darkness, He Himself is not under the control of these material modes or attributes. Everyone else falls under the purview of these three material modes with the exception of those who have surrendered to Him. He says that the greatest souls surrender to Him, and attain

Him through devotion while the ones with impious souls find other objects of worship.

Lord Krishna reveals to Arjuna that those who do not surrender to Him remain covered in illusion and Maya and can never know Him. But, those who realise that it is Krishna who is the cause of all causes and worship Him with unswerving devotion become dear to Krishna, and these rare souls are sure to attain Him. Krishna is the essence of everything that exists from the heat in fire, the taste of water, the sound of the wind, the light of the sun, the luminance of the moon, the ability in Man, and the fragrance of the earth. He is all-pervading, the intelligence of the intelligent, and the life of all living beings.

1

श्रीभगवानुवाच
मय्यासक्तमनाः पार्थ
योगं युञ्जन्मदाश्रयः ।
असंशयं समग्रं मां
यथा ज्ञास्यसि तच्छृणु॥

śrībhagavān uvāca
mayy āsakta-manāḥ pārtha
yogaṁ yuñjanmad-āśrayaḥ
asaṁśayaṁ samagraṁ māṁ
yathā jñāsyasi tacchṛṇu ||

śrībhagavānuvāca—the Supreme Lord said; mayi—unto Me; āsakta-manāḥ—mind attached; pārtha—O son of Pṛthā; yogam—self-realisation; yuñjan— so practicing; mat-āśrayaḥ—in consciousness of Me (Kṛṣṇa consciousness); asaṁśayam—without doubt; samagram — completely; mām—unto Me; yathā—as much as; jñāsyasi—you can know; tat—that; śṛṇu— try to hear.

Meaning: The Glorious Lord said: Hear, O Partha, how with mind attached to Me, by practising Yoga reliant on Me, you can know Me to the fullest, free from all doubts.

2

ज्ञानं तेऽहं सविज्ञानमिदं
वक्ष्याम्यशेषतः।
यज्ज्ञात्वा नेह भूयो
ऽन्यज्ज्ञातव्यमवशिष्यते॥

jñānaṁ te 'haṁ sa-vijñānam idaṁ
vakṣyāmyaśeṣataḥ
yajjñātvānehabhūyo
'nyaj jñātavyam avaśiṣyate||

jñānam—phenomenal knowledge; te—unto you; aham—I; sa—with; vijñānam—noumenal knowledge; idam—this; vakṣyāmi—shall explain; aśeṣataḥ—in full; yat—which; jñātvā—knowing; na—not; iha—in this world; bhūyaḥ—further; anyat—anything more; jñātavyam—knowable; avaśiṣyate— remains to be known.

Meaning: I shall now declare to you this wisdom fully, the knowledge of which will leave nothing else here to be known.

3

मनुष्याणां सहस्रेषु
कश्चिद्यतति सिद्धये।
यततामपि सिद्धानां
कश्चिन्मां वेत्ति तत्त्वतः॥

manuṣyāṇāṁ sahasreṣu
kaścidyatati siddhaye
yatatāmapi siddhānāṁ
kaścinmāṁ vetti tattvataḥ||

manuṣyāṇām—of men; sahasreṣu—out of many thousands; kaścit—someone; yatati—endeavors; siddhaye—for perfection; yatatām—of those so endeavoring; api—indeed; siddhānām—of those who have achieved perfection; kaścit—someone; mām—Me; vetti—does know; tattvataḥ—in fact.

Meaning: Of the many men in the world, barely one in a thousand may strive for perfection. But, even among the ones that have achieved perfection, hardly one knows Me truly.

4

भूमिरापोऽनलो वायुः
खं मनो बुद्धिरेव च ।
अहङ्कार इतीयं मे
भिन्ना प्रकृतिरष्टधा॥

bhūmirāpo'nalo vāyuḥ
khaṁ mano buddhireva ca
ahaṅkāra itīyaṁ me
bhinnāprakṛtir aṣṭadhā ||

bhūmiḥ—earth; āpaḥ—water; analaḥ—fire; vāyuḥ—air; kham—ether; manaḥ—mind; buddhiḥ—intelligence; eva—certainly; ca—and; ahaṅkāraḥ—false ego; iti—thus; iyam—all these; me—My; bhinnā—separated; prakṛtiḥ —energies; aṣṭadhā—total eight.

Meaning: Earth, water, fire, air, ether, mind, understanding and egoism: thus eightfold is My active Nature divided.

5

अपरेयमितस्त्वन्यां
प्रकृतिं विद्धि मे पराम्।
जीवभूतां महाबाहो
ययेदं धार्यते जगत्।।

apareyam itas tv anyāṁ
prakṛtiṁ viddhi me parām
jīva-bhūtāṁ mahā-bāho
yayedaṁ dhāryate jagat ||

aparā—inferior; iyam—this; itaḥ—besides this; tu—but; anyām—another; prakṛtim—energy; viddhi—just try to understand; me—My; parām—superior; jīva-bhūtām—the living entities; mahā-bāho—O mighty-armed one; yayā—by whom; idam—this; dhāryate—being utilised or exploited; jagat—the material world.

Meaning: This is the inferior Nature of Mine, O Arjuna. But know My other active Nature which is the Superior, manifested in the soul of creatures, by which the universe is sustained, O mighty-armed.

6

एतद्योनीनि भूतानि
सर्वाणीत्युपधारय ।
अहं कृत्स्नस्य जगतः
प्रभवः प्रलयस्तथा॥

etad yonīni bhūtāni
sarvāṇītyupadhāraya
ahaṁ kṛtsnasya jagataḥ
prabhavaḥ pralayastathā ||

etat—these two natures; yonīni—source of birth; bhūtāni—everything created; sarvāṇi—all; iti—thus; upadhāraya—know; aham—I; kṛtsnasya—all-inclusive; jagataḥ—of the world; prabhavaḥ—source of manifestation; pralayaḥ—annihilation; tathā—as well as.

Meaning: Know that all the living creatures have been born from this womb. I am the cause of the origin and also the dissolution of all that is material and spiritual in this universe.

7

मत्तः परतरं नान्यति
कञ्चिदस्ति धनंजय ।
मयि सर्वमिदं प्रोतं
सूत्रे मणिगणा इव॥

mattaḥ parataraṁ nānyat
kiñcidastidhanañjaya
mayisarvamidaṁprotaṁ
sūtre maṇi-gaṇā iva ||

mattaḥ—beyond Myself; parataram—superior; na—not; anyat— anything else; kiñcit—something; asti—there is; dhanañjaya—O conquerer of wealth; mayi—in Me; sarvam—all that be; idam—which we see; protam —strung; sūtre—on a thread; maṇi-gaṇāḥ—pearls; iva—likened.

Meaning: O Dhananjaya, there is no Truth that is superior to Me. Everything in this universe rests upon Me like pearls hang on a thread.

8

रसोऽहमप्सु कौन्तेय
प्रभास्मि शशिसूर्ययोः ।
प्रणवः सर्ववेदेषु
शब्दः खे पौरुषं नृषु॥

raso'hamapsukaunteya
prabhāsmiśaśi-sūryayoḥ
praṇavaḥ sarva-vedeṣu
śabdaḥkhepauruṣaṁnṛṣu||

rasaḥ—taste; aham—I; apsu—in water; kaunteya—O son of Kuntī; prabhā asmi—I am the light; śaśi-sūryayoḥ—in the sun and the moon; praṇavaḥ—the three letters A.U.M.; sarva—in all; vedeṣu—in the Vedas; śab daḥ—sound vibration; khe—in the ether; pauruṣam—ability; nṛṣu—in man.

Meaning: O son of Kunti, I am the taste of the waters, the beaming light of the sun and the moon, the vital syllable 'Om' in the Vedas, the sound in ether, and abilty in Man.

9

पुण्यो गन्धः पृथिव्यां च
तेजश्चास्मि विभावसौ।
जीवनं सर्वभूतेषु
तपश्चास्मि तपस्विषु।।

puṇyo gandhaḥ pṛthivyāṁ ca
tejaś cāsmi vibhāvasau
jīvanaṁ sarva-bhūteṣu
tapaścāsmi tapasviṣu||

puṇyaḥ—original; gandhaḥ—fragrance; pṛthivyām—in the earth; ca—also; tejaḥ—temperature; ca—also; asmi—I am; vibhāvasau—in the fire; jīvanam—life; sarva—all; bhūteṣu—living entities; tapaḥ—penance; ca—also; asmi—I am; tapasviṣu—in those who practice penance.

Meaning: I am the pure fragrance in earth, the heat in fire, the life in all that lives, and the penance of ascetics.

10

बीजं मां सर्वभूतानां
विद्धि पार्थ सनातनम्।
बुद्धिर्बुद्धिमतामस्मि
तेजस्तेजस्विनामहम्॥

bījaṁ māṁ sarva-bhūtānāṁ
viddhipārthasanātanam
buddhirbuddhimatāmasmi
tejas tejasvinām aham||

bījam—seed; mām—unto Me; sarva-bhūtānām—of all living entities; viddhi—try to understand; pārtha—O son of Pṛthā; sanātanam—original, eternal; buddhiḥ—intelligence; buddhimatām—of the intelligent; asmi—I am; tejaḥ—prowess; tejasvinām—of the powerful; aham—I am.

Meaning: Know me, O Partha, as the original seed of all existence. I am the intelligence of the intelligent, and the energy of the energetic.

11

बलं बलवतां चाहं
कामरागविवर्जितम्।
धर्माविरुद्धो भूतेषु
कामोऽस्मि भरतर्षभः॥

balaṁ balavatāṁ cāhaṁ
kāma-rāga-vivarjitam
dharmāviruddho bhūteṣu
kāmo'smi bharatarṣabha||

balam—strength; balavatām—of the strong; ca—and; aham—I am; kāma—passion; rāga—attachment; vivarjitam—devoid of; dharma-aviruddha—not against the religious principles; bhūteṣu—in all beings; kāmaḥ—sex-life; asmi—I am; bharatarṣabha—O lord of the Bhāratas.

Meaning: I am the strength of the strong, devoid of desire and passion. I am desire in creatures not contrary to religious principles, O Lord of the Bharatas.

12

ये चैव सात्त्विका भावा
राजसास्तामसाश्चये।
मत्त एवेति तान्विद्धि
न त्वहं तेषु ते मयि॥

ye caiva sāttvikā bhāvā
rājasāstāmasāścaye
mattaevetitān viddhi
na tvahaṁteṣu te mayi||

ye—all those; ca—and; eva—certainly; sāttvikāḥ—in goodness; bhāvāḥ—states of being; rājasāḥ—mode of passion; tāmasāḥ—mode of ignorance; ca—also; ye—although; mattaḥ—from Me; eva—certainly; iti—thus; tān—those; viddhi—try to know; na—not; tu—but; aham—I; teṣu—in those; te— they; mayi—unto Me.

Meaning: All states of being whether they are good-natured and dark or passionate are manifested by My energy. Know them to be Me; but not that I am in them, or they are in Me. I am independent and not under the modes of material nature.

13

त्रिभिर्गुणमयैर्भावैरेभिः
सर्वमिदं जगत्।
मोहितं नाभिजानाति
मामेभ्यः परमव्ययम्॥

tribhir guṇamayair bhāvair ebhiḥ
sarvamidaṁ jagat
mohitaṁ nābhijānāti
māmebhyaḥ paramavyayam ||

tribhiḥ—three; guṇamayaiḥ—by the three guṇas; bhāvaiḥ—state of being; ebhiḥ—all this; sarvam—the whole world; idam—in this world; jagat—universe; mohitam—deluded; na abhijānāti—do not know; mām—unto Me; ebhyaḥ—above these; param—the Supreme; avyayam—inexhaustible.

Meaning: Confounded by the three modes of goodness, passion, and ignorance, the world does not seek to know Me, the Supreme beyond them, the Immutable.

14

दैवी ह्येषा गुणमयी
मम माया दुरत्यया ।
मामेव ये प्रपद्यन्ते
मायामेतां तरन्ति ते॥

daivī hy eṣā guṇamayī
mamamāyāduratyayā
mām eva ye prapadyante
māyāmetāṁtarantite||

daivī—transcendental; hi—certainly; eṣā—this; guṇamayī—consisting of the three modes of material nature; mama—My; māyā—energy; duratyayā—very difficult to overcome; mām—unto Me; eva—certainly; ye—those; prapadyante—surrender; māyāmetām—this illusory energy; taranti—overcome; te—they.

Meaning: This divine energy of Mine, My Maya is indeed divine and difficult to overcome. Only those who seek refuge in Me and surrender to Me can swim easily across this sea of Maya.

15

न मां दुष्कृतिनो मूढाः
प्रपद्यन्ते नराधमाः।
माययापहृतज्ञाना आसुरं
भावमाश्रिताः॥

na māṁ duṣkṛtino mūḍhāḥ
prapadyantenarādhamāḥ
māyayāpahṛta-jñānāāsuraṁ
bhāvamāśritāḥ ||

na—not; mām—unto Me; duṣkṛtinaḥ—miscreants; mūḍhāḥ—foolish; prapadyante—surrender; narādhamāḥ—lowest among mankind; māyayā—by the illusory energy; apahṛta—stolen by illusion; jñānāḥ—knowledge; asuram—demonic; bhāvam—nature; āśritāḥ—accepting.

Meaning: The confounded evil-doers who are totally foolish, the lowest men among mankind, robbed of reason by illusion, and taking part in activities of demonic nature, do not surrender unto Me.

16

चतुर्विधा भजन्ते मां जनाः
सुकृतिनोऽर्जुन।
आर्तो जिज्ञासुरर्थार्थी
ज्ञानी च भरतर्षभ॥

catur-vidhā bhajante māṁ janāḥ
sukṛtino 'rjuna
ārto-jijñāsurarthārthī
jñānī ca bharatarṣabha ||

catur-vidhāḥ—four kinds of; bhajante—render services; mām—unto Me; janāḥ—persons; sukṛtinaḥ—those who are pious; arjuna—O Arjuna; ārtaḥ — the distressed; jijñāsuḥ—the inquisitive; artha-arthī—one who desires material gain; jñānī—one who knows things as they are; ca—also; bharatarṣabha—O great one amongst the descendants of Bharata.

Meaning: O best among the Bharatas, four kinds of devoted men surrender themselves to Me: the afflicted, the inquisitive, the one searching for knowledge of the Absolute, and the wise.

17

तेषां ज्ञानी नित्ययुक्त
एकभक्तिर्विशिष्यते।
प्रियो हि ज्ञानिनोऽत्यर्थमहं
स च मम प्रियः॥

teṣāṁ jñānī nitya-yukta
eka-bhaktirviśiṣyate
priyo hi jñānino 'tyartham ahaṁ
sa ca mama priyaḥ||

teṣām—out of them; jñānī—one in full knowledge; nitya-yuktaḥ—always engaged; eka—only one; bhaktiḥ—devotional service; viśiṣyate—especially; priyaḥ—very dear; hi—certainly; jñāninaḥ—person in knowledge; atyartham —highly; aham—I am; saḥ—he; ca—also; mama—Mine; priyaḥ—dear.

Meaning: Among these, the wise man is the most distinguished, always settled in Yoga and devoted to Me with full knowledge and pure devotional service. I am very dear to him, and he is dear to Me too.

18

उदाराः सर्व एवैते
ज्ञानी त्वात्मैव मे मतम्।
आस्थितः स हि युक्तात्मा
मामेवानुत्तमां गतिम्॥

udārāḥsarva evaite
jñānītvātmaiva me matam
āsthitaḥ sa hi yuktātmā
māmevānuttamāṁ gatim||

udārāḥ—magnanimous; sarve—all; eva—certainly; ete—these; jñānī —one who is in knowledge; tu—but; ātmāeva—just like Myself; me—Mine; matam—opinion; āsthitaḥ—situated; saḥ—he; hi—certainly; yukta-ātmā—engaged in devotional service; mām—unto Me; eva—certainly; anuttamām—the highest goal; gatim—destination.

Meaning: All these four kinds of devotees are noble, but the wise man who is situated in knowledge of Me, I consider to dwell in Me. With the self settled in Yoga, he attains Me.

19

बहूनां जन्मनामन्ते
ज्ञानवान्मां प्रपद्यते ।
वासुदेवः सर्वमिति
स महात्मा सुदुर्लभः ॥

bahūnāṁ janmanām ante
jñānavānmāṁ prapadyate
vāsudevaḥ sarvamiti
sa mahātmā sudurlabhaḥ ||

bahūnām—many; janmanām—births; ante—after; jñānavān—he possessing knowledge; mām—unto Me; prapadyate—surrenders; vāsudevaḥ —cause of all causes; sarvam—all; iti—thus; saḥ—such; mahātmā—great soul; sudurlabhaḥ—very rare.

Meaning: After the end of his numerous births, he finally knows that 'Vasudeva is all', and surrenders unto Me. Such a great soul is very rare in this world.

20

कामैस्तैस्तैर्हृतज्ञाना:
प्रपद्यन्तेऽन्यदेवता:।
तं तं नियममास्थाय
प्रकृत्या नियता: स्वया।।

kāmais tais tair hṛta-jñānāḥ
prapadyante'nya-devatāḥ
taṁ taṁ niyamam āsthāya
prakṛtyāniyatāḥsvayā ||

kamaiḥ—by desires; taiḥ—by those; taiḥ—by those; hṛta—distorted; jñānāḥ—knowledge; prapadyante—surrender; anya—other; devatāḥ—demigods; tam—that; tam—that; niyamam—rules; āsthāya—following; prakṛtyā —by nature; niyatāḥ—controlled; svayā—by their own.

Meaning: Those who are robbed of wisdom by several desires, surrender to other gods, following their respective rules and regulations of worship in accordance with their respective natures.

21

यो यो यां यां तनुं भक्तः
श्रद्धयार्चितुमिच्छति।
तस्य तस्याचलां श्रद्धां
तामेव विदधाम्यहम्।।

yoyoyāṁyāṁtanuṁbhaktaḥ
śraddhayārcitum icchati
tasya tasyācalāṁ śraddhāṁ
tāmevavidadhāmyaham||

yaḥ—that; yaḥ—that; yām—which; yām—which; tanum—form of the demigods; bhaktaḥ—devotee; śraddhayā—with faith; arcitum—to worship; icchati—desires; tasya—of that; tasya—of that; acalām—steady; śraddhām—faith; tam—him; eva—surely; vidadhāmi—give; aham—I.

Meaning: Whatever the form or deity a devotee desires to worship with faith, I ordain that faith for him by making it steady. I am present in every heart as the Supersoul.

22

स तया श्रद्धया
युक्तस्तस्याराधनमीहते।
लभते च ततः कामान्मयैव
विहितान्हि तान्।।

satayāśraddhayā
yuktas tasyārādhanam īhate
labhatecatataḥkāmān mayaiva
vihitān hi tān||

saḥ—he; tayā—with that; śraddhayā—with faith; yuktaḥ—endowed; tasya—his; ārādhanam—worship; īhate—seeks; labhate—obtains; ca—and; tataḥ—from which; kāmān—desires; mayā—by Me; eva—alone; vihitān—regulated; hi—for; tān—those.

Meaning: Endowed with such a faith, he strives to worship that particular form and thus gains the desires he seeks, but bestowed by Me alone.

23

अन्तवत्तु फलं तेषां
तद्भवत्यल्पमेधसाम्।
देवान्देवयजो यान्ति
मद्भक्ता यान्ति मामपि।।

antavattuphalaṁ teṣāṁ
tadbhavatyalpa-medhasām
devān deva-yajo yānti
mad-bhaktāyāntimāmapi ||

antavat tu—limited and temporary; phalam—fruits; teṣām—their; tat—that; bhavati—becomes; alpa-medhasām—of those of small intelligence; devān—demigods' planets; deva-yajaḥ—worshipers of demigods; yānti—achieve; mat—My; bhaktāḥ—devotees; yānti—attain; mām—unto Me; api—surely.

Meaning: But for these men of small intelligence, their fruits of devotion are temporary and limited. The worshippers of the gods go to the planets of the gods, but My devotee reaches My Supreme planet.

24

अव्यक्तं व्यक्तिमापन्नं
मन्यन्ते मामबुद्धयः।
परं भावमजानन्तो
ममाव्ययमनुत्तमम्॥

avyaktaṁ vyaktim āpannaṁ
manyantemāmabuddhayaḥ
paraṁ bhāvam ajānanto
mamāvyayamanuttamam ||

avyaktam—non manifested; vyaktim—personality; āpannam—achieved; manyante—think; mām—unto Me; abuddhayaḥ—less intelligent persons; param—supreme; bhāvam—state of being; ajānantaḥ—without knowing; mama—My; avyayam—imperishable; anuttamam—the finest.

Meaning: The unintelligent men, unaware of my supreme nature think that I have assumed this form. Because of their ignorance, they are unaware of My higher nature which is supreme, imperishable, and unexcelled.

25

नाहं प्रकाशः
सर्वस्य योगमायासमावृतः।
मूढोऽयं नाभिजानाति
लोको मामजमव्ययम्॥

nāhaṁ prakāśaḥ
sarvasyayoga-māyā-samāvṛtaḥ
mūḍho'yaṁ nābhijānāti
lokomāmajamavyayam ||

na—nor; aham—I; prakāśaḥ—manifest; sarvasya—to everyone; yoga- māyā—internal potency; samāvṛtaḥ—covered; mūḍhaḥ—foolish; ayam—this; na— not; abhijānāti—can understand; lokaḥ—such less intelligent persons; mām— Me; ajam—unborn; avyayam—inexhaustible.

Meaning: I am never discovered by the foolish and unintelligent. The deluded know Me not as the Unborn and the Imperishable as for them I am surrounded by the combinative Power of Yoga-Maya.

26

वेदाहं समतीतानि
वर्तमानानि चार्जुन।
भविष्याणि च भूतानि
मां तु वेद न कश्चन॥

vedāhaṁ samatītāni
vartamānānicārjuna
bhaviṣyāṇica bhūtāni
āṁ tu veda na kaścana||

veda—know; aham—I; sama—equally; atītāni—past; vartamānāni—present; ca—and; arjuna—O Arjuna; bhaviṣyāṇi—future; ca—also; bhūtāni—living entities; mām—Me; tu—but; veda—knows; na—not; kaścana—anyone.

Meaning: O Arjuna, I know everything that has happened in the past, all that is taking place in the present, and all things that are yet to come. I also know all the living creatures, but no one knows Me.

27

इच्छाद्वेषसमुत्थेन
द्वन्द्वमोहेन भारत।
सर्वभूतानि सम्मोहं
सर्गे यान्ति परन्तप॥

icchā-dveṣa-samutthena
dvandva-mohenabhārata
sarva-bhūtāni sammohaṁ
sarge yānti parantapa ||

icchā—desire; dveṣa—hate; samutthena—born; dvandva—duality; mohena —overcome; bhārata—O scion of Bharata; sarva—all; bhūtāni— living entities; sammoham—into delusion; sarge—in creation; yānti—go; parantapa—O conquerer of enemies.

Meaning: O Bharata, all living beings are born to the dual delusion that arises from desire and hate, O conquerer of foes.

28

येषां त्वन्तगतं पापं
जनानां पुण्यकर्मणाम्।
ते द्वन्द्वमोहनिर्मुक्ता
भजन्ते मां दृढव्रताः॥

yeṣāṁ tv anta-gataṁ pāpaṁ
janānāṁpuṇya-karmaṇām
te dvandva-moha-nirmuktā
bhajante māṁ dṛḍha-vratāḥ||

yeṣām—whose; tu—but; anta-gatam—completely eradicated; pāpam —sin; janānām—of the persons; puṇya—pious; karmaṇām—previous activities; te—they; dvandva—duality; moha—delusion; nirmuktāḥ—free from; bhajante—worship; mām—Me; dṛḍha-vratāḥ—with determination.

Meaning: The men of meritous deeds performed in pervious lives and in this life, whose sins are completely washed away, they are freed from the duality of delusion, devoting themselves to My service with determined vows.

29

जरामरणमोक्षाय
मामाश्रित्य यतन्ति ये।ते ब्रह्म
तद्विदुः कृत्स्नमध्यात्मं
कर्म चाखिलम्।।

jarā-maraṇa-mokṣāya
māmāśritya yatanti yete brahma
tadviduḥ kṛtsnam adhyātmaṁ
karma cākhilam||

jarā—old age; maraṇa—death; mokṣāya—for the purpose of liberation; mām—unto Me; āśritya—taking shelter of; yatanti—endeavor; ye—all those; te—such persons; brahma—Brahman; tat—actually that; viduḥ—they know; kṛtsnam—everything; adhyātmam—transcendental; karma—fruitive activities; ca—also; akhilam—entirely.

Meaning: The ones who strive for liberation from old age and death and are reliant on Me, know That Brahma, the all-presiding Self, and the all-encompassing Act.

30

साधिभूताधिदैवं मां
साधियज्ञं च ये विदुः।
प्रयाणकालेऽपि च
मां ते विदुर्युक्तचेतसः॥

sādhibhūtādhidaivaṁ māṁ
sādhiyajñaṁ ca ye viduḥ
prayāṇa-kāle 'pi ca
māṁ teviduryukta-cetasaḥ||

sa-adhibhūta—the governing principle of the material manifestation; adhidaivam—underlying all the demigods; mām—Me; sa-adhiyajñam—sustaining all sacrifices; ca—and; ye—those; viduḥ—know; prayāṇa—of death; kāle—at the time; api—even; ca—and; mām—Me; te—they; viduḥ— know; yukta-cetasaḥ—with steadfast mind.

Meaning: They also know Me as the Supreme Lord of creatures and spirits of nature (adhidaiva, adhibhuta) and as Lord of sacrifice (adhiyajna). Those with a Yoga-settled mind know Me even at the time of their death.

ॐ तत्सदिति श्रीमद्भगवद्गीतासूपनिषत्सु ब्रह्मविद्यायां योगशास्त्रे
श्रीकृष्णार्जुनसंवादे ज्ञानविज्ञानयोगो नाम सप्तमोऽध्यायः।

Thus in the Upanishad of the Glorious Divine Lay, the Science of Brahma, the Ordinance of Yoga, the Discourse between the Glorious Lord Krishna and Arjuna, the Seventh Chapter titled 'Jnyana Vijnyana Yoga' (The Yoga of Knowledge and Realisation).

CHAPTER 8

AKSHARA BRAHMA YOGA (THE YOGA OF THE IMPERISHABLE BRAHMAN)

CHAPTER 8

AKSHARA BRAHMA YOGA (THE YOGA OF THE IMPERISHABLE BRAHMAN)

Chapter Eight deals with the attainment of salvation where Lord Krishna lays stress on the science of Yoga. He also informs Arjuna how the material world was created and how it was made distinguishable and different from the spiritual world. Lord Krishna says that one attains whatever one remembers at the last phase of one's life. This means the very last thought at the moment of death. Lord Krishna lays most emphasis on this thought as if one remembers Lord Krishna devotedly throughout one's life, and particularly at the time of death, one successfully attains His Supreme abode and escapes this material world.

Arjuna asks Lord Krishna the following seven questions about attaining the Supreme. What is Brahman? What is the Self? What are fruitive activities? What is meant by material manifestation? Who are the demigods? Who is called the Lord of sacrifice? How can those who are engaged in devotional service of the Lord know Krishna at the time of death?

Lord Krishna replies that 'brahman' is a reference to the living entity that is imperishable and indestructible, the 'self' refers to the soul's intrinsic nature of service, 'fruitive actions' refer to the actions performed by the embodied ones desirous of fruits or results from those actions, material manifestation refers to the physical nature that is always changing, the demigods and their planets are a part of the universal form of the Supreme Lord, and the Lord of sacrifice is Lord Krishna Himself as the Supersoul, the combination of the souls of all the living entities as well as their origin. Knowing Krishna at the time of death is totally dependent on one's consciousness. The basic principle underlying this is that whatever state of being one remembers when one is about to quit the body, he will attain that state without fail. Lord Krishna states to Arjuna that whover quits his body remembering Him only attains His nature without a doubt. Therefore, he tells Arjuna that he should always think of Him in the form of Krishna and simultaneously engage in his prescribed duty of fighting in the battle of Kurukshetra. He tells Arjuna that by performing actions that are dedicated to Him and his intelligence fixed on Him, Arjuna will undoubtedly attain Him.

Lord Krishna also explains the process of creation and dissolution to Arjuna. During each day of Brahma, all living creatures are manifested, and during the night of Brahma, all of them merge into the unmanifested nature. The life span of living beings is a day of Brahma, and although there are auspicious as well as inauspicious times for leaving the body, true devotees of Krishna do not care about them. This is because by engaging in pure devotional service to the Lord, they are automatically assured of all the results that can be obtained by extensive study of the Vedas or by performing sacrifices, charity, or engagement in philosophical speculation. Such devotees reach the Lord's Supreme Eternal Abode with the greatest of ease.

1

अर्जुन उवाच
किं तद्ब्रह्म किमध्यात्मं
किं पुरुषोत्तम।
अधिभूतं च किं प्रोक्तमधिदैवं
किमुच्यते।।

arjunauvāca
kiṁtad-brahmakimadhyātmaṁ
kiṁ karma puruṣottama
adhibhūtaṁcakiṁproktam adhidaivaṁ
kim ucyate||

arjunaḥuvāca—Arjuna said; kim—what; tat—that; brahma—Brahman; kim—what; adhyātmam—the self; kim—what; karma—fruitive activities; puruṣottama—O Supreme Person; adhibhūtam—the material manifestation; ca—and; kim—what; proktam—is called; adhidaivam—the demigods; kim—what; ucyate—is called.

Meaning: Arjuna said: O Being Most High, O most Supreme One, what is Brahman? What is the self? What is Karma? And what is declared Adhibhuta and what is called Adhidaiva?

2

अधियज्ञः कथं कोऽत्र
देहेऽस्मिन्मधुसूदन।
प्रयाणकाले च कथं
ज्ञेयोऽसि नियतात्मभिः॥

adhiyajñaḥ kathaṁ ko 'tra
dehe'sminmadhusūdana
prayāṇa-kāle ca kathaṁ
jñeyo'siniyatātmabhiḥ||

adhiyajñaḥ—the Lord of sacrifice; katham—how; kaḥ—who; atra—here; dehe—in the body; asmin—in this; madhusūdana—O Madhusūdana; prayāṇa-kāle—at the time of death; ca—and; katham—how; jñeyaḥ—be known; asi—You can; niyata-ātmabhiḥ—by the self-controlled.

Meaning: How does the Lord of sacrifice reside in the body and where does he live, O Madhusudana? And how do people engaged in devotional service know You at the time of their death?

3

श्रीभगवानुवाच
अक्षरं ब्रह्म परमं
स्वभावोऽध्यात्ममुच्यते।
भूतभावोद्भवकरो
विसर्गः कर्मसंज्ञितः॥

śrī bhagavān uvāca
akṣaraṁbrahmaparamaṁ
svabhāvo'dhyātmamucyate
bhūta-bhāvodbhava-karo
visargaḥkarma-saṁjñitaḥ||

śrībhagavānuvāca—the Supreme Personality of Godhead said; akṣaram indestructible; brahma—Brahman; paramam—transcendental; svabhāvaḥ; eternal nature; adhyātmam—the self; ucyate—is called; bhūta-bhāva- udbhava-karaḥ—action producing the material bodies of the living entities; visargaḥ—creation; karma—fruitive activities; saṁjñitaḥ—is called.

Meaning: The Glorious Lord said: The indestructible one is the Supreme Brahma or the Brahman and His eternal nature is called Adhyatma or the Paramount Self. The action pertinent to the development and evolution of these material bodies is called Karma.

4

अधिभूतं क्षरो भावः
पुरुषश्चाधिदैवतम्।
अधियज्ञोऽहमेवात्र
देहे देहभृतां वर॥

adhibhūtaṁ kṣaro bhāvaḥ
puruṣaścādhidaivatam
adhiyajño'hamevātra
dehedeha-bhṛtāṁvara ||

adhibhūtam—the physical manifestation; kṣaraḥ—constantly changing; bhāvaḥ—nature; puruṣaḥ—the Universal Form; ca—and; adhidaivatam—including all demigods like the sun and moon; adhiyajñaḥ—the Supersoul; aham—I (Kṛṣṇa); eva—certainly;atra—in this; dehe—body; deha-bhṛtām—of the embodied; vara—the Supreme.

Meaning: Adhibhuta is the physical nature that is known to change endlessly (phenomena), and the Presiding Spirit is called Adhidaivata. The universe is the cosmic form of the Supreme Lord, and in this body I am Adhiyajna or the Lord of sacrifice, O best of men.

5

अंतकाले च मामेव
स्मरन्मुक्त्वा कलेवरम्।
यः प्रयाति स मद्भावं
याति नास्त्यत्र संशयः॥

anta-kālecamāmeva
smaranmuktvākalevaram
yaḥ prayāti sa mad-bhāvaṁ
yātināstyatrasaṁśayaḥ ||

anta-kāle—at the end of life; ca—also; mām—unto Me; eva—certainly; smaran—remembering; muktvā—quitting; kalevaram—the body; yaḥ—he who; prayāti—goes; saḥ—he; mad-bhāvam—My nature; yati—achieves; na—not; asti—there is; atra—here; saṁśayaḥ—doubt.

Meaning: And who, at the time of death remembers Me in his last moments before he departs from his body, attains to My nature instantly. There is no doubt in this.

6

यं यं वापि स्मरन्भावं
त्यजत्यन्ते कलेवरम्।
तं तमेवैति कौन्तेय
सदा तद्भावभावितः॥

yaṁyaṁvāpismaranbhāvaṁ
tyajaty ante kalevaram
taṁtamevaitikaunteya
sadātad-bhāva-bhāvitaḥ ||

yam yam—whatever; vā—either; api—also; smaran—remembering; bhāvam—nature; tyajati—give up; ante—at the end; kalevaram—this body; tam tam —similar; eva—certainly; eti—gets; kaunteya—O son of Kuntī; sadā—always; tat—that; bhāva—state of being; bhāvitaḥ—remembering.

Meaning: Whatever the nature one contemplates when he quits his body at the time of death, that is the nature he attains having been constantly affected by that nature, O son of Kunti.

7

तस्मात्सर्वेषु कालेषु
मामनुस्मर युध्य च।
मय्यर्पितमनो
बुद्धिर्मामेवैष्यस्यसंशयम्।।

tasmātsarveṣukāleṣu
māmanusmarayudhya ca
mayy arpita-mano
buḍdhir māmevaiṣyasyasaṁśayaḥ ||

tasmāt—therefore; sarveṣu—always; kāleṣu—time; mām—unto Me; anusmara—go on remembering; yudhya—fight; ca—also; mayi—unto Me; arpita—surrender; manaḥ—mind; buddhiḥ—intellect; mām—unto Me; eva—surely; eṣyasi—will attain; asaṁśayaḥ—beyond a doubt.

Meaning: Therefore, O Arjuna, think of Me earnestly always and fight. By dedicating your will and understanding to Me, you will undoubtedly attain Me.

8

अभ्यासयोगयुक्तेन
चेतसा नान्यगामिना।
परमं पुरुषं दिव्यं याति
पार्थानुचिन्तयन्॥

abhyāsa-yoga-yuktena
cetasānānya-gāminā
paramaṁ puruṣaṁ divyaṁ yāti
pārthānucintayan||

abhyāsa—practice; yoga-yuktena—being engaged in meditation; cetasā — by the mind and intelligence; na anya-gāminā—without being deviated; paramam—the Supreme; puruṣam—Personality of Godhead; divyam—transcendental; yāti—achieves; pārtha—O son of Pṛthā; anucintayan —constantly thinking of.

Meaning: The one who meditates on the Supreme Divine with a mind that never deviates, settled by constant practice, he, O Partha, is sure to reach Me.

9

कविं पुराणमनुशासितार-
मणोरणीयांसमनुस्मरेद्यः।
सर्वस्य धातारमचिन्त्यरूपम्
आदित्यवर्णं तमसः परस्तात्॥

kaviṁ purāṇamanuśāsitāram
aṇoraṇīyāṁsamanusmaredyaḥ
sarvasya dhātāram acintya-rūpam
āditya-varṇaṁtamasaḥ parastāt||

kavim—one who knows everything; purāṇam—the oldest; anuśāsitāram the controller; aṇoḥ—of the atom; aṇīyāṁsam—smaller than; anusmaret always thinking; yaḥ—one who; sarvasya—of everything; dhātāram—maintainer; acintya—inconceivable; rūpam—form; āditya-varṇam—illuminated like the sun; tamasaḥ—of the darkness; parastāt— transcendental.

Meaning: One should meditate upon the Supreme Presiding Spirit Divine as the one who is the Omniscient, the most Ancient, the ruler of all, the Atom of atoms, the Controller of form unimaginable, shining like the luminous sun beyond the darkness.

10

प्रयाण काले मनसाचलेन भक्त्या
युक्तो योगबलेन चैव ।
भ्रुवोर्मध्ये प्राणमावेश्य सम्यक्
सतं परं पुरुषमुपैति दिव्यम्॥

prayāṇa-kālemanasā'calena bhaktyā
yukto yoga-balena caiva
bhruvormadhyeprāṇamāveśyasamyak
sataṁ paraṁ puruṣamupaiti divyam||

prayāṇa-kāle—at the time of death; manasā—by the mind; acalena—without being deviated; bhaktyā—in full devotion; yuktaḥ—engaged; yoga- balena—by the power of mystic yoga; ca—also; eva—certainly; bhruvoḥ—between the two eyebrows; madhye—in; prāṇam—the life air; āveśya—establishing; samyak—completely; saḥ—he; tam—that; param—transcendental; puruṣam—Personality of Godhead; upaiti—achieves; divyam—in the spiritual kingdom.

Meaning: The one who, at the time of death, fixes his life air between the eyebrows with unswerving will, aided by devotion and Yoga-power, and remembers the Supreme Lord will certainly attain the Supreme Presiding Spirit Divine.

11

यदक्षरं वेदविदो वदन्ति विशन्ति
यद्यतयो वीतरागाः।
यदिच्छन्तो ब्रह्मचर्यं चरन्ति तत्ते
पदं संग्रहेण प्रवक्ष्ये॥

yad akṣaraṁ veda-vido vadanti
viśantiyadyatayo vīta-rāgāḥ
yadicchanto brahmacaryaṁ caranti tatte
padaṁ saṅgraheṇa pravakṣye||

yat—that which; akṣaram—inexhaustible; veda-vidaḥ—a person conversant with the Vedas; vadanti—say; viśanti—enters; yat—in which; yatayaḥ—great sages; vīta-rāgāh—in the renounced order of life; yat—that which; icchantaḥ—desiring; brahmacaryam—celibacy; caranti—practices; tat—that; te—unto you; padam—situation; saṅgraheṇa—in summary; pravakṣye—I shall explain.

Meaning: The learned in the Vedas who are great sages enter into Brahman. The dispassionate ascetics practice celibacy to master such perfection. I shall now declare to you this process by which one may attain salvation.

12

सर्वद्वाराणि संयम्य
मनो हृदि निरुध्य च।
मूर्ध्न्याधायात्मनः प्राणमास्थितो
योगधारणाम्॥

sarva-dvārāṇi saṁyamya
mano hṛdi nirudhya ca
mūrdhnyādhāyātmanaḥprāṇam āsthito
yoga-dhāraṇām||

sarva-dvārāṇi—allthe doorsofthe body;saṁyamya—controlling; manaḥ—mind; hṛdi—in the heart; nirudhya—confined; ca—also; mūrdhni—on the head; ādhāya—fixed; ātmanaḥ—soul; prāṇam—the life air; āsthitaḥ—situated; yoga-dhāraṇām—the yogic situation.

Meaning: The yogic state demands detachment from all sensual pursuits by closing all the gates of the senses, confining the mind in the heart, and settling the life air at the top of the head to be firmly established in the constancy of Yoga.

13

ओमित्येकाक्षरं ब्रह्म
व्याहरन्मामनुस्मरन्।
यः प्रयाति त्यजन्देहं
स याति परमां गतिम्॥

oṁ ity ekākṣaraṁ brahma-
vyāharanmāmanusmaran
yaḥ prayāti tyajan dehaṁ
sa yāti paramāṁ gatim||

om—the combination of letters, omkāra; iti—thus; eka-akṣaram—supreme, indestructible; brahma—absolute; vyāharan—vibrating; mām— Me (Kṛṣṇa); anusmaran—remembering; yaḥ—anyone; prayāti—leaves; tyajan— quitting; deham—this body; saḥ—he; yāti—achieves; paramām— supreme; gatim— destination.

Meaning: After being situated in the practice of Yoga, reciting the sacred syllable 'Om', if one earnestly remembers Me while departing from the body, he will reach the Supreme Goal.

14

अनन्यचेताः सततं यो
मां स्मरति नित्यशः।
तस्याहं सुलभः पार्थ
नित्ययुक्तस्य योगिनः॥

ananya-cetāḥsatataṁ yo
māṁsmaratinityaśaḥ
tasyāhaṁ sulabhaḥ pārtha
nitya-yuktasya yoginaḥ||

ananya-cetāḥ—without deviation; satatam—always; yaḥ—anyone; mām— Me (Kṛṣṇa); smarati—remembers; nityaśaḥ—regularly; tasya—to him; aham —I am; sulabhaḥ—very easy to achieve; pārtha—O son of Pṛthā; nitya— regularly; yuktasya—engaged; yoginaḥ—of the devotee.

Meaning: He who always remembers Me with unwavering devotion, obtains Me easily. O Partha, this is because of the Yogi's constant engagement in devotional service that I am easily accessible to him.

15

मामुपेत्य पुनर्जन्म
दुःखालयमशाश्वतम्।
नाप्नुवन्ति महात्मानः
संसिद्धिं परमां गताः॥

māṁ upetya punar janma
duḥkhālayamaśāśvatam—
nāpnuvanti mahātmānaḥ
saṁsiddhiṁparamāṁgatāḥ||

mām—unto Me; upetya—achieving; punaḥ—again; janma—birth; duḥkha- ālayam—place of miseries; aśāśvatam—temporary; na—never; āpnuvanti—attain; mahātmānaḥ—the great souls; saṁsiddhim—perfection; paramām—ultimate; gatāḥ—achieved.

Meaning: The great souls who are the Yogis in devotion never return to the temporary world full of miseries after attaining Me as they have attained the highest perfection.

16

आब्रह्मभुवनाल्लोकाः
पुनरावर्तिनोऽर्जुन।
मामुपेत्य तु कौन्तेय
पुनर्जन्म न विद्यते॥

ābrahma-bhuvanāl lokāḥ
punarāvartino›rjuna
mām upetya tu kaunteya
punarjanmanavidyate ||

ābrahma—up to the Brahmaloka planet; bhuvanāt—from the planetary systems; lokāḥ—planets; punaḥ—again; āvartinaḥ—returning; arjuna—O Arjuna; mām—unto Me; upetya—arriving; tu—but; kaunteya—O son of Kuntī; punaḥ janma—rebirth; na—never; vidyate—takes to.

Meaning: From the highest planet in Brahma's world down to the lowest like this are places of misery with birth and death taking place repeatedly. But, O son of Kunti, there is no rebirth for the one who reaches My abode.

17

सहस्रयुगपर्यन्तमहर्यद्
ब्रह्मणो विदुः।
रात्रिं युगसहस्रान्तां
तेऽहोरात्रविदो जनाः।।

sahasra-yuga-paryantamaharyad
brahmaṇo viduḥ
rātriṁ yuga-sahasrāntāṁ
te'ho-rātra-vidojanāḥ||

sahasra—thousand; yuga—millenniums; prayantam—including; ahaḥ—day; yat—that; brahmaṇaḥ—of Brahmā; viduḥ—know it; rātrim—night; yuga—millenniums; sahasra-antām—similarly, at the end of one thousand; te—that; ahaḥ-rātra—day and night; vidaḥ—understand; janāḥ—people.

Meaning: One day of Brahma is a thousand cycles according to human calculation. So is the duration of one night of Brahma.

18

अव्यक्ताद्व्यक्तयः सर्वाः
प्रभवन्त्यहरागमे।
रात्र्यागमे प्रलीयन्ते
तत्रैवाव्यक्तसंज्ञके।।

avyaktādvyaktayaḥsarvāḥ
prabhavantyahar-āgame
rātry-āgame pralīyante
tatraivāvyakta-saṁjñake ||

avyaktāt—from the unmanifest; vyaktayaḥ—living entities; sarvāḥ—all; prabhavanti—come into being; ahaḥ-āgame—at the beginning of the day; rātri-āgame—at the fall of night; pralīyante—are annihilated; tatra—there; eva—certainly; avyakta—the unmanifest; saṁjñake—called.

Meaning: When Brahma's day is manifest, all manifestations of living beings come forth. At the arrival of Brahma's night, they dissolve into the unmanifested, and are annihilated.

19

भूतग्रामः स एवायं
भूत्वा भूत्वा प्रलीयते।
रात्र्यागमेऽवशः पार्थ
प्रभवत्यहरागमे।।

bhūta-grāmaḥ sa evāyaṁ
bhūtvābhūtvāpralīyate
rātry-āgame'vaśaḥpārtha
prabhavatyahar-āgame ||

bhūta-grāmaḥ—the aggregate of all living entities; saḥ—they; eva—certainly; ayam—this; bhūtvā bhūtvā—taking birth; pralīyate—annihilate; rātri—night; āgame—on arrival; avaśaḥ—automatically; pārtha—O son of Pṛthā; prabhavanti—manifest; ahaḥ—during daytime; āgame—on arrival.

Meaning: The day comes again and again as the group of creatures appear again and dissolve helplessly as Brahma's night falls, O Partha.

20

परस्तस्मात्तु भावो
ऽन्योऽव्यक्तोऽव्यक्तात्सनातनः।
यः स सर्वेषु भूतेषु
नश्यत्सु न विनश्यति।।

paras tasmāt tu bhāvo
'nyo'vyakto'vyaktātsanātanaḥ
yaḥ sa sarveṣu bhūteṣu
naśyatsu na vinaśyati ||

paraḥ—transcendental; tasmāt—from that; tu—but; bhāvaḥ—nature; anyaḥ—another; avyaktaḥ—unmanifest; avyaktāt—from the unmanifest; sanātanaḥ—eternal; yaḥ—that; saḥ—which; sarveṣu—all; bhūteṣu—manifestation; naśyatsu—being annihilated; na—never; vinaśyati—annihilated.

Meaning: But higher than that manifested and unmanifested matter, there is another nature, eternal and transcendental in comparison. When all the creatures and the world perishes, this unmanifested Being Eternal remains.

21

अव्यक्तोऽक्षर इत्युक्तस्तमाहुः
परमां गतिम्।
यं प्राप्य न निवर्तन्ते
तद्धाम परमं मम॥

avyakto'kṣaraityuktas tamāhuḥ
paramāṁ gatim
yaṁ prāpya na nivartante
taddhāma paramaṁ-mama

avyaktaḥ—unmanifested; akṣaraḥ—infallible; iti—thus; uktaḥ—said; tam—that which; āhuḥ—is known; paramām—ultimate; gatim—destination; yam—that which; prāpya—gaining; na—never; nivartante—comes back; tat- dhāma—that abode; paramam—supreme; mama—Mine.

Meaning: This Unmanifested is called the Imperishable, and is the Supreme Being and the Supreme Destination, attaining which no one returns. That is My supreme abode.

22

पुरुषः स परः पार्थ
भक्त्या लभ्यस्त्वनन्यया।
यस्यान्तः स्थानि भूतानि
येन सर्वमिदं ततम्॥

puruṣaḥ sa paraḥ pārtha
bhaktyālabhyastvananyayā
yasyāntaḥsthāni bhūtāni
yenasarvamidaṁtatam ||

puruṣaḥ—the Supreme Personality; saḥ—He; paraḥ—the Supreme, than whom no one is greater; pārtha—O son of Pṛthā; bhaktyā—by devotional service; labhyaḥ—can be achieved; tu—but; ananyayā—unalloyed, undeviating devotion; yasya—His; antaḥsthāni—within; bhūtāni—all this material manifestation; yena—by whom; sarvam—all; idam—whatever we can see; tatam—distributed.

Meaning: But that Supreme Presiding Spirit, O Partha, greater than all, in whom all beings abide and by whom everything is pervaded can be attained by undeviating devotion.

23

यत्र काले त्वनावत्तिमावृत्तिं
चैव योगिनः।
प्रयाता यान्ति तं कालं
वक्ष्यामि भरतर्षभः।।

yatra kāle tv anāvṛttim āvṛttiṁ
caivayoginaḥ
prayātā yānti taṁ kālaṁ
vakṣyāmibharatarṣabha ||

yatra—in that; kāle—time; tu—but; anāvṛttim—no return; āvṛttim—return; ca—also; eva—certainly; yoginaḥ—of different kinds of mystics; prayātāḥ—one who goes; yānti—departs; tam—that; kālam—time; vakṣyāmi—describing; bharatarṣabha—O best of the Bhāratas.

Meaning: O mighty Bharata, I shall now explain to you the different times at which departed Yogis find return or no return into this world.

24

अग्निर्ज्योतिरहः शुक्लः
षण्मासा उत्तरायणम्।
तत्र प्रयाता गच्छन्ति
ब्रह्म ब्रह्मविदो जनाः॥

agnir jyotir ahaḥ śuklaḥ
ṣaṇ-māsāuttarāyaṇam
tatraprayātā gacchanti
brahmabrahma-vidojanāḥ ||

agniḥ—fire; jyotiḥ—light; ahaḥ—day; śuklaḥ—white; ṣaṭ-māsāḥ—six months; uttarāyaṇam—when the sun passes on the northern side; tatra—there; prayātāḥ—one who goes; gacchanti—passes away; brahma—the Absolute; brahma-vidaḥ—one who knows the Absolute; janāḥ—person.

Meaning: The ones with the knowledge of the Supreme Brahman exit this world under the influence of fire, in the light, at an auspicious time, during the fortnight of the moon, and in the six-monthly northward course of the sun.

25

धूमो रात्रिस्तथा
कृष्ण षण्मासा दक्षिणायनम्।
तत्र चान्द्रमसं ज्योतिर्योगी-
प्राप्य निवर्तते।।

dhūmo rātris tathā
kṛṣṇaḥ ṣaṇ-māsādakṣiṇāyanam
tatra cāndramasaṁ jyotir yogī
prāpya nivartate||

dhūmaḥ—smoke; rātriḥ—night; tathā—also; kṛṣṇaḥ—the fortnight of the dark moon; ṣaṭ-māsāḥ—the six months; dakṣiṇa-ayanam—when the sun passes on the southern side; tatra—there; cāndramasam—the moon planet; jyotiḥ—light, yogī—the mystic; prāpya—achieves; nivartate—comes back.

Meaning: The Yogi who passes away from this world during night time, smoke, the dark fortnight, or in the six-monthly southward course of the Sun, or who reached the lunar planet, returns again to this world.

26

शुक्ल कृष्णे गती ह्येते
जगतः शाश्वते मते।
एकया यात्यनावृत्ति
मन्ययावर्तते पुनः॥

śukla-kṛṣṇe gatī hy ete
jagataḥśāśvatemate
ekayā yāty anāvṛtti
manyayāvartate punaḥ ||

śukla—light; kṛṣṇe—darkness; gatī—passing away; hi—certainly; ete— all these; jagataḥ—of the material world; śāśvate—the Vedas; mate—in the opinion; ekayā—by one; yāti—goes; anāvṛttim—no return; anyayā—by the other; āvartate—comes back; punaḥ—again.

Meaning: The Vedas state that the two ways of passing from this world is in light and in darkness. The one who passes in light does not return to this world, but the one who passes in darkness returns.

27

नैते सृती पार्थ
जानन्योगी मुह्यति कश्चन।
तस्मात्सर्वेषु कालेषु
योगयुक्तो भवार्जुन॥

naite sṛtī pārtha
jānan yogīmuhyatikaścana
tasmātsarveṣukāleṣu
yoga-yuktobhavārjuna||

na—never; ete—all these; sṛtī—different paths; pārtha—O son of Pṛthā; jānan—even if they know; yogī—the devotees of the Lord; muhyati—bewildered; kaścana—anyone; tasmāt—therefore; sarveṣu kāleṣu—always; yoga-yuktaḥ—being engaged in Kṛṣṇa consciousness; bhava—just become; arjuna—O Arjuna.

Meaning: The Yogi who is aware of these two eternal paths is never bewildered. Therefore, O Arjuna, be fixed in devotion always.

28

वेदेषु यज्ञेषु तपःसु चैव
दानेषु यत्पुण्यफलं प्रदिष्टम्।
अत्येत तत्सर्वमिदं विदित्वा
योगी परं स्थानमुपैति चाद्यम्।।

vedeṣuyajñeṣutapaḥ su caiva
dāneṣuyatpuṇya-phalaṁpradiṣṭam
atyeti tat sarvam idaṁ viditvā
yogī paraṁ sthānamupaiti cādyam ||

vedeṣu—in the study of the Vedas; yajñeṣu—in the performances of yajña,sacrifice; tapaḥsu—undergoing different types of austerities; ca—also; eva—certainly; dāneṣu—in giving charities; yat—that which; puṇya-phalam—the result of pious work; pradiṣṭam—directed; atyeti—surpasses; tat—all those; sarvam idam—all those described above; viditvā—knowing; yogī—the devotee; param—supreme; sthānam—abode; upaiti—achieved peace; ca—also; ādyam—original.

Meaning: The Yogi who is aware of these paths of devotional service passes beyond the sacrifices, penances, and charity mentioned in the Vedas to gain the fruit of merit and passes to the abode of the Supreme Being.

ॐ तत्सदिति श्री मद्भगवद्गीतासूपनिषत्सु ब्रह्मविद्यायां योगशास्त्रे

श्री कृष्णार्जुनसंवादे अक्षरब्रह्मयोगोनामाष्टमोऽध्यायः।

Thus in the Upanishad of the Glorious Divine Lay, the Science of Brahma, the Ordinance of Yoga, the Discourse between the Glorious Lord Krishna and Arjuna, the Eighth Chapter titled 'Akshara Brahma Yoga' (The Yoga of the Imperishable Brahman).

CHAPTER 9
RAJA VIDYA RAJAGUHYA YOGA
(THE YOGA OF KNOWLEDGE OF THE SOVEREIGN MYSTERY)

CHAPTER 9

RAJA VIDYA RAJAGUHYA YOGA (THE YOGA OF KNOWLEDGE OF THE SOVEREIGN MYSTERY)

In the two previous chapters, Lord Krishna declared to Arjuna that bhakti or devotion is the highest path and yet the simplest one of attaining Yoga or the union with the Supreme One. In Chapter Nine, Lord Krishna reveals His supreme glories that bring about devotion, reverence, and awe. But, although Lord Krishna stands before Arjuna in his human form, He should not be mistaken to have a human personality.

In this chapter, Lord Krishna reveals the Most Confidential Knowledge which is the knowledge of devotional service. He says it is the purest form of knowledge which is everlasting and the most important form of education. By perfecting religion, one gains a direct perception to the self.

Lord Krishna explains how His unmanifested form pervades everything but that he Himself remains detached from matter. It is He who creates, pervades, maintains, and destroys the entire material existence where all the living beings are under his supervision and protection. He is the supreme object of worship. Everything is in Him and He is in everything as the soul is related to Him eternally.

Lord Krishna reveals that different worshippers wish to achieve different goals. The ones who worship the demigods wish to attain the heavenly planets and take birth in their midst to bask in the pleasures of heavenly delights. But, after the fruits of their pious deeds are exhausted, they return to earth again. Those who worship their ancestors go to the palace of their ancestors and the ones who worship ghosts become ghosts themselves. But, the ones who worship Krishna with unparalleled devotion are reunited with Him forever. Whatever Krishna's devotee eats, does, offers, or gives away as charity, he does so as an offering to the Lord who responds by giving His devotee what he lacks and preserving what He has. Even people of low birth can reach the Supreme destination if they take refuge in Krishna.

1

श्रीभगवानुवाच
इदं तु ते गुह्यतमं
प्रवक्ष्याम्यनसूयवे।
ज्ञानं विज्ञानसहितं
यज्ज्ञात्वा मोक्ष्यसेऽशुभात्॥

śrī bhagavān uvāca
idaṁ tu te guhyatamaṁ
pravakṣyāmyanasūya-ve
jñānaṁ vijñāna-sahitaṁ
yajjñātvāmokṣyase'śubhāt||

śrībhagavanuvāca—the Supreme Personality of Godhead said; idam— this; tu—but; te—unto you; guhyatamam—most confidential; pravakṣyāmi —I am speaking; anasūyave—to the non envious; jñānam—knowledge; vijñāna—realised knowledge; sahitam—with; yat—which; jñātvā —knowing; mokṣyase—be released; aśubhāt—from this miserable material existence.

Meaning: The Glorious Lord said: Now, dear Arjuna, as you are never envious of Me, I shall declare to you the most secret wisdom, along with discriminate wisdom, knowing which you will free yourself from the miseries and evils of material existence.

2

राजविद्या राजगुह्यं
पवित्रमिदमुत्तमम्।
प्रत्यक्षावगमं धर्म्यं
सुसुखं कर्तुमव्ययम्॥

rāja-vidyā rāja-guhyaṁ
pavitramidamuttamam
pratyakṣāvagamaṁ dharmyaṁ
susukhaṁkartumavyayam||

rāja-vidyā—the king of education; rāja-guhyam—the king of confidential knowledge; pavitram—the purest; idam—this; uttamam—transcendental; pratyakṣa—directly experienced; avagamam—understood; dharmyam—the principle of religion; susukham—very happy; kartum—to execute; avyayam—everlasting.

Meaning: This sovereign knowledge, the sovereign science, the sovereign mystery is the most mysterious of all secrets, and the highest of all sciences. It is the most righteous and purest form of knowledge, directly felt by realisation, undiminishing, and easily performed.

3

अश्रद्दधानाः पुरुषा
धर्मस्यास्य परन्तप।
अप्राप्य मां निवर्तन्ते
मृत्युसंसारवर्त्मनि॥

aśraddadhānāḥ puruṣā
dharmasyāsyaparantapa
aprāpya māṁ nivartante
mṛtyu-saṁsāra-vartmani ||

aśraddadhānāḥ—those who are faithless; puruṣāḥ—such persons; dharmasya—of this process of religion; asya—of it; parantapa—O killer of the enemies; aprāpya—without obtaining; mām—Me; nivartante—come back; mṛtyu—death; saṁsāra—material existence; vartmani—on the path of.

Meaning: The ones who are unfaithful in this devotion, O destroyer of foes, cannot attain Me, and return to the cycle of death and birth in this material world.

4

मया ततमिदं
सर्व जगदव्यक्तमूर्तिना।
मत्स्थानि सर्वभूतानि
न चाहं तेषवस्थितः।।

mayā tatam idaṁ
sarvaṁ jagadavyakta-mūrtinā
mat-sthānisarva-bhūtāni
na cāhaṁ teṣvavasthitaḥ ||

mayā—by Me; tatam—spread; idam—all these manifestations; sarvam—all; jagat—cosmic manifestation; avyakta-mūrtinā—unmanifested form; mat-sthāni—unto Me; sarva-bhūtāni—all living entities; na—not; ca—also; aham— I; teṣu—in them; avasthitaḥ—situated.

Meaning: I pervade the entire universe in My unmanifested form. All creatures are dependent upon Me, but I do not depend on them.

5

न च मत्स्थानि भूतानि
पश्य मे योगमैश्वरम्।
भूतभृन्न च भूतस्थो
ममात्मा भूतभावनः॥

na ca mat-sthāni bhūtāni
paśyameyogamaiśvaram
bhūta-bhṛn na ca bhūta-stho
mamātmābhūta-bhāvanaḥ||

na—never; ca—also; mat-sthāni—situated in Me; bhūtāni—all creation; paśya—just see; me—My; yogam aiśvaram—inconceivable mystic power; bhūta-bhṛt—maintainer of all living entities; na—never; ca—also; bhūta- sthaḥ—in the cosmic manifestation; mama—My; ātmā—Self; bhūta-bhāvanaḥ—isthe source of all manifestations.

Meaning: But everything that has been created does not depend on Me. Behold my divine opulence! Although I am the sustainer of all living beings, My Self which is the source of creation, is aloof from all creatures.

6

यथाकाशस्थितो नित्यं वायुः
सर्वत्रगो महान्।
तथा सर्वाणि भूतानि
मत्स्थानीत्युपधारय॥

yathākāśa-sthito nityaṁvāyuḥ
sarvatra-gomahān
tathāsarvāṇi bhūtāni
mat-sthānītyupadhāraya||

yathā—as much as; ākāśa-sthitaḥ—situated in space; nityam—always; vāyuḥ—wind; sarvatra-gaḥ—blowing everywhere; mahān—great; tathā—similarly; sarvāṇi—everything, bhūtāni—created beings; mat-sthāni—situated in Me; iti—thus; upadhāraya—try to understand.

Meaning: Just as the mighty wind blows everywhere, know that the creatures everywhere are placed in My ethereal space.

7

सर्वभूतानि कौन्तेय
प्रकृतिं यान्ति मामिकाम्।
कल्पक्षये पुनस्तानि
कल्पादौ विसृजाम्यहम्॥

sarva-bhūtāni kaunteya
prakṛtiṁyāntimāmikām
kalpa-kṣaye punas tāni
kalpādauvisṛjāmyaham||

sarva-bhūtāni—all created entities; kaunteya—O son of Kuntī; prakṛtim—nature; yānti—enter; māmikām—unto Me; kalpa-kṣaye—at the end of the millennium; punaḥ—again; tāni—all those; kalpa-ādau—in the beginning of the millennium; visṛjāmi—I create; aham—I.

Meaning: O son of Kunti, all creatures enter into My nature at the end of the expiry of the said term. Again, at the beginning of another millennium, I create and send them forth by My potency.

8

प्रकृतिं स्वामवष्टभ्य
विसृजामि पुनः पुनः।
भूतग्राममिमं कृत्स्नमवशं
प्रकृतेर्वशात्॥

prakṛtiṁsvāmavaṣṭabhya
visṛjāmipunaḥpunaḥ
bhūta-grāmamimaṁ kṛtsnam-avaśaṁ
prakṛter vaśāt||

prakṛtim—material nature; svām—of My personal self; avaṣṭabhya—enter in; visṛjāmi—create; punaḥpunaḥ—again,again; bhūta-grāmam—all these cosmic manifestations; imam—this; kṛtsnam—total; avaśam—automatically; prakṛteḥ—by the force of nature; vaśāt—under obligation.

Meaning: The entire cosmic order is under Me. It is manifested again and again by My will, and it is My will that it is destroyed in the end.

9

न च मां तानि कर्माणि
निबध्नन्ति धनंजय।
उदासीनवदासीनमसक्तं
तेषु कर्मसु।।

na ca māṁ tāni karmāṇi
nibadhnantidhanañjaya
udāsīnavad āsīnam asaktaṁ
teṣu karmasu||

na—never; ca—also; mām—Me; tāni—all those; karmāṇi—activities; nibadhnanti—bind; dhanañjaya—O conquerer of riches; udāsīnavat—as neutral; āsīnam—situated; asaktam—without attraction; teṣu—in them; karmasu—in activities.

Meaning: But all these acts cannot bind Me, O Dhananjaya. I am always detached, sitting on a high and neutral seat.

10

मयाध्यक्षेण प्रकृतिः
सूयते सचराचरम।
हेतुनानेन कौन्तेय
जगद्विपरिवर्तते॥

mayādhyakṣeṇa prakṛtiḥ
sūyatesa-carācaram
hetunānena kaunteya
jagadviparivartate||

mayā—by Me; adhyakṣeṇa—by superintendence; prakṛtiḥ—material nature; sūyate—manifest; sa—with; carācaram—moving and non moving; hetunā—for this reason; anena—this; kaunteya—O son of Kuntī; jagat— the cosmic manifestation; viparivartate—is working.

Meaning: I preside over the working of the material nature, O son of Kunti, producing the universe of mobile and immobile beings. By the rule of Nature, this manifestation is created and destroyed again and again.

11

अवजानन्ति मां मूढा
मानुषीं तनुमाश्रितम्।
परं भावमजानन्तो
मम भूतमहेश्वरम्।।

avajānanti māṁ mūḍhā
mānuṣīṁtanumāśritam
paraṁ bhāvam ajānanto
mamabhūta-maheśvaram||

avajānanti—deride; mām—Me; mūḍhāḥ—foolish men; mānuṣīm—in a human form; tanum—body; āśritam—assuming; param—transcendental; bhāvam—nature; ajānantaḥ—not knowing; mama—Mine; bhūta—everything that be; maheśvaram—supreme proprietor.

Meaning: The counfounded, unaware of My supreme nature as the great Lord of all creatures, disregard Me when I descend on earth in My human form.

12

मोघाशा मोघकर्माणो
मोघज्ञाना विचेतसः।
राक्षसीमासुरीं चैव प्रकृतिं
मोहिनीं श्रिताः॥

moghāśā mogha-karmāṇo
mogha-jñānā vicetasaḥ
rākṣasīm āsurīṁ caiva prakṛtiṁ
mohinīṁ śritāḥ||

moghāśāḥ—baffled hope; mogha-karmāṇaḥ—baffled in fruitive activities; mogha-jñānāḥ—baffled in knowledge; vicetasaḥ—bewildered; rākṣasīm—demonic; āsurīm—atheistic; ca—and; eva—certainly; prakṛtim—nature; mohinīm—bewildering; śritāḥ—taking shelter of.

Meaning: The wrong-minded who are confounded with hopes, deeds, and wisdom in vain, and attracted by atheistic, greedy, and demonic views cannot perform fruitive activities or gain true knowledge as they defeat the purpose and hopes of their liberation.

13

महात्मानस्तु मां
पार्थ दैवीं प्रकृतिमाश्रिताः।
भजन्त्यनन्यमनसो ज्ञात्वा
भूतादिमव्ययम्।।

mahātmānas tu māṁ
pārtha daivīṁ prakṛtimāśritāḥ
bhajanty ananya-manaso jñātvā
bhūtādimavyayam ||

mahātmānaḥ—the great souls; tu—but; mām—unto Me; pārtha—O son of Pṛthā; daivīm—divine; prakṛtim—nature; āśritāḥ—taken shelter of; bhajanti—render service; ananya-manasaḥ—without deviation of the mind; jñātvā —knowing; bhūta—creation; ādim—original; avyayam— inexhaustible.

Meaning: O Partha, the high-souled are not deluded and are sheltered in the divine nature. They perform devotional service to Me with undeviating will, knowing that I am the original and Inexhaustible Supreme One who is the source of all creatures.

14

सततं कीर्तयन्तो
मां यतन्तश्च दृढव्रताः ।
नमस्यन्तश्च मां भक्त्या
नित्ययुक्ता उपासते।।

satataṁ kīrtayanto
māṁ yatantaśca dṛḍha-vratāḥ
namasyantaśca māṁ bhaktyā
nitya-yuktā upāsate ||

satatam—always; kīrtayantaḥ—chanting; mām—Me; yatantaḥ ca—fully endeavoring also; dṛḍha-vratāḥ—with determination; namasyantaḥ ca—offering obeisances; mām—unto Me; bhaktyā—in devotion; nitya-yuktāḥ—perpetually engaged; upāsate—worship.

Meaning: They chant My glories always, worshipping Me with undeviated devotion, preaching about Me and bowing down before Me.

15

ज्ञानयज्ञेन चाप्यन्ते
यजन्तो मामुपासते।
एकत्वेन पृथक्त्वेन
बहुधा विश्वतोमुखम्॥

jñāna-yajñena cāpy anye
yajantomāmupāsate
ekatvena pṛthaktvena
bahudhāviśvato-mukham||

jñāna-yajñena—by cultivation of knowledge; ca—also; api—certainly; anye—others; yajantaḥ—worshiping; mām—Me; upāsate—worship; ekatvena—in oneness; pṛthaktvena—in duality; bahudhā—diversity; viśvataḥ-mukham —in the universal form.

Meaning: Others, who are engaged in cultivating wisdom and offering knowledge-sacrifice, worship Me as the Supreme Lord, who is without a second and diverse in many in the Universal Form.

16

अहं क्रतुरहं यज्ञः
स्वधाहमहमौषधम्।
मंत्रोऽहमहमेवाज्य-
महमग्निरहं हुतम्॥

ahaṁ kratur ahaṁ yajñaḥ
svadhāhamahamauṣadham
mantro 'ham aham evājyam-
ahamagnirahaṁhutam||

aham—I; kratuḥ—ritual; aham—I; yajñaḥ—sacrifice; svadhā—oblation; aham—I ; aham—I; auṣadham—healing herb ; mantraḥ—transcendental chant; aham—I; aham—I; eva—certainly; ajyam—melted butter; aham—I; agniḥ—fire; aham—I; hutam—offering.

Meaning: I am the Vedic sacrifice and the ancestral offering. I am the healing herb, the formula, and even the butter I am. I am the sacred chant, the fire, and the burnt offering.

17

पिताहमस्य जगतो माता
धाता पितामहः।
वेद्यं पवित्रमोङ्कार
ऋक्साम यजुरेव च॥

pitāhamasya jagato mātā
dhātā pitāmahaḥ
vedyaṁ pavitram oṁkāra
ṛksāmayajureva ca ||

pitā—father; aham—I; asya—of this; jagataḥ—of the universe; mātā—mother; dhātā—supporter; pitāmahaḥ—grandfather; vedyam—what is to be known; pavitram—that which purifies; omkāraḥ—the syllable om; ṛk—the Ṛg-veda; sāma—the Sāma-veda; yajuḥ—the Yajur-veda; eva—certainly; ca—and.

Meaning: I am the father, mother, the support, and the grandsire of this universe. I am the object of knowledge, the purifier, the holy syllable 'Om', and the Rik, Sama, and the Yajur Vedas.

18

गतिर्भर्ता प्रभुः
साक्षी निवासः शरणं सुहृत्।
प्रभवः प्रलयः स्थानं
निधानं बीजमव्ययम्॥

gatir bhartā prabhuḥ
sākṣī nivāsaḥśaraṇaṁsuhṛt
prabhavaḥ pralayaḥ sthānaṁ
nidhānaṁbījamavyayam||

gatiḥ—goal; bhartā—sustainer; prabhuḥ—Lord; sākṣī—witness; nivāsaḥ — abode; śaraṇam—refuge; suhṛt—most intimate friend; prabhavaḥ— creation; pralayaḥ—dissolution; sthānam—ground; nidhānam—resting place; bījam— seed; avyayam—imperishable.

Meaning: I am the goal, the nourisher, the master, the spectator, the abode, the shelter, the lover, friend, manifester, dissolver, the resting place, the nursery, and the eternal unperishing seed.

19

तपाम्यहमहं वर्षं
निगृह्णाम्युत्सृजामि च।
अमृतं चैव मृत्युश्च
सदसच्चाहमर्जुन।।

tapāmyahamahaṁ varṣaṁ
nigṛhṇāmy utsṛjāmi ca
amṛtaṁ caiva mṛtyuś ca
sadasaccāhamarjuna||

tapāmi—give heat; aham—I; aham—I; varṣam—rain; nigṛhṇāmi—withold; utsṛjāmi—send forth; ca—and; amṛtam—immortality; ca—and; eva—certainly; mṛtyuḥ—death; ca—and; sat—being; asat—nonbeing; ca—and; aham—I; arjuna—O Arjuna.

Meaning: I am the source and controller of heat, rain, and drought. I am immortality and also death personified. Both the real and unreal are in Me, O Arjuna.

20

त्रैविद्या मां सोमपाः पूतपापा
यज्ञैरिष्ट्वा स्वर्गतिं प्रार्थयन्ते।
ते पुण्यमासाद्य सुरेन्द्रलोक
मश्नन्ति दिव्यान्दिवि देवभोगान्॥

trai-vidyā māṁ soma-pāḥ pūta-pāpā
yajñairiṣṭvāsvargatiṁprārthayante
te puṇyam āsādya surendra-lokam
aśnantidivyāndivideva-bhogān ||

trai-vidyāḥ—the knowers of the three Vedas; mām—unto Me; soma-pāḥ— drinkers of soma juice; pūta—purified; pāpāḥ—sins; yajñaiḥ—with sacrifices; iṣṭvā—after worshiping; svargatim—passage to heaven; prārthayante—pray; te—they; puṇyam—virtue; āsādya—enjoying; surendra—of Indra; lokam—world; aśnanti—enjoy; divyān—celestial; divi—in heaven; deva-bhogān— pleasures of the gods.

Meaning: The students of the Triple Science of the Vedas who are also drinkers of the soma juice and freed from sin, worship Me indirectly to seek the heavenly planets of gratification. They take birth on Indra's planet where they revel in the excellent enjoyment of the gods in heaven.

21

ते तं भुक्त्वा स्वर्गलोकं विशालं
क्षीणे पुण्य मर्त्यलोकं विशन्ति।
एवं त्रयीधर्ममनुप्रपन्ना
गतागतं कामकामा लभन्ते॥

te taṁ bhuktvā svarga-lokaṁ viśālaṁ
kṣīṇepuṇyemartya-lokaṁviśanti
evaṁ trayī-dharmam anuprapannā
gatāgataṁkāma-kāmālabhante ||

te—they; tam—that; bhuktvā—enjoying; svarga-lokam—heaven; viśālam —vast; kṣīṇe—being exhausted; puṇye—merits; martya-lokam—mortal earth; viśanti—fall down; evam—thus; trayī—three Vedas; dharmam—doctrines; anuprapannāḥ—following; gata-agatam—death and birth; kāma-kāmāḥ—desiring sense enjoyments; labhante—attain.

Meaning: After they have enjoyed the heavenly delights, they return to this mortal world again after the exhaustion of their merits. They rely on the Vedic principles to achieve momentary happiness by going backward and forward as their reward.

22

अनन्याश्चिन्तयन्तो
मां ये जनाः पर्युपासते।
तेषां नित्याभियुक्तानां
योगक्षेमं वहाम्यहम्॥

ananyāś cintayanto
māṁ yejanāḥparyupāsate
teṣāṁnityābhiyuktānāṁ
yoga-kṣemaṁvahāmy aham||

ananyāḥ—no other; cintayantaḥ—concentrating; māṁ—unto Me; ye—who; janāḥ—persons; paryupāsate—properly worship; teṣām—their; nitya—always; abhiyuktānām—fixed in devotion; yoga-kṣemam—requirements; vahāmi— carry; aham—I.

Meaning: To the ones who worship Me with unwavering devotion, constantly settled in Yoga, I carry the burden of supplying to them and protecting them.

23

येऽप्यन्यदेवता भक्ता
यजन्ते श्रद्धयान्विताः।
तेऽपि मामेव कौन्तेय
यजन्त्यविधिपूर्वकम्॥

ye 'py anya-devatā-bhaktā
yajanteśraddhayānvitāḥ
te 'pi mām eva kaunteya
yajantyavidhi-pūrvakam ||

ye—those; api—also; anya—other; devatā—demigods; bhaktāḥ —devotees; yajante—worship; śraddhaya-anvitāḥ—with faith; te—they; api—also; mām—Me; eva—even; kaunteya-O son of Kuntī; yajanti—sacrifice; avidhi- pūrvakam—in a wrong way.

Meaning: Even if those devotees who faithfully make sacrificial offerings to other gods, O son of Kunti, that sacrifice is actually meant for Me alone, and is offered without true knowledge.

24

अहं हि सर्वयज्ञानां
भोक्ता च प्रभुरेव च।
न तु मामभिजानन्ति
तत्त्वेनातश्च्यवन्ति ते॥

ahaṁ hi sarva-yajñānāṁ
bhoktā ca prabhureva ca
na tu mām abhijānanti
tattvenātaścyavanti te||

aham—I; hi—surely; sarva—of all; yajñānām—sacrifices; bhoktā—enjoyer; ca—and; prabhuḥ—Lord; eva—also; ca—and; na—not; tu—but; mām—Me; abhijānanti—know; tattvena—in reality; ataḥ—therefore; cyavanti—fall down; te—they.

Meaning: I am the consumer and the object of all sacrifices. Those who do not seek to know Me in truth, are born again.

25

यान्ति देवव्रता
देवान्पितृन्यान्ति पितृव्रताः।
भूतानि यान्ति भूतेज्या
यान्ति मद्याजिनोऽपि माम्।

yānti deva-vratā
devān pitṝnyāntipitṛ-vratāḥ
bhūtāniyānti bhūtejyā
yāntimad-yājino'pimām||

yānti—achieve; deva-vratāḥ—worshipers of demigods; devān—to demigods; pitṝn—to ancestors; yānti—go; pitṛ-vratāḥ—worshipers of ancestors; bhūtāni—to ghosts and spirits; yānti—go; bhūtejyāḥ—worshipers of ghosts and spirits; yānti—go; mat—My; yājinaḥ—devotees; api—also; mām—unto Me.

Meaning: The worshippers of the gods will take birth among them and those who worship spirits and ghosts will be born among such beings. Those who worship their ancestors go to them and those who worship Me will come to live with Me.

26

पत्रं पुष्पं फलं तोयं
यो मे भक्त्या प्रयच्छति।
तदहं भक्त्युपहृतमश्नामि
प्रयतात्मनः॥

patraṁ puṣpaṁ phalaṁ to yaṁ
yomebhaktyāprayacchati
tad ahaṁ bhakty-upahṛtam aśnāmi
prayatātmanaḥ||

patram—aleaf; puṣpam—a flower; phalam—a fruit; toyam—water; yaḥ —whoever; me—unto Me; bhaktyā—with devotion; prayacchati—offers; tat —that; aham—I; bhakti-upahṛtam—offered in devotion; aśnāmi—accept; prayata-ātmanaḥ—of one in pure consciousness.

Meaning: If a leaf, a flower, a fruit, or even water is offered to Me with love and devotion, I will accept that offering of love from the self-controlled.

27

यत्करोषि यदश्नासि
यज्जुहोषि ददासि यत्।
यत्तपस्यसि कौन्तेय
तत्कुरुष्व मदर्पणम्॥

yatkaroṣiyadaśnāsi
yajjuhoṣidadāsiyat
yat tapasyasi kaunteya
tatkuruṣvamadarpaṇam||

yat—what; karoṣi—you do; yat—whatever; aśnāsi—you eat; yat— whatever; juhoṣi—you offer; dadāsi—you give away; yat—whatever; yat— whatever; tapasyasi—austerities you perform; kaunteya—O son of Kuntī; tat—that; kuruṣva—make; mat—unto Me; arpaṇam—offering.

Meaning: Whatever you perform, whatever you eat, whatever you sacrifice, whatever you give away, whatever austerity you perform, O son of Kunti, dedicate it to Me.

28

शुभाशुभफलैरेवं
मोक्ष्य से कर्मबंधनैः।
सन्न्यासयोगमुक्तात्मा
विमुक्तो मामुपैष्यसि।।

śubhāśubha-phalair evaṁ
mokṣyasekarma-bandhanaiḥ
sannyāsa-yoga-yuktātmā
vimuktomāmupaiṣyasi ||

śubha—good; aśubha—evil; phalaiḥ—results; evam—thus; mokṣyase —free; karma—action; bandhanaiḥ—bondage; sannyāsa—of renunciation; yoga—the yoga; yukta-ātmā—having the mind firmly set on; vimuktaḥ —liberated; mām—to Me; upaiṣyasi—you will attain.

Meaning: Thus you shall be released from the bonds of action of good and evil deeds. With your self aligned to Yoga and Sannyasa you shall be completely freed and come to Me.

29

समोऽहं सर्वभूतेषु
न मे द्वेष्योऽस्ति न प्रियः।
ये भजन्ति तु मां भक्त्या
मयि ते तेषु चाप्यहम्॥

samo'haṁsarva-bhūteṣu
na me dveṣyo'sti na priyaḥ
ye bhajanti tu māṁ bhaktyā
mayi te teṣu cāpyaham||

samaḥ—equally disposed; aham—I; sarva-bhūteṣu—to all living entities; na—no one; me—Mine; dveṣyaḥ—hateful; asti—is; na—nor; priyaḥ—dear; ye—those; bhajanti—render transcendental service; tu—yet; mām—unto Me; bhaktyā—in devotion; mayi—unto Me; te—such persons; teṣu—in them; ca—also; api—certainly; aham—I.

Meaning: I am equal to all beings. I envy no one and no one is dear to Me. But who serves Me with devotion, they are in Me, and I am in them.

30

अपि चेत्सुदुराचारो
भजते मामनन्यभाक्।
साधुरेव स मन्तव्यः
सम्यग्व्यवसितो हि सः॥

apicet sudurācāro
bhajatemāmananya-bhāk
sādhur eva sa mantavyaḥ
samyagvyavasito hi saḥ||

api—in spite of; cet—although; sudurācāraḥ—one committing the most abominable actions; bhajate—engaged in devotional service; mām—unto Me; ananya-bhāk—without deviation; sādhuḥ—saint; eva—certainly; saḥ—he; mantavyaḥ—to be considered; samyak—completely; vyavasitaḥ—situated; hi—certainly; saḥ—he.

Meaning: Even if one is most ill-behaved, but serves Me with undying devotion, he should be considered good indeed as he is rightly located.

31

क्षिप्रं भवति धर्मात्मा
शश्वच्छान्तिं निगच्छति।
कौन्तेय प्रतिजानीहि
न मे भक्तः प्रणश्यति॥

kṣipraṁ bhavati dharmātmā
śaśvac-chāntiṁ nigacchati
kaunteya pratijānīhi
na me bhaktaḥ praṇaśyati ||

kṣipram—very soon; bhavati—becomes; dharma-ātmā—righteous; śaśvat- śāntim—lasting peace; nigacchati—attains; kaunteya—O son of Kuntī; pratijānīhi—justly declare; na—never; me—Mine; bhaktaḥ—devotee; praṇaśyati—perishes.

Meaning: He speedily becomes righteous and attains everlasting peace. O son of Kunti, declare boldly that My devotee never perishes.

32

मां हि पार्थ व्यपाश्रित्य
येऽपि स्यु पापयोनयः।
स्त्रियो वैश्यास्तथा शूद्रास्तेऽपि
यान्ति परां गतिम्॥

māṁhipārthavyapāśritya
ye'pisyuḥpāpa-yonayaḥ
striyo vaiśyās tathā śūdrās te'pi
yāntiparāṁgatim||

mām—unto Me; hi-certainly; pārtha—O son of Pṛthā; vyapāśrītya—particularly taking shelter; ye—anyone; api—also; syuḥ—becomes; pāpa-yonayaḥ—born of a lower family; striyaḥ—women; vaiśyāḥ—mercantile people; tathā—also; śūdrāḥ—lower class men; te api—even they; yānti— go; parām—supreme; gatim—destination.

Meaning: Those who take refuge in Me, O Partha, even if they may be of lower birth, women, Vaishyas as well as Shudras, they can reach the Supreme Goal.

33

किं पुनर्ब्राह्मणाः पुण्या
भक्ता राजर्षयस्तथा।
अनित्यमसुखं लोकमिमं
प्राप्य भजस्व माम्॥

kiṁpunarbrāhmaṇāḥpuṇyā
bhaktā rājarṣayas tathā
anityamasukhaṁlokam imaṁ
prāpyabhajasvamām||

kim—how much; punaḥ—again; brāhmaṇāḥ-brāhmaṇas; puṇyāḥ—righteous; bhaktāḥ—devotees; rājarṣayaḥ—saintly kings; tathā—also; anityam—temporary; asukham—sorrowful; lokam—planets; imam—this; prāpya—gain ing; bhajasva—are engaged in loving service; mām—untoMe.

Meaning: How much greater then are the holy Brahmanas, the devout sages and kings, who in this temporary world of evil devote themselves in My loving service.

34

मन्मना भव मद्भक्तो
मद्याजी मां नमस्कुरु।
मामेवैष्यसि युक्त्वैवमा
अत्मानं मत्परायणः॥

man-manā bhava mad-bhakto
mad-yājīmāṁnamaskuru
mām evaiṣyasi yuktvaivam
ātmānaṁmat-parāyaṇaḥ||

man-manāḥ—always thinking of Me; bhava—become; mad—My; bhaktaḥ—devotee; mad—My; yājī—worshipper; mām—unto Me; eva—certainly; eṣhyasi—you will come; yuktvā—united with Me; evam—thus; ātmānam—your mind and body; mat-parāyaṇaḥ—having dedicated to Me

Meaning: Fix your mind on Me, be My devotee, worship Me, and offer sacrifice to Me. Thus disposing the self, fixing the supreme goal in Me, and being completely absorbed in Me, you will come to Me indeed.

ॐ तत्सदिति श्रीमद्भगवद्गीतासूपनिषत्सु ब्रह्मविद्यायां योगशास्त्रे

श्री कृष्णार्जुनसंवादे राजविद्याराजगुह्ययोगो नाम नवमोऽध्यायः।

Thus in the Upanishad of the Glorious Divine Lay, the Science of Brahma, the Ordinance of Yoga, the Discourse between the Glorious Lord Krishna and Arjuna, the Ninth Chapter titled 'Raja Vidya Rajaguhya Yoga' (The Yoga of Knowledge of the Sovereign Mystery).

CHAPTER 10

VIBHUTI YOGA

(THE YOGA OF DIVINE MANIFESTATIONS)

CHAPTER 10

VIBHUTI YOGA (THE YOGA OF DIVINE MANIFESTATIONS)

In Chapter Ten, Lord Krishna reveals the Infinite Glory of the Ultimate Truth as the cause of all causes, which is the support and essence of everything that exists. Lord Krishna also specifies His opulence and special manifestations to Arjuna. The real devotees of Krishna know that He is the unborn, the One without beginnings, the Supreme Lord of the three worlds, the creator of all living entities, and the origin of everything that exists in the Universe.

All the good qualities as well as the bad like understanding, knowledge, truthfulness, control of the mind and senses, non-violence, fearlessness, austerity, birth, death, fear, distress, and infamy among others are all created by Krishna. One can cultivate all the good qualities and remove the bad qualities from the system by engaging in Krishna's devotional service.

The ones who submerge themselves lovingly in Krishna's devotional service are full of faith in terms of His mystic powers, opulence, and all-pervading qualities. The thought of such devotees is always on Krishna's mind. These dovotees devote their entire lives to the service of Krishna and they gain the greatest satisfaction, joy, and bliss by speaking about Him to each other and enlightening the uninitiated.

Even if such devotees do not have adequate knowledge of the Vedic scriptures or are not educated, thanks to the pure devotional service that they engage in, they are aided from within by Krishna so that the darkness that is born out of ignorance within them is destroyed.

By the end of the chapter, Arjuna has fully realised that Lord Krishna is none other than the Supreme One, who is the Imperishable and the Absolute Truth. He is the greatest, the unborn, the original, the purest, the transcendental, and the Lord of all things. Now, Arjuna wishes to know more. Krishna answers his queries, concluding with, "All opulent, beautiful, and glorious creations rise from a spark of My splendour."

1

श्रीभगवानुवाच
भूय एव महाबाहो
शृणु मे परमं वचः।
यत्तेऽहं प्रीयमाणाय
वक्ष्यामि हितकाम्यया॥

śrī bhagavān uvāca
bhūyaevamahā-bāho
śṛṇumeparamaṁvacaḥ
yat te ‹haṁ prīyamāṇāya
vakṣyāmihita-kāmyayā ||

śrībhagavānuvāca—the Supreme Personality of Godhead said; bhūyaḥ—again; eva—certainly; mahā-bāho—O mighty-armed; śṛṇu—just hear; me—My; paramaṁ—supreme; vacaḥ—information; yat—that which; te—to you; aham—I; prīyamāṇāya—thinking you dear to Me; vakṣyāmi—say;hita-kāmyayā—for your benefit.

Meaning: The Glorious Lord said: Listen again to My supreme word, O mighty-armed Arjuna. I shall declare this to you for your own good and which will give you great joy.

2

न मे विदुः सुरगणाः
प्रभवं न महर्षयः।
अहमादिर्हि देवानां
महर्षीणां च सर्वशः॥

nameviduḥ sura-gaṇāḥ
prabhavaṁ na maharṣayaḥ
aham ādir hi devānāṁ
maharṣīṇāṁca sarvaśaḥ||

na—never; me—My; viduḥ—knows; sura-gaṇāḥ—demigods; prabhavam— opulences; na—never; maharṣayaḥ—great sages; aham—I am; ādiḥ—the origin; hi—certainly; devānām—of the demigods; maharṣīṇām—of the great sages; ca—also; sarvaśaḥ—in all respects.

Meaning: Neither the gods or the great saints are aware of all My manifestations, for, in every respect, I am the origin of the gods and great sages.

3

यो मामजमनादिं च
वेत्ति लोकमहेश्वरम्।
असम्मूढः स मर्त्येषु
सर्वपापैः प्रमुच्यते ॥

yo mām ajam anādiṁ ca
vettiloka-maheśvaram
asammūḍhaḥ sa martyeṣu
sarva-pāpaiḥpramucyate ||

yaḥ—anyone; mām—unto Me; ajam—unborn; anādim—without beginning; ca—also; vetti—knows; loka—the planets; maheśvaram— supreme master; asaṁmūḍhaḥ—without doubt; saḥ—he; martyeṣu—among those subject to death; sarva-pāpaiḥ—from all sinful reactions; pramucyate—is delivered.

Meaning: He who knows Me as the Unborn, the Beginningless, the Supreme Lord of the universe, he, the unerring among men, is freed from all his sins.

4-5

बुद्धिर्ज्ञानमसम्मोहः
क्षमा सत्यं दमः शमः।
सुखं दुःखं भवोऽभावो
भयं चाभयमेव च॥

अहिंसा समता तुष्टिस्तपो
दानं यशोऽयशः।
भवन्ति भावा भूतानां
मत्त एव पृथग्विधाः॥

buddhir jñānam asammohaḥ
kṣamāsatyaṁ damaḥ śamaḥ
sukhaṁduḥkhaṁbhavo'bhāvo
bhayaṁ cābhayam eva ca||

ahiṁsā samatā tuṣṭistapo
dānaṁyaśo'yaśaḥ
bhavanti bhāvā bhūtānāṁ
mattaevapṛthag-vidhāḥ||

buddhiḥ—intelligence; jñānam—knowledge; asam-mohaḥ—freedom from doubt; kṣamā—forgiveness; satyam—truthfulness; damaḥ—control of the senses; śamaḥ—control of the mind; sukham—happiness; duḥkham— distress; bhavaḥ—birth; abhāvaḥ—death; bhayam—fear; ca—also; abhayam—without fear; eva—also; ca—and; ahiṁsā—non violence; samatā—equilibrium; tuṣṭiḥ— satisfaction; tapaḥ—penance; dānam—charity; yaśaḥ—fame; ayaśaḥ—infamy; bhavanti—become; bhāvāḥ—natures; bhūtānām—of living entities; mattaḥ—from Me; eva—certainly; pṛthak- vidhāḥ—differently arranged.

Meaning: Understanding, knowledge, freedom from doubt and delusion, forgiveness, truthfulness, dispassionateless, tranquility, pleasure, pain, energy, birth, death, fear, fearlessness, nonviolence, equanimity, satisfaction, austerity, charity, fame, and infamy are the good characteristics of beings that have been created by Me.

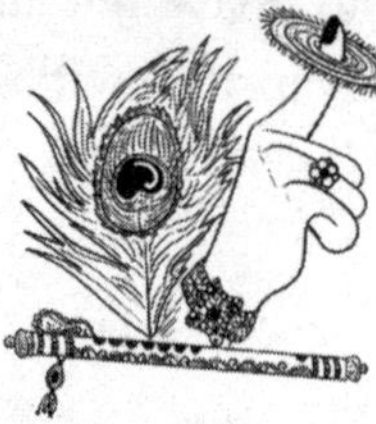

6

महर्षयः सप्त पूर्वे
चत्वारो मनवस्तथा।
मद्भावा मानसा जाता
येषां लोक इमाः प्रजाः।।

maharṣayaḥ sapta pūrve
catvāromanavastathā
mad-bhāvā mānasā
jātā yeṣāṁlokaimāḥprajāḥ||

maharṣayaḥ—the great sages; sapta—seven; pūrve—before; catvāraḥ —four; manavaḥ—Manus; tathā—also; mat-bhāvāḥ—born of Me; mānasāḥ—from the mind; jātāḥ—born; yeṣām—of them; loke—the planets; imāḥ— all this; prajāḥ—population.

Meaning: The seven great sages, and before them the four other great sages, and the Manus, from whom all beings of mankind in the planet have descended, have all derived their characteristics from Me and have been born out of My will.

7

एतां विभूतिं योगं च
मम यो वेत्ति तत्त्वतः।
सोऽविकम्पेन योगेन
युज्यते नात्र संशयः॥

etāṁ vibhūtiṁ yogaṁ ca
mamayovettitattvataḥ
so 'vikalpena yogena
yujyatenātrasaṁśayaḥ||

etām—all this; vibhūtiṁ—opulence; yogam ca—also mystic power; mama—of Mine; yaḥ—anyone; vetti—knows; tattvataḥ—factually; saḥ—he; avikalpena—without division; yogena—in devotional service; yujyate—engaged; na—never; atra—here; saṁśayaḥ—doubt.

Meaning: Whoever grasps this about My diversification and combination adopts Yoga without any hesitation. In this there can be no doubt.

8

अहं सर्वस्य प्रभवो
मत्तः सर्वं प्रवर्तते।
इति मत्वा भजन्ते मां
बुधा भावसमन्विताः।।

aham̐ sarvasya prabhavo
mattaḥsarvam̐pravartate
iti matvā bhajante mām̐
budhā bhāva-samanvitāḥ ||

aham—I; sarvasya—of all; prabhavaḥ—source of generation; mattaḥ—from Me; sarvam—everything; pravartate—emanates; iti—thus; matvā— knowing; bhajante—becomes devoted; mām—unto Me; budhāḥ—learned; bhāva- samanvitāḥ—with great attention.

Meaning: I am the manifester of all spiritual and material worlds. Everything evolves from Me. The wise who are aware of this devote themselves to Me and worship Me whole-heartedly.

9

मच्चित्ता मद्गतप्राणा
बोधयन्तः परस्परम्।
कथयन्तश्च मां नित्यं
तुष्यन्ति च रमन्ति च ॥

mac-cittā mad-gata-prāṇā
bodhayantaḥ parasparam
kathayantaścamāṁnityaṁ
tuṣyanti ca ramanti ca ||

mat-cittāḥ—minds fully engaged in Me; mat-gata-prāṇāḥ—lives devoted to the service of Kṛṣṇa; bodhayantaḥ—preaching; parasparam—among themselves; kathayantaḥ ca—talking also; mām—about Me; nityam—perpetually; tuṣyanti—are pleased; ca—also; ramanti—enjoy transcendental bliss; ca—also.

Meaning: Those pure devotees who have devoted their minds totally to Me and have surrendered their lives to Me, derive great comfort and delight instructing and enlightening everyone about Me.

10

तेषां सततयुक्तानां
भजतां प्रीतिपूर्वकम्।
ददामि बद्धियोगं तं
येन मामुपयान्ति ते ॥

teṣāṁ satata-yuktānāṁ
bhajatāṁprīti-pūrvakam
dadāmibuddhi-yogaṁ taṁ
yena mām-upayānti te||

teṣām—unto them; satata-yuktānām—always engaged; bhajatām—in devotional service; prīti-pūrvakam—in loving ecstasy; dadāmi—I give; buddhi-yogam—real intelligence; tam—that; yena—by which; mām—unto Me; upayānti—come; te—they.

Meaning: To those who are always devoted heartily to Me, and worship Me with love and devotion, I provide that understanding by which they can come to Me.

11

तेषामेवानुकम्पार्थमहम
ज्ञानजं तमः।
नाशयाम्यात्मभावस्थो
ज्ञानदीपेन भास्वता।।

teṣām evānukampārtham-aham
ajñāna-jaṁtamaḥ
nāśayāmy ātma-bhāvastho
jñāna-dīpenabhāsvatā ||

teṣām—for them; eva—certainly; anukampā-artham—to show special mercy; aham—I; ajñāna-jam—due to ignorance; tamaḥ—darkness; nāśayāmi—dispel; ātma—within; bhāvasthaḥ—themselves; jñāna—of knowledge; dīpena—with the lamp; bhāsvatā—glowing.

Meaning: For the sake of compassion for these devotees, I reside in their hearts and destroy the darkness born of ignorance with the shining lamp of wisdom.

12-13

अर्जुन उवाच

परं ब्रह्म परं धाम
पवित्रं परमं भवान्।
पुरुषं शाश्वतं
दिव्यमादिदेवमजं विभुम्।।

आहुस्त्वामृषयः
सर्वे देवर्षिर्नारदस्तथा।
असितो देवलो व्यासः
स्वयं चैव ब्रवीषि मे ।।

arjunauvāca
paraṁ brahma paraṁ dhāma
pavitraṁparamaṁbhavān
puruṣaṁ śāśvataṁ
divyam ādi-devamajaṁvibhum||

āhus tvām ṛṣayaḥ
sarve devarṣirnāradastathā
asitodevalo vyāsaḥ
svayaṁcaivabravīṣime||

arjunaḥuvāca—Arjunasaid; param—supreme; brahma—truth; param — supreme; dhāma—sustenance; pavitram—purest; paramam—supreme; bhavān—Yourself; puruṣam—personality; śāśvatam—original; divyam —transcendental; ādi-devam—original Lord; ajam—unborn; vibhum —greatest; āhuḥ—say; tvām—unto You; ṛṣayaḥ—sages; sarve—all; devarṣiḥ—the sage among the demigods; nāradaḥ—Nārada; tathā—also; asitaḥ—Asita; devalaḥ—Devala; vyāsaḥ—Vyāsa; svayam—personally; ca—also; eva—certainly; bravīṣi—explaining; me—unto me.

Meaning: Arjuna said: You are the Supreme Brahma, the Supreme Abode, the Supreme Holiness, the Absolute Truth, and the Eternal Divinity. You are the Primeval God, original and transcendental, the Unborn with all-pervading beauty, the Manifold Being. All the great sages like Narada, Asita, Devala, and Vyasa proclaim this of You, and You are now Yourself declaring this to me.

14

सर्वमेतदृतं मन्ये
यन्मां वदसि केशव।
न हि ते भगवन्व्यक्तिं
विदुर्देवा न दानवाः॥

sarvam etad ṛtaṁ manye
yanmāṁvadasikeśava
na hi te bhagavan vyaktiṁ
vidurdevānadānavāḥ ||

sarvam—all; etat—these; ṛtam—truths; manye—accept; yat—which; mām— unto me; vadasi—You tell; keśava—O Kṛṣṇa; na—never; hi—certainly; te—Your;bhagavan—O Personality of Godhead; vyaktim—revelation; viduḥ—can know; devaḥ—the demigods; na—nor; dānavāḥ—the demons.

Meaning: O Keshava, I totally accept whatever that You have told me as the truth. Neither the gods nor the demons know Your manifestation, O Lord.

15

स्वयमेवात्मनात्मानं
वेत्थ त्वं पुरुषोत्तम।
भूतभावन भूतेश
देवदेव जगत्पते॥

svayam evātmanātmānaṁ
vetthatvaṁpuruṣottama
bhūta-bhāvana bhūteśa
deva-devajagat-pate ||

svayam—personality; eva—certainly; ātmanā—by Yourself; ātmānam—Yourself; vettha—know; tvam—You; puruṣottama—O greatest of all persons; bhūta-bhāvana—O origin of everything; bhūteśa—O Lord of everything; deva-deva—O Lord of all demigods; jagat-pate—O Lord of the entire universe.

Meaning: You alone know Yourself, the self by the self, by Your own potencies, O Being most High, Lord of all creatures, God of gods, O Lord of the universe!

16

वक्तुमर्हस्यशेषेण
दिव्या ह्यात्मविभूतयः।
याभिर्विभूतिभिर्लोकानिमांस्त्वं
व्याप्य तिष्ठसि ॥

vaktumarhasyaśeṣeṇa
divyāhyātma-vibhūtayaḥ
yābhir vibhūtibhir lokān imāṁstvaṁ
vyāpya tiṣṭhasi ||

vaktum—to say; arhasi—deserve; aśeṣeṇa—in detail; divyā—divine; hi—certainly; ātma—Yourself; vibhūtayaḥ—opulences; yābhiḥ—by which; vibhūtibhiḥ—opulences; lokān—all the planets; imān—these; tvam—You; vyāpya—pervading; tiṣṭhasi—remain.

Meaning: Please tell me about Your divine powers in detail by which You engage in the diversification of Your self which pervade all these worlds You abide.

17

कथं विद्यामहं योगिंस्त्वां
सदा परिचिन्तयन्।
केषु केषु च भावेषु
चिन्त्योऽसि भगवन्मया।।

kathaṁvidyāmahaṁyogiṁs tvāṁ
sadā paricintayan
keṣukeṣucabhāveṣu
cintyo'sibhagavanmayā ||

katham—how; vidyām aham—shall I know; yogin—O supreme mystic; tvām—You; sadā—always; paricintayan—thinking; keṣu—in which; ca—also; bhāveṣu—nature; cintyaḥ asi—You are remembered; bhagavan—O Supreme; mayā—by me.

Meaning: How should I know You by meditation? In what various forms should You be contemplated by me, O Lord?

18

विस्तरेणात्मनो योगं
विभूतिं च जनार्दन।
भूयः कथय तृप्तिर्हि
शृण्वतो नास्ति मेऽमृतम् ॥

vistareṇātmano yogaṁ
vibhūtiṁcajanārdana
bhūyaḥ kathaya tṛptir hi
śṛṇvatonāstime'mṛtam ||

vistareṇa—indescription; ātmanaḥ—of Yourself; yogam—mystic power; vibhūtim—opulences; ca—also; janārdana—O killer of the atheists; bhūyaḥ—again; kathaya—describe; tṛptiḥ—satisfaction; hi—certainly; śṛṇvataḥ —hearing; naasti—there is no; me—my; amṛtam—nectar.

Meaning: Tell me again in detail, O Janardana, about the combination and diversification of Your Self as I am never tired of hearing about Your glory.

19

श्रीभगवानुवाच
हन्त ते कथयिष्यामि
दिव्या ह्यात्मविभूतयः ।
प्राधान्यतः कुरुश्रेष्ठ
नास्त्यन्तो विस्तरस्य मे ॥

śrī bhagavān uvāca

hantatekathayiṣyāmi
divyāhyātma-vibhūtayaḥ
prādhānyataḥ kuru-śreṣṭha
nāstyanto vistarasya me ||

śrībhagavānuvāca—the Supreme Personality of Godhead said; hanta—yes; te—unto you; kathayiṣyāmi—I shall speak; divyāḥ—divine; hi—certainly; ātma-vibhūtayaḥ—personal opulences; prādhānyataḥ—principally; kuruśreṣṭha—O best of the Kurus; naasti—there is no; antaḥ—limit; vistarasya—to the extent; me—My.

Meaning: The Glorious Lord said: Blessing on you! I shall declare to you the splendour of My manifestations, but I shall reveal only the prominent ones, O best of the Kurus, for there is no limit to My expansion.

20

अहमात्मा गुडाकेश
सर्वभूताशयस्थितः।
अहमादिश्च मध्यं च
भूतानामन्त एव च ॥

ahamātmā guḍākeśa
sarva-bhūtāśaya-sthitaḥ
ahamādiścamadhyaṁ ca
bhūtānāmanta eva ca||

aham—I; ātmā—soul; guḍākeśa—O Arjuna; sarva-bhūta—all living entities; āśaya-sthitaḥ—situated within; aham—I am; ādiḥ—origin; ca— also; madhyam—middle; ca—also; bhūtānām—all living entities; antaḥ—end; eva—certainly; ca—and.

Meaning: O Gudakesha, I am the self seated in the hearts of every creature. I am the beginning, the middle, and also the end of all creatures.

— 21 —

आदित्यानामहं
विष्णुर्ज्योतिषां रविरंशुमान्।
मरीचिर्मरुतामस्मि
नक्षत्राणामहं शशी ॥

ādityānām ahaṁ
viṣṇur jyotiṣāṁraviraṁśumān
marīcir marutām asmi
nakṣatrāṇāmahaṁśaśī ||

ādityānām—of the Ādityas; aham—I am; viṣṇuḥ—the Supreme Lord; jyotiṣām—of all luminaries; raviḥ—the sun; aṁśumān—radiant; marīciḥ—Marīci; marutām—of the Marutas; asmi—I am; nakṣatrāṇām—of stars; aham—I am; śaśī—the moon.

Meaning: I am Vishnu among the Adityas, the radiant sun among lights, Marichi among the Maruts, and the moon among the stars of the night.

22

वेदानां सामवेदोऽस्मि
देवानामस्मि वासवः।
इंद्रियाणां मनश्चास्मि
भूतानामस्मि चेतना ॥

vedānāṁ sāma-vedo 'smi
devānāmasmivāsavaḥ
indriyāṇāṁ manaś cāsmi
bhūtānāmasmicetanā ||

vedānām—of all the Vedas; sāma-vedaḥ—the Sāma-veda; asmi—I am; devānām—of all the demigods; asmi—I am; vāsavaḥ—heavenly king; indriyāṇām—of all the senses; manaḥ—the mind; ca—also; asmi—I am; bhūtānām—of all living entities; asmi—I am; cetanā—the living force.

Meaning: I am the Sama-veda among the Vedas, Indra among the Gods, the mind among the senses, and consciousness among the creatures.

23

रुद्राणां शङ्करश्चास्मि
वित्तेशो यक्षरक्षसाम्।
वसूनां पावकश्चास्मि
मेरुः शिखरिणामहम्॥

rudrāṇāṁ śaṅkaraś cāsmi
votteśoyakṣa-rakṣasām
vasūnāṁ pāvakaś cāsmi
meruḥśikhariṇāmaham

rudrāṇām—of all the Rudras; śaṅkaraḥ—Lord Śiva; ca—also; asmi—I am; vitteśaḥ—the lord of the treasury; yakṣa-rakṣasām—of the Yakṣas and Rākṣasas; vasūnām—of the Vasus; pāvakaḥ—fire; ca—also; asmi—I am; meruḥ—Meru; śikhariṇām—of all mountains; aham—I am.

Meaning: I am Lord Shiva among the Rudras, Kubera (the lord of wealth) among the Yakshas and the Rakshasas, Agni (Fire) among the Vasus, and Meru among the mountains.

24

पुरोधसां च मुख्यं मां
विद्धि पार्थ बृहस्पतिम्।
सेनानीनामहं स्कन्दः
सरसामस्मि सागरः॥

purodhasāṁcamukhyaṁmāṁ
viddhi pārtha bṛhaspatim
senānīnām ahaṁ skandaḥ
sarasāmasmisāgaraḥ

purodhasām—of all priests; ca—also; mukhyam—chief; mām—Me; viddhi—understand; pārtha—O son of Pṛthā; bṛhaspatim—Bṛhaspati; senānīnām—of all commanders; aham—I am; skandaḥ—Kārtikeya; sarasām—of all reservoirs of water; asmi—I am; sāgaraḥ—the ocean.

Meaning: O Arjuna, also know Me as Vrihaspati, the chief of the household priests, Skanda, the lord of war among generals, and the ocean among the bodies of water.

25

महर्षीणां भृगुरहं
गिरामस्म्येकमक्षरम्।
यज्ञानां जपयज्ञोऽस्मि
स्थावराणां हिमालयः॥25॥

maharṣīṇāṁ bhṛgur ahaṁ
girāmasmyekamakṣaram
yajñānāṁ japa-yajño 'smi
sthāvarāṇāṁhimālayaḥ

maharṣīṇām—among the great sages; bhṛguḥ—Bhṛgu; aham—I am; girām —of vibrations; asmi—I am; ekam akṣaram-praṇava; yajñānām—of sacrifices; japa-yajñaḥ—chanting; asmi—I am; sthāvarāṇām—ofimmovable things; himālayaḥ—the Himalayan mountains.

Meaning: I am Brighu among the great sages, the one-lettered among words, the recital of the holy names of sacrifices, and the Himalayas among immovable things.

26

अश्वत्थः सर्ववृक्षाणां
देवर्षीणां च नारदः।
गन्धर्वाणां चित्ररथः
सिद्धानां कपिलो मुनिः॥

aśvatthaḥ sarva-vṛkṣāṇāṁ
devarṣīṇāṁcanāradaḥ
gandharvāṇāṁ citrarathaḥ
siddhānāṁkapilomuniḥ

aśvatthaḥ—the banyan tree; sarva-vṛkṣāṇām—of all trees; devarṣīṇām— of all the sages amongst the demigods; ca—and; nāradaḥ—Nārada; gandharvā-ṇām—the citizens of the Gandharva planet; citrarathaḥ—Citraratha; siddhānām—of all those who are perfected; kapilaḥmuniḥ—KapilaMuni.

Meaning: I am the Ashwathha (holy fig tree) among all trees, Narada among the godly sages, Chitraratha among the Gandharvas, and Kapila the sage among the perfected beings.

27

उच्चैःश्रवसमश्वानां
विद्धि माममृतोद्भवम्।
ऐरावतं गजेन्द्राणां
नराणां च नराधिपम्।।

uccaiḥ śravasam aśvānāṁ
viddhi māmamṛtodbhavam
airāvataṁ gajendrāṇāṁ
narāṇāṁ ca narādhipam

uccaiḥśravasam—Uccaiḥśravā; aśvānām—among horses; viddhi—know; mām—Me; amṛta-udbhavam—produced from the churning of the ocean; airāvatam—Airāvata; gajendrāṇām—of elephants; narāṇām—among human beings; ca—and; narādhipam—the king.

Meaning: Among horses, I am the erect-eared Ucchaishrava who rose out of the ocean, born of the elixir of immortality, I am Airavata of the lordly elephants, and I am the monarch of men among men.

28

आयुधानामहं वज्रं
धेनूनामस्मि कामधुक्।
प्रजनश्चास्मि कन्दर्पः
सर्पाणामस्मि वासुकिः॥

āyudhānām ahaṁ vajraṁ
dhenūnāmasmikāmadhuk
prajanaścāsmikandarpaḥ
sarpāṇāmasmivāsukiḥ

āyudhānām—of all weapons; aham—I am; vajram—the thunderbolt;
dhenūnām—ofcows; asmi—I am; kāmadhuk—the surabhi cows; prajanaḥ
—for begetting children; ca—and; asmi—I am; kandarpaḥ—Cupid; sarpāṇām— of all snakes; asmi—I am; vāsukiḥ—Vāsuki.

Meaning: I am the thunderbolt or Vajra among the divine weapons, and the Surabhi among cows, the giver of abundant milk. I am Kandarpa, the god of love, and Vasuki among serpents.

29

अनन्तश्चास्मि नागानां
वरुणो यादसामहम् ।
पितॄणामर्यमा चास्मि
यमः संयमतामहम् ॥

anantaś cāsmi nāgānāṁ
varuṇoyādasāmaham
pitṝṇāmaryamācāsmi
yamaḥsaṁyamatāmaham

anantaḥ—Ananta; ca—also; asmi—I am; nāgānām—of all serpents; varuṇaḥ—the demigod controlling the water; yādasām—of all aquatics; aham—I am; piṭṝnām—of the ancestors; aryamā—Aryāma; ca—also; asmi—Iam; yamaḥ—the controller of death; saṁyamatām—of all regulators; aham—I am.

Meaning: I am Ananta among the unhooded Naga snakes, Varuna among the water deities, Aryama of departed ancestors, and Yama, the lord of death among the dispensers of law and justice.

30

प्रह्लादश्चास्मि दैत्यानां
कालः कलयतामहम्।
मृगाणां च मृगेन्द्रोऽहं
वैनतेयश्च पक्षिणाम्॥

prahlādaścāsmidaityānāṁ
kālaḥ kalayatām aham
mṛgāṇāṁcamṛgendro'haṁ
vainateyaścapakṣiṇām

prahlādaḥ—Prahlāda; ca—also; asmi—I am; daityānām—of the demons; kālaḥ—time; kalayatām—of subduers; aham—I am; mṛgāṇām—of animals; ca—and; mṛgendraḥ—the lion; aham—I am; vainateyaḥ—Garuḍa; ca—also; pakṣiṇām—of birds.

Meaning: I am the devoted Prahlada among the Daityas and demons, Time among the reckoners, the lion among the beasts, and Garuda, the carrier of Vishnu among the birds.

31

पवनः पवतामस्मि
रामः शस्त्रभृतामहम्।
झषाणां मकरश्चास्मि
स्रोतसामस्मि जाह्नवी।।

pavanaḥpavatāmasmi
rāmaḥśastra-bhṛtāmaham
jhaṣāṇāṁ makaraś cāsmi
srotasāmasmijāhnavī

pavanaḥ—the wind; pavatām—of all that purifies; asmi—I am; rāmaḥ— Rāma; śastra-bhṛtām—of the carriers of weapons; aham—I am; jhaṣāṇām —of all aquatics; makaraḥ—shark; caasmi—I am also; srotasām—of flowing rivers; asmi—I am; jāhnavī—the River Ganges.

Meaning: I am the wind among the purifiers, Rama among the armed men, the crocodile among the fishes, and Ganges of the flowing rivers.

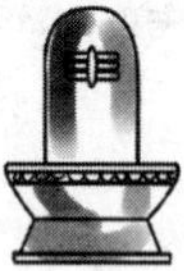

32

सर्गाणामादिरन्तश्च
मध्यं चैवाहमर्जुन ।
अध्यात्मविद्या विद्यानां
वादः प्रवदतामहम् ॥

sargāṇām ādir antaś ca
madhyaṁcaivāhamarjuna
adhyātma-vidyā vidyānāṁ
vādaḥpravadatāmaham

sargāṇām—of all creations; ādiḥ—beginning; antaḥ—end; ca—and; madhyam—middle; ca—also; eva—certainly; aham—I am; arjuna—O Arjuna; adhyātma-vidyā—spiritual knowledge; vidyānām—of all education; vādaḥ—natural conclusion; pravadatām—of arguments; aham—I am.

Meaning: I am the beginning, the middle, and the end of all creation, O Arjuna. I am the spiritual science of all the sciences, and the conclusive truth of logicians.

33

अक्षराणामकारोऽस्मि
द्वंद्वः सामासिकस्य च ।
अहमेवाक्षयः कालो
धाताहं विश्वतोमुखः ॥

akṣarāṇām akāro 'smi
dvandvaḥsāmāsikasya ca
aham evākṣayaḥ kālo
dhātāhaṁviśvato-mukhaḥ||

akṣarāṇām—of letters; akāraḥ—the first; asmi—I am; dvandvaḥ—dual; sāmāsikāsya—compounds;ca—and; aham—I am; eva—certainly; akṣayaḥ—eternal; kālaḥ—time; dhātā—creator; aham—I am; viśvato-mukhaḥ— Brahmā.

Meaning: I am the letter 'A' of letters, and the dual word of composite words. I am also inexhaustible Time, and Brahma of the creators, his manifold faces turned everywhere in the universe.

34

मृत्युः सर्वहरश्चाहम
उद्भवश्च भविष्यताम्।
कीर्तिः श्रीर्वाक्च नारीणां
स्मृतिर्मेधा धृतिः क्षमा।।

mṛtyuḥ sarva-haraś cāham
udbhavaścabhaviṣyatām
kīrtiḥ śrīr vāk ca nārīṇāṁ
smṛtirmedhādhṛtiḥkṣamā

mṛtyuḥ—death; sarva-haraḥ—all-devouring; ca—also; aham—I am; udbhavaḥ—generation; ca—also; bhaviṣyatām—of the future; kīrtiḥ—fame; śrīḥvāk—beautiful speech; ca—also; nārīṇāṁ—of women; smṛtiḥ—memory; medhā—intelligence; dhṛtiḥ—faithfulness; kṣamā—patience.

Meaning: I am all-absorbing death and the creator of all things yet to be. In women, I am fame, prosperity, good speech, memory, intelligence, faithfulness, patience, and forgiveness.

35

बृहत्साम तथा साम्नां
गायत्री छन्दसामहम्।
मासानां मार्गशीर्षोऽहमृ
तूनां कुसुमाकरः॥

bṛhat-sāma tathā sāmnāṁ
gāyatrī chandasāmaham
māsānāṁ mārga-śīrṣo'hamṛ
tūnāṁ kusumākaraḥ

bṛhat-sāma—the Bṛhat-sāma; tathā—also; sāmnām—of the Sāma-veda song; gāyatrī—the Gāyatrī hymns; chandasām—of all poetry; aham—I am; māsānām—of months; mārga-śīrṣo 'ham—the month of November- December; aham—I am; ṛtūnām—of all seasons; kusumākaraḥ—spring.

Meaning: I am also the Vrihat-Sama of the Samas, the Gayatri among the mantras, the Margashirsha among the months, and the flowering spring among the seasons.

36

द्यूतं छलयतामस्मि
तेजस्तेजस्विनामहम्।
जयोऽस्मि व्यवसायोऽस्मि
सत्त्वं सत्त्ववतामहम्॥

dyūtaṁ chalayatām asmi
tejastejasvināmaham
jayo 'smi vyavasāyo 'smi
sattvaṁ sattvavatāmaham||

dyūtam—gambling; chalayatām—of all cheats; asmi—I am; tejaḥ—splendid; tejasvinām—of everything splendid; aham—I am; jayaḥ—victory; asmi—I am; vyavasāyaḥ—adventure; asmi—I am; sattvam—strength; sattvavatām—of all the strong; aham—I am.

Meaning: I am the dice of the gamblers and cheats, the radiance of the radiant. I am victory, true knowledge, and the goodness in the good.

37

वृष्णीनां वासुदेवोऽस्मि
पाण्डवानां धनंजयः।
मुनीनामप्यहं व्यासः
कवीनामुशना कविः॥

vṛṣṇīnāṁ vāsudevo 'smi
pāṇḍavānāṁdhanañjayaḥ
munīnāmapyahaṁvyāsaḥ
kavīnām uśanā kaviḥ||

vṛṣṇīnām—of the descendants of Vṛṣṇi; vāsudevaḥ—Kṛṣṇa in Dvāraka; asmi—I am; pāṇḍavānām—of the Pāṇḍavas; dhanañjayaḥ—Arjuna; munīnām—of the sages; api—also; aham—I am; vyāsaḥ—Vyāsa, the compiler of all Vedic literature; kavīnām—of all great thinkers; uśanā— Uśanā; kaviḥ—the thinker.

Meaning: I am Vasudeva among the Vrishnis, Arjuna among the Pandavas, and Vyasa among the sages, and Ushana among the great thinkers.

38

दण्डो दमयतामस्मि
नीतिरस्मि जिगीषताम्।
मौनं चैवास्मि गुह्यानां
ज्ञानं ज्ञानवतामहम्॥

daṇḍodamayatāmasmi
nītirasmi jigīṣatām
maunaṁ caivāsmi guhyānāṁ
jñānaṁjñānavatāmaham||

daṇḍaḥ—punishment; damayatām—of all separation; asmi—Iam; nītiḥ—morality; asmi—I am; jigīṣatām—of the victorious; maunam—silence; ca—and; eva—also; asmi—I am; guhyānām—of secrets; jñānam—knowledge; jñānavatām—of the wise; aham—I am.

Meaning: I am the scepter of chastisement, the policy and morality of the victorious, the reticence of silent workers, the reason of the rational, and the wisdom of the wise.

39

यच्चापि सर्वभूतानां
बीजं तदहमर्जुन ।
न तदस्ति विना यत्स्यान्
मया भूतं चराचरम्।।

yac cāpi sarva-bhūtānāṁ
bījaṁtadahamarjuna
na tad asti vinā yat syān
mayā bhūtaṁcarācaram||

yat—whatever; ca—also; api—may be; sarva-bhūtānām—of all creations; bījam—the seed; tat—that; aham—I am; arjuna—OArjuna; na—not; tat—that; asti—there is; vinā—without; yat—that; syāt—exists; mayā—by Me; bhūtam—created; carācaram—moving and unmoving.

Meaning: And, O Arjuna, I am the generating seed of all creatures. There is no being, moving or unmoving, that exists without Me.

40

नान्तोऽस्ति मम दिव्यानां
विभूतीनां परन्तप।
एष तूद्देशतः प्रोक्तो
विभूतेर्विस्तरो मया॥

nānto 'sti mama divyānāṁ
vibhūtīnāṁ parantapa
eṣa tūddeśataḥ prokto
vibhūtervistaro mayā ||

na—nor; antaḥ—a limit; asti—is there; mama—of My; divyānām—divine; vibhūtīnam—opulences; parantapa—O conquerer of the enemies; eṣaḥ—all this; tu—that; uddeśataḥ—examples; proktaḥ—spoken; vibhūteḥ—opulences; vistaraḥ—expanded; mayā—by Me.

Meaning: O mighty conqueror of foes, there is no end to My glorious diversifications. I have merely declared to you an indicative expansion of my divine and infinite diversifications.

41

यद्यद्विभूतिमत्सत्त्वं
श्रीमदूर्जितमेव वा।
तत्तदेवावगच्छ त्वं
मम तेजोंऽशसम्भवम् ॥

yadyadvibhūtimatsattvaṁ
śrīmad ūrjitam eva vā
tattadevāvagacchatvaṁ
mamatejo'ṁśa-sambhavam||

yat yat—whatever; vibhūti—opulences; mat—having; sattvam— existence; śrīmat—beautiful; ūrjitam—glorious; eva—certainly; vā—or; tat tat—all those; eva—certainly; avagaccha—you must know; tvam—you; mama—My; tejaḥ—splendor; aṁśa—partly; sambhavam—born of.

Meaning: Know that all singular, glorious, or energetic entitities have risen from but a spark of My Splendour.

42

अथवा बहुनैतेन किं
ज्ञातेन तवार्जुन।
विष्टभ्याहमिदं कृत्स्नमे
ंकांशेन स्थितो जगत्॥

athavā bahunaitena kiṁ
jñātena tavārjuna
viṣṭabhyāhamidaṁkṛtsnam
ekāṁśenasthitojagat||

athavā—or; bahunā—many; etena—by this kind; kim—what; jñātena—knowing; tava—you; arjuna—O Arjuna; viṣṭabhya—entire; aham—I; idam—this; kṛtsnam—all manifestations; eka—one; aṁśena—part; sthithaḥ—situated; jagat—in the universe.

Meaning: But what need do you have for this detailed knowledge, O Arjuna? Know that I pervade and support this entire universe with a single fragment of Myself.

ॐ तत्सदिति श्रीमद्भगवद्गीतासूपनिषत्सु ब्रह्मविद्यायांयोगशास्त्रे
श्रीकृष्णार्जुनसंवादे विभूतियोगो नाम दशमोऽध्यायः।

Thus in the Upanishad of the Glorious Divine Lay, the Science of Brahma, the Ordinance of Yoga, the Discourse between the Glorious Lord Krishna and Arjuna, the Tenth Chapter titled 'Vibhuti Yoga' (The Yoga of Divine Manifestations).

CHAPTER 11

VISHVARUPA DARSHAN YOGA (YOGA OF THE VISION OF THE ABSOLUTE DIVINE FORM)

CHAPTER 11

VISHVARUPA DARSHAN YOGA (YOGA OF THE VISION OF THE ABSOLUTE DIVINE FORM)

In the previous chapter, Lord Krishna had described His divine vibhutis or opulence to nurture and magnify Arjuna's devotion. Lord Krishna had mentioned towards the end that all the glory, beauty, and power is but a spark of His immeasurable splendour. This revelation naturally made Arjuna curious.

In Chapter Eleven of the Bhagavad Gita, Arjuna requests Lord Krishna to reveal His Vishvarupa or Universal Form, the infinite cosmic form that anyone who claims to be God should be willing to show. Lord Krishna grants Arjuna divine vision first as no one can see the Glorious Universal Form that comprises all universes with the eyes of a mortal. Then, Lord Krishna exhibits his spectacular universal form that displays all that is in existence in the Universe and the three worlds. By doing so, he proves His divinity to Arjuna. Through His Universal Form, Lord Krishna shows everything that ever was, and everything that now is, and everything that will ever be, in one place.

Arjuna is spellbound at this sight of Lord Krishna's mystical Universal Form with unlimited eyes, mouths, and arms. The various forms of the Lord were decorated resplendently with splendid ornaments and attire, holding divine weapons. The Lord was garlanded with divine flowers and the scent of celestial perfume over his bodies. In this magnificent and luminous form, Arjuna saw all the powerful gods. He saw the entire universe in the form of the Lord, and unlimited expansions of this universe that were divided into many thousands in His form. A spellbound Arjuna falls to his feet with folded hands and pays obeisances to the Lord as the spell of illusion and confoundedness he was under is broken. Lord Krishna tells him that apart from the five Pandavas, all the warriors assembled on the battlefield of Kurukshetra will be killed in due course of time. Hence, Lord Krishna urges Arjuna to fight as His instrument and assures Arjuna of victory and a prosperous kingdom. A frightened Arjuna requests Lord Krishna to withdraw His fearful form and display His original form. Lord Krishna then displays His four-armed form to Arjuna holding various weapons, and then finally returns to his human two-armed form. Arjuna's mind rests at ease on seeing the Lord's beautiful human form. Only one who is engaged in pure devotional service of the Lord is lucky enough to see such a form.

1

अर्जुन उवाच
मदनुग्रहाय परमं
गुह्यमध्यात्मसंज्ञितम्।
यत्त्वयोक्तं वचस्तेन
मोहोऽयं विगतो मम।।

arjunauvāca
mad-anugrahāya paramaṁ
guhyamadhyātma-saṁjñitam
yat tvayoktaṁ vacas tena
moho'yaṁvigatomama||

arjunaḥ uvāca—Arjuna said; mat-anugrahāya—just to show me favor; paramam—supreme; guhyam—confidential; adhyātma—spiritual; saṁjñitam —in the matter of; yat—what; tvayā—by You; uktam—said; vacaḥ—words; tena—by that; mohaḥ—illusion; ayam—this; vigataḥ—is educated; mama—my.

Meaning: Arjuna said: My confusion and illusion has disappeared by that word, the Supreme Secret that you have declared to me so kindly.

2

भवाप्ययौ हि भूतानां
श्रुतौ विस्तरशो मया।
त्वत्तः कमलपत्राक्ष
माहात्म्यमपि चाव्ययम्॥

bhavāpyayau hi bhūtānāṁ
śrutau vistaraśo mayā
tvattaḥ kamala-patrākṣa
māhātmyamapi cāvyayam||

bhava—appearance; apyayau—disappearance; hi—certainly; bhūtānām—of all living entities; śrutau—have heard; vistaraśaḥ—detail; mayā—by me; tvattaḥ—from You; kamala-patrākṣa—O lotus-eyed one; māhātmyam—glories; api—also; ca—and; avyayam—inexhaustible.

Meaning: O lotus-eyed one, I have heard in great detail from You of the creation and dissolution of creatures and about the High Selfhood that is imperishable.

3

एवमेतद्यथात्थ
त्वमात्मानं परमेश्वर।
द्रष्टुमिच्छामि ते
रूपमैश्वरं पुरुषोत्तम।।

evametad yathāttha
tvamātmānaṁ parameśvara
draṣṭum icchāmi te
rūpam aiśvaraṁ puruṣottama ||

evam—that; etat—this; yathāttha—as it is; tvam—You; ātmānam—the soul; parameśvara—the Supreme Lord; draṣṭum—tosee; icchāmi—I wish; te—You; rūpam—form; aiśvaram—divine; puruṣottama—O best of personalities.

Meaning: O Lord Supreme, though I see You here before me, I feel the curiosity to witness Your Lordly form in its cosmic manifestation.

4

मन्यसे यदि तच्छक्यं
मया द्रष्टुमिति प्रभो ।
योगेश्वर ततो मे त्वं
दर्शयात्मानमव्ययम्॥

manyase yadi tac chakyaṁ
mayā draṣṭumiti prabho
yogeśvara tato me tvaṁ
darśayātmānamavyayam||

manyase—if You think; yadi—if; tat—that; śakyam—able to see; mayā—by me; draṣṭum—to see; iti—thus; prabho—O Lord; yogeśvara—the Lord of all mystic power; tataḥ—then; me—unto me; tvam—You; darśaya—show; ātmānam—Yourself; avyayam—eternal.

Meaning: If You think that I am capable of witnessing Your cosmic form, O Lord, O beholder of all mystic power, kindly show me that universal and imperishable self.

5

श्रीभगवानुवाच
पश्य मे पार्थ रूपाणि
शतशोऽथ सहस्रशः।
नानाविधानि दिव्यानि
नानावर्णाकृतीनि च ॥

śrī bhagavān uvāca
paśya me pārtha rūpāṇi
śataśo›tha sahasraśaḥ
nānā-vidhāni divyāni
nānā-varṇākṛtīni ca||

śrībhagavānuvāca—the Supreme Personality of Godhead said; paśya— just see; me—Mine; pārtha—O son of Pṛthā; rūpāṇi—forms; śataśaḥ—hundreds; atha—also; sahasraśaḥ—thousands; nānā-vidhāni— variegated; divyāni— divine; nānā—variegated; varṇa—colored; akṛtīni— forms; ca—also.

Meaning: The Glorious Lord said: Behold, O Arjuna, My forms by the hundreds and thousands, varied and divine in nature, glorious and various in colour and shape.

6

पश्यादित्यान्वसून्रुद्रान-
श्विनौ मरुतस्तथा।
बहून्यदृष्टपूर्वाणि
पश्याश्चर्याणि भारत।।

paśyādityān vasūn rudrān
aśvinau marutastathā
bahūny adṛṣṭa-pūrvāṇi
paśyāś caryāṇi bhārata||

paśya—see; ādityān—the twelve sons of Aditi; vasūn—the eight Vasus; rudrān—the eleven forms of Rudra; aśvinau—the two Asvins; marutaḥ—the forty-nine Maruts (demigods of the wind); tathā—also; bahūni—many; adṛṣṭa—that you have not heard or seen; pūrvāṇi—before; paśya—there see; āścaryāṇi—all the wonderful; bhārata—O best of the Bhāratas.

Meaning: O Bharata, behold the Adityas, the Vasus, the Rudras, the twin Ashwins and the Maruts. Behold the many marvels that have been unseen or unheard before.

7

इहैकस्थं जगत्कृत्स्नं
पश्याद्य सचराचरम्।
मम देहे गुडाकेश
यच्चान्यद्द्रष्टुमिच्छसि।।

ihaikasthaṁ jagat kṛtsnaṁ
paśyādyasa-carācaram
mama dehe guḍākeśa
yacc-ānyaddraṣṭum icchasi ||

iha—in this; ekastham—in one; jagat—the universe; kṛtsnam—completely; paśya—see; adya—immediately; sa—with; cara—moving; acaram—not moving; mama—My; dehe—in this body; guḍākeśa—O Arjuna; yat—that; ca— also; anyat—other; draṣṭum—to see; icchasi—you like.

Meaning: Behold today in My body, O Gudakesha, the entire universe of the moving and the unmoving together and everything else that you desire to see.

8

न तु मां शक्यसे
द्रष्टमनेनैव स्वचक्षुषा।
दिव्यं ददामि ते चक्षुः
पश्य मे योगमैश्वरम्।।

na tu māṁ śakyase
draṣṭum anenaiva sva-cakṣuṣā
divyaṁ dadāmi te cakṣuḥ
paśya me yogam aiśvaram||

na—never; tu—but; mām—Me; śakyase—able; draṣṭum—to see; anena—by this; eva—certainly; sva-cakṣuṣā—with your own eyes; divyam—divine; dadāmi—I give; te—you; cakṣuḥ—eyes; paśya—see; me—My; yogam aiśvaram—inconceivable mystic power.

Meaning: But you will not be able to see Me with your present eyes. Therefore, I shall grant you divine eyes through which you can see My mystic opulence.

9

संजय उवाच

एवमुक्त्वा ततो
राजन्महायोगेश्वरो हरिः।
दर्शयामास पार्थाय
परमं रूपमैश्वरम्॥

sañjaya uvāca
evam uktvā tato
rājan mahā-yogeśvaro hariḥ
darśayāmāsa pārthāya
paramaṁ rūpamaiśvaram ||

sañjayaḥ uvāca—Sanjaya said; evam—thus; uktvā—saying; tataḥ— thereafter; rājan—O King; mahā-yogeśvaraḥ—the most powerful mystic; hariḥ—the Supreme Personality of Godhead, Kṛṣṇa;darśayāmāsa—showed; pārthāya—unto Arjuna; paramam—divine; rūpam—universal form; aiśvaram — opulences.

Meaning: Sanjaya said: O King, the Supreme, the Lord of everything, speaking thus, displayed His Universal Form to Arjuna.

10-11

अनेकवक्त्रनयन-
मनेकाद्भुतदर्शनम्।
अनेकदिव्याभरणं
दिव्यानेकोद्यतायुधम्॥
दिव्यमाल्याम्बरधरं
दिव्यगन्धानुलेपनम्।
सर्वाश्चर्यमयं देवम-
नन्तं विश्वतोमुखम्॥

aneka-vaktra-nayanam
anekādbhuta-darśanam
aneka-divyābharaṇaṁ
divyānekodyatāyudham||
divya-mālyāmbara-dharaṁ
divya-gandh-ānulepanam
sarvāścarya-mayaṁ devam
anantaṁviśvato-mukham||

aneka—various; vaktra—mouths; nayanam—eyes; aneka—various; adbhuta—wonderful; darśanam—sight; aneka—many; divya—divine; ābharaṇam—ornaments; divya—divine; aneka—

various; udyata—uplifted; āyudham weapons; divya—divine; mālya—garlands; ambara-dharam—covered with the dresses; divya—divine; gandha—fragrance; anulepanam— smeared; sarva— all; aścaryamayam—wonderful; devam—shining; anantam—unlimited; viśvataḥ-mukham—all-pervading.

Meaning: In that mystical universal form, Arjuna saw unlimited eyes and unlimited mouths. It featured wondrous sights and the forms were decorated with splendid ornaments and dressed in fine garbs, holding shining weapons. The Lord was garlanded splendidly with many celestial scents on His body. He was magnificent, luminous, boundless, and universe-facing.

12

दिवि सूर्यसहस्रस्य
भवेद्युगपदुत्थिता।
यदि भाः सदृशी सा
स्याद्भासस्तस्य महात्मनः।।

divi sūrya-sahasrasya
bhavedyugapadutthitā
yadi bhāḥ sadṛśī sā syād
bhāsastasya-mahātmanaḥ||

divi—in the sky; sūrya—sun; sahasrasya—of many thousands; bhavet—there were; yugapat—simultaneously; utthitā—present; yadi—if; bhāḥ—light; sadṛśī—like that; sā—that; syāt—may be; bhāsaḥ—effulgence; tasya—there is; mahātmanaḥ—of the great Lord.

Meaning: If the splendour of hundreds of thousands of suns were to light up the sky, they might resemble the luminousity of the Supreme One in His Universal Form.

13

तत्रैकस्थं जगत्कृत्स्नं
प्रविभक्तमनेकधा।
अपश्यद्देवदेवस्य
शरीरे पाण्डवस्तदा।।

tatraikasthaṁ jagat kṛtsnaṁ
pravibhakta-manekadhā
apaśyad deva-devasya
śarīre pāṇḍavastadā ||

tatra—there; ekastham—one place; jagat—universe; kṛtsnam—completely; pravibhaktam—divided in; anekadhā—many kinds; apaśyat—could see; deva-devasya—of the Supreme Personality of Godhead; śarīre—in the universal form; pāṇḍavaḥ—Arjuna; tadā—at that time.

Meaning: Arjuna then saw the whole universe together in the form of the Lord, and unlimited expansions of the universe divided manifold into many, many thousands in His body.

14

ततः स विस्मयाविष्टो
हृष्टरोमा धनंजयः ।
प्रणम्य शिरसा देवं
कृताञ्जलिरभाषत।।

tataḥ sa vismayāviṣṭo
hṛṣṭa-romā dhanañjayaḥ
praṇamya śirasā devaṁ
kṛtāñjalir-abhāṣata ||

tataḥ—thereafter; saḥ—he; vismayāviṣṭaḥ—being overwhelmed with wonder; hṛṣṭa-romā—with his bodily hairs standing on end due to his great ecstasy; dhanañjayaḥ—Arjuna; praṇamya—offering obeisances; śirasā—with the head; devam—to the Supreme Personality of Godhead; kṛtāñjaliḥ—with folded hands; abhāṣata—began to say.

Meaning: Then, overwhelmed with astonishment, hair standing on end, Arjuna bowed his head, and began praying to the Supreme Lord with folded hands.

15

अर्जुन उवाच
पश्यामि देवांस्तव देव देहे
सर्वास्तथा भूतविशेषसङ्घान्।
ब्रह्माणमीशं कमलासनस्थ
मृषींश्च सर्वानुरगांश्च दिव्यान् ॥

arjunauvāca
paśyāmi devāṁstava deva dehe
sarvāṁstathā bhūta-viśeṣa-saṅghān
brahmāṇam īśaṁ kamalāsana-stham
ṛṣīṁśca sarvānuragāṁśca divyān||

arjunaḥ uvāca—Arjuna said; paśyāmi—I see; devān—all the demigods; tava—Your; deva—O Lord; dehe—in the body; sarvān—all; tathā—also; bhūta—living entities; viśeṣa-saṅghān—specifically assembled; brahmāṇam— Lord Brahmā; īśam—Lord Śiva; kamala-āsana-stham—sitting on the lotus flower; ṛṣīn—great sages; ca—also; sarvān—all; uragān—serpents; ca—also; divyān—divine.

Meaning: Arjuna said: In your body, O Lord, I see all the celestial beings and several other living beings. I see Lord Brahma seated on his lotus seat as well as Lord Shiva, several sages, and the divine serpents.

16

अनेकबाहूदरवक्त्रनेत्रं
पश्यामि त्वां सर्वतोऽनन्तरूपम्।
नान्तं न मध्यं न पुनस्तवादिं
पश्यामि विश्वेश्वर विश्वरूप॥

aneka-bāhūdara-vaktra-netraṁ
paśyāmi tvāṁ sarvato'nanta-rūpam
nāntaṁ na madhyaṁ na punas tavādiṁ
paśyāmi viśveśvara viśva-rūpa||

aneka—many; bāhū—arms; udara—bellies; vaktra—mouths; netram—eyes; paśyāmi—I see; tvām—unto You; sarvataḥ—from all sides; ananta- rūpam—unlimited form; na antam—there is no end; na madhyam—there is no middle; na punaḥ—nor again; tava—Your; ādim—beginning; paśyāmi—I see; viśveśvara—O Lord of the universe; viṣva-rūpa—in the form of the universe.

Meaning: I see You everywhere with numerous arms, mouths, eyes, and bellies, in form expanded and limitless. I find no beginning and no end, and neither is there a middle, O Lord of the Universe, O Form Universal.

17

किरीटिनं गदिनं चक्रिणं च
तेजोराशिं सर्वतो दीप्तिमन्तम्।
पश्यामि त्वां दुर्निरीक्ष्यं समन्ता
द्दीप्तानलार्कद्युतिमप्रमेयम्।।

kirīṭinaṁ gadinaṁ cakriṇaṁ ca
tejo-rāśiṁ sarvato dīptimantam
paśyāmi tvāṁ durnirīkṣyaṁ samantād
dīptānalārka-dyutimaprameyam ||

kirīṭinam—with helmets; gadinam—with maces; cakriṇam—with discs; ca—and; tejorāśim—effulgence; sarvataḥ—all sides; dīptimantam—glowing; pasyāmi—I see; tvām—You; durnirīkṣyam—difficult to see; samantāt—spreading; dīpta-anala—blazing fire; arka—sun; dyutim— sunshine; aprameyam—immeasurable.

Meaning: Your form, adorned with several crowns, scepters, and clubs and discus in hand is difficult to behold bercause of its glaring luminosity and splendour. It is fiery, immeasurable, and dazzling just like the Sun.

18

त्वमक्षरं परमं वेदितव्यं
त्वमस्य विश्वस्य परं निधानम्।
त्वमव्ययः शाश्वतधर्मगोप्ता
सनातनस्त्वं पुरुषो मतो मे॥

tvamakṣaraṁ paramaṁ veditavyaṁ
tvamasya viśvasya paraṁ nidhānam
tvam avyayaḥ śāśvata-dharma-goptā
sanātanastvaṁ puruṣo mato me||

tvam—You; akṣaram—inexhaustible; paramam—supreme; veditavyam —to be understood; tvam—You; asya—of this; viśvasya—of the universe; param—supreme; nidhānam—basis; tvam—You are; avyayaḥ —inexhaustible; śāśvata-dharma-goptā—maintainer of the eternal religion; sanātanaḥ—eternal; tvam—You; puruṣaḥ—Supreme Personality; mataḥme —is my opinion.

Meaning: You are the Immutable, the Supreme primal objective. You are the First Nursery of the Universe and the best. You are the Unperishing Guardian of Eternal Virtue. You are the Eternal Presiding Being.

19

अनादिमध्यान्तमनन्तवीर्य
मनन्तबाहुं शशिसूर्यनेत्रम्।
पश्यामि त्वां दीप्तहुताशवक्त्रं
स्वतेजसा विश्वमिदं तपन्तम्॥

anādi-madhyāntam ananta-vīryam
ananta-bāhuṁśaśi-sūrya-netram
paśyāmi tvāṁ dīpta-hutāśa-vaktraṁ
sva-tejasā viśvamidaṁ tapantam||

anādi—without beginning; madhya—without middle; antam—without end; ananta—unlimited; vīryam—glorious; ananta—unlimited; bāhum—arms; śaśi—moon; sūrya—sun; netram—eyes; paśyāmi—I see; tvām— You; dīpta—blazing; hutāśa-vaktram—fire coming out of Your mouth; sva- tejasā—by Your; viśvam—this universe; idam—this; tapantam—heating.

Meaning: You are the origin without any beginning, middle, or end. You are unlimited in power with numberless arms, with the sun and the moon among Your eyes and the blazing fire as Your mouth. With your splendour, you heat up this entire universe.

20

द्यावापृथिव्योरिदमन्तरं हि
व्याप्तं त्वयैकेन दिशश्च सर्वाः ।
दृष्ट्वाद्भुतं रूपमुग्रं तवेदं
लोकत्रयं प्रव्यथितं महात्मन्॥

dyāv āpṛthivyor idam antaraṁ hi
vyāptaṁ tvayaikena diśaśca sarvāḥ
dṛṣṭvādbhutaṁ rūpam ugraṁ tavedaṁ
loka-trayaṁ pravyathitaṁ mahātman||

dyau—in outer space; āpṛthivyoḥ—of the earth; idam—this; antaram—in between; hi—certainly; vyāptam—pervaded; tvayā—by You; ekena—by one; diśaḥ—directions; ca—and; sarvāḥ—all; dṛṣṭvā—by seeing; adbhutam—wonderful; rūpam—form; ugram—terrible; tava—Your; idam—this; loka—planetary system; trayam—three; pravyathitam—perturbed; mahātman— O great one.

Meaning: You fill the entire space between the sky and the planets and all the space between even though You are one. The triple world is perplexed by the sight of Your marvellous and terrible form that I now behold, O Great Self.

21

अमी हि त्वां सुरसङ्घा विशन्ति,
केचिद्भीताः प्राञ्जलयो गृणन्ति।
स्वस्तीत्युक्त्वा महर्षिसिद्धसङ्घाः
स्तुवन्ति त्वां स्तुतिभिः पुष्कलाभिः॥

amī hi tvāṁ sura-saṅghā viśanti
kecidbhītāḥ prāñjalayo gṛṇanti
svastīty-uktvā maharṣi-siddha-saṅghāḥ
stuvanti tvāṁ stutibhiḥ puṣkalābhiḥ||

amī—all those; hi—certainly; tvām—unto You; sura-saṅghāḥ—groups of demigods; viśanti—entering; kecit—some of them; bhītāḥ—out of fear; prāñjalayaḥ—with folded hands; gṛṇanti—offering prayers unto; svasti—all peace; iti—thus; uktvā—speaking like that; maharṣi—great sages; siddha- saṅghāḥ—perfect sages; stuvanti—singing hymns; tvām—unto You; stutibhiḥ —with prayers; puṣkalābhiḥ—Vedic hymns.

Meaning: All the celestial gods are surrendering to You and entering You. They look terrified as they sing the Vedic hymns in Your praise with folded hands.

22

रुद्रादित्या वसवो ये च साध्या-
विश्वेऽश्विनौ मरुतश्चोष्मपाश्च ।
गंधर्वयक्षासुरसिद्धसङ्घा-
वीक्षन्ते त्वां विस्मिताश्चैव सर्वे॥

rudrādityā vasavo ye ca sādhyā
viśve'śvinau marutaścoṣmapāśca
gandharva-yakṣāsura-siddha-saṅghā
vīkṣante tvāṁ vismitāścaiva sarve||

rudra—manifestations of Lord Śiva; ādityāḥ—the Ādityas; vasavaḥ—the Vasus; ye—all those; ca—and; sādhyāḥ—the Sādhyas; viśve—the Viśvadevas; aśvinau — the Aśvinīkumāras; marutaḥ—the Maruts; ca — and; uṣmapāḥ — the forefathers; ca—and; gandharva —the Gandharvas; yakṣa—the Yakṣas; asura- siddha—the demons and the perfected demigods; saṅghāḥ—assemblies; vīkṣante —are seeing; tvām—You; vismitāḥ —in wonder; ca—also; eva—certainly; sarve—all.

Meaning: Your various manifestations of Lord Shiva, the Adityas, the Vasus, the Sadhyas, the Vishwas, the twin Ashwins, the Maruts, the forefathers, the Gandharvas, Yakshas, Asuras, the celestials, and the perfected are all gazing at You in wonder.

23

रूपं महत्ते बहुवक्त्रनेत्रं
महाबाहो बहुबाहूरुपादम्।
बहूदरं बहुदंष्ट्राकरालं
दृष्ट्वा लोकाः प्रव्यथितास्तथाहम्॥

rūpaṁ mahat te bahu-vaktra-netraṁ
mahā-bāhobahu-bāhūru-pādam
bahūdaraṁ bahu-daṁṣṭrā-karālaṁ
dṛṣṭvā lokāḥ pravyathitāstathāham

rūpam—form; mahat—very great; te—of You; bahu—many; vaktra— faces; netram—eyes; mahā-bāho—Omighty-armed one;bahu—many; bāhu—arms; ūru—thighs; pādam—legs; bahu-udaram—many bellies; babu- daṁṣṭrā—many teeth; karālam—horrible; dṛṣṭvā—seeing; lokāḥ—all the planets; pravyathitāḥ—perturbed; tathā—similarly; aham—I.

Meaning: Witnessing Your grand form with numerous eyes, mouths, arms, thighs, feet, breasts and terrible teeth, O mighty-armed One, the worlds are in awe, and so am I.

24

नभःस्पृशं दीप्तमनेकवर्णं
व्यात्ताननं दीप्तविशालनेत्रम्।
दृष्ट्वा हि त्वां प्रव्यथितान्तरात्मा
धृतिं न विन्दामि शमं च विष्णो॥

nabhaḥ spṛśaṁ dīptam aneka-varṇaṁ
vyāttānanaṁ dīpta-viśāla-netram
dṛṣṭvā hi tvāṁ pravyathit-āntarātmā
dhṛtiṁ navindāmi śamaṁ ca viṣṇo

nabhaḥ spṛśam—touching the sky; dīptam—glowing; aneka—many; varṇam—color; vyāttā—open; ānanam—mouth; dīpta—glowing; viśāla— very great; netram—eyes; dṛṣṭvā—by seeing; hi—certainly; tvām—You; pravyathitā —perturbed; antaḥ—within; ātmā—soul; dhṛtim—steadiness; na—no;vindāmi—and have; śamam—mental tranquility; ca—also; viṣṇo— O Lord Viṣṇu.

Meaning: O all-pervading Vishnu, seeing Your multicoloured, sky-reaching form with radiant colours, open mouth, and blazing eyes, I am losing my balance, firmness, and comfort, and I am afraid.

25

दंष्ट्राकरालानि च ते मुखानि
दृष्ट्वैव कालानलसन्निभानि।
दिशो न जाने न लभे च शर्म
प्रसीद देवेश जगन्निवास॥

daṁṣṭrā-karālāni ca te mukhāni
dṛṣṭvaivakālānala-sannibhāni
diśo na jāne na labhe ca śarma
prasīdadeveśajagan-nivāsa ||

daṁṣṭrā—teeth; karālāni—like that; ca—also; te—Your; mukhāni—faces; dṛṣṭvā—seeing; eva—thus; kālānala—the fire of death; sannibhāni—as if blazing; diśaḥ—directions; najāne—do not know; nalabhe—nor obtain; caśarma—andgrace; prasīda—be pleased; deveśa—O Lord of all lords; jagat-nivāsa—refuge of the worlds.

Meaning: Seeing Your mouths wide open with terrible teeth like the insatiable fire of Time, I cannot find ease of mind, and I am losing my balance. Have mercy upon Me, O Lord of the Lords, O Refuge of the Universe.

26-27

अमी च त्वां धृतराष्ट्रस्य पुत्राः
सर्वे सहैवावनिपालसंघैः।
भीष्मो द्रोणः सूतपुत्रस्तथासौ
सहास्मदीयैरपि योधमुख्यैः॥

वक्त्राणि ते त्वरमाणा विशन्ति
दंष्ट्राकरालानि भयानकानि।
केचिद्विलग्ना दशनान्तरेषु
सन्दृश्यन्ते चूर्णितैरुत्तमाङ्गैः॥

amī ca tvāṁ dhṛtarāṣṭrasya putrāḥ
sarvesahaivāvanipāla-saṅghaiḥ
bhīṣmo droṇaḥ sūta-putras tathāsau
sahāsmadīyairapiyodha-mukhyaiḥ ||

vaktrāṇi te tvaramāṇā viśanti
daṁṣṭrā-karālānibhayānakāni
kecid vilagnā daśanāntareṣu
sandṛśyante cūrṇitairuttamāṅgaiḥ ||

amī—all those; ca—also; tvām—You; dhṛtarāṣṭasya—of Dhṛtarāṣṭra; putrāḥ—sons; sarva—all; sahaeva—along with; avanipāla—warrior kings; saṅghaiḥ—with the groups; bhīṣmaḥ—Bhīṣmadeva; droṇaḥ—Droṇācārya; sūta-putraḥ—Karṇa; tathā—also; asau—that; saha—with; asmadīyaiḥ— our; api—also; yodha-mukhyaiḥ—chief among the warriors; vaktrāṇi— mouths; te—Your; tvaramāṇāḥ—fearful; viśanti—entering; daṁṣṭrā— teeth; karālāni—terrible; bhayānakāni—very fearful; kecit—some of them; vilagnāḥ—being attacked; daśanāntareṣu—between the teeth; sandṛśyante—being seen; cūrṇitaiḥ—smashed; uttama-aṅgaiḥ—by the head.

Meaning: I can see all the sons of Dhritarashtra along with their allied kings, Bheeshma, Drona, and Karna rushing into Your mouths as Your fearful teeth crushes their heads and bodies.

— 28 —

यथा नदीनां बहवोऽम्बुवेगाः
समुद्रमेवाभिमुखा द्रवन्ति।
तथा तवामी नरलोकवीराविशन्ति
वक्त्राण्यभिविज्वलन्ति॥

yathā nadīnāṁ bahavo 'mbu-vegāḥ
samudramevābhimukhā dravanti
tathā tavāmī nara-loka-vīrāviśanti
vaktrāṇy-abhivijvalanti||

yathā—as; nadīnām—of the rivers; bahavaḥ—many; ambu-vegāḥ; —waves of the waters; samudram—ocean; eva—certainly; abhimukhāḥ—towards; dravanti—gliding; tathā—similarly; tava—Your; amī—all those;nara-lokavīrāḥ—the kings of human society; viśanti—entering; vaktrāṇi—into the mouths; abhivijvalanti—blazing.

Meaning: As the rivers flow forward into the great ocean, I see these great heroes of the world enter Your mouths blazing from all sides with great speed and perish.

29

यथा प्रदीप्तं ज्वलनं पतंगा
विशन्ति नाशाय समृद्धवेगाः।
तथैव नाशाय विशन्ति लोकास्तवापि
वक्त्राणि समृद्धवेगाः॥

yathā pradīptaṁ jvalanaṁ pataṅgā
viśanti nāśāya samṛddha-vegāḥ
tathaiva nāśāya viśanti lokāstavāpi
vaktrāṇi samṛddha-vegāḥ ||

yathā—as; pradīptam—blazing; jvalanam—fire; pataṅgāḥ—moths; viśanti—enters; nāśāya—destruction; samṛddha—full; vegāḥ—speed; tathā eva—similarly; nāśāya—for destruction; viśanti—entering; lokāḥ—all people; tava—unto You; api—also; vaktrāṇi—in the mouths; samṛddha- vegāḥ—with full speed.

Meaning: I see all the people rushing with great speed into Your mouths just like moths fly into a blazing fire to die.

30

लेलिह्यसे ग्रसमानः समन्ता-
ल्लोकान्समग्रान्वदनैर्ज्वलद्भिः।
तेजोभिरापूर्य जगत्समग्रं -
भासस्तवोग्राः प्रतपन्ति विष्णो ॥

lelihyase grasamānaḥ samantāl-
lokānsamagrān-vadanairjvaladbhiḥ
tejobhir āpūrya jagat samagraṁ-
bhāsastavograḥ pratapantiviṣṇo ||

lelihyase—licking; grasamānaḥ—devouring; samantāt—from all directions; lokān—people; samagrān—completely; vadanaiḥ—by the mouth; jvaladbhiḥ—with blazing; tejobhiḥ—by effulgence; āpūrya— covering; jagat—the universe; samagram—all; bhāsaḥ—illuminating; tava—Your; ugrāḥ—terrible; pratapanti—scorching; viṣṇo—O all-pervading Lord.

Meaning: O Vishnu, I see You devouring everyone in Your blazing mouths and filling the entire universe with your immeasurable radiance. The rays emanating from Your body scorch the earth.

31

आख्याहि मे को भवानुग्ररूपो-
नमोऽस्तु ते देववर प्रसीद।
विज्ञातुमिच्छामि भवन्तमाद्यं
न हि प्रजानामि तव प्रवृत्तिम्॥

ākhyāhi me ko bhavān ugra-rūpo
namo›stutedeva-varaprasīda
vijñātumicchāmi bhavantamādyaṁ
na hi prajānāmi tava pravṛttim||

ākhyāhi—please explain; me—unto me; kaḥ—who; bhavān—You; ugra- rūpaḥ—fierce form; namaḥ astu—obeisances; te—unto You; deva-vara— the great one amongst the demigods; prasīda—be gracious; vijñātum—just to know; icchāmi—I wish; bhavantam—You; ādyam—the original; na— never; hi—certainly; prajānāmi—do I know; tava—Your; pravṛttim— mission.

Meaning: Please tell me who You are with so severe a form, O Lord of lords. I bow to You and ask You to have mercy on me. O Primeval One, I seek to understand You as I do not comprehend Your motive.

32

श्रीभगवानुवाच
कालोऽस्मि लोकक्षयकृत्प्रवृद्धो
लोकान्समाहर्तुमिह प्रवृत्तः ।
ऋतेऽपि त्वां न भविष्यन्ति सर्वे
येऽवस्थिताः प्रत्यनीकेषु योधाः।।

śrībhagavān uvāca
kālo 'smi loka-kṣaya-kṛt pravṛddho
lokānsamāhartumiha pravṛttaḥ
ṛte'pi tvāṁ na bhaviṣyanti sarve
ye'vasthitāḥ pratyanīkeṣu yodhāḥ ||

śrībhagavānuvāca—the Personality of Godhead said; kālaḥ—time; asmi—I am; loka—the worlds; kṣaya-kṛt—destroyer; pravṛddhaḥ—to engage; lokān—all people; samāhartum—to destroy; iha—in this world; pravṛttaḥ— to engage; ṛte api—without even; tvām—you; na—never; bhaviṣyanti—will be; sarve—all; ye—who; avasthitāḥ—situated; pratyanīkeṣu—on the opposite side; yodhāḥ—the soldiers.

Meaning: The Glorious Lord said: I am Time, the matured destroyer of the world and have come now to engage all people. Even with your intention, all the soldiers gathered here on both sides will be killed with the exception of you, the Pandavas.

33

तस्मात्त्वमुत्तिष्ठ यशो लभस्व
जित्वा शत्रून्भुङ्क्ष्व राज्यं समृद्धम्।
मयैवैते निहताः पूर्वमेव
निमित्तमात्रं भव सव्यसाचिन्॥

tasmāttvamuttiṣṭha yaśo labhasva
jitvā śatrūnbhuṅkṣva rājyaṁ samṛddham
mayaivaite nihatāḥ pūrvam eva
nimitta-mātraṁ bhava savyasācin||

tasmāt—therefore; tvām—you; uttiṣṭha—get up; yaśaḥ—fame; labhasva —gain; jitvā—conquering; śatrūn—enemies; bhuṅkṣva—enjoy; rājyam —kingdom; samṛddham—flourishing; mayā—by Me; eva—certainly; ete —all these; nihatāḥ—already killed; pūrvam eva—by previous elements; nimitta-mātram—just become the cause; bhava—become; savyasācin—O Savyasācin.

Meaning: Therefore, stand up and fight, O Arjuna. Conquer your foes to enjoy a prosperous kingdom. I have already killed your enemies by My arrangement, and you, O ambidextrous one, can be but an instrument in this battle.

34

द्रोणं च भीष्मं च जयद्रथं च
कर्णं तथान्यान पियोधवीरान्।
मया हतांस्त्वं जहि मा व्यथिष्ठा-
युध्यस्व जेतासिरणे सपत्नान्॥

dronaṁ ca bhīṣmaṁ ca jayadrathaṁ ca
karṇaṁ tathānyāna piyodha-vīrān
mayā hatāṁstvaṁ jahi mā vyathiṣṭhā
yudhyasva jetāsi raṇe sapatnān||

droṇam ca—also Droṇa; bhīṣmam ca—also Bhīṣma; jayadratham ca—also Jayadratha; karṇam—also Karṇa; tathā—also; anyān—others; api—certainly; yodha-vīrān—great warriors; mayā—by Me; hatān—already killed; tvam—you; jahi—become victorious; mā—never; vyathiṣṭhāḥ—be disturbed; yudhyasva—just fight; jetāsi—just conquer; raṇe—in the fight; sapatnān— enemies.

Meaning: All the great heroes like Bhishma, Drona, Karna, and Jayadrath have been slain by Me already. Do not worry. Just fight and you shall conquer your enemies in battle.

35

संजय उवाच

एतच्छ्रुत्वा वचनं केशवस्य
कृतांजलिर्वेपमानः किरीटी।
नमस्कृत्वा भूय एवाह कृष्णं
सगद्गदं भीतभीतः प्रणम्य॥

sañjaya uvāca
etacchrutvā vacanaṁ keśavasya
kṛtāñjalir vepamānaḥ kirītī
namaskṛtvā bhūya evāha kṛṣṇaṁ
sagadgadaṁ bhīta-bhītaḥ praṇamya ||

sañjayaḥ uvāca—Sañjaya said; etat—thus; śrutvā—hearing; vacanam— speech; keśavasya—of Kṛṣṇa; kṛtāñjaliḥ—with folded hands; vepamānaḥ—trembling; kirītī—Arjuna; namaskṛtvā—offering obeisances; bhūyaḥ—again; eva—also; āhakṛṣṇam—said unto Kṛṣṇa; sa-gadgadam—faltering; bhīta-bhītaḥ—fearful; praṇamya—offering obeisances.

Meaning: Sanjaya said to Dhritarashra: O King, after hearing these words from the Supreme Lord, Arjuna trembled in fear and prostrated himself with joined hands at Lord Krishna's feet. In an awed and choked voice, he addressed the Lord humbly as follows:

36

अर्जुन उवाच
स्थाने हृषीकेश तव प्रकीर्त्या
जगत्प्रहृष्यत्यनुरज्यते च।
रक्षांसि भीतानि दिशो द्रवन्ति
सर्वे नमस्यन्ति च सिद्धसङ्घाः।।

arjunauvāca
sthāne hṛṣīkeśa tava prakīrtyā
jagat prahṛṣyatyanurajyate ca
rakṣāṁsi bhītāni diśo dravanti
sarve namasyanti ca siddha-saṅghāḥ||

arjunaḥ uvāca—Arjuna said; sthāne—rightly; hṛṣīkeśa—O master of all senses; tava—Your; prakīrtya—glories; jagat—the entire world; prahṛṣyati—rejoicing; anurajyate—becoming attached; rakṣāṁsi—the demons; bhītāni—out of fear; diśaḥ—directions; dravanti—fleeing; sarve—all; namasyanti—offering respect; ca—also; siddha-saṅghāḥ—the perfect human beings.

Meaning: Arjuna said: O Hrishikesha, Your glory delights the world that becomes joyful on hearing Your name, making everyone attached to You and love You. As the perfected ones offer obeisance to You, the frightened demons fly to every quarter of the world at the very sight of You.

37

कस्माच्च ते न नमेरन्महात्मन्
गरीयसे ब्रह्मणोऽप्यादिकर्त्रे।
अनन्त देवेश जगन्निवास
त्वमक्षरं सदसत्तत्परं यत्॥

kasmāc ca te na nameran mahātman
garīyase brahmaṇo'pyādi-kartre
ananta deveśa jagan-nivāsa
tvamakṣaraṁ sad-asattatparaṁ yat ||

kasmāt—why; ca—also; te—unto You; na—not; nameran—offer proper obeisances; mahātman—O great one; garīyase—You are better than; brahmaṇaḥ—Brahmā; api—although; ādi-kartre—the supreme creator; ananta—unlimited; deveśa-God of the gods; jagat-nivāsa—O refuge of the universe; tvam—You are; akṣaram—imperishable; sat-asat—cause and effect; tat-param—transcendental; yat—because.

Meaning: O Great Self, why should they not offer homage to You who are greater than even Brahma and are the original master of his cause. O Infinite one, You are the Home of the universe, the invincible source, the cause of all causes, and that which is Supreme.

38

त्वमादिदेवः पुरुषः पुराणस्त्व-
मस्य विश्वस्य परं निधानम्।
वेत्तासि वेद्यं च परं च धाम
त्वया ततं विश्वमनन्तरूप॥

tvamādi-devaḥpuruṣaḥ purāṇas tvam-
asyaviśvasyaparaṁnidhānam
vettāsi vedyaṁ ca paraṁ ca dhāma
tvayā tataṁ viśvamananta-rūpa||

tvam—You; ādi-devaḥ—the original Supreme God; puruṣaḥ— personality; purāṇaḥ—old; tvam—You; asya—this; viśvasya—universe; param—transcenddental; nidhānam—refuge; vettā—knower; asi—You are; vedyamca—and the knowable; paramca—and transcendental; dhāma—refuge; tvayā—by You; tatam—pervaded; viśvam—universe; ananta- rūpa—unlimited form.

Meaning: You are the original God, the most ancient Primal being. You are the only sanctuary of this universe as well as its last resting-place. You are the Knower of everything, the Object to be known, and the Supreme Abode. O Infinite Form, You pervade the entire universe.

39

वायुर्यमोऽग्निर्वरुणः शशाङ्कः
प्रजापतिस्त्वं प्रपितामहश्च।
नमो नमस्तेऽस्तु सहस्रकृत्वः
पुनश्च भूयोऽपि नमो नमस्ते॥

vāyur yamo 'gnir varuṇaḥ śaśāṅkaḥ
prajāpatistvaṁ prapitāmahaś ca
namo namaste'stusahasra-kṛtvaḥ
punaśca bhūyo'pi namo namaste ||

vāyuḥ—air; yamaḥ—controller; agniḥ—fire; varuṇaḥ—water; śaśāṅkaḥ — moon; prajāpatiḥ—Brahmā; tvam—You; prapitāmahaḥ—grandfather; ca— also; namaḥ—offering respects; namaḥ te—again I offer my respects unto You; astu—are being; sahasra-kṛtvaḥ—a thousand times; punaḥ ca— and again;

bhūyaḥ—again; api—also; namaḥ—offer my respects; namaḥte—offering my respects unto You.

Meaning: You are Vayu, Yama, Agni, Varuna, and the Moon! You are the Lord of all creatures and the Supreme Controller most ancient. I offer my salutations to You a thousand times, again and again!

40

नमः पुरस्तादथ पृष्ठतस्ते
नमोऽस्तु ते सर्वत एव सर्व।
अनन्तवीर्यामितविक्रमस्त्वं
सर्वं समाप्नोषि ततोऽसि सर्वः॥

namaḥ purastād atha pṛṣṭhatas te
namo'stu te sarvata eva sarva
ananta-vīryāmita-vikramas tvaṁ
sarvaṁ samāpnoṣitato'sisarvaḥ||

namaḥ—offering obeisances; purastāt—from the front; atha—also; pṛṣṭhataḥ—from behind; te—You; namaḥ astu—offer my respects; te—unto You; sarvataḥ—from all sides; eva sarva—because You are everything; ananta-vīrya—unlimited potency; amita-vikramaḥ—unlimited force; tvam—You;

sarvam—everything; samāpnoṣi—cover;tataḥasi—therefore You are; sarvaḥ—everything.

Meaning: I offer my obeisances to You from the front, behind, and from all sides. You are of immeasurable strength and unbounded power. You are all-pervading, and thus You are everything!

41-42

सखेति मत्वा प्रसभं यदुक्तं
हे कृष्ण हे यादव हे सखेति।
अजानता महिमानं तवेदं-
मया प्रमादात्प्रणयेन वापि॥

यच्चावहासार्थमसत्कृतोऽसि
विहारशय्यासनभोजनेषु।
एकोऽथवाप्यच्युत तत्समक्षं
तत्क्षामये त्वामहमप्रमेयम्॥

sakheti matvā prasabhaṁ yaduktaṁ
he kṛṣṇa he yādava he sakheti
ajānatā mahimānaṁ tavedaṁ-
mayā pramādātpraṇayena vāpi ||

yac cāvahāsārtham asatkṛto 'si
vihāra-śayyāsana-bhojaneṣueko
'thavāpyacyutatat-samakṣaṁ
tatkṣāmaye tvāmaham-aprameyam ||

sakhā—friend; iti—thus; matvā—thinking; prasabham—temporary; yat—whatever; uktam—said; he krṣṇa—O Kṛṣṇa; he yādava—O Yādava; he sakhāiti—O my dear friend; ajānatā—without knowing; mahimānam—glories; tava—Your; idam—this; mayā—by me; pramādāt—out of foolishness; pranayena—out of love; vāapi—either; yat—whatever; ca—also; avahāsārtham—for joking; asatkṛtaḥ—dishonor; asi—have been done; vihāra —in relaxation; śayyā—in joking; āsana—in a resting place; bhojaneṣu—or while eating together; ekaḥ—alone; athavā—or; api—others; acyuta—O infallible one; tat-samakṣam—as Your competitor; tat—all those; kṣāmaye— excuse; tvām—You; aham—I; aprameyam— immeasurable.

Meaning: In the past, I have addressed You as a friend, being ignorant of Your glories, my Lord. Please forgive me for words I have uttered in love and intimacy such as 'O Krishna', 'O Yadava', and 'O my friend' that have dishonoured You. I ask You, the Immeasurable, to forgive the irreverence that I have made towards You in jest at play, rest, during meals, and alone in Your company.

43

पितासि लोकस्य चराचरस्य
त्वमस्य पूज्यश्च गुरुर्गरीयान्।
न त्वत्समोऽस्त्यभ्यधिकः
कुतोऽन्योलोकत्रयेऽप्यप्रतिमप्रभाव।।

pitāsilokasya carācarasya
tvamasya pūjyaśca gururgarīyān
na tvat-samo'styabhyadhikaḥ
kuto'nyo loka-traye'pyapratima-prabhāva ||

pitā—father; asi—You are; lokasya—of all the world; cara—moving; acarasya—non moving; tvam—You are; asya—of this; pūjyaḥ—worshipable; ca—also; guruḥ—master; garīyān—glorious; na—never; tvat-samaḥ—equal to You; asti—there is; abhyadhikaḥ—greater; kutaḥ—how is it possible; anyaḥ—other; loka-traye—in three planetary systems; api—also; apratima—immeasurable; prabhāva—power.

Meaning: O father of this world of cosmic manifestation of the moving and the unmoving, You are the spiritual master and no one is equal to You. There is no one greater than You in all the three worlds, O Lord of incomparable power.

44

तस्मात्प्रणम्य प्रणिधाय कायं
प्रसादये त्वामहमीशमीड्यम्।
पितेव पुत्रस्य सखेव सख्युः
प्रियः प्रियायार्हसि देव सोढुम्॥

tasmāt praṇamya praṇidhāya kāyaṁ
prasādaye tvāmahamīśamīḍyam
piteva putrasya sakheva sakhyuḥ
priyaḥ priyāyārhasi deva soḍhum||

tasmāt—therefore; praṇamya—after offering obeisances; praṇidhāya— laying down; kāyam—body; prasādaye—to beg mercy; tvām—unto you; aham—I; īśam—unto the Supreme Lord; īḍyam—who is worshipable; pitā iva—like a father; putrasya—of a son; sakhāiva—like a friend; sakhyuḥ—of a friend; priyaḥ—lover; priyāyāḥ—of the dearmost; arhasi—You should; deva—my Lord; soḍhum—tolerate.

Meaning: Therefore, I lay my body prostrate before You, and ask for Your grace, the Supreme Lord to be worshipped by everyone. Please forgive the wrongs that I have done to You as a father bears with his son, a friend with his friend, and a lover with his beloved, O Lord.

45

अदृष्टपूर्वं हृषितोऽस्मि दृष्ट्वा
भयेन च प्रव्यथितं मनो मे।
तदेव मे दर्शय देवरूपं
प्रसीद देवेश जगन्निवास॥

adṛṣṭa-pūrvaṁ hṛṣito 'smi dṛṣṭvā
bhayena ca pravyathitaṁ mano me
tad-eva me darśaya deva rūpaṁ
prasīda-deveśajagan-nivāsa ||

adṛṣṭa-pūrvam—never seen before; hṛṣitaḥ—gladdened; asmi—I am; dṛṣṭvā—by seeing; bhayena—out of fear; ca—also; pravyathitam —perturbed; manaḥ—mind; me—mine; tat—therefore; eva—certainly; me —unto me; darśaya—show; deva—O Lord; rūpam—the form; prasīda—just be gracious; deveśa—O Lord of lords; jagat-nivāsa—the refuge of the universe.

Meaning: I have had the pleasure of witnessing Your Universal Form, one that was never seen before. I am happy, and yet, my mind is troubled with fear. Therefore, O Lord of the Universe, please be gracious and reveal Your other form to me.

46

किरीटिनं गदिनं चक्रहस्त-
मिच्छामि त्वां द्रष्टुमहं तथैव।
तेनैव रूपेण चतुर्भुजेन
सहस्रबाहो भव विश्वमूर्ते॥

kirīṭinaṁgadinaṁcakra-hastam
icchāmi tvāṁ draṣṭumahaṁ tathaiva
tenaiva rūpeṇa catur-bhujena
sahasra-bāho bhavaviśva-mūrte||

kirīṭinam—with helmet; gadinam—with club; cakra-hastam—disc in hand; icchāmi—I wish; tvām—You; draṣṭum—to see; aham—I; tathāeva—in that position; tenaeva—by that; rūpeṇa—with form; catur-bhujena—four-handed; sahasra-bāho—O thousand-handed one; bhava—just become; viśva-mūrte— O universal form.

Meaning: I wish to see You as before, in Your four-armed form, sceptered, diademed, and holding the discus, club, wheel, conch, and lotus flower. Appear again in that form, O Universal Lord of a thousand arms.

47

श्रीभगवानुवाच
मया प्रसन्नेन तवार्जुनेदं
रूपं परं दर्शितमात्मयोगात्।
तेजोमयं विश्वमनन्तमाद्यं
यन्मे त्वदन्येन न दृष्टपूर्वम्॥

śrībhagavān uvāca
mayā prasannena tavārjunedaṁ
rūpaṁ paraṁ darśitamātma-yogāt
tejomayaṁ viśvam anantam ādyaṁ
yanme tvad-anyena na dṛṣṭa-pūrvam ||

śrībhagavānuvāca—the Supreme Personality of God head said; mayā—by Me; prasannena—happily; tava—unto you; arjuna—O Arjuna; idam— this; rūpam—form; param—transcendental; darśitam—shown; ātma-yogāt—by My internal potency; tejomayam—full of effulgence; viśvam—the entire universe; anantam—unlimited; ādyam—original; yat me—that which is Mine; tvat-anyena—besides you; na dṛṣṭa-pūrvam—no one has previously seen.

Meaning: The Glorious Lord said: O dear Arjuna, I shall happily reveal My Universal Form within this material world by using My internal potency. You will be the first one to witness this unlimited, supreme, and radiant form as no one else has seen it before.

48

न वेदयज्ञाध्ययनैर्न दानैर्न च
क्रियाभिर्न तपोभिरुग्रैः।
एवं रूपः शक्य अहं नृलोके
द्रष्टुं त्वदन्येन कुरुप्रवीर॥

naveda-yajñādhyayanairna dānair naca
kriyābhirna tapobhirugraiḥ
evaṁ rūpaḥ śakya ahaṁ nṛloke
draṣṭuṁtvad-anyenakuru-pravīra||

na—never; veda—Vedic study; yajña—sacrifice; adhyayanaiḥ—studying; na dānaiḥ—by charity; na—never; ca—also; kriyābhiḥ—by pious activities; natapobhiḥ—by serious penances; ugraiḥ—severe; evam— thus; rūpaḥ—form; śakyaḥ—can be seen; aham—I; nṛloke—in this material world; draṣṭum—to see; tvat—you; anyena—by another; kuru-pravīra—O best among the Kuru warriors.

Meaning: This Universal Form of Mine cannot be witnessed by studying the Vedas, performing sacrifices and austerities, or giving charities, O hero of the Kurus.

49

मा ते व्यथा मा च विमूढभावो
दृष्ट्वा रूपं घोरमीदृङ्ममेदम्।
व्यतेपभीः प्रीतमनाः पुनस्त्वं
तदेव मे रूपमिदं प्रपश्य।।

mātevyathāmācavimūḍha-bhāvo
dṛṣṭvā rūpaṁ ghoramīdṛṅmam-edam
vyapetabhīḥ prīta-manāḥ punas tvaṁ
tadeva me rūpamidaṁ prapaśya||

mā—let it not be; te—unto you; vyathā—trouble; mā—let it not be; ca— also; vimūḍha-bhāvaḥ—bewilderment; dṛṣṭvā—by seeing; rūpam—form; ghoram—horrible; īdṛk—like this; mama—My; idam—as it is; vyapetabhīḥ—just become free from all fear; prīta-manāḥ—be pleased in mind; punaḥ—again; tvam—you; tat—that; eva—thus; me—My; rūpam—form; idam—this; prapaśya—just see.

Meaning: Your mind has been troubled and confused seeing this stern and terrible form of Mine. Now, be free of terror and happy to behold My other form that you so desire. Behold!

50

संजय उवाच

इत्यर्जुनं वासुदेवस्तथोक्त्वा
स्वकं रूपं दर्शयामास भूयः।
आश्वासयामास च भीतमेनंभूत्वा
पुनः सौम्यवपुर्महात्मा।।

sañjaya uvāca
ityarjunaṁ vāsudev-astathoktvā
svakaṁ rūpaṁ darśayāmāsa bhūyaḥ
āśvāsayāmāsa ca bhītam enaṁ bhūtvā
punaḥsaumya-vapurmahātmā ||

sañjayaḥ uvāca—Sañjaya said; iti—thus; arjunam—unto Arjuna; vāsudevaḥ—Kṛṣṇa; tathā—that way; uktvā—saying; svakam—His own; rūpam—form; darśayāmāsa—showed; bhūyaḥ—again; āśvāsayāmāsa—also convinced him; ca—also; bhītam—fearful; enam—him; bhūtvāpunaḥ—becoming again; saumya-vapuḥ—beautiful form; mahātmā—the great one.

Meaning: Sanjaya said to Dhritarashtra: The Supreme Lord addressing Arjuna, displayed His real four-armed form and thus comforted the terrified Arjuna.

51

अर्जुन उवाच
दृष्ट्वेदं मानुषं रूपं
तव सौम्यं जनार्दन।
इदानीमस्मि संवृत्तः
सचेताः प्रकृतिं गतः॥

arjunauvāca
dṛṣṭvedaṁ mānuṣaṁ rūpaṁ
tava saumyaṁ janārdana
idānīmasmi saṁvṛttaḥ
sa-cetāḥ prakṛtiṁ gataḥ||

arjunaḥ uvāca—Arjuna said; dṛṣṭvā—seeing; idam—this; mānuṣam— human being; rūpam—form; tava—Your; saumyam—very beautiful; janārdana—O chastiser of the enemies; idānīm—just now; asmi—I am; saṁvṛttaḥ—settled; sa-cetāḥ—in my consciousness; prakṛtim—my own; gataḥ—I am.

Meaning: Arjuna said: Witnessing Your gentle human-like form, O Janardana, my mind is now peaceful, and I am restored to my previous faculties, consciousness, and nature.

52

श्रीभगवानुवाच
सुदुर्दर्शमिदं रूपं
दृष्टवानसि यन्मम।
देवा अप्यस्य रूपस्य
नित्यं दर्शनकाङ्क्षिणः॥

śrī bhagavān uvāca
sudurdarśamidaṁ rūpaṁ
dṛṣṭavānasi yanmama
devā apy asya rūpasya
nityaṁdarśana-kāṅkṣiṇaḥ

śrī bhagavān uvāca—the Supreme Personality of Godhead said; sudur- darśana— very difficult to be seen; idam—this;rūpam—form; dṛṣṭavān asi— as you have seen; yat—which; mama—of Mine; devāḥ—the demigods; api asya—also this; rūpasya—of the form; nityam—eternally; darśana-kāṅkṣiṇaḥ—always aspire to see.

Meaning: The Glorious Lord said: It is very difficult to see Me in this form that you have witnessed, O Arjuna. Even the gods are always eager to behold this form of Mine or have a glimpse of it.

53

नाहं वेदैर्न तपसा
न दानेन न चेज्यया।
शक्य एवं विधो द्रष्टुं
दृष्ट्वानसि मां यथा।।

nāhaṁ vedair na tapasā
na dānena na cejyayā
śakya evaṁ-vidho draṣṭuṁ
dṛṣṭavānasi māṁ yathā ||

na—never; aham—I; vedaiḥ—by study of the Vedas; na—never; tapasā— by serious penances; na—never; dānena—by charity; na—never; ca— also; ijyayā—by worship; śakyaḥ—is it possible; evam-vidhaḥ—like this; draṣṭum—to see; dṛṣṭavān—seeing; asi—you are; mām—Me; yathā—as.

Meaning: Neither through the Vedas, nor through austerity, charity, or sacrifice can this form of Mine be seen like you have seen Me.

54

भक्त्या त्वनन्यया
शक्य अहमेवंविधोऽर्जुन।
ज्ञातुं द्रष्टुं च तत्त्वेन
प्रवेष्टुं च परन्तप॥

bhaktyā tv ananyayā
śakya ahamevaṁ-vidho'rjuna
jñātuṁ draṣṭuṁ ca tattvena
praveṣṭuṁ ca parantapa||

bhaktyā—by devotional service; tu—but; ananyayā—without being mixed with fruitive activities or speculative knowledge; śakyaḥ—possible; aham—I; evam-vidhaḥ—like this; arjuna—O Arjuna; jñātum—to know; draṣṭum—to see; tattvena—in fact; praveṣṭum—and to enter into; ca—also; parantapa—O mighty-armed one.

Meaning: It is only by undivided devotion that I can be truly known, seen, and felt, O Arjuna just as you can see me directly, O terror of foes.

55

मत्कर्मकृन्मत्परमो
मद्भक्तः सङ्गवर्जितः।
निर्वैरः सर्वभूतेषु
यः स मामेति पाण्डव।।

mat-karma-kṛnmat-paramo
mad-bhaktaḥsaṅga-varjitaḥ
nirvairaḥ sarva-bhūteṣu
yaḥ sa māmeti pāṇḍava||

mat-karma-kṛt—engaged in doing My work; mat-paramaḥ—concerning Me, the Supreme; mat-bhaktaḥ—engaged in My devotional service; saṅga-varjitaḥ—freed from the contamination of previous activities and mental speculation; nirvairaḥ—without an enemy; sarva-bhūteṣu—to every living entity; yaḥ—one who; saḥ—he; mām—unto Me; eti—comes; pāṇḍava—O son of Pāṇḍu.

Meaning: O Pandava, the one who is engaged in My pure devotional service, considering Me as the supreme goal, and has cast off all other attachment, who is not the enemy to any living being, he most certainly comes to Me.

ॐ तत्सदिति श्रीमद्भगवद्गीतासूपनिषत्सु ब्रह्मविद्यायांयोगशास्त्रे श्रीकृष्णार्जुनसंवादे विश्वरूपदर्शनयोगो नामैकादशोऽध्यायः।

Thus in the Upanishad of the Glorious Divine Lay, the Science of Brahma, the Ordinance of Yoga, the Discourse between the Glorious Lord Krishna and Arjuna, the Eleventh Chapter titled 'Vishvarupa Darshan Yoga' (Yoga of the Vision of the Absolute Divine Form).

CHAPTER 12

BHAKTI YOGA

(THE YOGA OF DEVOTION)

CHAPTER 12
BHAKTI YOGA
(THE YOGA OF DEVOTION)

In Chapter Twelve of the Bhagavad Gita, Lord Krishna highlights the virtues and the glory of devotion to God. He also explains to Arjuna the various forms of spiritual disciplines and tells him about the attributes of the devotees who engage in such devotional activities to become dear to Him.

Arjuna asks Lord Krishna about who is more perfect- the devotee that worships the Lord's personal form by engaging in devotional service or the Yogi who meditates upon the impersonal Brahman or the Self? Hence, this chapter focuses on the difference between Bhakti Yoga and the sheer devotional love for Lord Krishna, which is considered the highest form of spiritual existence.

Lord Krishna replies that the devotee who has his mind fixed on His personal form is the perfect one. This is because devotional service engages the mind and the senses in the best way possible, and is a simple and natural way for the embodied soul to reach the abode of the Supreme One. On the other hand, the impersonal path is a difficult one because it is unnatural and is not recommended for devotees by Lord Krishna.

The highest stage of devotional service is one where the consciousness is totally fixed on Krishna. A step that is lower than that is the practice of regulated devotional service. Lower than that step is that of Karma-Yoga, where one renounces the fruits of action. The indirect processes that are there to attain the Supreme One comprise the cultivation of knowledge and meditation.

A devotee who is pure, proficient, tolerant, possesses control of the self, is equal in all emotion, is non-envious, is free from false ego, and behaves the same with both friends and enemies, is the one who is most dear to the Lord.

1

अर्जुन उवाच
एवं सततयुक्ता ये
भक्तास्त्वां पर्युपासते।
ये चाप्यक्षरमव्यक्तं
तेषां के योगवित्तमाः।।

arjunauvāca
evaṁsatata-yuktāye
bhaktāstvāṁ paryupāsate
ye cāpy akṣaram avyaktaṁ
teṣāṁ ke yoga-vittamāḥ ||

arjunaḥ uvāca—Arjuna said; evam—thus; satata—always; yuktāḥ—engaged; ye—those; bhaktāḥ—devotees; tvām—unto You; paryupāsate—properly worship; ye—those; ca—also; api—again; akṣaram—beyond the senses; avyaktam—unmanifested; teśām—of them; ke—who; yoga-vittamāḥ—the most perfect.

Meaning: Arjuna said: Who is said to have attained perfection in the instruction of Yoga: the ones who are constantly engaged in Your devotional service, or the ones who worship the unmanifested, indestructible Brahman?

2

श्रीभगवानुवाच
मय्यावेश्य मनो ये मां
नित्ययुक्ता उपासते।
श्रद्धया परयोपेतास्
ते मे युक्ततमा मताः॥

śrībhagavān uvāca
mayyāveśya mano ye māṁ
nitya-yuktā upāsate
śraddhayā parayopetās
te me yuktatamā matāḥ ||

śrī bhagavān uvāca—the Supreme Personality of Godhead said; mayi— unto Me; āveśya—fixing; manaḥ—mind; ye—one who; mām—unto Me; nitya—always; yuktāḥ—engaged; upāsate—worships; śraddhayā—with faith; parayā—transcendental; upetāḥ—engages; te—they; me—Mine; yuktatamāḥ—most perfect; matāḥ—I consider.

Meaning: The Glorious Lord said: The one whose attention is always fixed on My personal form, and he who worships me with the greatest devotion is considered by Me to be the most perfect in Yoga.

3-4

ये त्वक्षरमनिर्देश्यम-
व्यक्तं पर्युपासते।
सर्वत्रगमचिन्त्यं च
कूटस्थमचलं ध्रुवम्।।
सन्नियम्येन्द्रियग्रामं
सर्वत्र समबुद्धयः।
ते प्राप्नुवन्ति मामेव
सर्वभूतहिते रताः।।

ye tv akṣaram anirdeśyam
avyaktaṁparyupāsate
sarvatra-gam acintyaṁ ca
kūṭasthamacalaṁ dhruvam||
sanniya-myendriya-grāmaṁ
sarvatrasama-buddhayaḥ
te prāpnuvanti mām eva
sarva-bhūta-hiteratāḥ||

ye—those; tu—but; akṣaram—which is beyond the perception of the senses; anirdeśyam—indefinite; avyaktam—unmanifested; paryupāsate—completely engages; sarvatra-gam—all-pervading; acintyam—

inconceivable; ca—also; kūṭastham—in the center; acalam—immovable; dhruvam—fixed; sanniyamya —controlling; indriya-grāmam—all the senses; sarvatra—everywhere; sama- buddayaḥ—equally disposed; te— they; prāpnuvanti—achieve; mām—unto Me; eva—certainly; sarva-bhūta- hite—all living entities' welfare; ratāḥ—engaged.

Meaning: But those who worship the unmanifested fully that is indefinite, all-pervading, unimagining, fixed, unchanging, and stable by regulating the various senses and being focussed on the welfare of all creatures, such persons also achieve Me.

5

क्लेशोऽधिकतरस्तेषा-
मव्यक्तासक्तचेतसाम्।
अव्यक्ता हि गतिर्दुःखं
देहवद्भिरवाप्यते॥

kleśo 'dhikataras teṣām-
avyaktāsakta-cetasām
avyaktā hi gatir duḥkhaṁ
dehavadbhiravāpyate ||

kleśaḥ—trouble; adhikataraḥ—more troublesome; teṣām—of them; avyakta—unmanifested; āsakta—being attached; cetasām—of those whose minds; avyaktā—unmanifested; hi—certainly; gatiḥ duḥkham—progress is troublesome; dehavadbhiḥ—of the embodiments; avāpyate—achieve.

Meaning: For the ones whose minds are fixed on the unmanifested, impersonal feature of the Supreme, the trouble is greater for advancement. For the embodied one, it is always difficult to pursue this discipline of unmanifest course.

6-7

ये तु सर्वाणि कर्माणि
मयि सन्नयस्य मत्पराः।
अनन्येनैव योगेन
मां ध्यायन्त उपासते।।
तेषामहं समुद्धर्ता
मृत्युसंसारसागरात्।
भवामि नचिरात्पार्थ
मय्यावेशितचेतसाम्।।

yetusarvāṇi karmāṇi
mayisannyasyamat-parāḥ
ananyenaiva yogena
māṁdhyāyantaupāsate||

teṣām ahaṁ samuddhartā
mṛtyu-saṁsāra-sāgarāt
bhavāmi na cirāt pārtha
mayyāveśita-cetasām||

ye—one who; tu—but; sarvāṇi—everything; karmāṇi—activities; mayi—unto Me; sannyasya—giving up; mat-parāḥ—being attached to Me; ananyena—without division; eva—certainly; yogena—by practice of such bhakti-yoga; mām—unto Me; dhyāyantaḥ—meditating; upāsate—worship; teṣām—of them; aham—I; samuddhartā—deliverer; mṛtyu—that; saṁsāra—material existence; sāgarāt—from the ocean; bhavāmi—become; nacirāt—not a long time; pārtha—O son of Pṛthā; mayi—unto Me; āveśita—fixed; cetasām—of those whose minds are like that.

Meaning: But the one who surrenders all his actions totally to Me, regarding Me as supreme and is devoted without deviation, meditating on Me, O Partha, is delivered quickly from the ocean of birth and death by Me.

8

मय्येव मन आधत्स्व
मयि बुद्धिं निवेशय।
निवसिष्यसि मय्येव
अत ऊर्ध्वं न संशयः॥

mayy eva mana ādhatsva
mayi buddhiṁniveśaya
nivasiṣyasi mayyeva
ata ūrdhvaṁ na saṁśayaḥ||

mayi—unto Me; eva—certainly; manaḥ—mind; ādhatsva—fix; mayi—upon Me; buddhim—intelligence; niveśaya—apply; nivasiṣyasi—you lead; mayi—unto Me; eva—certainly; ataḥ—therefore; ūrdhvam—up; na—never; saṁśayaḥ—doubt.

Meaning: Fix your mind on Me and introduce all your intelligence into Me. Thus, you shall reside in Me always without doubt.

9

अथ चित्तं समाधातुं
न शक्नोषि मयि स्थिरम्।
अभ्यासयोगेन ततो
मामिच्छाप्तुं धनंजय।।

atha cittaṁ samādhātuṁ
na śaknoṣi mayi sthiram
abhyāsa-yogena tato
mām icchāptuṁ dhanañjaya||

atha—if, therefore; cittam—mind; samādhātam—fixing; na—not; śaknoṣi—able; mayi—upon Me; sthiram—fixed; abhyāsa—practice; yogena—by devotional service; tataḥ—therefore; mām—Me; icchā—desire; āptum—to get; dhanañjaya—O Arjuna.

Meaning: O Arjuna, O winner of wealth, if you cannot fix your mind upon Me without deviation, you should follow the regulated principles of bhakti-yoga to develop the desire to attain into Me.

10

अभ्यासेऽप्यसमर्थोऽसि
मत्कर्मपरमो भव।
मदर्थमपि कर्माणि
कुर्वन्सिद्धिमवाप्स्यसि॥

abhyāse'pyasamartho 'si
mat-karma-paramobhava
mad-artham api karmāṇi
kurvansiddhim avāpsyasi||

abhyāse—in the practice of; api—even; asamarthaḥ—unable; asi—you are; mat-karma—My work; paramaḥ—supreme; bhava—you become; mat- artham—for My sake; api—even though; karmāṇi—what; kurvan—performing; siddhim—perfection; avāpsyasi—achieve.

Meaning: If you fail to practice the regulated principles of bhakti-yoga, you must try to work for Me, because by doing so you will reach the perfect stage.

11

अथैतदप्यशक्तोऽसि
कर्तुं मद्योगमाश्रितः।
सर्वकर्मफलत्यागं
ततः कुरु यतात्मवान्॥

athaitadapyaśakto'si
kartuṁmad-yogamāśritaḥ
sarva-karma-phala-tyāgaṁ
tataḥ kuru yatātmavān||

atha—even though; etat—this; api—also; aśaktaḥ—unable; asi—you are; kartum—to perform; mat—unto Me; yogam—devotional service; āśritaḥ—refuge; sarva-karma—all activities; phala—result; tyāgam—for renunciation; tataḥ—therefore; kuru—do; yata-ātmavan—self-situated.

Meaning: If you do not have the strength to work in this consciousness, renounce the fruit of all your actions by being self-controlled and resigning yourself to Me.

12

श्रेयो हि ज्ञानमभ्यासा-
ज्ज्ञानाद्ध्यानं विशिष्यते।
ध्यानात्कर्मफलत्याग-
स्त्यागाच्छान्तिरनन्तरम्॥

śreyo hi jñānam abhyāsāj
jñānāddhyānaṁ viśiṣyate
dhyānāt karma-phala-tyāgas
tyāgācchāntir-anantaram ||

śreyaḥ—better; hi—certainly; jñānam—knowledge; abhyāsāt—by practice; jnānāt—better than knowledge; dhyānam—meditation; viśiṣyate—especially considered; dhyānāt—from meditation; karma-phala-tyāgaḥ—renunciation of the results of fruitive action; tyāgāt—by such renunciation; śāntiḥ—peace; anantaram—thereafter.

Meaning: If you cannot engage in this practice, then cultivate knowledge. Meditation is however, better than knowledge, and better than meditation is renouncing the fruits of action, for by doing so one attains peace of mind.

13-14

अद्वेष्टा सर्वभूतानां
मैत्रः करुण एव च।
निर्ममो निरहङ्कारः
समदुःखसुखः क्षमी॥

संतुष्टः सततं योगी
यतात्मा दृढ़निश्चयः।
मय्यर्पितमनोबुद्धिर्यो
मद्भक्तः स मे प्रियः॥

adveṣṭā sarva-bhūtānāṁ
maitraḥ karuṇa eva ca
nirmamo nirahaṅkāraḥ
sama-duḥkha-sukhaḥ kṣamī||

santuṣṭaḥ satataṁ yogī
yatātmādṛḍha-niścayaḥ
mayy-arpita-mano-buddhiryo
mad-bhaktaḥ sa me priyaḥ||

adveṣṭā—not envious; sarva-bhūtānām—for all living entities; maitraḥ—friendly; karuṇaḥ—kindly; eva—certainly; ca—also; nirmamaḥ—with no sense of proprietorship; nirahaṅkāraḥ—without false ego; sama—equally; duḥkhaḥ—distress; sukhaḥ—happiness; kṣamī—forgiving; santuṣṭaḥ—satisfied; satatam—satisfied; yogī—engaged in devotion; yatā-atmā—endeavoring; dṛdḥaniścayaḥ—with determination; mayi—upon Me; arpita—engaged; manaḥ—mind; buddhiḥ—intelligent; yaḥ—one who; mat-bhaktaḥ—My devotee; saḥ me priyaḥ—he is dear to Me.

Meaning: One who is loving to all living creatures, who is friendly, forgiving, and not envious, who holds nothing as his own, is free from false ego, alike in pleasure and pain, and is engaged in unwavering devotion towards Me, is very dear to Me.

15

श्रीभगवानुवाच
यस्मान्नोद्विजते लोको
लोकान्नोद्विजते च यः।
हर्षामर्षभयोद्वेगैर्मुक्तो
यः स च मे प्रियः॥

śrī-bhagavān uvāca
yasmān nodvijate loko
lokānnodvijate ca yaḥ
harṣāmarṣa-bhayodvegairmukto-
yaḥ sa came priyaḥ||

śrī-bhagavān uvāca: śrī-bhagavān said: yasmān—from whom; na—never; udvijate—agītātes; lokaḥ—persons; lokāt —persons; na—never; advijate—disturbed; ca—also; yaḥ—anyone; harṣa—happiness; amarṣa—distress; bhaya—fearfulness; udvegaiḥ—with anxiety; muktaḥ—freed; yaḥ—who; saḥ—anyone; ca—also; me—My; priyaḥ—very dear.

Meaning: He who is not disturbed by the world or anxiety, who is free from exultation, anger, and fear, is steady in happiness and sadness, is also very dear to Me.

16

अनपेक्षः शुचिर्दक्ष
उदासीनो गतव्यथः।
सर्वारम्भपरित्यागी
यो मद्भक्तः स मे प्रियः॥

anapekṣaḥ śucir dakṣa
udāsīnogata-vyathaḥ
sarvārambha-parityāgī
yomad-bhaktaḥsamepriyaḥ||

anapekṣaḥ—neutral; śuciḥ—pure; dakṣaḥ—expert; udāsīnaḥ—free from care; gata-vyathaḥ—freed from all distress; sarva-ārambha—all endeavors; parityāgī—renouncer; yaḥ—anyone; mat-bhaktaḥ—My devotee; saḥ—he; me—Me; priyaḥ—very dear

Meaning: A devotee of Mine who has renounced every undertaking and is an expert, pure, free from all pains, without care or dependence on anything, and not striving for a result, is very dear to Me.

17

यो न हृष्यति न द्वेष्टि
न शोचति न काङ्क्षति।
शुभाशुभपरित्यागी
भक्तिमान्यः स मे प्रियः॥

yo na hṛṣyati na dveṣṭi
na śocati na kāṅkṣati
śubhāśubha-parityāgī
bhaktimānyaḥ same priyaḥ||

yaḥ—one who: na—never; hṛṣyati—takes pleasure; na—never; dveṣṭi—grieves; na—never; śocati—laments; na—never; kāṅkṣati—desires; śubha—auspicious; aśubha—inauspicious; parityāgī—renouncer; bhaktimān—devotee; yaḥ—one who; saḥ—he is; me—My; priyaḥ—dear.

Meaning: He who is devout, neither laments nor desires, exults or hates, does not take part in pleasure or grief, seeks neither good nor evil, renounces things both auspicious and inauspicious, is very dear to Me.

18-19

समः शत्रौ च मित्रे च
तथा मानापमानयोः।
शीतोष्णसुखदुःखेषु
समः सङ्गविवर्जितः॥

तुल्यनिन्दास्तुतिर्मौनी
सन्तुष्टो येन केनचित्।
अनिकेतः स्थिरमति-
र्भक्तिमान्मे प्रियो नरः॥

samaḥ śatrau ca mitre ca
tathā mānāpamānayoḥ
śītoṣṇa-sukha-duḥkheṣu
samaḥ saṅga-vivarjitaḥ||
tulya-nindā-stutir maunī
santuṣṭoyenakenacit
aniketaḥ sthira-matir
bhaktimānme priyo naraḥ||

samaḥ—equal; śatrau—to the enemy; ca—also; mitre—to friends; ca— also; tatha—so; māna—honour; apamānayoḥ—dishonour; śīta—cold; uṣṇa— heat; sukha—happiness; duḥkheṣu—distress; samaḥ—equiposed; saṅga- vivarjitaḥ— free from all association; tulya—equal; nindā—defamation; stutiḥ—repute; maunī—silent; santuṣṭaḥ—satisfied; yena—somehow; kena—or other; cit—if; aniketaḥ—having no residence; sthira—fixed; matiḥ—determination; bhaktimān—engaged in devotion; me—My; priyaḥ—dear; naraḥ—a man.

Meaning: One who is the same to a friend and foe, equal in honour and dishonour, in heat or cold, happiness and pain, alike in criticism or praise, silent and reticent, satisfied with everything and anything, homeless, firm in principle, and devout, is the one who is very dear to Me.

20

ये तु धर्म्यामृतमिदं
यथोक्तं पर्युपासते।
श्रद्धाना मत्परमा
भक्तास्तेऽतीव मे प्रियाः॥

ye tu dharmāmṛtam idaṁ
yathoktaṁ paryupāsate
śraddadhānā mat-paramā
bhaktāsteīva me priyāḥ||

ye—one who; tu—but; dharmya—generosity; amṛtam—understanding; idam—this; yathā—as; uktam—said; paryupāsate—completely engages; sraddadhānāḥ—with faith; mat-paramāḥ—taking the Supreme Lord as everything; bhaktāḥ—devotees; te—such persons; atīva—very, very; me— Me; priyāḥ—dear.

Meaning: But the devotees who are most dear to Me are the ones who are completely full of faith and devotion. This devotee considers Me as the Supreme One and makes Me his supreme goal, and is very, very dear to Me.

ॐ तत्सदिति श्रीमद्भगवद्गीतासूपनिषत्सु ब्रह्मविद्यायांयोगशास्त्रे श्रीकृष्णार्जुनसंवादे भक्तियोगो नाम द्वादशोऽध्यायः।

Thus in the Upanishad of the Glorious Divine Lay, the Science of Brahma, the Ordinance of Yoga, the Discourse between the Glorious Lord Krishna and Arjuna, the Twelfth Chapter titled 'Bhakti Yoga' (The Yoga of Devotion).

CHAPTER 13

KSETRA-KSETRAJNA-VIBHAGA YOGA

(THE YOGA OF THE DIFFERENCE BETWEEN THE FIELD AND ITS KNOWER)

CHAPTER 13
KSETRA-KSETRAJNA-VIBHAGA YOGA (THE YOGA OF THE DIFFERENCE BETWEEN THE FIELD AND ITS KNOWER)

In Chapter Thirteen of the Bhagavad Gita, Lord Krishna explains the fundamental difference between the physical body that is perishable and the imperishable immortal soul.

Arjuna inquires of Lord Krishna about Nature (prakriti), the Enjoyer (purusa), the Field (ksetra), the Knower of the Field (ksetra-jna), Knowledge (jnana), and the Object of Knowledge (gnaya) and wishes to know the respective terms and their application to our lives.

Lord Krishna reveals to Arjuna that the Field is nothing but the field of activity of the conditioned soul in the body. Both the living entity as well as the Supreme Lord live within it and are therefore known as the Knowers of the Field. Knowledge refers to the understanding of the body and its knowers. Knowledge is perfected thanks to qualities like non-violence, humility, tolerance, self-control, cleanliness, lack of false ego, and being equal and even-minded in the face of both pleasant and unpleasant events in life.

The Object of Knowledge is none other than the Supersoul. Nature is the cause of all material causes and effects and the two Enjoyers are the living entity and the Supersoul. The one who can see that the individual soul and the Supersoul undergo no change at all regardless of the several types of material bodies they enter and exit is the one who possesses the eternal vision. It is only after thorough understanding of the difference between the body and the knower of the body and after comprehension of the process of liberation from material bondage and the birth and death cycles, does one reach the supreme goal to attain the Supreme One.

1-2

अर्जुन उवाच
प्रकृतिं पुरुषं चैव
क्षेत्रं क्षेत्रज्ञमेव च।
एतद्वेदितुमिच्छामि
ज्ञानं ज्ञेयं च केशव॥
श्रीभगवानुवाच
इदं शरीरं कौन्तेय
क्षेत्रमित्यभिधीयते।
एतद्यो वेत्ति तं प्राहुः
क्षेत्रज्ञ इति तद्विदः॥

arjunauvāca
prakṛtiṁ puruṣaṁ caiva
kṣetraṁkṣetrajñameva ca
etadveditumicchāmi
jñānaṁ jñeyaṁ ca keśava
śrī bhagavān uvāca
idaṁ śarīraṁ kaunteya
kṣetramityabhidhīyate
etad yo vetti taṁ prāhuḥ
kṣetrajñaḥit itad-vidaḥ

arjunaḥ uvāca—Arjuna said; prakṛtim—nature; puruṣam—the enjoyer; ca—also; eva—certainly; kṣetram—body; kṣetrajñam—knower of the body; eva—certainly; ca—also; etat—all this; veditum—to understand; icchāmi—I wish; jñānam—knowledge; jñeyam—the object of knowledge; ca—also; keśava—O Kṛṣṇa; śrī bhagavān uvāca—the Personality of Godhead said; idam—this; śarīram—body; kaunteya—O son of Kuntī; kṣetram—the field; iti—thus; abhidhīyate—is called; etat—this; yaḥ—anyone; vetti—knows; tam—him; prāhuḥ—is called; kṣetrajñaḥ—knower of the body; iti—thus; tat-vidaḥ—one who knows.

Meaning: Arjuna said: O dear Krishna, I wish to know about Nature, the Enjoyer, the Field, and the Knower of this Field. The Glorious Lord said: O son of Kunti, this body is called the Field, and the one who knows this body is called the knower of the Field. Thus say the knowers of That.

3

श्रीभगवानुवाच
क्षेत्रज्ञं चापि मां विद्धि
सर्वक्षेत्रेषु भारत।
क्षेत्रक्षेत्रज्ञयोर्ज्ञानं
यत्तज्ज्ञानं मतं मम।।

śrībhagavān uvāca
kṣetrajñaṁ cāpi māṁ viddhi
sarva-kṣetreṣu bhārata
kṣetra-kṣetrajñayorjñānaṁ
yattajjñānaṁ mataṁ mama

śrībhagavānuvāca—the Supreme Personality of Godhead said; kṣetrajñam—the knower; ca—also; api—certainly; mām—Me; viddhi—know; sarva—all; kṣetreṣu—in bodily fields; bhārata—O son of Bharata; kṣetra—field of activities (the body); kṣetrajñayoḥ—the knower of the field; jñānam—knowledge; yat—that which is taught; tat—that; jñānam—knowledge; matam—opinion; mama—that.

Meaning: Know Me also as the Field-knower in all Fields, O Bharata. In me, I hold all that is known as wisdom, what is known as wisdom about the Field, and the knower of the Field.

4-5

तत्क्षेत्रं यच्च यादृक्च
यद्विकारि यतश्च यत्।
स च यो यत्प्रभावश्च
तत्समासेन मे शृणु॥
ऋषिभिर्बहुधा गीतं
छन्दोभिर्विविधैः पृथक्।
ब्रह्मसूत्रपदैश्चैव
हेतुमद्भिर्विनिश्चितैः॥

tatkṣetraṁyaccayādṛkca
yad vikāri yataś ca yat
sa ca yo yatprabhāvaśca
tatsamāsenameśṛṇu||

ṛṣibhir bahudhā gītaṁ
chandobhirvividhaihpṛthak
brahma-sūtra-padaiś caiva
hetumadbhirviniścitaiḥ||

tat—that; kṣetram—field of activities; yat—as ; ca—also; yādṛk—asitis; ca—also;yat—whatis;vikāri—changes;yataḥ—fromwhich;ca—also;yat—one; saḥ—he; ca—also; yaḥ—one; yat—which;

prabhāvaḥ ca— influence also; tat—that; samāsena—in detail; me—from Me; śṛṇu— understand. ṛṣibhiḥ—by the wise sages; bahudhā—in many ways; gītām—described; chandobhiḥ—Vedic hymns; vividhaiḥ—in various; pṛthak—variously; brahma-sūtra—the Vedānta; padaiḥ—aphorism; ca—also; eva—certainly; hetumadbhiḥ—with cause and effect; viniścitaiḥ—ascertain.

Meaning: O Bharata, you have to understand what that Field is, the character of this Field, into what this Field can be modified, and the powers it possesses. Hear from Me in detail about all this. That knowledge about what the Field of activities and the knower of activities is made up of, from where it is produced, who that knower is, and what he is influenced by. This knowledge has been sung by several sages in several verses, as well as recorded in the Vedic writings, particularly in the Vedanta Sutra, and has in it all reasoning regarding cause and effect.

6-7

महाभूतान्यहङ्कारो
बुद्धिरव्यक्तमेव च।
इन्द्रियाणि दशैकं च
पञ्च चेन्द्रियगोचराः॥

इच्छा द्वेषः सुखं दुःखं
सङ्घातश्चेतना धृतिः।
एतत्क्षेत्रं समासेन
सविकारमुदाहृतम्॥

mahā-bhūtāny ahaṅkāro
buddhiravyaktameva ca
indriyāṇi daśaikaṁ ca
pañca cendriya-gocarāḥ||
icchā dveṣaḥ sukhaṁ duḥkhaṁ
saṅghātaścetanādhṛtiḥ etat
kṣetraṁ samāsena
sa-vikāramudāhṛtam||

mahā-bhūtāni—great elements; ahaṅkāraḥ—false ego; buddhiḥ—intelligence; avyaktam—the unmanifested; eva—certainly; ca—also; indriyāṇi—senses ; daśa ekam—eleven; ca—also; pañca—five; ca—also; indriya-gocarāḥ— objects of the senses; icchā—desire; dveṣaḥ—hatred; sukham—happiness; duḥkham—distress; saṅghātaḥ—the aggregate; cetanā—living symptoms; dhṛtiḥ—conviction; etat—all this; kṣetram—field of activities; samāsena—in summary; sa-vikāram—interaction; udāhṛtam—exemplified.

Meaning: The vast elements, false ego, intelligence, the unmanifested, the ten senses, the mind, and the five sense objects in desire, hatred, pleasure, pain, the compound which is the life-receptacle- all these in summary, are considered to be the field of activities and its interactions.

8-12

अमानित्वमदम्भित्वम-
हिंसा क्षान्तिरार्जवम्।
आचार्योपासनं शौचं
स्थैर्यमात्मविनिग्रहः॥
इन्द्रियार्थेषु वैराग्यम-
नहङ्कार एव च।
जन्ममृत्युजराव्याधि-
दुःखदोषानुदर्शनम्॥
असक्तिरनभिष्वङ्गः -
पुत्रदारगृहादिषु।
नित्यं च समचित्तत्वमिष्टा-
निष्टोपपत्तिषु॥
मयि चानन्ययोगेन
भक्तिरव्यभिचारिणी।
विविक्तदेशसेवित्व-
मरतिर्जनसंसदि॥

अध्यात्मज्ञाननित्यत्वं
तत्त्वज्ञानार्थदर्शनम्।
एतज्ज्ञानमिति प्रोक्तम-
ज्ञानं यदतोऽन्यथा।।

amānitvam adambhitvam
ahiṁsā kṣāntirārjavam
ācāryopāsanaṁ śaucaṁ
sthairyamātma-vinigrahaḥ||

indriyārtheṣuvairāgyam
anahaṅkāra eva ca
janma-mṛtyu-jarā-vyādhi-
duḥkha-doṣānudarśanam||

asaktir anabhiṣvaṅgaḥ
putra-dāra-gṛhādiṣu
nityaṁcasama-cittatvamiṣṭ-
āniṣṭopapattiṣu||

mayi cānanya-yogena
bhaktiravyabhicāriṇī
vivikta-deśa-sevitvam-
aratirjana-saṁsadi||

adhyātma-jñāna-nityatvaṁ
tattva-jñānārtha-darśanam
etaj jñānam iti proktam
ajñānaṁyadato'nyathā||

amānitvam—humility; adambhitvam—pridelessness; ahiṁsā— nonviolence; kṣāntiḥ—tolerance; ārjavam—simplicity; ācārya-upāsanam—approaching a bonafide spiritual master; śaucam—cleanliness; sthairyam—steadfastness; ātma-vinigrahaḥ—control; iṇdriya-artheṣu—in the matter of the senses; vairāgyam—renunciation; anahaṅkāraḥ—being without false egoism; eva—certainly; ca—also; janma—birth; mṛtyu—death; jarā—old age; vyādhi—disease; duḥkha—distress; doṣa—fault; anudarśanam— observing; asaktiḥ—without attachment; anabhiṣvaṅgaḥ—without association; putra—son; dāra—wife; gṛha-ādiṣu—home,etc.; nityam —eternal; ca—also; sama-cittatvam—equilibrium; iṣṭa—desirable; aniṣṭaḥ—undesirable; upapattiṣu—having obtained; mayi—unto Me; ca—also; ananya-yogena—by devotional service; bhaktiḥ—devotion; avyabhicāriṇī—constant, unalloyed; vivikta—solitary; deśa—place; sevitvam—aspiring; aratiḥ—without attachment; jana—people in general; saṁsadi—mass;

adhyātma—pertaining to the self; jñāna—knowledge; nityatvam—eternity; tattva-jñāna—knowledge of the truth; artha—the object; darśanam—philosophy; etat—all this; jñānam—knowledge; iti—thus; proktam — declared; ajñānam—ignorance; yat—that which; ataḥ—from this; anyathā— others.

Meaning: Pridelessness, humility, non-violence, forgiveness, tolerance, simplicity, attention to a spiritual master, purity, steadiness, self control, renunciation of the objects of sense gratification, non-egoism, the perception of birth, death, infirmity, disease and old age, non-attachment to children, wife, home and the rest, having a constant mind among desirable and undesirable events, constant and unswerving devotion to Me, living in solitary places and detachment from promiscuous society, realising the importance of self-realisation and true wisdom, and the philosophical quest for the Absolute Truth- all of these I declare thus to be knowledge, and what differs from this is termed as ignorance.

13-14

ज्ञेयं यत्तत्प्रवक्ष्यामि
यज्ज्ञात्वामृतमश्नुते।
अनादिमत्परं ब्रह्म
न सत्तन्नासदुच्यते॥
सर्वतः पाणिपादं तत्सर्वतो-
ऽक्षिशिरोमुखम्।
सर्वतः श्रुतिमल्लोके
सर्वमावृत्य तिष्ठति॥

jñeyaṁ yat tat pravakṣyāmi
yajjñātvā'mṛtamaśnute
anādi mat-paraṁ brahma
na sattannā-saducyate||
sarvataḥ pāṇi-pādaṁ tat sarvato-
'kṣi-śiro-mukham
sarvataḥ śrutimal loke
sarvamāvṛtya tiṣṭhati||

jñeyam—knowable; yat—that; tat—which; pravakṣyāmi—I shall now explain; yat—which; jñātvā—knowing; amṛtam—nectar; aśnute—taste; anādi—beginningless; mat-param—subordinate to

Me; brahma—spirit; na—neither; sat—cause; tat—that; na—nor; asat—effect; ucyate—is called. sarvataḥ—everywhere; pāṇi—hands; pādam—legs; tat—that; sarvataḥ—everywhere; akṣi—eyes; śiraḥ—head; mukham—face; sarvataḥ—everywhere; śrutimat—hearing; loke—in the world; sarvam—everywhere, āvṛtya—covering; tiṣṭhati—exists.

Meaning: I will now declare That which is the Object to be known, the knowledge of which will make you taste immortality. That is the Beginningless Brahman that culminates in Me, and is declared to be the phenomenal, neither the Real nor the Unreal that lies beyond the cause and effect of this material world.

15-16

सर्वेन्द्रियगुणाभासं
सर्वेन्द्रियविवर्जितम्।
असक्तं सर्वभृच्चैव
निर्गुणं गुणभोक्तृ च।।
बहिरन्तश्च भूतानाम-
चरं चरमेव च।
सूक्ष्मत्वात्तदविज्ञयं
दूरस्थं चान्तिके च तत्।।

sarvendriya-guṇābhāsaṁ
sarvendriya-vivarjitam
asaktaṁ sarva-bhṛc caiva
nirguṇaṁguṇa-bhoktṛca||
bahir antaś ca bhūtānām-
acaraṁcaramevaca
sūkṣmatvāt tad avijñeyaṁ
dūrasthaṁ cāntikecatat||

sarve—all; indriya—senses; guṇa—qualities; ābhāsam—original source; sarva—all; indriya—senses; vivarjitam—being without; asaktam—without attachment; sarva-bhṛt—maintainer of everyone; ca—also; eva—certainly; nirguṇam—without material qualities; guṇa-bhoktṛ—simultaneously master of the guṇas; ca—also. bahiḥ—outside; antaḥ—inside; ca—also; bhūtānām—of all living entities; acaram—not moving; caram—moving; eva—also; ca—and; sūkṣmatvāt—on account of being subtle; tat—that; avijñeyam—unknowable; dūrasthaṁ— far away; ca antike—near also; ca—and; tat—that.

Meaning: This Supersoul is the original source of all the sense-attributes, yet entirely distinct from all the senses. The Supersoul is unattached to the senses, and yet supports all of them, maintaining all living creatures, being inside and outside them, moving and unmoving. He transcends all the modes of material nature and yet, is the master of them all.

17

अविभक्तं च भूतेषु
विभक्तमिव च स्थितम्।
भूतभर्तृ च तज्ज्ञेयं
ग्रसिष्णु प्रभविष्णु च॥

avibhaktaṁ ca bhūteṣu
vibhaktamiva ca sthitam
bhūta-bhartṛ ca taj jñeyaṁ
grasiṣṇu prabhaviṣṇu ca||

avibhaktam—without division; ca—also; bhūteṣu—in every living being; vibhaktam—divided; iva—as if; ca—also; sthitam—situated; bhūta-bhartṛ—maintainer of all living entities; ca—also; tat—that; jñeyam—to be understood; grasiṣṇu—devours; prabhaviṣṇu—develops; ca—also.

Meaning: The Supersoul gives the impression that it is divided, but He never is. He is located as one, and is the sustainer of all creatures. It is to be understood that He creates and absorbs all.

18

ज्योतिषामपि तज्ज्योति-
स्तमसः परमुच्यते।
ज्ञानं ज्ञेयं ज्ञानगम्यं
हृदि सर्वस्य विष्ठितम्॥

jyotiṣām api taj jyotis
tamasaḥparamucyate
jñānaṁjñeyaṁjñāna-gamyaṁ
hṛdi sarvasya viṣṭhitam||

jyotiṣām—in all luminous objects; api—also; tat—that; jyotiḥ—source of light; tamasaḥ—of the darkness; param—beyond; ucyate—is said; jñānam—knowledge; jñeyam—to be known; jñāna-gamyam—to be approached by knowledge; hṛdi—in the heart; sarvasya—of everyone; viṣṭhitam—situated.

Meaning: The Supersoul is the Light of lights, illuminating every object, being their source of light. He is said to be beyond darkness and is unmanifested. He is wisdom and knowledge as well as their goal, and is seated in everyone's heart.

19

इति क्षेत्रं तथा ज्ञानं
ज्ञेयं चोक्तं समासतः।
मद्भक्त एतद्विज्ञाय
मद्भावायोपपद्यते॥

iti kṣetraṁ tathā jñānaṁ
jñeyaṁ coktuṁ samāsataḥ
mad-bhakta etad vijñāya
mad-bhāvāyopapadyate||

iti—thus; kṣetram—field of activities (the body); tathā—also; jñānam—knowledge; jñeyam—knowable; ca—also; uktam—describe; samāsataḥ—in summary; mat-bhaktaḥ—My devotee; etat—all this; vijñāya—after understanding; mat-bhāvāya—My nature; upapadyate—attains.

Meaning: Thus the Field of activities, knowledge, and the Object of knowledge have been summarised and described by Me. My devotee that knows all of this thoroughly can easily attain to My nature.

20

प्रकृतिं पुरुषं चैव
विद्ध्यनादी उभावपि।
विकारांश्च गुणांश्चैव
विद्धि प्रकृतिसम्भवान्।।

prakṛtiṁ puruṣaṁ caiva
viddhyanādīubhāvapi
vikārāṁś ca guṇāṁś caiva
viddhiprakṛti-sambhavān||

prakṛtim—material nature; puruṣam—living entities; ca—also; eva— certainly; viddhi—must know; anādī—without beginning; ubhau—both; api—also; vikārān—transformation; ca—also; guṇān—three modes of nature; ca—also; eva—certainly; viddhi—know; prakṛti—material nature; sambhavān—produced of.

Meaning: Know that both material nature and the living beings are to be known as beginningless. Their variations, transformation, and attributes are influenced by Nature.

21

कार्यकरणकर्तृत्वे
हेतुः प्रकृतिरुच्यते।
पुरुषः सुखदुःखानां
भोक्तृत्वे हेतुरुच्यते॥

kārya-kāraṇa-kartṛtve
hetuḥprakṛtirucyate
puruṣaḥsukha-duḥkhānāṁ
bhoktṛtve heturucyate||

kārya—effect; kāraṇa—cause; kartṛtve—in the matter of creation; hetuḥ— instrument; prakṛtiḥ—material nature; ucyate—is said to be; puruṣaḥ—the living entities; sukha—happiness; duḥkhānām—of distresses; bhoktṛtve—in enjoyment; hetuḥ—instrument; ucyate—is said to be.

Meaning: It is said that Nature is the cause of all material activities and effects while the Presiding Being is the source of all the pleasure and pain in this world.

22

पुरुषः प्रकृतिस्थो हि
भुङ्क्ते प्रकृतिजान्गुणान्।
कारणं गुणसंगोऽस्य
सदसद्योनिजन्मसु॥

puruṣaḥ prakṛti-stho hi
bhuṅkteprakṛti-jānguṇān
kāraṇaṁ guṇa-saṅgo'syasad-
asad-yoni-janmasu ||

puruṣaḥ—the living entity; prakṛti-sthaḥ—being situated in the material energy; hi—certainly; bhuṅkte—enjoys; prakṛti-jān—produced by the material nature; guṇān—modes of nature; kāraṇam—cause; guṇa-saṅgaḥ— association with the modes of nature; asya—of the living entity; sat-asat— good and bad; yoni—species of life; janmasu—birth.

Meaning: The living entity, seated in Nature is thus affected in the ways of life by the three Nature-born attributes because of his association with the attributes of that material nature. Thus, he encounters both good and evil amongst several species.

23

उपद्रष्टानुमन्ता च भर्ता
भोक्ता महेश्वरः।
परमात्मेति चाप्युक्तो
देहेऽस्मिन्पुरुषः परः॥

upadraṣṭānumantā ca bhartā
bhoktāmaheśvaraḥ
paramātmeti cāpy ukto
dehe'sminpuruṣaḥparaḥ||

upadraṣṭā—overseer; anumantā—permitter; ca—also; bhartā—master; bhoktā—supreme enjoyer; maheśvaraḥ—the Supreme Lord; paramātmā—Supersoul; iti—also; ca—and; apiuktaḥ—is said; dehe—in this body; asmin—this; puruṣaḥ—enjoyer; paraḥ—transcendental.

Meaning: Yet in this body there exists another Supreme Presiding Body who is none other than the Great Lord who is also called the Supreme Self. He exists as the overseer and the appraiser, and is known as the Supersoul.

24

य एवं वेत्ति पुरुषं
प्रकृतिं च गुणैः सह।
सर्वथा वर्तमानोऽपि
न स भूयोऽभिजायते।।

ya evaṁ vetti puruṣaṁ
prakṛtiṁ ca guṇaiḥ saha
sarvathā vartamāno'pi
nasa bhūyo 'bhijāyate||

yaḥ—anyone; evam—thus; vetti—understands; puruṣam—the living entities; prakṛtim—material nature; ca—and; guṇaiḥ—modes of material nature; saha—with; sarvathā—by all means; vartamānaḥ—situated; api—in spite of; na—never; saḥ—he; bhūyaḥ—again; abhijāyate—takes his birth.

Meaning: The one who understands the philosophy of the Presiding Being and the interacting attributes of Nature is certain of attaining liberation. Regardless of his present position, he is freed from the cycle of birth and death.

25

ध्यानेनात्मनि पश्यन्ति
केचिदात्मानमात्मना।
अन्ये साङ्ख्येन योगेन
कर्मयोगेन चापरे॥

dhyānenātmani paśyanti
kecidātmānamātmanā
anye sāṅkhyena yogena
karma-yogenacāpare ||

dhyānena—by meditation; ātmani—self; paśyanti—see; kecit—one; ātmānam—Supersoul; ātmanā—by the mind; anye—others; sāṅkhyena—by philosophical discussion; yogena—by the yoga system; karma-yogena—by activities without fruitive desire; ca—also; apare—others.

Meaning: Some see the Supersoul, seeing the self by the self in the self through meditation, and some by cultivating knowledge and others by working without the lack of fruitive desire.

26

अन्ये त्वेवमजानन्तः
श्रुत्वान्येभ्य उपासते।
तेऽपि चातितरन्त्येव
मृत्युं श्रुतिपरायणाः॥

anye tv evam ajānantaḥ
śrutvānyebhyaupāsate
te'picātitarantyeva
mṛtyuṁ śruti-parāyaṇāḥ ||

anye—others; tu—but; evam—this; ajānantaḥ—without spiritual knowledge; śrutvā—by hearing; anyebhyaḥ—from others; upāsate—begin to worship; te—they; api—also; ca—and; atitaranti—transcend; eva—certainly; mṛtyum—the path of death; śruti-parāyaṇāḥ—inclined to the process of hearing.

Meaning: There are also those who are not versed with spiritual knowledge and begin to worship the Supreme One from whatever they have heard about Him from others. Even these people, with the highest aim to follow whatever they have heard, cross beyond the cycles of birth and death.

27

यावत्सञ्जायते किञ्चि-
त्सत्त्वं स्थावरजङ्गमम्।
क्षेत्रक्षेत्रज्ञसंयोगा-
त्तद्विद्धि भरतर्षभ।।

yāvatsaṁjāyate kiñcit
sattvaṁsthāvara-jaṅgamam
kṣetra-kṣetrajña-saṁyogāt
tadviddhi bharatarṣabha ||

yāvat—whatever; saṁjāyate—takes place; kiñcit—anything; sattvam—existence; sthāvara—not moving; jaṅgamam—moving; kṣetra—the body; kṣetrajña—knower of the body; saṁyogāt—union between; tat viddhi— you must know it; bharatarṣabha—O chief of the Bhāratas.

Meaning: Whatever thing is born, moving or unmoving, do know it to be derived from the union of the Field of activities and the knower of the Field, O chief of the Bharatas.

28

समं सर्वेषु भूतेषु
तिष्ठन्तं परमेश्वरम्।
विनश्यत्स्वविनश्यन्तं
यः पश्यति स पश्यति॥

samaṁ sarveṣu bhūteṣu
tiṣṭhantaṁ parameśvaram
vinaśyatsv avinaśyantaṁ
yaḥ paśyati sa paśyati||

samam—equally; sarveṣu—in all; bhūteṣu—living entities; tiṣṭhantam—residing; parameśvaram—the Supersoul; vinaśyatsu—in the destructible; avinaśyantam—not destroyed; yaḥ—anyone; paśyati—see; saḥ—he; paśyati—actually sees.

Meaning: One who sees the Supreme Soul seated the same way in the individual soul of all living beings, and who understands that the soul or the Supersoul can never be destroyed is the one who really sees.

29

समं पश्यन्हि सर्वत्र
समवस्थितमीश्वरम्।
न हिनस्त्यात्मनात्मानं
ततो याति परां गतिम्॥

samaṁ paśyan hi sarvatra
samavasthitam-īśvaram
na hinastyātm-anātmānaṁ
tato yāti parāṁ gatim||

samam—equally; paśyan—seeing; hi—certainly; sarvatra—everywhere; samavasthitam—equally situated; īśvaram—Supersoul; na—does not; hinasti—degrade; ātmanā—by the mind; ātmānam—the soul; tataḥ yāti— then reaches; parām—the transcendental; gatim—destination.

Meaning: One who can see the Supersoul equally in every living being everywhere does not degrade the self by the self and reaches the Highest Goal.

30

प्रकृत्यैव च कर्माणि
क्रियमाणानि सर्वशः।
यः पश्यति तथात्मानम-
कर्तारं स पश्यति॥

prakṛtyaiva ca karmāṇi
kriyamāṇānisarvaśaḥ
yaḥ paśyati tathātmānam
akartāraṁsapaśyati||

prakṛtyā—material nature; eva—certainly; ca—also; karmāṇi—activities; kriyamāṇāni—engaged in performing; sarvaśaḥ—in all respects; yaḥ— anyone who; paśyati—sees; tathā—also; ātmānam—himself; akartāram— non-doer; saḥ—he; paśyati—sees perfectly.

Meaning: One who sees that all actions are wholly performed by Nature, and that the self is a non-actor in this performance, actually sees.

31

यदा भूतपृथग्भाव-
मेकस्थमनुपश्यति।
तत एव च विस्तारं
ब्रह्म सम्पद्यते तदा॥

yadābhūta-pṛthag-bhāvam
eka-stham anupaśyati
tata eva ca vistāraṁ
brahma sampadyate tadā ||

yadā—when; bhūta—living entities; pṛthak-bhāvam—separated entities; eka-stham—situated in one; anupaśyati—tries to see through authority; tataḥ eva—thereafter; ca—also; vistāram—expanded; brahma—the Absolute; sampadyate—attains; tadā—at that time.

Meaning: When he sees the varied nature of all creatures rooted in the One, and that the original of expansion is there itself, then he realises Brahma.

32

अनादित्वान्निर्गुणत्वा-
त्परमात्मायमव्ययः।
शरीरस्थोऽपि कौन्तेय
न करोति न लिप्यते॥

anāditvān nirguṇatvāt
paramātmāyam-avyayaḥ
śarīra-stho ‹pi kaunteya
nakarotina lipyate||

anāditvāt—due to eternity; nirguṇatvāt—due to transcendental; param— beyond material nature; ātmā—spirit; ayam—this; avyayaḥ—inexhaustable; śarīra-sthaḥ api—though dwelling in the body; kaunteya—O son of Kuntī; na karoti—never does anything; na lipyate—nor is he entangled.

Meaning: This Imperishable Supreme Self, without any beginning and attributes, neither acts nor is contaminated by actions even though it rests in the body, O son of Kunti.

33

यथा सर्वगतं सौक्ष्म्यादा-
काशं नोपलिप्यते।
सर्वत्रावस्थितो देहे
तथात्मा नोपलिप्यते॥

yathāsarva-gataṁsaukṣmyād-
ākāśaṁ nopalipyate
sarvatrāvasthito dehe
tathātmā nopalipyate||

yathā—as; sarva-gatam—all-pervading; saukṣmyāt—due to being subtle; ākāśam—the sky; na—never; upalipyate—mixes; sarvatra—everywhere; avasthitaḥ—situated; dehe—in the body; tathā—such; ātmā—the self; na—never; upalipyate—mixes.

Meaning: Just as the all-pervading sky does not mix with anything because of its subtle nature, in the same way, the soul located in the Brahman vision does not mix with the body even though it is located in it.

34

यथा प्रकाशयत्येकः
कृत्स्नं लोकमिमं रविः।
क्षेत्रं क्षेत्री तथा कृत्स्नं
प्रकाशयति भारत॥

yathā prakāśayaty ekaḥ
kṛtsnaṁ lokamimaṁ raviḥ
kṣetraṁ kṣetrī tathā kṛtsnaṁ
prakāśayati bhārata||

yathā—as; prakāśayati—illuminates; ekaḥ—one; kṛtsnam—the whole; lokam—universe; imam—this; raviḥ—the sun, kṣetram—this body; kṣetrī —the soul; tathā—similarly; kṛtsnam—all; prakāśayati—illuminates; bhārata—O son of Bharata.

Meaning: As a single sun illuminates the whole world, O son of Bharata, so does the Lord of the Field within the body illuminate the whole body by consciousness.

35

क्षेत्रक्षेत्रज्ञयोरेवमन्तरं
ज्ञानचक्षुषा।
भूतप्रकृतिमोक्षं च ये
विदुर्यान्ति ते परम्॥

kṣetra-kṣetrajñayor evam antaraṁ
jñāna-cakṣuṣā
bhūta-prakṛti-mokṣaṁ ca ye
viduryānti teparam||

kṣetra—body; kṣetrajñayoḥ—of the proprietor of the body; evam—that;
antaram—difference; jñāna-cakṣuṣā—by vision of knowledge; bhūta
—living entity; prakṛti—material nature; mokṣam—liberation; ca—also; ye
—one who; viduḥ—knows; yānti—approaches; te—they; param—Supreme.

Meaning: The ones that possess the eye of reason to see this difference between the Field and the Knower of the Field (the body and the owner of the body) and can comprehend the process of liberation from the bondage of birth, death, and rebirth, they attain to the Supreme Goal.

ॐ तत्सदिति श्रीमद्भगवद्गीतासूपनिषत्सु ब्रह्मविद्यायांयोगशास्त्रे

श्रीकृष्णार्जुनसंवादे क्षेत्रक्षेत्रज्ञविभागयोगो नाम त्रयोदशोऽध्यायः।

Thus in the Upanishad of the Glorious Divine Lay, the Science of Brahma, the Ordinance of Yoga, the Discourse between the Glorious Lord Krishna and Arjuna, the Thirteenth Chapter titled 'Ksetra-Ksetrajna-Vibhaga Yoga' (The Yoga of the Difference Between the Field and its Knower).

CHAPTER 14

GUNATRAYA VIBHAGA YOGA (THE YOGA OF THE DIVISION OF THE THREE GUNAS)

CHAPTER 14

GUNATRAYA VIBHAGA YOGA (THE YOGA OF THE DIVISION OF THE THREE GUNAS)

In Chapter Fourteen of the Bhagavad Gita, Lord Krishna reveals to Arjuna that all embodied souls fall under the control of the three attributes or modes or qualities of material nature. These three modes are that of goodness, passion, and darkness or ignorance and they influence everything that falls in the domain of material existence.

The source of the three modes of material nature in goodness, passion and ignorance is the total material substance. There is intense competition between these three modes as they exert their influence upon the conditioned soul to be the dominant resident force. Observation of these three modes at work make us realise that it is they that are active and not us, and that we are not separate from each other. Once we understand this, the influence of material nature over us declines gradually and we attain the spiritual nature of Lord Krishna.

The mode of goodness illuminates us by freeing us from all the sinful reactions. It brings about a condition of joy and knowledge and the person who dies in the mode of goodness attains the higher planets as a result. However, a person who falls under the influence of the mode of passion experiences the need of unlimited desires for excessive material enjoyment, particularly pleasures of the flesh. To satisfy those passionate desires, he is forced to be a seeker of wealth and this binds him to sinful reactions of which the end result is always misery. A person who is in the mode of passion is never satisfied with what he has or the position he has already attained. Hence, after his death, he takes birth on earth again among the people engaged in fruitive activities.

The third mode, the mode of darkness or ignorance means delusion of the highest kind. This quality gives rise to madness, laziness, indolence, and foolishness. If one dies while in the mode of ignorance, his next birth on earth is in the animal kingdom or in the hellish worlds.
The one who manages to transcend the three modes is known to be steadfast in his behaviour, aloof from the activities of the temporary material body, and equal in behaviour towards both his friends and his enemies. Such transcendental qualities can only evolve in someone who is fully engaged in devotional service. Lord Krishna advises Arjuna to free himself from ignorance and passion to walk on the path of pure goodness till he acquires the ability to transcend them.

1

श्रीभगवानुवाच
परं भूयः प्रवक्ष्यामि
ज्ञानानं मानमुत्तमम्।
यज्ज्ञात्वा मुनयः सर्वे
परां सिद्धिमितो गताः॥

śrībhagavān uvāca
paraṁ bhūyaḥ pravakṣyāmi
jñānānāṁjñāna-muttamam
yaj jñātvā munayaḥ sarve
parāṁ siddhimito gatāḥ||

śrībhagavānuvāca—the Supreme Personality of Godhead said; param—transcendental; bhūyaḥ—again; pravakṣyāmi—I shall speak; jñānānām—of all knowledge; jñānam—knowledge; uttamam—the supreme; yat—which; jñātvā—knowing; munayaḥ—the sages; sarve—all; parām—transcendental; siddhim—perfection; itaḥ—from this world; gatāḥ—attain.

Meaning: The Glorious Lord said: I shall again declare to you the Supreme wisdom, the highest form of all wisdom, knowing which sages have gone on to attain supreme perfection.

2

इदं ज्ञानमुपाश्रित्य
मम साधर्म्यमागताः।
सर्गेऽपि नोपजायन्ते
प्रलये न व्यथन्ति च॥

idaṁjñānamupāśritya
mama sādharmyamāgatāḥ
sarge'pi nopajāyante
pralaye na vyathantica ||

idam—this; jñānam—knowledge; upāśritya—taking shelter of; mama— My; sādharmyam—nature; āgatāḥ—attain; sargeapi—even in the creation; na— never; upajāyante—comes in; pralaye—in the annihilation; na—nor; vyathanti—disturbed; ca—also.

Meaning: By becoming reliant on this wisdom, they attain a comformity to My righteous nature. So established, they are subject to no further evolution at the time of creation nor experience troubles at the time of dissolution.

3

मम योनिर्महद्ब्रह्म
तस्मिन्गर्भं दधाम्यहम्।
सम्भवः सर्वभूतानां
ततो भवति भारत।।

mamayonirmahad-brahma
tasmingarbhaṁ dadhāmyaham
sambhavaḥ sarva-bhūtānāṁ
tato bhavati bhārata||

mama—My; yoniḥ—source of birth; mahat—the total material existence; brahma—supreme; tasmin—in that; garbham—pregnancy; dadhāmi—create; aham—I; sambhavaḥ—possibility; sarva-bhūtānām—of all living entities; tataḥ—thereafter; bhavati—becomes; bhārata—O son of Bharata.

Meaning: The total material substance is the Vast Brahman which is my womb. It is the source of all birth, and I impregnate the Brahman so that the births of all living things can take place, O son of Bharata.

4

सर्वयोनिषु कौन्तेय
मूर्तयः सम्भवन्ति याः।
तासां ब्रह्ममहद्योनिरहं
बीजप्रदः पिता॥

sarva-yoniṣu kaunteya
mūrtayaḥ sambhavanti yāḥ
tāsāṁ brahmamaha-dyonir ahaṁ
bīja-pradaḥ pitā ||

sarva-yoniṣu—in all species of life; kaunteya—O son of Kuntī; mūrtayaḥ
—forms; sambhavanti—as they appear; yāḥ—which; tāsām—all of them; brahma—supreme; mahat yoniḥ—the source of birth in the material substance; aham—Myself; bīja-pradaḥ—seed-giving; pitā—father.

Meaning: All species of life are produced by birth in this material nature, O son of Kunti. The vast Brahman is their womb, and I am their seed-supplying father.

5

सत्त्वं रजस्तम इति
गुणाः प्रकृतिसम्भवाः।
निबध्नन्ति महाबाहो
देहे देहिनमव्ययम्।।

sattvaṁ rajastama iti
guṇāḥprakṛti-sambhavāḥ
nibadhnanti mahā-bāho
dehe dehinam avyayam||

sattvam—mode of goodness; rajaḥ—mode of passion; tamaḥ—mode of ignorance; iti—thus; guṇāḥ—qualities; prakṛti—material nature; sambhavāḥ—produced of; nibadhnanti—does condition; mahā-bāho—O mighty-armed one; dehe—in this body; dehinam—the living entity; avyayam—eternal.

Meaning: The three Nature-born attributes are Goodness, Passion, and Darkness, O mighty-armed. The living entity is encompassed by these attributes or modes when He comes into contact with Nature.

6

तत्र सत्त्वं निर्मलत्वा-
त्प्रकाशकमनामयम्।
सुखसङ्गेन बध्नाति
ज्ञानसङ्गेन चानघ॥

tatra sattvaṁ nirmalatvāt
prakāśakam-anāmayam
sukha-saṅgena badhnāti
jñāna-saṅgenacānagha ||

tatra—thereafter; sattvam—mode of goodness; nirmalatvāt—being purest in the material world; prakāśakam—illuminating; anāmayam—without any sinful reaction; sukha—happiness; saṅgena—association; badhnāti—conditions; jñāna—knowledge; saṅgena—association; ca—also; anagha—O sinless one.

Meaning: Among these , the attribute of goodness is purer than the others because it is free from impurity, illuminating, healthy, and frees one from sinless reactions. The ones situated in this attribute acquire knowledge, but may become used to the concept of happiness, O sinless one.

7

रजो रागात्मकं विद्धि
तृष्णासङ्गसमुद्भवम्।
तन्निबध्नाति कौन्तेय
कर्मसङ्गेन देहिनम्॥

rajorāgātmakaṁ viddhi
tṛṣṇā-saṅga-samudbhavamtan
nibadhnāti kaunteya
karma-saṅgena dehinam||

rajaḥ—mode of passion; rāga-ātmakam—born of desire or lust; viddhi—know; tṛṣṇā—hankering; saṅga—association; samudbhavam—produced of; tat—that; nibadhnāti—is bound; kaunteya—O son of Kuntī; karma-saṅgena—association with fruitive activity; dehinam—of the embodied.

Meaning: The attribute of Passion springs forth from the thirst for unlimited desire and longings, O son of Kunti. It binds the embodied one to attachment to material fruitive activity.

8

तमस्त्वज्ञानजं विद्धि
मोहनं सर्वदेहिनाम्।
प्रमादालस्यनिद्रा-
भिस्तन्निबध्नाति भारत ॥

tamas tv ajñāna-jaṁ viddhi
mohanaṁsarva-dehinām
pramādālasya-nidrā-
bhistannibadhnāti bhārata||

tamaḥ—mode of ignorance; tu—but; ajñāna-jam—products of ignorance; viddhi—knowing; mohanam—delusion; sarva-dehinām—of all embodied beings; pramāda—madness; ālasya—indolence; nidrābhiḥ—sleep; tat—that; nibadhnāti—binds; bhārata—O son of Bharata.

Meaning: But know that Darkness is born out of ignorance and causes all living beings to be deluded. This attribute causes error, sloth, and sleep, which limit the conditioned soul, O son of Bharata.

9

सत्त्वं सुखे सञ्जयति
रजः कर्मणि भारत।
ज्ञानमावृत्य तु तमः
प्रमादे सञ्जयत्युत॥

sattvaṁ sukhe sañjayati
rajaḥ karmaṇi bhārata
jñānam āvṛtya tu tamaḥ
pramāde sañjayatyuta||

sattvam—mode of goodness; sukhe—in happiness; sañjayati—develops; rajaḥ—mode of passion; karmaṇi—fruits of activities; bhārata—O son of Bharata; jñānam—knowledge; āvṛtya—covering; tu—but; tamaḥ—the mode of ignorance; pramāde—in madness; sañjayati—develops; uta—it is said.

Meaning: Goodness gives birth to happiness, and Passion to action, O Bharata. But Darkness, on the other hand, envelops all reason and leads from ignorance to error to madness.

10

रजस्तमश्चाभिभूय
सत्त्वं भवति भारत।
रजः सत्त्वं तमश्चैव
तमः सत्त्वं रजस्तथा ॥

rajas tamaś cābhibhūya
sattvaṁbhavatibhārata
rajaḥ sattvaṁ tamaś caiva
tamaḥ sattvaṁ rajastathā||

rajaḥ—mode of passion; tamaḥ—mode of ignorance; ca—also; abhibhūya—also surpassing; sattvam—mode of goodness; bhavati— becomes prominent; bhārata—O son of Bharata; rajaḥ—mode of passion; sattvam—mode of goodness; tamaḥ—mode of ignorance; ca—also; eva— like that; tamaḥ—mode of ignorance; sattvam—mode of goodness; rajaḥ—mode of passion; tathā—as in this.

Meaning: Sometimes, Goodness is defeated by Passion which becomes dominant, O Bharata. Sometimes, Goodness defeats Passion to become the dominant mode, and at other times the attribute of Darkness defeats both Goodness and Passion. In this way, the three modes always battle for supremacy.

11

सर्वद्वारेषु देहेऽस्मि-
न्प्रकाश उपजायते।
ज्ञानं यदा तदा विद्या-
द्विवृद्धं सत्त्वमित्युत॥

sarva-dvāreṣudehe'smin
prakāśa upajāyate
jñānaṁ yadā tadā vidyād
vivṛddhaṁ sattvamityuta||

sarva-dvāreṣu—all the gates; dehe asmin—in this body; prakāśaḥ —quality of illumination; upajāyate—develops; jñānam—knowledge; yadā —when; tadā—at that time; vidyāt—must know; vivṛddham—increased; sattvam—mode of goodness; iti—thus; uta—said.

Meaning: When the light of knowledge illuminates all the gates of the body, let it be known that the mode of Goodness is experienced, which increases.

12

लोभः प्रवृत्तिरारम्भः
कर्मणामशमः स्पृहा।
रजस्येतानि जायन्ते
विवृद्धे भरतर्षभ॥

lobhaḥ pravṛttir ārambhaḥ
karmaṇāmaśamaḥ spṛhā
rajasy etāni jāyante
vivṛddhe bharatarṣabha||

lobhaḥ—greed; pravṛttiḥ—hankering; ārambhaḥ—endeavor; karmaṇām—of activities; aśamaḥ—uncontrollable; spṛhā—desire; rajasi—in the mode of passion; etāni—all this; jāyante—develop; vivṛddhe—when there is excess; bharatarṣabha—O chief of the descendants of Bharata.

Meaning: With an increase in the attribute of Passion, there is the birth and development of symptoms like greed, attachment, desire, rufflement, and undertaking of actions, O mighty Bharata.

13

अप्रकाशोऽप्रवृत्तिश्च
प्रमादो मोह एव च।
तमस्येतानि जायन्ते
विवृद्धे कुरुनन्दन ॥

aprakāśo 'pravṛttiś ca
pramādomohaevaca
tamasy etāni jāyante
vivṛddhekuru-nandana||

aprakāśaḥ—darkness; apravṛttiḥ—inactivity; ca—and; pramādaḥ—madness; mohaḥ—illusion; eva—certainly; ca—also; tamasi—of the mode of ignorance; etāni—these; jāyante—are manifested; vivṛddhe—is developed; kuru-nandana—O son of Kuru.

Meaning: With an increase in the mode of Darkness, O son of Kuru, gloominess, inertia, illusion, and error are born, O son of the Kurus.

14

यदा सत्त्वे प्रवृद्धे तु
प्रलयं याति देहभृत्।
तदोत्तमविदां लोकान-
मलान्प्रतिपद्यते ॥

yadā sattve pravṛddhe tu
pralayaṁ yāti deha-bhṛt
tadottama-vidāṁ lokān
amalān pratipadyate ||

yadā—when; sattve—mode of goodness; pravṛddhe—in development; tu—but; pralayam—dissolution; yāti—goes; deha-bhṛt—embodied; tadā—at that time; uttama-vidām—of the great sages; lokān—the planets; amalān—pure; pratipadyate—attains.

Meaning: When one experiences the mode of Goodness, he goes into a state of dissolution to attain the pure and higher planets of the knowers of the Most High.

15

रजसि प्रलयं गत्वा
कर्मसङ्गिषु जायते।
तथा प्रलीनस्तमसि
मूढयोनिषु जायते।।

rajasi pralayaṁ gatvā
karma-saṅgiṣujāyate
tathā pralīnas tamasi
mūḍha-yoniṣujāyate||

rajasi—in passion; pralayam—dissolution; gatvā—attaining; karma-saṅgiṣu—in the association of fruitive activities; jāyate—takes birth; tathā—thereafter; pralīnaḥ—being dissolved; tamasi—in ignorance; mūḍha—animal; yoniṣu—species; jāyate—take birth.

Meaning: When one goes into dissolution or dies in Passion, he takes birth again among action-loving people. Likewise, he who dies in the mode of Darkness, takes birth in the wombs of the deluded ones.

16

कर्मणः सुकृतस्याहुः
सात्त्विकं निर्मलं फलम्।
रजसस्तु फलं दुःखम-
ज्ञानं तमसः फलम्॥

karmaṇaḥ sukṛtasyāhuḥ
sāttvikaṁ nirmalaṁ phalam
rajasas tu phalaṁ duḥkham-
ajñānaṁ tamasaḥ phalam||

karmaṇaḥ—of work; sukṛtasya—in the mode of goodness; āhuḥ—said; sāttvikam—mode of goodness; nirmalam—purified; phalam—result; rajasaḥ—of the mode of passion; tu—but; phalam—result; duḥkham—misery; ajñānam—nonsense; tamasaḥ—of the mode of ignorance; phalam—result.

Meaning: The fruit that springs from the action of Goodness is said to be pure and spotless, but the fruit of Passion is pain and the fruit of the actions of Darkness is ignorance and foolishness.

17

सत्त्वात्सञ्जायते ज्ञानं
रजसो लोभ एव च।
प्रमादमोहौ तमसो
भवतोऽज्ञानमेव च।।

sattvātsañjāyate jñānaṁ
rajaso lobha eva ca
pramāda-mohau tamaso
bhavato'jñānameva ca||

sattvāt—from the mode of goodness; sañjāyate—develops; jñānam—knowledge; rajasaḥ—from the mode of passion; lobhaḥ—greed; eva—certainly; ca—also; pramāda—madness; mohau—illusion; tamasaḥ—from the mode of ignorance; bhavataḥ—develops; ajñānam—nonsense; eva—certainly; ca—also.

Meaning: Wisdom which is real knowledge arises from Goodness, greed and grief results from the mode of Passion, and from the attribute of Darkness springs error, confusion, and foolishness.

18

ऊर्ध्वं गच्छन्ति सत्त्वस्था
मध्ये तिष्ठन्ति राजसाः।
जघन्यगुणवृत्तिस्था
अधो गच्छन्ति तामसाः॥

ūrdhvaṁgacchantisattva-sthā
madhye tiṣṭhanti rājasāḥ
jaghanya-guṇa-vṛtti-sthā
adho gacchanti tāmasāḥ||

ūrdhvam—upwards; gacchanti—goes; sattva-sthāḥ—one who is situated in the mode of goodness; madhye—in the middle; tiṣṭhanti—dwell; rājasāḥ—those who are situated in the mode of passion; jaghanya—abominable; guṇa—quality; vṛtti-sthāḥ—occupation; adhaḥ—down; gacchanti—go; tāmasāḥ—persons in the mode of ignorance.

Meaning: Those located in the mode of Goodness eventually go upwards to the higher planets while the Passionate stop midway to live on the earthly planets. The ones seated in the mode of Darkness, the lowest attribute of them all, descend to the hellish worlds.

19

नान्यं गुणेभ्यः कर्तारं
यदा द्रष्टानुपश्यति।
गुणेभ्यश्च परं वेत्ति
मद्भावं सोऽधिगच्छति।।

nānyaṁ guṇebhyaḥ kartāraṁ
yadā draṣṭānupaśyati
guṇebhyaśca paraṁ vetti
mad-bhāvaṁ so'dhigacchati||

na—never; anyam—other than; guṇebhyaḥ—from the qualities; kartāram—the performer; yadā—when; draṣṭā anupaśyati—he who sees properly; guṇebhyaḥ ca—from the modes of nature; param—transcendental; vetti—know; mat-bhāvam—My spiritual nature; saḥ—he; adhigacchati—is promoted.

Meaning: When the discerner sees that nothing exists beyond these modes of nature in all his activities of merely an actor in this life, aware that the Supreme Lord is transcendental to these modes, then he attains to My spiritual nature.

20

गुणानेतानतीत्य त्री-
न्देही देहसमुद्भवान्।
जन्ममृत्युजरादुःखै-
र्विमुक्तोऽमृतमश्नुते॥

guṇānetānatītya trīn-
dehīdeha-samudbhavān
janma-mṛtyu-jarā-duḥkhair-
vimukto'mṛtamaśnute||

guṇān—qualities; etān—all these; atītya—transcending; trīn—three; dehī— body; deha—body; samudbhavān—produced of; janma—birth; mṛtyu—death; jarā—old age; duḥkhaiḥ—distresses; vimuktaḥ—being freed from; amṛtam—nectar; aśnute—enjoys.

Meaning: When the embodied one transcends these three body-born attributes or modes, he is released from the bondage of birth, death, old age and their miseries, and tastes the nectar of immortality even in this lifetime.

21

अर्जुन उवाच
कैर्लिङ्गैस्त्रीन्गुणानेता-
नतीतो भवति प्रभो।
किमाचारः कथं चैतांस्त्री
-गुणानतिवर्तते॥

arjunauvāca
kairliṅgaistrīnguṇānetān
atīto bhavati prabho
kimācāraḥ kathaṁ caitāṁs trīn
guṇān ativartate||

arjunaḥuvāca—Arjuna said; kaiḥ—by which; liṅgaiḥ—symptoms; trīn—three; guṇān—qualities; etān—all this; atītaḥ—transcend; bhavati—become; prabho—my Lord; kim—what; ācāraḥ—behavior; katham—what; ca—also; etān—these; trīn—three; guṇān—qualities; ativartate—transcend.

Meaning: Arjuna said: O Lord, what are the symptoms by which one who transcends these three modes of nature can be identified? What is his conduct? By what means does he transcend these three modes?

22-25

श्रीभगवानुवाच

प्रकाशं च प्रवृत्तिं च
मोहमेव च पाण्डव।
न द्वेष्टि सम्प्रवृत्तानि न
निवृत्तानि काङ्क्षति॥

उदासीनवदासीनो
गुणैर्यो न विचाल्यते।
गुणा वर्तन्त इत्येवं
योऽवतिष्ठति नेङ्गते॥

समदुःखसुखः स्वस्थः
समलोष्टाश्मकाञ्चनः।
तुल्यप्रियाप्रियो धीरस्तुल्य-
निन्दात्मसंस्तुतिः॥

मानापमानयोस्तुल्य-
स्तुल्यो मित्रारिपक्षयोः।
सर्वारम्भपरित्यागी
गुणातीतः स उच्यते॥

śrī-bhagavān uvāca

prakāśaṁca pravṛttiṁca
mohamevaca pāṇḍava
na dveṣṭi sampravṛttāni
na nivṛttāni kāṅkṣati ||

udāsīnavad āsīno
guṇairyo na vicālyate
guṇā vartanta ity evaṁ
yo 'vatiṣṭhati neṅgate ||

sama-duḥkha-sukhaḥ-svasthaḥ
sama-loṣṭāśma-kāñcanaḥ
tulya-priyāpriyo dhīrastulya-
nindātma-saṁstutiḥ ||

mānāpamānayos tulyas
tulyo mitrāri-pakṣayoḥ
sarvārambha-parityāgī
guṇātītaḥsaucyate ||

śrī bhagavān uvāca—the Supreme Personality of Godhead said; prakāśamca—andillumination; pravṛttimca—and attachment; moham—illusion; eva ca—also; pāṇḍava—O son of Pāṇḍu; na dveṣṭi—does not hate; sampravṛttāni—although developed; na nivṛttāni—nor stop development; kāṅkṣati—desires; udāsīnavat—as if neutral; āsīnaḥ— situated; guṇaiḥ—by the qualities; yaḥ—one who; na—never; vicālyate—is agitated; guṇāḥ—the qualities; vartante—is situated; iti evam—knowing thus; yaḥ—one who; avatiṣṭhati—remains; na —never; iṅgate—flickering; sama—equally; duḥkha—in distress; sukhaḥ—in happiness; svasthaḥ— being situated himself; sama—equally; loṣṭa—a lump of earth; aśma— stone;kāñcanaḥ—gold; tulya—equally disposed; priya—dear; apriyaḥ—undesirable; dhīraḥ—steadily; tulya—equally; nindā—in defamation; ātma-saṁstutiḥ—in praise of himself; māna—honour; apamānayoḥ—dishonour; tulyaḥ—equally; tulyaḥ—equally; mitra—friend; ari—enemy; pakṣayoḥ—in party; sarva—all; ārambhaḥ—endeavor; parityāgī— renouncer; guṇa-atītaḥ—transcendental to the material modes of nature; saḥ—he; ucyate—is said to be.

Meaning: The Glorious Lord said: O Pandava, the one who does not dislike illumination and flowing energy, attachment, and delusion when they are present and does not seek them when they are absent, the one who is seated like on a high seat unconcerned, unmoved by the three material attributes and beyond them, remains firm and immovable in the knowledge that the attributes are moving, who is alike in pleasure and pain, self-centred, regards a lump of earth, stone, and a piece of gold the same, is alike with the agreeable and the disagreeable, remains unchanged in honour and dishonour, treats his friends and enemies alike, and has renounced all fruitive undertakings, such a man is said to be above all the three modes of nature.

26

मां च योऽव्यभिचारेण
भक्तियोगेन सेवते।
स गुणान्समतीत्यैता-
न्ब्रह्मभूयाय कल्पते।।

māṁcayo'vyabhicāreṇa
bhakti-yogenasevate
sa guṇān samatītyaitān
brahma-bhūyāya kalpate||

mām—unto Me; ca—also; yaḥ—person; avyabhicāreṇa — without fail; bhakti-yogena — by devotional service; sevate—renders service; saḥ — he; guṇān—all the modes of material nature; samatītya—transcending; etān—all this; brahma-bhūyāya—to be elevated on the Brahman platform; kalpate—is considered.

Meaning: He who serves Me with unswerving devotional service transcends the attributes of material nature immediately and completely, and thus attains the level of Brahman.

27

ब्रह्मणो हि प्रतिष्ठाहम-
मृतस्याव्ययस्य च।
शाश्वतस्य च धर्मस्य
सुखस्यैकान्तिकस्य च॥

brahmaṇohipratiṣṭhāham
amṛtasyāvyayasya ca
śāśvatasya ca dharmasya
sukhasyaikāntikasya ca||

brahmaṇaḥ—of the impersonal brahmajyoti; hi—certainly; pratiṣṭhā— the rest; aham—I am; amṛtasya—of the imperishable; avyayasya—immortal; ca—also; śāśvatasya—of eternal; ca—and; dharmasya—of the constitutional position; sukhasya—happiness; aikāntikasya—ultimate; ca—also.

Meaning: For I am the image of Brahman, the Immortal and Imperishable, of eternal Righteousness, and of the sheer joy of culminating into the Supreme One.

ॐ तत्सदिति श्रीमद्भगवद्गीतासूपनिषत्सु ब्रह्मविद्यायांयोगशास्त्रे

श्रीकृष्णार्जुनसंवादे गुणत्रयविभागयोगो नामचतुर्दशोऽध्यायः॥

Thus in the Upanishad of the Glorious Divine Lay, the Science of Brahma, the Ordinance of Yoga, the Discourse between the Glorious Lord Krishna and Arjuna, the Fourteenth Chapter titled 'Gunatraya Vibhaga Yoga' (The Yoga of the Division of the Three Gunas).

CHAPTER 15

PURUSHOTTAMA YOGA (THE YOGA OF THE SUPREME ONE)

CHAPTER 15

PURUSHOTTAMA YOGA (THE YOGA OF THE SUPREME ONE)

In Chapter Fifteen of the Bhagavad Gita, Lord Krishna tells Arjuna about the glories, virtues, and transcendental characteristics of the omnipotent Lord. Lord Krishna draws a comparison between the fig tree and the 'tree of life'. The tree of the material world is a reflection of the real tree equated with the spiritual world. Just like a fig tree's reflection is located on the water, the material reflection of the spiritual world is located on desire, and no one is aware of its origin or end point. The three modes of material nature provide this tree with nourishment, and the Vedic hymns serve as the leaves of the spiritual tree, while the branches are the objects of the senses.

The one who wants to disengage himself from this tree must use the weapon of non-attachment to cut himself free to seek refuge in the Supreme God. In this material world, everyone perishes. But, in the spiritual world everyone is imperishable. And, beyond everyone is the Supreme One who is Krishna.

Lord Krishna also explains the reason and the value about knowing God and how He can be attained and realised. The one who comes to know about Lord Krishna's identity as the Supreme Imperishable One surrenders to Him totally by engaging in His devotional service. The devotees who instill self-discipline in themselves and diligently follow the path of Yoga realise God in themselves as their Self.

1

श्रीभगवानुवाच
ऊर्ध्वमूलमधः शाख-
मश्वत्थं प्राहुरव्ययम्।
छन्दांसि यस्य पर्णानि
यस्तं वेद स वेदवित्॥

śrībhagavān uvāca
ūrdhva-mūlam adhaḥ-śākham
aśvatthaṁ prāhuravyayam
chandāṁsi yasya parṇāni
yastaṁ veda sa veda-vit||

śrībhagavānuvāca—the Supreme Personality of Godhead said; ūrdhva-mūlam—with roots above; adhaḥ—downwards; śākham—branches; aśvattham—banyan tree; prāhuḥ—said; avyayam—eternal; chandāṁsi— Vedic hymns; yasya—of which; parṇāni—the leaves; yaḥ—anyone; tam— that; veda—knows; saḥ—he; veda-vit—the knower of the Vedas.

Meaning: The Glorious Lord said: The Ashwattha or the fig tree which has its roots upwards and its branches downwards has leaves like the Vedic verses. The one who knows this, is learned in the Vedas.

2

अधश्चोर्ध्वं प्रसृतास्तस्य शाखा
गुणप्रवृद्धा विषयप्रवालाः।
अधश्च मूलान्यनुसन्ततानि
कर्मानुबन्धीनि मनुष्यलोके॥

adhaścordhvaṁ prasṛtāstasya śākhā
guṇa-pravṛddhā viṣaya-pravālāḥ
adhaś ca mūlāny anusantatāni
karmānu-bandhīni manuṣya-loke||

adhaḥ—downward; ca—and; ūrdhvam—upward; prasṛtāḥ—extended; tasya —its; śākhāḥ—branches; guṇa—modes of material nature; pravṛddhāḥ—developed; viṣaya—sense objects; pravālāḥ—twigs; adhaḥ—downward; ca—and; mūlāni—roots; anusantatāni—extended; karma—according to work; anubandhīni—bound; manuṣya-loke—in the world of human society.

Meaning: The branches of the fig tree spread downward and upwards, deriving its nourishment from the three attributes of material nature. The twigs signify the budding sense-objects and the roots that extend downwards follow the fruitive actions into the world of human society.

3-4

न रूपमस्येह तथोपलभ्यते
नान्तो न चादिर्न च सम्प्रतिष्ठा।
अश्वत्थमेनं सुविरूढमूल
मसङ्गशस्त्रेण दृढेन छित्त्वा।।
ततः पदं तत्परिमार्गितव्यं
यस्मिन्गता न निवर्तन्ति भूयः।
तमेव चाद्यं पुरुषं प्रपद्ये
यतः प्रवृत्तिः प्रसृता पुराणी।।

na rūpam asyeha tathopalabhyate
nānto na cādirna ca sampratiṣṭhā
aśvattham enaṁ suvirūḍha-mūlam
asaṅga-śastreṇa dṛḍhena chittvā ||
tataḥ padaṁ tat parimārgitavyaṁ
yasmingatā na nivartanti bhūyaḥ
tameva cādyaṁ puruṣaṁ prapadye
yataḥ pravṛttiḥ prasṛtā purāṇī ||

na—not; rūpam—form; asya—of this tree; iha—in this; tathā—also; upalabhyate—can be perceived; na—never; antaḥ—end; na—never; ca— also; ādiḥ—beginning; na—never; ca—also; sampratiṣṭhā—the foundation; aśvattham—banyan tree; enam—this; suvirūḍha—strongly; mūlam— rooted; asaṅga-śastreṇa—by the weapon of detachment; dṛḍhena—strong; chittvā— by cutting; tataḥ—thereafter; padam—situation; tat—that; parimārgitavyam —has to be searched out; yasmin—where; gatāḥ—going; na—never; nivartanti—comes back; bhūyaḥ—again; tam—to him; eva— certainly; ca—also; ādyam— original; puruṣam—the Personality of Godhead; prapadye—surrender; yataḥ—from whom; pravṛttiḥ— beginning; prasṛtā—extension; purāṇī—very old.

Meaning: The real form of this fig tree is inconceivable in this world. No one can understand its end, origin, or foundation. One can only cut down this firmly-rooted tree with the sharp weapon of non-attachment. By doing so, one must seek that Goal, from where one never returns after reaching, and surrender at the feet of that Supreme Ancient Presiding Being, from whom everything is abiding since the advent of time, and from whom all ancient impulse has bloomed.

5

निर्मानमोहा जितसङ्गदोषा
अध्यात्मनित्या विनिवृत्तकामाः।
द्वन्द्वैर्विमुक्ताः सुखदुःखसञ्ज्ञै-
र्गच्छन्त्यमूढाः पदमव्ययं तत्॥

nirmāna-mohā jita-saṅga-doṣā
adhyātma-nityāvinivṛtta-kāmāḥ
dvandvairvimuktāḥ sukhaduḥkha saṁjñair
gacchantya-mūḍhāḥ padamavyayaṁtat||

nir—without; māna—respect; mohāḥ—illusion; jita—having conquered; saṅga—association; doṣāḥ—faulty; adhyātma—spiritual; nityāḥ—eternity; vinivṛtta—associated; kāmāḥ—lusts; dvandvaiḥ—with duality; vimuktāḥ—liberated; sukha-duḥkha—happiness and distress; saṁjñaiḥ—named; gacchanti—attains; amūḍhāḥ—unbewildered; padam—situation; avyayam—eternal; tat—that.

Meaning: The one who is free from false pride and illusion, has won over the evils of attachment, has understood the eternal and surrendered to the Supreme Lord, is liberated from the duality of pleasure and pain, and goes undeluded to that eternal kingdom.

6

न तद्भासयते सूर्यो न
शशाङ्को न पावकः।
यद्गत्वा न निवर्तन्ते
तद्धाम परमं मम॥

natadbhāsayate sūryo na
śaśāṅko na pāvakaḥ
yad gatvā na nivartante
taddhāma paramaṁ mama||

na—not; tat—that; bhāsayate—illuminates; sūryaḥ—sun; na—nor; śaśāṅkaḥ—the moon; na—nor; pāvakaḥ—fire, electricity; yat—where; gatvā—going; na—never; nivartante—comes back; tat dhāma—that abode; paramam—supreme; mama—My.

Meaning: My abode is not illuminated by the sun, moon, or fire, and reaching it none can return from there to the material world. That supreme world is Mine.

7

मममैवांशो जीवलोके
जीवभूतः सनातनः।
मनः षष्ठानीन्द्रियाणि
प्रकृतिस्थानि कर्षति॥

mamaivāṁśo jīva-loke
jīva-bhūtaḥ sanātanaḥ
manaḥ ṣaṣṭhānīndriyāṇi
prakṛti-sthāni karṣati||

mama—My; eva—certainly; aṁśaḥ—fragmental particles; jīva-loke—world of conditional life; jīva-bhūtaḥ—the conditioned living entities; sanātanaḥ—eternal; manaḥ—mind; ṣaṣṭhāni—six; indriyāṇi—senses; prakṛti— material nature; sthāni—situated; karṣati—struggling hard.

Meaning: My everlasting fragments make up the living beings of this world, manifested as a creature-soul in the world of creature-souls. The living creatures live a conditioned life, and are struggling to come to terms with the six senses, which include the mind as the sixth sense.

8

शरीरं यदवाप्नोति
यच्चाप्युत्क्रामतीश्वरः।
गृहीत्वैतानि संयाति
वायुर्गन्धानिवाशयात्॥

śarīraṁyad avāpnoti
yaccāpyutkrāmatīśvaraḥ
gṛhītvaitāni saṁyāti
vāyurgandhānivāśayāt||

śarīram—body; yat—as much as; avāpnoti—gets; yat—that which; ca—also; api—virtually; utkrāmati—gives up; īśvaraḥ—the lord of the body; gṛhītvā—taking; etāni—all these; saṁyāti—goes away; vāyuḥ—air; gandhān— smell; iva—like; āśayāt—from the flower.

Meaning: When the living entity enters a body from another, he carries his different conceptions of life just as the wind carries fragrances.

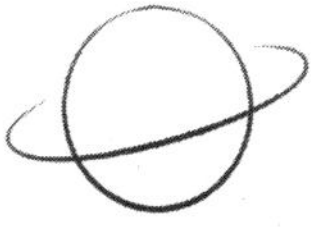

9

श्रोत्रं चक्षुः स्पर्शनं
च रसनं घ्राणमेव च।
अधिष्ठाय मनश्चायं
विषयानुपसेवते॥

śrotraṁcakṣuḥsparśanaṁ
carasanaṁ ghrāṇameva ca
adhiṣṭhāya manaś cāyaṁ
viṣayānupasevate||

śrotram—ears; cakṣuḥ—eyes; sparśanam—touch; ca—also; rasanam—tongue; ghrāṇam—smelling power; eva—also; ca—and; adhiṣṭhāya—being situated; manaḥ—mind; ca—also; ayam—this; viṣayān—sense objects; upasevate—enjoys.

Meaning: When the living entity enters a body, he is seated upon the eye, the touch, the smell, the taste, and also upon the mind to enjoy sense objects.

10

उत्क्रामन्तं स्थितं वापि
भुञ्जानं वा गुणान्वितम्।
विमूढा नानुपश्यन्ति
पश्यन्ति ज्ञानचक्षुषः।।

utkrāmantaṁ sthitaṁ vāpi
bhuñjānaṁvāguṇānvitam
vimūḍhā nānupaśyanti
paśyantijñāna-cakṣuṣaḥ||

utkrāmantam—quitting the body; sthitam—situated in the body; vāpi—either; bhuñjānam—enjoying; vā—or; guṇa-anvitam—under the spell of the modes of material nature; vimūḍhāḥ—foolish persons; na—never; anupaśyanti—can see; paśyanti—one can see; jñāna-cakṣuṣaḥ—one who has the eyes of knowledge.

Meaning: The bewildered cannot see or understand how a living entity can quit a body to enter another. Neither can they comprehend how he enjoys the spell of the attributes of nature. But the one with the eyes of wisdom sees and understands this.

11

यतन्तो योगिनश्चैनं
पश्यन्त्यात्मन्यवस्थितम्।
यतन्तोऽप्यकृतात्मानो
नैनं पश्यन्त्यचेतसः॥

yatanto yoginaś cainaṁ
paśyantyātmanyavasthitam
yatanto 'py kṛtātmāno
nainaṁ paśyantyacetasaḥ||

yatantaḥ—endeavouring; yoginaḥ—transcendentalists; ca—also; enam— this; paśyanti—cansee; ātmani—in the self; avasthitam—situated; yatantaḥ—although endeavouring; api—although; akṛta-ātmānaḥ—without self-realisation; na—does not; enam—this; paśyanti—can see; acetasaḥ—undeveloped mind.

Meaning: The Yogi, who is located in self-realisation can see the living entity residing in the Self. Men who are thoughtless and untrained cannot witness this even if they try to.

12

यदादित्यगतं तेजो
जगद्भासयतेऽखिलम्।
यच्चन्द्रमसि यच्चाग्नौ
तत्तेजो विद्धि मामकम्।।

yadāditya-gataṁtejo
jagadbhāsayate'khilam
yac candramasi yac cāgnau
tattejo viddhi māmakam||

yat—that which; āditya-gatam—in the sunshine; tejaḥ—splendor; jagat—the whole world; bhāsayate—illuminates; akhilam—entirely; yat—that which; candramasi—in the moon; yat—that which; ca—also; agnau—in the fire; tat—that; tejaḥ—splendor; viddhi—understand; māmakam—from Me.

Meaning: The splendour of the sun, which illuminates the entire world by dispelling darkness originates from Me. The splendour of the moon and fire also come from Me.

13

गामाविश्य च भूतानि
धारयाम्यहमोजसा।
पुष्णामि चौषधीः सर्वाः
सोमो भूत्वा रसात्मकः॥

gām āviśya ca bhūtāni
dhārayāmyahamojasā
puṣṇāmi cauṣadhīḥ sarvāḥ
somo bhūtvā rasātmakaḥ||

gām—the planets; āviśya—entering; ca—also; bhūtāni—living entities; dhārayāmi—sustaining; aham—I; ojasā—by My energy; puṣṇāmi—nourishing; ca—and; auṣadhīḥ—all vegetables; sarvāḥ—all; somaḥ—the moon; bhūtvā— becoming; rasa-ātmakaḥ—supplying the juice.

Meaning: Pervading the universe, I enter into each planet, making they stay in orbit with My energy. With My power I nourish all the creatures and provide nourishment to the plants by becoming the watery Soma.

14

अहं वैश्वानरो भूत्वा
प्राणिनां देहमाश्रितः।
प्राणापानसमायुक्तः
पचाम्यन्नं चतुर्विधम्॥

aham̐ vaiśvānaro bhūtvā
prāṇinām̐ dehamāśritaḥ
prāṇāpāna-samāyuktaḥ
pacāmyannam̐ catur-vidham||

aham—I; vaiśvānaraḥ—by My plenary portion as the digesting fire; bhūtvā—becoming; prāṇinām—of all living entities; deham—body; āśritaḥ—situated; prāṇa—outgoing air; apāna—downgoing air; samāyuktaḥ— keep balance; pacāmi—digest; annam—foodstuff; catur-vidham—four kinds of.

Meaning: I am the fire of digestion sheltered in every living body, and I am the air of life both incoming and outgoing to digest the four kinds of food.

15

सर्वस्य चाहं हृदि सन्निविष्टोमत्तः
स्मृतिर्ज्ञानमपोहनं च।
वेदैश्च सर्वैरहमेव वेद्योवेदान्त
कृद्वेदविदेव चाहम्।।

sarvasya cāhaṁ hṛdi sanniviṣṭomattaḥ
smṛtirjñānamapohanaṁca
vedaiś ca sarvair aham eva vedyovedānta
kṛdveda-videvacāham ||

sarvasya—of all living beings; ca—and; aham—I; hṛdi—in the heart; sanniviṣṭaḥ—being situated; mattaḥ—from Me; smṛtiḥ—remembrance; jñānam—knowledge; apohanam ca—and forgetfulness; vedaiḥ—by the Vedas; ca—also; sarvaiḥ—all; aham—I am; eva—certainly; vedyaḥ— knowable; vedānta-kṛt—the compiler of the Vedānta; veda-vit—the knower of the Vedas; eva—certainly; ca—and; aham—I.

Meaning: I am seated in everyone's heart. Memory, reason, and belief originate from Me. I am the object to be known by the study of all the Vedas, and I am also the compiler of Vedanta and the knower of the Vedas.

16

द्वाविमौ पुरुषौ लोके
क्षरश्चाक्षर एव च।
क्षरः सर्वाणि भूतानि
कूटस्थोऽक्षर उच्यते॥

dvāv imau puruṣau loke
kṣaraścākṣara eva ca
kṣaraḥ sarvāṇi bhūtāni
kūṭastho'kṣaraucyate||

dvau—two; imau—in this (world); puruṣau—living entities; loke—in the world; kṣaraḥ—fallible; ca—and; akṣaraḥ—infallible; eva—certainly; ca—and; kṣaraḥ—the fallible; sarvāṇi—all; bhūtāni—living entities; kūṭasthaḥ—in oneness; akṣaraḥ—infallible; ucyate—is said.

Meaning: There are two classes of beings in this world in the Perishable and the Imperishable. The Perishable includes all beings in the material world and all entities in the spiritual world are called the Imperishable.

17

उत्तमः पुरुषस्त्वन्यः
परमात्मेत्युदाहृतः।
यो लोकत्रयमाविश्य
बिभर्त्यव्यय ईश्वरः॥

uttamaḥ puruṣas tv anyaḥ
paramātmetyudāhṛtaḥ
yo loka-trayam āviśya
bibhartyavyaya īśvaraḥ||

uttamaḥ—the best; puruṣaḥ—personality; tu—but; anyaḥ—another; param —the Supreme; ātmā—Self; iti—thus; udāhṛtaḥ—said; yaḥ—one who; loka— of the universe; trayam—the three divisions; āviśya—entering; bibharti— maintaining; avyayaḥ—inexhaustible; īśvaraḥ—the Lord.

Meaning: But the Presiding Being that is Most High and the greatest living personality is called the Supreme Self, who as the Imperishable Lord sustains the three worlds.

18

यस्मात्क्षरमतीतो-
ऽहमक्षरादपि चोत्तमः।
अतोऽस्मि लोके वेदे च
प्रथितः पुरुषोत्तमः॥

yasmāt kṣaram atīto
'ham akṣarādapicottamaḥ
ato 'smi loke vede ca
prathitaḥ puruṣottamaḥ||

yasmāt—because; kṣaram—the fallible; atītaḥ—transcendental; aham—I; akṣarāt—from the infallible; api—better than that; ca—and; uttamaḥ—the best; ataḥ—therefore; asmi—I am; loke—in the world; vede—in the Vedic literature; ca—and; prathitaḥ—celebrated; puruṣottamaḥ—as the Supreme Personality.

Meaning: I am beyond the Perishable and the Imperishable, being transcendental and also because I am the Supreme One. That is why I am celebrated both in the world and in the Vedas as the Highest Presiding Being.

19

यो मामेवमसम्मूढो
जानाति पुरुषोत्तमम्।
स सर्वविद्भजति मां
सर्वभावेन भारत॥

yo māmevamasammūḍho
jānāti puruṣottamam
sa sarva-vid bhajati māṁ
sarva-bhāvenabhārata ||

yaḥ—anyone; mām—unto Me; evam—certainly; asammūḍhaḥ—without adoubt; jānāti—knows; puruṣottamam—the Supreme Personality of Godhead; saḥ—he; sarva-vit—knower of everything; bhajati—renders devotional service; mām—unto Me; sarva-bhāvena—in all respects; bhārata—O son of Bharata.

Meaning: He who is not bewildered, and knows Me as the Supreme Presiding Being without any doubt is to be known as the knower of everything, and is therefore devoted to Me with all his nature, O son of Bharata.

20

इति गुह्यतमं शास्त्र-
मिदमुक्तं मयानघ।
एतद्बुद्ध्वा बुद्धिमान्स्या-
त्कृतकृत्यश्च भारत॥

iti guhyatamaṁ śāstram
idamuktaṁmayānagha
etadbuddhvā buddhimānsyāt
kṛta-kṛtyaś ca bhārata||

iti—thus; guhyatamam—the most confidential; śāstram—revealed scriptures; idam—this; uktam—disclosed; mayā—by Me; anagha—O sinless one; etat—this; buddhvā—understanding; buddhimān—intelligent; syāt—one becomes; kṛta-kṛtyaḥ—the most perfect; ca—and; bhārata—O son of Bharata.

Meaning: Thus the greatest secret of the Vedic scriptures has been declared now by Me, O sinless one. The one who understands this becomes wise and duty-accomplished so that his actions will know perfection, O Bharata.

ॐ तत्सदिति श्रीमद्भगवद्गीतासूपनिषत्सु ब्रह्मविद्यायां योगशास्त्रे श्रीकृष्णार्जुन संवादे पुरुषोत्तमयोगो नाम पंचदशोऽध्यायः।

Thus in the Upanishad of the Glorious Divine Lay, the Science of Brahma, the Ordinance of Yoga, the Discourse between the Glorious Lord Krishna and Arjuna, the Fifteenth Chapter titled 'Purushottam Yoga' (The Yoga of the Supreme One).

CHAPTER 16

DAIVASURA SAMPAD VIBHAGA YOGA

(THE YOGA OF THE DIVISION BETWEEN THE DIVINE AND THE DEMONIC)

CHAPTER 16

DAIVASURA SAMPAD VIBHAGA YOGA (THE YOGA OF THE DIVISION BETWEEN THE DIVINE AND THE DEMONIC)

In Chapter Sixteen of the Bhagavad Gita, Lord Krishna informs Arjuna in detail about the two classes of created creatures, the divine and the demonic. Both of these classes are endowed with different qualities. Divine men like Arjuna are blessed with the divine qualities in which are included gentleness, modesty, charity, self-control, forgiveness, austerity, cleanliness, simplicity, non-violence, tranquility, truthfulness, fearlessness, freedom from anger, cultivation of spiritual knowledge, compassion for all living beings, aversion to fault-finding, freedom from covetousness, and steady determination. The ones in possession of divine qualities and leading regulated lives abiding by the spiritual authority laid down by the holy scriptures are the ones who attain spiritual perfection.

On the other hand, the demonic qualities are made up of anger, pride, envy, arrogance, harshness, ignorance, uncleanliness, impudence, and improper behaviour. These qualities trap people in a vicious cycle of illusion that keeps pushing them back in the cycle of life and death to be born among the demonic species of life. People in possession of demonic qualities live a whimsical life, not following the regulations laid down in the holy scriptures. So, the only thing they inherit after their death is lower births than before and more material bondage. Unable to rid themselves of their demonic qualities, these people are unable to attain the Supreme God, and gradually descend to hell.

Lord Krishna also reveals that the two kinds of action in regulated and unregulated action produce completely different results. The one who disregards the rules laid down by the scriptures fails to attain spiritual perfection, happiness as well as the spiritual destination. But the devotees who are regulated by the scriptures comprehend the difference between duty and what cannot be termed as duty. They are the ones who perform acts beneficial to self-realisation to gradually reach the supreme destination to be united with the Supreme Lord.

1-3

श्रीभगवानुवाच

अभयं सत्त्वसंशुद्धि-
र्ज्ञानयोगव्यवस्थितिः।
दानं दमश्च यज्ञश्च
स्वाध्यायस्तप आर्जवम्॥
अहिंसा सत्यमक्रोध-
स्त्यागः शान्तिरपैशुनम्।
दया भूतेष्वलोलुप्त्वं
मार्दवं ह्रीरचापलम्॥
तेजः क्षमा धृतिः शौचम-
द्रोहोनातिमानिता।
भवन्ति सम्पदं दैवीम-
भिजातस्य भारत॥

śrī bhagavān uvāca
abhayaṁsattva-saṁśuddhir
jñāna-yoga-vyavasthitiḥ
dānaṁ damaś ca yajñaś ca
svādhyāyastapa ārjavam||

ahiṁsā satyam akrodhas
tyāgaḥ śāntirapaiśunam
dayā bhūteṣv aloluptvaṁ
mārdavaṁ-hrīracāpalam ||

tejaḥ kṣamā dhṛtiḥ śaucam
adroho nātimānitā
bhavanti sampadaṁ daivīm-
abhijātasya bhārata ||

śrī bhagavān uvāca—the Supreme Personality of Godhead said; abhayam —fearlessness; sattva-saṁśuddhiḥ—purification of one's existence; jñāna— knowledge; yoga—of linking up; vyavasthitiḥ—the situation; dānam—charity; damaḥca—and controlling the mind; yajñaḥca—and performance of sacrifice; svādhyāyaḥ—study of Vedic literature; tapaḥ—austerity; ārjavam—simplicity; ahiṁsā—non violence; satyam—truthfulness; akrodhaḥ—freedom from anger; tyāgaḥ—renunciation; śāntiḥ—tranquility; apaiśunam —aversion to fault finding; dayā—mercy; bhūteṣu—towards all living entities; aloluptvam—freedom from greed; mārdavam—gentleness; hrīḥ—modesty; acāpalam—determination; tejaḥ—

vigor; kṣamā—forgiveness; dhṛtiḥ—fortitude; śaucam—cleanliness; adrohaḥ—freedom from envy; na—not; atimānitā—expectation of honor; bhavanti—become; sampadam—qualities; daivīm—transcendental; abhijātasya—one who is born of; bhārata—O son of Bharata.

Meaning: The Glorious Lord said: Fearlessness, purity of heart, cultivation of spiritual knowledge and Yoga, charity, self-control, safcrifice, study of the Vedas, austerity and simplicity, non-violence, truthfulness, harmlessness, freedom from anger, renunciation, peacefulness, aversion to faultfinding, compassion to creatures, freedom from covetousness, mildness, modesty, unfickleness, energy, forgiveness, steadfastness, cleanliness, freedom from enmity and pride- these are the transcendental quailities of the one who belongs to men endowed with divine nature, O Bharata.

4

दम्भो दर्पोऽभिमानश्च
क्रोधः पारुष्यमेव च।
अज्ञानं चाभिजातस्य
पार्थ सम्पदमासुरीम्॥

dambho darpo 'bhimānaś ca
krodhaḥ pāruṣyameva ca
ajñānaṁ cābhijātasya
pārtha sampadamāsurīm||

dambhaḥ—pride; darpaḥ—arrogance; abhimānaḥ—conceit; ca—and; krodaḥ—anger; pāruṣyam—harshness; eva—certainly; ca—and; ajñānam—ignorance; ca—and; abhijātasya—one who is born; pārtha—O son of Pṛthā; sampadam—nature; āsurīm—demonic.

Meaning: Pride, arrogance, anger, conceit, wrath, harshness, and ignorance- these qualities belong to the one who is born into demonic nature, O Partha.

5

दैवी सम्पद्विमोक्षाय
निबन्धायासुरी मता।
मा शुचः सम्पदं दैवीम-
भिजातोऽसि पाण्डव॥

daivī sampad vimokṣāya
nibandhāyāsurī matā
mā śucaḥ sampadaṁ daivīm-
abhijāto 'si pāṇḍava||

daivī—transcendental; sampat—nature; vimokṣāya—meant for liberation; nibandhāya—for bondage; āsurī—demonic qualities; matā—it is considered; mā—do not; śucaḥ—worry; sampadam—nature; daivīm— transcendental; abhijātaḥ—born; asi—you are; pāṇḍava—O son of Pandu.

Meaning: The godly endowment is suitable for liberation and the demonic qualities make for bondage. Do not grieve, O Pandava, for you are born with the divine qualities.

6

द्वौ भूतसर्गौ लोके-
ऽस्मिन्दैव आसुर एव च।
दैवो विस्तरशः प्रोक्त
आसुरं पार्थ मे शृणु॥

dvaubhūta-sargauloke-
'smin daiva āsura eva ca
daivo vistaraśaḥ prokta
āsuraṁ pārtha me śṛṇu||

dvau—two; bhūta-sargau—created living beings; loke—in this world; asmin—this; daivaḥ—godly; āsuraḥ—demonic; eva—certainly; ca—and; daivaḥ—divine; vistaraśaḥ—at great length; proktaḥ—said; āsuram— demonic; pārtha—O son of Pṛthā; me—from Me; śṛṇu—just hear.

Meaning: This world contains two streams of creatures: the godly and the demonic. I have already described the divine qualities at length. Now hear from Me of the demonic qualities, O Partha.

7

प्रवृत्तिं च निवृत्तिं च
जना न विदुरासुराः।
न शौचं नापि चाचारो
न सत्यं तेषु विद्यते॥

pravṛttiṁ ca nivṛttiṁ ca
janā na vidurāsurāḥ
na śaucaṁ nāpi cācāro
na satyaṁ teṣu vidyate ||

pravṛttim—proper action; ca—also; nivṛttim—improper action; ca—and; janāḥ—persons; na—never; viduḥ—know; āsurāḥ—in demonic quality; na—never; śaucam—cleanliness; na—nor; api—also; ca—and; ācāraḥ—behavior; na—never; satyam—truth; teṣu—in them; vidyate—there is.

Meaning: The demonic people are not aware what is to be done and what is not to be done. They are unknowing when to follow an impulse and when to control it. Neither purity nor behaviour nor cleanliness is to be found in them.

8

असत्यमप्रतिष्ठं ते
जगदाहुरनीश्वरम्।
अपरस्परसम्भूतं
किमन्यत्कामहैतुकम्॥

asatyam apratiṣṭhaṁ te
jagadāhuranīśvaram
aparaspara-sambhūtaṁ
kimanyatkāma-haitukam||

asatyam—unreal; apratiṣṭham—without foundation; te—they; jagat—the cosmic manifestation; āhuḥ—is said; anīśvaram—with no controller; aparaspara—by mutual lust; sambhūtam—caused; kim anyat—there is no other cause; kāma-haitukam—it is due to lust only.

Meaning: The demonic are of the opinion that this world is without truth and principle, and there is no God controlling it. The demonic evolves from the union of the inferior and superior, and is the source of desire and has no other cause other than lust.

9

एतां दृष्टिमवष्टभ्य
नष्टात्मानोऽल्पबुद्धयः।
प्रभवन्त्युग्रकर्माणः
क्षयाय जगतोऽहिताः॥

etāṁ dṛṣṭim avaṣṭabhya
naṣṭātmāno'lpa-buddhayaḥ
prabhavantyugra-karmāṇaḥ
kṣayāya jagato 'hitāḥ||

etām—thus; dṛṣṭim—vision; avaṣṭabhya—accepting; naṣṭa—lost; ātmānaḥ—self; alpa-buddhayaḥ—less intelligent; prabhavanti—flourish; ugra-karmāṇaḥ—in painful activities; kṣayāya—for destruction; jagataḥ—of the world; ahitāḥ—unbeneficial.

Meaning: The demonic of ruined and lost selves with no intelligence become the performers of fierce and horrible deeds, and prove to be enemies who are intent on destroying the world.

10

काममाश्रित्य दुष्पूरं
दम्भमानमदान्विताः।
मोहाद्गृहीत्वासद्ग्राहा-
न्प्रवर्तन्ते ऽशुचिव्रताः॥

kāmam āśritya duṣpūraṁ
dambha-māna-madānvitāḥ
mohād gṛhītvāsad-grāhān
pravartante'śuci-vratāḥ ||

kāmam—lust; āśritya—takings helter of; duṣpūram—insatiable; dambha—pride; māna—false prestige; mada-anvitāḥ—absorbed in conceit; mohāt—by illusion; gṛhītvā—taking; asat—non permanent; grāhān—things; pravartante—flourish; aśuci—unclean; vratāḥ—avowed.

Meaning: Taking shelter in insatiable desires and lust, the demonic is possessed with pride and false ego, conceit, and arrogance to be totally disillusioned by the doctrines of delusion, and is prone to engaging in action with impious objectives.

11-12

चिन्तामपरिमेयां च
प्रलयान्तामुपाश्रिताः।
कामोपभोगपरमा
एतावदिति निश्चिताः॥
आशापाशशतैर्बद्धाः
कामक्रोधपरायणाः।
ईहन्ते कामभोगार्थम-
न्यायेनार्थसंचयान्॥

cintām aparimeyāṁ ca
pralayāntāmupāśritāḥ
kāmopabhoga-paramā
etāvad iti niścitāḥ ||
āśā-pāśa-śatair baddhāḥ
kāma-krodha-parāyaṇāḥ
īhante kāma-bhogārtham-
anyāyenārtha-sañcayān ||

cintām—fears and anxieties; aparimeyām—unmeasurable; ca—and; pralaya-antām—unto the point of death; upāśritāḥ—having taken shelter of them; kāma-upabhoga—sense gratification; paramāḥ—the highest goal of life; etāvat—thus; iti—in this way; niścitāḥ—ascertain; āśā-pāśa—entanglement in the network of hope; śataiḥ—by hundreds; baddhāḥ—being bound; kāma—lust; krodha—anger; parāyaṇāḥ—always situated in that mentality; īhante—desire; kāma—lust; bhoga—sense enjoyment; artham—for that purpose; anyāyena—illegally; artha—wealth; sañcayān—accumulate.

Meaning: The demonic believe that surrendering the senses to the gratification of lust is the highest aim of their life till their death. Thus there is no end for their worries as desire and anger are their highest impulses. Bound by hundreds and thousands of desires, they seek the accumulation of wealth and power by illegal means to gratify their senses.

13-15

इदमद्य मया लब्धमिमं
प्राप्स्ये मनोरथम्।
इदमस्तीदमपि मे
भविष्यति पुनर्धनम्।।
असौ मया हतः
शत्रुर्हनिष्ये चापरानपि।
ईश्वरोऽहमहं भोगी
सिद्धोऽहं बलवान्सुखी।।
आढ्योऽभिजनवानस्मि
कोऽन्योऽस्ति सदृशो मया।
यक्ष्ये दास्यामि मोदिष्य
इत्यज्ञानविमोहिताः।।

idam adya mayā labdhamimaṁ
prāpsyemanoratham
idam astīdam api me
bhaviṣyati punardhanam ||
asau mayā hataḥ
śatrurhaniṣye cāparānapi
īśvaro ‹ham ahaṁ bhogī
siddho›haṁbalavānsukhī ||

āḍhyo ‹bhijanavān asmi
ko›nyo›stisadṛśomayā
yakṣye dāsyāmi modiṣya
ityajñāna-vimohitāḥ ||

idam—this; adya—today; mayā—by me; labdham —gained; imam—this; prāpsye—I shall gain; manoratham — according to my desires; idam — this; asti—there is; idam—this; api—also; me—mine; bhaviṣyati — will increase in the future; punaḥ—again; dhanam — wealth; asau—that; mayā—by me; hataḥ—has been killed; śatruḥ—enemy; haniṣye—I shall kill; ca—also; aparān —others; api—certainly; īśvaraḥ—the lord; aham—I am; aham—I am; bhogī—the enjoyer;siddhah—perfect;aham—I am; balavān—powerful; sukhī—happy; āḍhyaḥ—wealthy; abhijanavān—surrounded by aristocratic relatives; asmi —I am; kaḥ—who else; anyaḥ—other; asti —there is; sadṛśaḥ—like; mayā—me; yakṣye—I shall sacrifice; dāsyāmi—I shall give in charity; modiṣye — I shall rejoice; iti— thus; ajñāna —ignorance; vimohitāḥ — deluded by.

Meaning: The demonic one thinks, I have gained so much wealth today which is mine, and I will obtain even more wealth that will be mine again. I have killed that enemy of mine, and I will kill others also. I am the lord of everything, I am the enjoyer. I am successful, powerful, and happy. I possess great wealth and I am surrounded by men whom I possess. Who else is my equal? I shall perform sacrifices, give alms, and thus I shall rejoice. This is the way the demonic people deluded by ignorance think and speak.

16

अनेकचित्तविभ्रान्ता
मोहजालसमावृताः।
प्रसक्ताः कामभोगेषु
पतन्ति नरकेऽशुचौ॥

aneka-citta-vibhrāntā
moha-jāla-samāvṛtāḥ
prasaktāḥ kāma-bhogeṣu
patanti narake'śucau ||

aneka—numerous; citta-vibhrāntāḥ—perplexed by anxieties; moha—of illusions; jāla—by a network; samāvṛtāḥ—surrounded; prasaktāḥ— attached; kāma—lust; bhogeṣu—sense gratification; patanti—glides down; narake— into hell; aśucau—unclean.

Meaning: Perplexed by many worrying thoughts, and caught in a network of illusion, the demonic develops a strong attachment to the enjoyment of the senses and descends into an unclean hell.

17

आत्मसम्भाविताः स्तब्धा
धनमानमदान्विताः।
यजन्ते नामयज्ञैस्ते
दम्भेनाविधिपूर्वकम्॥

ātma-sambhāvitāḥ stabdhā
dhana-māna-madānvitāḥ
yajante nāma-yajñais te
dambhenāvidhi-pūrvakam||

ātma-sambhāvitāḥ—self-complacent; stabdhāḥ—impudent; dhana-māna—wealth and false prestige; mada-anvitāḥ—absorbed inpride; yajante—perform sacrifices; nāma—in name only; yajñaiḥ—with such a sacrifice; te—they; dambhena—out of pride; avidhi-pūrvakam—without following any rules and regulations.

Meaning: Indulging in self-glory, stubborn, intoxicated with wealth and false honour, the demonic irregularly perform nominal sacrifices without following the proper rules and regulations.

18

अहङ्कारं बलं दर्पं
कामं क्रोधं च संश्रिताः।
मामात्मपरदेहेषु
प्रद्विषन्तोऽभ्यसूयकाः॥

ahaṁkāraṁ balaṁ darpaṁ
kāmaṁ krodhaṁ ca saṁśritāḥ
mām ātma-para-deheṣu
pradviṣanto'bhyasūyakāḥ||

ahaṁkāram—false ego; balam—strength; darpam—pride; kāmam—lust; krodham—anger; ca—also; saṁśritāḥ—having taken shelter of; mām—Me; ātma—one's own; para-deheṣu—in other bodies; pradviṣantaḥ—blasphemes; abhyasūyakāḥ—envious.

Meaning: Taking shelter in false ego, power, pride, lust, and wrath, the demonic becomes envious of the Supreme Lord who is sheltered in his own body and the body of others, and maliciously tries to harm Him. The demonic continuously blasphemes against the real God.

19

तानहं द्विषतः क्रूरा-
न्संसारेषु नराधमान्।
क्षिपाम्यजस्रमशुभाना-
सुरीष्वेव योनिषु॥

tān ahaṁ dviṣataḥ krūrān
saṁsāreṣunarādhamān
kṣipāmyajasramaśubhān
āsurīṣv eva yoniṣu ||

tān—those; aham—I; dviṣataḥ—envious; krūrān—mischievous; saṁsāreṣu—into the ocean of material existence; narādhamān—the lowest of mankind; kṣipāmi—put; ajasram—innumerable; aśubhān—inauspicious; āsurīṣu—demonic; eva—certainly; yoniṣu—in the wombs.

Meaning: The envious, criel and wretched haters of Me are the lowest among men, and I cast them continuously into demonic wombs of various demonic species of life in the ocean of material existence.

20

आसुरीं योनिमापन्ना
मूढा जन्मनि जन्मनि।
मामप्राप्यैव कौन्तेय
ततो यान्त्यधमां गतिम्॥

āsurīṁ yonim āpannā
mūḍhā janmani janmani
māmaprāpyaiva kaunteya
tato yāntyadhamāṁ gatim||

āsurīm—demonic; yonim—species; āpannāḥ—gaining; mūḍhāḥ—the foolish; janmani janmani—in birth after birth; mām—unto Me; aprāpya—without achieving; eva—certainly; kaunteya—O son of Kuntī; tataḥ—thereafter; yānti—goes; adhamām—condemned; gatim—destination.

Meaning: Finding birth repeatedly in demonic wombs among demonic species of life, such persons can never attain Me, O son of Kunti. Deluded birth after birth, they tread the lowest path to gradually sink into the most miserable existence.

21

त्रिविधं नरकस्येदं
द्वारं नाशनमात्मनः।
कामः क्रोधस्तथा लोभस्त-
स्मादेतत्त्रयं त्यजेत्॥

tri-vidhaṁ narakasyedaṁ
dvāraṁ nāśana-mātmanaḥ
kāmaḥ krodhas tathā lobhas
tasmādetattrayaṁtyajet||

tri-vidham—three kinds of; narakasya—hellish; idam—this; dvāram—gate; nāśanam—destructive; ātmanaḥ—of the self; kāmaḥ—lust; krodhaḥ—anger; tathā—as well as; lobhaḥ—greed; tasmāt—therefore; etat—these; trayam— three; tyajet—must give up.

Meaning: The gates that lead to this hell are three in number- desire, wrath, and greed. Everyone should renounce this triad of evil as it causes the degradation of the soul.

22

एतैर्विमुक्तः कौन्तेय
तमोद्वारैस्त्रिभिर्नरः।
आचरत्यात्मनः श्रेयस्ततो
याति परां गतिम्॥

etairvimuktaḥ kaunteya
tamo-dvāraistribhirnaraḥ
ācaraty ātmanaḥ śreyastato
yāti parāṁ gatim||

etaiḥ—by these; vimuktaḥ—being liberated; kaunteya—O son of Kuntī; tamaḥ-dvāraiḥ—the gates of ignorance; tribhiḥ—three kinds of; naraḥ—a person; ācarati—performs; ātmanaḥ—self; śreyaḥ—benediction; tataḥ—thereafter; yāti—goes; parām—supreme; gatim—destination.

Meaning: The one who has avoided these three gates of hellish Darkness, O son of Kunti, performs action conducive to his own welfare and self-realisation to attain the Supreme Goal.

23

यः शास्त्रविधिमुत्सृज्य
वर्तते कामकारतः।
न स सिद्धिमवाप्नोति
न सुखं न परां गतिम्॥

yaḥ śāstra-vidhim utsṛjya
vartatekāma-kārataḥ
na sa siddhim-avāpnoti
na sukhaṁ na parāṁ gatim||

yaḥ—anyone; śāstra-vidhim—the regulations of the scriptures; utsṛjya—giving up; vartate—remains; kāma-kārataḥ—acting whimsically in lust; na—never; saḥ—he; siddhim—perfection; avāpnoti—achieves; na—never; sukham—happiness; na—never; parām—the supreme; gatim—perfectional stage.

Meaning: The one who rejects the scriptural injunctions of the Ordinance and acts according to his own whims to follow the workings of desire, neither attains perfection, happiness, nor the Supreme Goal.

24

तस्माच्छास्त्रं प्रमाणं
ते कार्याकार्यव्यवस्थितौ।
ज्ञात्वा शास्त्रविधानोक्तं
कर्म कर्तुमिहार्हसि॥

tasmācchāstraṁ pramāṇaṁ
tekāryākārya-vyavasthitau
jñātvā śāstra-vidhānoktaṁ
karma kartumih-ārhasi ||

tasmāt—therefore; śāstram—scriptures; pramāṇam—evidence; te—your; kārya—duty; akārya—forbidden activities; vyavasthitau—in determining; jñātvā—knowing; śāstra—of scripture; vidhāna—regulations; uktam—as declared; karma—work; kartum—to do; iha arhasi—you should do it.

Meaning: The regulations of the scriptures is the authority of what should be done or what should not be done. Knowing what is declared in such rules and regulations of the Ordinance, you should act at this moment to be gradually elevated.

ॐ तत्सदिति श्रीमद्भगवद्गीतासूपनिषत्सु ब्रह्मविद्यायां योगशास्त्रे
श्रीकृष्णार्जुन दैवासुरसम्पद्विभागयोगो नाम षोडशोऽध्यायः।

Thus in the Upanishad of the Glorious Divine Lay, the Science of Brahma, the Ordinance of Yoga, the Discourse between the Glorious Lord Krishna and Arjuna, the Sixteenth Chapter titled 'Daivasura Sampad Vibhaga Yoga (The Yoga of the Division Between the Divine and the Demonic).

CHAPTER 17

SHRADDHATREYA VIBHAGA YOGA (THE YOGA OF THE THREEFOLD DIVISION OF FAITH)

CHAPTER 17

SHRADDHATREYA VIBHAGA YOGA (THE YOGA OF THE THREEFOLD DIVISION OF FAITH)

In the earlier chapter, Lord Krishna explained the three gunas or the three modes of material nature and how they determine human behaviour. In Chapter Seventeen of the Bhagavat Gita, Lord Krishna delves deeper into this subject. He explains to Arjuna about the three divisions of faith or material existence in sattvic, rajasic, and tamasic or goodness, passion, and darkness. Arjuna inquires of Lord Krishna about the mode of nature that governs those who do not follow the regulations laid down by the scriptures but worship according to their own imagination. Lord Krishna replies by explaining in great detail the various kinds of faith, food, charity, susterity, sacrifice, and penance that characterise the three different modes of material nature and existence. He reveals that the character of all living beings is determined by these three divisions of faith. He warns Arjuna not to do things that go against the teachings of the scriptures as the study of the scriptures is of utmost importance. It is only by the devoted and focused study of the scriptures that a percon can love and worship the Supreme One armed with the Yoga of knowledge.

Lord Krishna reveals that the three holy words 'Om Tat Sat' are the symbolic representations of the Supreme Absolute Truth and have been chanted by the holy sages ever since the evolution of mankind. 'Om' is indicative of the Supreme, 'Tat' is used to become unattached from the material entanglements, and 'Sat' indicates that the objective of devotional service is the attainment of the Absolute Truth. Any charity, sacrifice, or penance that is performed without faith in the Supreme One is called 'asat' and is impermanent in nature.

Also, the acts performed by those whose faith rests in passion and ignorance does not yield results that are permanent, being material in nature. In comparison, the acts that are performed in goodness and in accordance with the spiritual injunctions, lead to the purification of the heart and bring about total faith and devotion in Lord Krishna.

1

अर्जुन उवाच
ये शास्त्रविधिमुत्सृज्य
यजन्ते श्रद्धयान्विताः।
तेषां निष्ठा तु का कृष्ण
सत्त्वमाहो रजस्तमः।।

arjunauvāca
ye śāstra-vidhim utsṛjya
yajante śraddhayānvitāḥ
teṣāṁ niṣṭhā tu kā kṛṣṇa
sattvamāho rajastamaḥ ||

arjunaḥ uvāca—Arjuna said; ye—those; śāstra-vidhim—the regulations of scripture; utsṛjya—giving up; yajante—worships; śraddhayā—full faith; anvitāḥ—possessed of; teṣām—of them; niṣṭhā—faith; tu—but; kā—what is that; kṛṣṇa—O Kṛṣṇa; sattvam—in goodness; āho—said; rajaḥ—in passion; tamaḥ—in ignorance.

Meaning: Arjuna said: But, O Keshava, what is the position of those who do not follow the principles of scripture but perform sacrifice with faith as per their own imagination? Is such a person in goodness, passion, or darkness?

2

श्रीभगवानुवाच
त्रिविधा भवति श्रद्धा
देहिनां सा स्वभावजा।
सात्त्विकी राजसी चैव
तामसी चेति तां शृणु॥

śrībhagavān uvāca
tri-vidhā bhavati śraddhā
dehināṁ sā svabhāva-jā
sāttvikī rājasī caiva
tāmasī ceti tāṁ śṛṇu||

śrībhagavānuvāca—the Supreme Personality of Godhead said; tri-vidhā— three kinds; bhavati—become; śraddhā—faith; dehinām—of the embodied; sā—that; sva-bhāva-jā—according to his mode of material nature; sāttvikī—mode of goodness; rājasī—mode of passion; ca—also; eva—certainly; tāmasī—mode of ignorance; ca—and; iti—thus; tām—that; sṛṇu—hear from Me.

Meaning: The Supreme Lord said: According to the threefold nature-born faith of the embodied one, it can be of three kinds- good, passionate, and dark. Now hear of these.

3

सत्त्वानुरूपा सर्वस्य
श्रद्धा भवति भारत।
श्रद्धामयोऽयं पुरुषो
यो यच्छ्रद्धः स एव सः॥

sattvānurūpā sarvasya
śraddhā bhavati bhārata
śraddhā-mayo›yaṁ puruṣo
yoyac-chraddhaḥ sa eva saḥ||

sattva-anurūpā—according to the existence; sarvasya—of everyone; śraddhā—faith; bhavati—becomes; bhārata—O son of Bhārata; śraddhā—faith; mayaḥ—full; ayam—this; puruṣaḥ—living entity; yaḥ—anyone; yat—that; śraddhaḥ—faith; saḥ—that; eva—certainly; saḥ—he.

Meaning: Everyone's faith is in accordance with his own nature, O Bharata. According to one's existence under the various branches of nature, one develops a particular faith. Man's faith constitutes him as he is what his faith is.

4

यजन्ते सात्त्विका देवा-
न्यक्षरक्षांसि राजसाः।
प्रेतान्भूतगणांश्चान्ये
जयन्ते तामसा जनाः॥

yajante sāttvikā devān
yakṣa-rakṣāṁsirājasāḥ
pretānbhūta-gaṇāṁścānye
yajante tāmasā janāḥ||

yajante—worship; sāttvikāḥ—those who are in the mode of goodness; devān—demigods; yakṣa-rakṣāṁsi rājasāḥ—those who are in the mode of passion worship demons; pretān—dead spirits; bhūta-gaṇān—ghosts; ca anye—and others; yajante—worship; tāmasāḥ—in the mode of ignorance; janāḥ—people.

Meaning: The good offer sacrifice to the gods, the passionate to Yakshas and Rakshasas who are the spirits of wealth and greed, and the dark people offer sacrifice to the groups of Preta and Bhutas, the existing and departed creature groups.

5-6

अशास्त्रविहितं घोरं
तप्यन्ते ये तपो जनाः।
दम्भाहङ्कारसंयुक्ताः
कामरागबलान्विताः॥
कर्शयन्तः शरीर-
स्थं भूतग्राममचेतसः।
मां चैवान्तःशरीरस्थं
तान्विद्ध्यासुरनिश्चयान्॥

aśāstra-vihitaṁ ghoraṁ
tapyante ye tapo janāḥ
dambhāhaṅkāra-saṁyuktāḥ
kāma-rāga-balānvitāḥ||
karṣayantaḥ śarīra-
sthaṁ bhūta-grāmamacetasaḥ
māṁ caivāntaḥ śarīra-sthaṁ
tānviddhyāsura-niścayān

aśāstra—not mentioned in the scriptures; vihitam—directed; ghoram—harmful to others; tapyante—undergo penances; ye—those; tapaḥ—austerities; janāḥ—persons; dambha—pride; ahaṅkāra—egotism; saṁyuktāḥ—engaged; kāma—lust; rāga—attachment; bala—force; anvitāḥ—impelled by; karṣayantaḥ—tormenting; śarīra-stham—situated within the body; bhūtagrāmam—combination of material elements; acetasaḥ—by such a misled mentality; mām—to Me; ca—also; eva—certainly; antaḥ—within; śarīra-stham —situated in the body; tān—them; viddhi—understand; āsura—demons; niścayān—certainly.

Meaning: Those who perform severe austerities and penances that are not mentioned in the scriptures, do so out of vanity, ego, lust, attachment, and driven by passion. Those who foolishly torture the organs of the body as well as the Supersoul that is Me, residing in that body, do know them to be of demonic resolves.

7

आहारस्त्वपि सर्वस्य
त्रिविधो भवति प्रियः।
यज्ञस्तपस्तथा दानं
तेषां भेदमिमं शृणु॥

āhārastvapi sarvasya
tri-vidho bhavati priyaḥ
yajñas tapas tathā dānaṁ
teṣāṁ bhedam imaṁ śṛṇu||

āhāraḥ—eating; tu—certainly; api—also; sarvasya—of everyone; trividhaḥ—three kinds; bhavati—there are; priyaḥ—dear; yajñaḥ—sacrifice; tapaḥ—austerity;tathā—also; dānam—charity; teṣām—of them; bhedam—differences; imam—thus; śṛṇu—hear.

Meaning: Food that all of us consume and which is dear to us all is also of three kinds according to the three attributes of material nature. The same is applicable for sacrifice, austerities, and charity. Hear this about their distinction.

8-10

आयुः सत्त्वबलारोग्य-
सुखप्रीतिविवर्धनाः।
रस्याः स्निग्धाः स्थिरा
हृद्या आहाराः सात्त्विकप्रियाः॥

कट्वम्ललवणा-
त्युष्णतीक्ष्णरूक्षविदाहिनः।
आहारा राजसस्येष्टा
दुःखशोकामयप्रदाः॥

यातयामं गतरसं
पूति पर्युषितं च यत्।
उच्छिष्टमपि चामेध्यं
भोजनं तामसप्रियम्॥

āyuḥ sattva-balārogya-
sukha-prīti-vivardhanāḥ
rasyāḥ snigdhāḥ sthirā
hṛdyā āhārāḥ sāttvika-priyāḥ ||

kaṭv-amla-lavaṇāty-
uṣṇa- tīkṣṇa-rūkṣa-vidāhinaḥ
āhārā rājasasyeṣṭā
duḥkha-śokāmaya-pradāḥ ||

yāta-yāmaṁ gata-rasaṁ
pūti paryuṣitaṁ ca yat
ucchiṣṭam api cāmedhyaṁ
bhojanaṁ tāmasa-priyam ||

āyuḥ—duration of life; sattva—existence; bala—strength; ārogya— health; sukha—happiness; prīti—satisfaction; vivardhanāḥ—increasing; rasyāḥ—juicy; snigdhāḥ—fatty; sthirāḥ—enduring; hṛdyāḥ—pleasing to the heart; āhārāḥ—food; sāttvika—goodness; priyāḥ—palatable; kaṭu— bitter; amla— sour; lavaṇa—salty; ati-uṣṇa—very hot; tīkṣṇa—pungent; rūkṣa—dry; vidāhinaḥ—burning; āhārāḥ—food; rājasasya—in the mode of passion; iṣṭāḥ—palatable; duḥkha—distress; śoka—misery; āmaya-pradāḥ—causing disease; yāta-yāmam—food cooked three hours before being eaten; gata- rasam—tasteless; pūti—bad smelling; paryuṣitam— decomposed; ca—also; yat—that which; ucchiṣṭam—remnants of food eaten by others; api—also; ca—and; amedhyam—untouchable; bhojanam— eating; tāmasa—to one in the mode of darkness; priyam—dear.

Meaning: Nourishing food that are in the attribute of goodness lead to longevity of life, goodness, health, strength, happiness and satisfaction. This type of food is sweet, juicy, succulent, nutritious, and palatable. They are dear to the good. Food that is bitter, sour, saline, overhot, pungent, dry, and hot are preferred by people living in the mode of passion. Such food brings about pain, regret, and disease. Food cooked for more than three hours before being eaten, which is stale, devoid of flavour and taste, putrid, uinclean, and spoiled, is agreeable to people living in the mode of Darkness.

11

अफलाकाङ्क्षिभिर्यज्ञो
विधिदृष्टो य इज्यते।
यष्टव्यमेवेति मनः
समाधाय स सात्त्विकः॥

aphalākāṇkṣibhir yajño
vidhi-dṛṣṭoyaijyate
yaṣṭavyam eveti manaḥ
samādhāya sa sāttvikaḥ||

aphala-kāñkṣibhiḥ—devoid of desire for result; yajñaḥ—sacrifice; vidhi— accordingly; dṛṣtaḥ—direction; yaḥ—anyone; ijyate—performs; yaṣṭavyam—must be performed; eva—certainly; iti—thus; manaḥ—mind; samādhāya— fixed in; saḥ—he; sāttvikaḥ—is in the mode of goodness.

Meaning: The sacrifice that is prescribed by rule and performed according to duty and the rules of scripture, and is performed by non-seekers of fruit, is considered good sacrifice.

12

अभिसन्धाय तु फलं
दम्भार्थमपि चैव यत्।
इज्यते भरतश्रेष्ठ
तं यज्ञं विद्धि राजसम्॥

abhisandhāya tu phalaṁ
dambhārthamapi caiva yat
ijyatebharata-śreṣṭha
taṁ yajñaṁ viddhi rājasam ||

abhisandhāya—desiring; tu—but; phalam—the result; dambha—pride; artham—material benefits; api—also; ca—and; eva—certainly; yat—that which; ijyate—worship; bharata-śreṣṭha—O chief of the Bhāratas; tam—that; yajñam—sacrifice; viddhi—know; rājasam—in the mode of passion.

Meaning: But that sacrifice which is performed for consideration of fruit or for pride or glory or for material benefit, know that sacrifice to be passionate, O best of the Bharatas.

13

विधिहीनमसृष्टान्नं
मन्त्रहीनमदक्षिणम्।
श्रद्धाविरहितं यज्ञं
तामसं परिचक्षते।।

vidhi-hīnam asṛṣṭānnaṁ
mantra-hīnamadakṣiṇam
śraddhā-virahitaṁ yajñam
tāmasaṁ paricakṣate ||

vidhi-hīnam—without scriptural direction; asṛṣṭa-annam—without distribution of prasādam; mantra-hīnam—with no chanting of the Vedic hymns; adakṣiṇam—with no remunerations to the priests; śraddhā—faith; virahitam—without; yajñam—sacrifice; tāmasam—in the mode of ignorance; paricakṣate—is to be considered.

Meaning: That sacrifice that is performed without rule and in defiance of the scriptural injunctions, which lacks a formula or proper distribution of spiritual food, where no Vedic hymns are chanted and no remunerations are offered to the priests, and which is without faith, is said to be dark.

14

देवद्विजगुरुप्राज्ञ-
पूजनं शौचमार्जवम्।
ब्रह्मचर्यमहिंसा च
शारीरं तप उच्यते॥

deva-dvija-guru-prājña-
pūjanaṁ śaucamārjavam
brahma-caryamahiṁsā ca
śārīraṁ tapa ucyate||

deva—the Supreme Lord; dvija—the brāhmaṇa; guru—the spiritual master; prājña—worshippable personalities; pūjanam—worship; śaucam—cleanliness; ārjavam—simplicity; brahma-caryam—celibacy; ahiṁsā—non violence; ca— also; śārīram—pertaining to the body; tapaḥ— austerity; ucyate—is said to be.

Meaning: Bodily austerity is made up of the worship of the Supreme Lord, the preceptors, the wise, and superiors like the father and mother. The real austerities of the body are cleanliness, simplicity, celibacy, and non-violence.

15

अनुद्वेगकरं वाक्यं
सत्यं प्रियहितं च यत्।
स्वाध्यायाभ्यसनं चैव
वाङ्मयं तप उच्यते॥

anudvega-karaṁ vākyaṁ
satyaṁpriya-hitaṁcayat
svādhyāyābhyasanaṁ caiva
vāṅmayaṁ tapa ucyate||

anudvega—not agitating; karam—producing; vākyam—words; satyam —truthful; priya—dear; hitam—beneficial; ca—also; yat—which; svādhyāya—Vedic study; abhyasanam—practice; ca—also; eva—certainly; vāṅmayaṁ— of the voice; tapaḥ—austerity; ucyate—is said to be.

Meaning: Austerity of speech is undisturbing speech that is truthful, agreeable, and beneficial as well as avoiding speech that offends someone. The practice of good reading by reciting the Vedas regularly is also deemed austerity of speech.

16

मनः प्रसादः सौम्यत्वं
मौनमात्मविनिग्रहः।
भावसंशुद्धिरित्येतत्तपो
मानसमुच्यते॥

manaḥ-prasādaḥ saumyatvaṁ
maunamātma-vinigrahaḥ
bhāva-saṁśuddhirityetat tapo
mānasamucyate||

manaḥ-prasādaḥ—satisfaction of the mind; saumyatvam—without duplicity towards others; maunam—gravity; ātma—self; vinigrahaḥ—control; bhāva—nature; saṁśuddhiḥ—purification; iti—thus; etat—that is; tapaḥ—austerity; mānasam—of the mind; ucyate—is said to be.

Meaning: Mental austerity or austerities of the mind is cheerfulness of the mind, serenity, gravity, simplicity, self-control, and purity of thought.

17

श्रद्धया परया तप्तं
तपस्तत्त्रिविधं नरैः।
अफलाकाङ्क्षिभिर्युक्तैः
सात्त्विकं परिचक्षते॥

śraddhayā parayā taptaṁ
tapastattri-vidhaṁnaraiḥ
aphalākāṅkṣibhir yuktaiḥ
sāttvikaṁ paricakṣate ||

śraddhayā—with faith; parayā—transcendental; taptam—executed; tapaḥ —austerity; tat—that; tri-vidham—three kinds; naraiḥ—by men; aphala-ākāṅkṣibhiḥ—without desires for fruits; yuktaiḥ—engaged; sāttvikam—in the mode of goodness; pari-cakṣate—is called.

Meaning: This threefold austerity is practised by men of superior faith whose goal is not being desirous of fruit but to please the Supreme One, and performed by those settled in Yoga. This austerity is considered good.

18

सत्कारमानपूजार्थं
तपो दम्भेन चैव यत्।
क्रियते तदिह प्रोक्तं
राजसं चलमध्रुवम्॥

satkāra-māna-pūjārtham
tapo dambhena caiva yat
kriyate tad iha proktaṁ
rājasaṁ calama-dhruvam ||

satkāra—respect; māna—honor; pūjā-artham—for worship; tapaḥ— austerity; dambhena—with pride; ca—also; eva—certainly; yat—which is; kriyate—performed; tat—that; iha—in this world; proktam—is said; rājasam—in the mode of passion; calam—flickering; adhruvam—temporary.

Meaning: That austerity which is for the sake of ostentation, or to gain respect, honour, and worship is said to be in the mode of passion. These are neither steady nor permanent in nature.

19

मूढग्राहेणात्मनो-
यत्पीडया क्रियते तपः।
परस्योत्सादनार्थं वा
तत्तामसमुदाहृतम्॥

mūḍha-grāheṇātmanaḥ
yatpīḍayā kriyate tapaḥ
parasyotsā-danārthaṁ vā
tattāmasamudā-hṛtam ||

mūḍha—foolish; grāheṇa—with endeavor; ātmanaḥ—of one's own self; yat—which; pīḍayā—by torture; kriyate—is performed; tapaḥ—penance; parasya—toothers; utsādanārtham—causing annihilation; vā—or; tat—that; tāmasam—in the mode of darkness; udāhṛtam—is said to be.

Meaning: That austerity which is performed foolishly with self-torture or with the object of destroying, injuring, or bringing about someone's ruin, is known as dark.

20

दातव्यमिति यद्दानं
दीयतेऽनुपकारिणे।
देशे काले च पात्रे च
तद्दानं सात्त्विकं स्मृतम्॥

dātavyamiti yaddānaṁ
dīyate 'nupakāriṇe
deśe kāle ca pātre ca
taddānaṁ sāttvikaṁ smṛtam ||

dātavyam—worth giving; iti—thus; yat—that which; dānam—charity; dīyate—given; anupakāriṇe—to any person irrespective of doing good; dese—in place; kāle—in time; ca—also; pātre—suitable person; ca—and; tat—that; dānam—charity; sāttvikam—in the mode of goodness; smṛtam—consider.

Meaning: That gift that should be made and which is given out of a sense of duty, at the right time and place to a worthy person, without any expectation of return, is considered to be charity in the mode of goodness.

21

यत्तु प्रत्युपकारार्थं
फलमुद्दिश्य वा पुनः।
दीयते च परिक्लिष्टं
तद्दानं राजसं स्मृतम्॥

yat tu pratyupakārārthaṁ
phalamuddiśya vā punaḥ
dīyateca parikliṣṭaṁ
taddānaṁ rājasaṁ smṛtam||

yat—that which; tu—but; prati-upakāra-artham—for the sake of getting some return; phalam—result; uddiśya—desiring; vā—or; punaḥ—again; dīyate—is given in charity; ca—also; parikliṣṭam—grudgingly; tat—that; dānam— charity; rājasam—in the mode of passion; smṛtam—is understood to be.

Meaning: But that gift is considered passionate and charity in the mode of passion, which is given with the expectation of some return, or made with a desire for fruitive results, or made grudgingly.

22

अदेशकाले यद्दानम-
पात्रेभ्यश्च दीयते।
असत्कृतमवज्ञातं
तत्तामसमुदाहृतम्॥22॥

adeśa-kāle yad dānam
apātrebhyaśca dīyate
asatkṛtamava-jñātaṁ
tattāmasamudā-hṛtam||

adesa—unpurified place; kāle—unpurified time; yat—that which is; dānam —charity; apātrebhyaḥ—to unworthy persons; ca—also; dīyate—is given; asatkṛtam—without respect; avajñātam—without proper attention; tat— that; tāmasam—in the mode of darkness; udāhṛtam—is said to be.

Meaning: Charity which is performed at an unfit place or time to people who are not worthy and made with unkindness, contempt, and without respect is considered to be charity in the mode of darkness.

23

ॐ तत्सदिति निर्देशो
ब्रह्मणस्त्रिविधः स्मृतः।
ब्राह्मणास्तेन वेदाश्च
यज्ञाश्च विहिताः पुरा॥23॥

om-tat-saditi nirdeśo
brahmaṇastri-vidhaḥsmṛtaḥ
brāhmaṇās tena vedāś ca
yajñāśca vihitāḥ purā ||

om—indication of the Supreme; tat—that; sat—eternal; iti—that; nirdeśaḥ—indication; brāhmaṇāḥ—of the Supreme; tri-vidhaḥ—three kinds; smṛtaḥ—consider; brahmaṇaḥ—the brāhmaṇas; tena—therefore; vedāḥ—the Vedic literature; ca—also; yajñāḥ—sacrifice; ca—also; vihitāḥ—sacrifice; purā—formerly.

Meaning: 'Om,Tat,Sat', these three syllables are perceived to be the triple index to Brahma from the beginning of creation. They have been used to signify the Supreme Absolute Truth or the Brahman. The three syllables were first uttered by brahmanas while chanting Vedic hymns and sacrifices to worship the Supreme One.

24

तस्मादोमित्युदाहृत्य
यज्ञदानतपः क्रियाः।
प्रवर्तन्ते विधानोक्तः
सततं ब्रह्मवादिनाम्।।

tasmād om ity udāhṛtya
yajña-dāna-tapaḥ-kriyāḥ
pravartante vidhānoktāḥ
satataṁbrahma-vādinām ||

tasmāt—thercfore; om—beginning with om; iti—thus; udāhṛtya—indicating; yajña—sacrifice; dāna—charity; tapaḥ—penance; kriyāḥ—performances; pravartante—begins; vidhāna-uktāḥ—according to scriptural regulation; satatam—always; brahma-vādinām—of the transcendentalists.

Meaning: Thus the ones who undertake sacrifice, charities, and austerities always utter 'Om' in the beginning as a rule prescribed to attain the Supreme.

25

तदित्यनभिसन्दाय
फलं यज्ञतपःक्रियाः।
दानक्रियाश्चविविधाः
क्रियन्ते मोक्षकाङ्क्षिभिः॥

tadity anabhisandhāya
phalaṁyajña-tapaḥ-kriyāḥ
dāna-kriyāś ca vividhāḥ
kriyante mokṣa-kāṅkṣibhiḥ ||

tat—that; iti—they; anabhisandhāya—without fruitive result; phalam —result of sacrifice; yajña—sacrifice; tapaḥ—penance; kriyāḥ—activities; dāna—charity; kriyāḥ—activities; ca—also; vividhāḥ—varieties; kriyante—done; mokṣa-kāṅkṣibhiḥ—those who actually desire liberation.

Meaning: The liberation-seekers should perform sacrifice, penance, and charity with the word 'tat' without thinking of the fruit derived from such actions and be free of material entanglement.

26-27

सद्भावे साधुभावे च
सदित्यतत्प्रयुज्यते।
प्रशस्ते कर्मणि तथा
सच्छब्दः पार्थ युज्यते॥

यज्ञे तपसि दाने च
स्थितिः सदिति चोच्यते।
कर्म चैव तदर्थीयं
सदित्यवाभिधीयते॥

sad-bhāvesādhu-bhāveca
sadityetat prayujyate
praśaste karmaṇi tathā
sac-chabdaḥpārthayujyate ||

yajñe tapasi dāne ca
sthitiḥ sad iticocyate
karmacaivatad-arthīyaṁ
sad ity evābhidhīyate ||

sat-bhāve—in the sense of the nature of the Supreme; sādhu-bhāve—in the sense of the nature of devotion; ca—also; sat—the Supreme; iti—thus; etat— this; prayujyate—is used; praśaste—bona fide; karmaṇi—activities; tathā—also; sat-śabdaḥ—sound; pārtha—O son of Pṛthā; yujyate—is used; yajñe—sacrifice; tapasi—inpenance; dāne—charity; ca—also; sthitiḥ—situated; sat— the Supreme; iti—thus; ca—and; ucyate—pronounced; karma—work;ca—also; eva—certainly; tat—that; arthīyam—are meant; sat—Supreme; iti—thus; eva—certainly; abhidhīyate—is practised.

Meaning: The word 'Sat' is used for reality and goodness to indicate the Absolute Truth as the object of devotional sacrifice. The word 'Sat' is also applied to commendable acts, O Partha. Perseverance in sacrifice, austerity, and charity is also known as 'Sat', and so is action performed to please the Supreme One, O son of Kunti.

28

अश्रद्धया हुतं दत्तं
तपस्तप्तं कृतं च यत्।
असदित्युच्यते पार्थ न
च तत्प्रेत्य नो इह।।

aśraddhayā hutaṁ dattaṁ
tapastaptaṁ kṛtaṁ ca yat
asadityucyate pārtha na
ca tatpretya no iha||

aśraddhayā—without faith; hutam—performed; dattam—given; tapaḥ— penance; taptam—executed; kṛtam—performed; ca—also; yat—that which; asat—falls; iti—thus; ucyate—is said to be; pārtha—O son of Pṛthā; na— never; ca—also; tat—that; pretya—after death; no—nor; iha—in this life.

Meaning: But the sacrifices, charity, and austerity performed without faith in the Supreme One are temporary and is known as 'Asat' (not good), O son of Kunti. It is useless both in this life as well as the next.

ॐ तत्सदिति श्रीमद्भगवद्गीतासूपनिषत्सु ब्रह्मविद्यायां योगशास्त्रे
श्रीकृष्णार्जुनसंवादेश्रद्धात्रयविभागयोगोनामसप्तदशोऽध्यायः।

Thus in the Upanishad of the Glorious Divine Lay, the Science of Brahma, the Ordinance of Yoga, the Discourse between the Glorious Lord Krishna and Arjuna, the Seventeenth Chapter titled 'Shraddhatreya Vibhaga Yoga' (The Yoga of the Threefold Division of Faith).

CHAPTER 18

MOKSHA SANNYASA YOGA (THE YOGA OF LIBERATION THROUGH RENUNCIATION)

CHAPTER 18

MOKSHA SANNYASA YOGA (THE YOGA OF LIBERATION THROUGH RENUNCIATION)

In the final chapter, Lord Krishna sums up the ultimate conclusion or summarises the gist of the Bhagavad Gita by describing the meaning of renunciation and attainment of salvation by walking on the path of Karma. The Final Revelations of the Ultimate Truth, Renouncement, and Relinquishment are given here by Lord Krishna. Arjuna asks Lord Krishna about the purpose of tyaga or renunciation and sannyasa or the order of renunciation of life. Lord Krishna explains the same as well as the five causes of action, the three factors that motivate action, and the three components of action. Lord Krishna also reveals to Arjuna about action, understanding, determination, happiness, and work according to each of the three modes or attributes of material nature.

The Lord says that one must offer everything without hesitation and unconditionally to God. The renouncement of actions should not be performed with any desire. Relinquishing means not having any sort of attachment to the fruits or results of such actions. Lord Krishna informs Arjuna that even action that is performed with a good intention in mind like worshipping the Lord, should be performed unconditionally without any attachment to the results of the worship. The highest platform of self-realisation is pure devotional service to Krishna. When one surrenders to Krishna unconditionally and lovingly, He frees him of all sins, and allows him to join His eternal spiritual abode. Lord Krishna insists that one must attain perfection by the performance of one's prescribed duty and not the prescribed duty or work of someone else. Prescribed duties remain unaffected by sinful reactions, and one should thus perform work as a matter of duty, without any sort of attachment or expecting any results from that work. No matter what happens, one must never abandon one's duty. However, all actions cannot be relinquished in this world. But the actions that must be rejected and relinquished are theft, adultery, consumption of alcohol, reproach, lying, untouchability, and anger. Actions performed for rearing children cannot be relinquished. Often, living beings are killed while farming and cooking which is completely intentional. The solution is to find a Complete Guru after which one does not incur sins for deeds done unwillingly.

Lord Krishna tells Arjuna to always rely upon Him, work under His shelter, and be conscious of Him. He tells Arjuna that even if he refuses to fight, he will be forced to fight as it is the prescribed duty of a Kshatriya. Still, it is up to Arjuna to decide what he wants to do. Thanks to Lord Krishna's grace and this wonderful discourse of shining light, Arjuna's illusion, bewilderment, and doubts are dispelled, and he picks up his bow again to fight as per Lord Krishna's instructions.

1

अर्जुन उवाच
सन्न्यासस्य महाबाहो-
तत्त्वमिच्छामि वेदितुम्।
त्यागस्य च हृषीकेश
पृथक्केशिनिषूदन॥

arjuna uvāca
sannyāsasya mahābāho
tattvamicchāmi veditum
tyāgasya ca hṛṣīkeśa
pṛthak keśīniṣūdana||

arjunaḥ uvāca—Arjuna said; sannyāsasya—renunciation; mahā-bāho— O mighty-armed one; tattvam—truth; icchāmi—I wish; veditum—to understand; tyāgasya—of renunciation; ca—also; hṛṣīkeśa—O master of the senses; pṛthak—differently; keśi-nisūdana—O killer of the Keśī demon.

Meaning: Arjuna said: O mighty-armed one, I desire to know the essence of Tyaga or renunciation and about the renounced order of life known as Sannyasa or surrender, O Hrishikesha, slayer of the Keshi demon.

2

श्रीभगवानुवाच
काम्यानां कर्मणा न्यासं
सन्न्यासं कवयो विदुः।
सर्वकर्मफलत्यागं
प्राहुस्त्यागं विचक्षणाः॥

śrībhagavān uvāca
kāmyānāṁ karmaṇāṁ nyāsaṁ
sannyāsaṁ kavayo viduḥ
sarva-karma-phala-tyāgaṁ
prāhustyāgaṁ vicakṣaṇāḥ||

śrī bhagavān uvāca—the Supreme Personality of Godhead said; kāmyānām—with desire; karmaṇām—activities; nyāsam—renunciation; sannyāsam—renounced order of life; kavayaḥ—the learned; viduḥ—know; sarva—all; karma—activities; phala—of results; tyāgam—renunciation; prāhuḥ—call; tyāgam—renunciation; vicakṣaṇāḥ—the experienced.

Meaning: The Supreme Lord said: The sages know Sannyasa or renunciation as the surrender of all activities that covet something for self gratification.

The great learned men call it the renounced order of life which is relinquishing all fruits of action.

3

त्याज्यं दोषवदित्येके
कर्म प्राहुर्मनीषिणः।
यज्ञदानतपःकर्म न
त्याज्यमिति चापरे॥

tyājyaṁ doṣavad ity eke
karma prāhurmanīṣiṇaḥ
yajña-dāna-tapaḥ-karmana-
tyājyamiti cāpare||

tyājyam—must be given up; doṣavat—as an evil; iti—thus; eke—one group; karma—work; prāhuḥ—said; manīṣiṇaḥ—of great thinkers; yajña—sacrifice; dāna—charity; tapaḥ—penance; karma—work; na—never; tyājyam —is to be given up; iti—thus; ca—certainly; apare—others.

Meaning: Some philosophers are of the opinion that all action should be renounced as an evil, but there are other sages who think that the action of sacrifice, charity, and austerity should never be renounced.

4

निश्चयं शृणु मे तत्र
त्यागे भरतसत्तम।
त्यागो हि पुरुषव्याघ्र
त्रिविधः सम्प्रकीर्तितः॥

niścayaṁ śṛṇu me tatra
tyāge bharata-sattama
tyāgo hi puruṣa-vyāghra
tri-vidhaḥ samprakīrtitaḥ ||

niścayam—certainly; śṛṇu—hear; me—from Me; tatra—there; tyāge—in the matter of renunciation; bharata-sattama—O best of the Bhāratas; tyāgaḥ—renunciation; hi—certainly; puruṣa-vyāghra—O tiger among human beings; tri-vidhaḥ—three kinds; samprakīrtitaḥ—is declared.

Meaning: O best of the Bharatas, listen to what I have to say now about that renunciation. The scriptures declare that there are three kinds of renunciation, O mighty man.

5

यज्ञदानतपःकर्म न
त्याज्यं कार्यमेव तत्।
यज्ञो दानं तपश्चैव
पावनानि मनीषिणाम्॥

yajña-dāna-tapaḥ-karma na
tyājyaṁ kāryameva tat
yajño dānaṁ tapaś caiva
pāvanāni manīṣiṇām||

yajña—sacrifice; dāna—charity; tapaḥ—penance; karma—activities; na — never; tyājyam—to be given up; kāryam—must be done; eva—certainly; tat— that; yajñaḥ—sacrifice; dānam—charity; tapaḥ—penance; ca—also; eva— certainly; pāvanāni—purifying; manīṣiṇām—even of the great souls.

Meaning: The action of sacrifice, charity, and austerity should not be abandoned or renounced but should be performed. This threefold activity has the power to purify even the great souls.

6

एतान्यपि तु कर्माणि
सङ्गं त्यक्त्वा फलानि च।
कर्तव्यानीति मे पार्थ
निश्चितं मतमुत्तमम्॥

etānyapi tu karmāṇi
saṅgaṁ tyaktvā phalāni ca
kartavyānīti me pārtha
niścitaṁ matam-uttamam||

etāni—all this; api—certainly; tu—must; karmāṇi—activities; saṅgam—association; tyaktvā—renouncing; phalāni—results; ca—also; kartavyāni—as duty; iti—thus; me—My; pārtha—O son of Pṛthā; niścitam—definite; matam—opinion; uttamam—the best.

Meaning: But even these three actions should be performed only after one has renounced all attachment and fruits of actions. This is My final opinion, O son of Kunti.

7

नियतस्य तु सन्न्यासः
कर्मणो नोपपद्यते।
मोहात्तस्य परित्याग-
स्तामसः परिकीर्तितः

niyatasya tu sannyāsaḥ
karmaṇo- nopapadyate
mohāt tasya parityāgas
tāmasaḥparikīrtitaḥ||

niyatasya—prescribed duties; tu—but; sannyāsaḥ—renunciation; karmaṇaḥ—activities; na—never; upapadyate—is deserved; mohāt—by illusion; tasya—of which; parityāgaḥ—renunciation; tāmasaḥ—in the mode of ignorance; parikīrtitaḥ—declared.

Meaning: The renunciation of lawful action is not deemed proper. If one gives up the prescribed duties out of illusion arising from the mode of Darkness, such renunciation is called dark.

8

दुःखमित्येव यत्कर्म
कायक्लेशभयात्त्यजेत्।
स कृत्वा राजसं त्यागं
नैव त्यागफलं लभेत्।।

duḥkham ity eva yat karma
kāya-kleśa-bhayāttyajet
sa kṛtvā rājasaṁ tyāgaṁ
naiva tyāga-phalaṁ labhet||

duḥkham—unhappy; iti—thus; eva—certainly; yat—that which; karma— work; kāya—body; kleśa—troublesome; bhayāt—out of; tyajet—fear; saḥ—that; kṛtvā—after doing; rājasam—in the mode of passion; tyāgam— renunciation; na eva—certainly not; tyāga—renounced; phalam—results; labhet—gain.

Meaning: When one renounces action by giving up the prescribed duties because they are bothersome, painful, or for fear of suffering of the body, such renunciation is said to be in the mode of passion. Such action does not fetch the fruit of renunciation.

9

कार्यमित्येव यत्कर्म
नियतं क्रियतेऽर्जुन।
सङ्गं त्यक्त्वा फलं चैव
स त्यागः सात्त्विको मतः॥

kāryam ity eva yat karma
niyataṁ kriyate'rjuna
saṅgaṁ tyaktvā phalaṁ caiva
sa tyāgaḥ sāttviko mataḥ||

kāryam—must be done; iti—thus; eva—thus; yat—that which; karma—work; niyatam—prescribed; kriyate—performed; arjuna—O Arjuna; saṅgam—association; tyaktvā—giving up; phalam—result; ca—also; eva—certainly; saḥ—that; tyāgaḥ—renunciation; sāttvikaḥ—in the mode of goodness; mataḥ—in My opinion.

Meaning: When one renounces all attachment, and performs his prescribed duty only because it should be performed, not desirous of any attachment to the fruit, his renunciation is said to attain the nature of goodness, O Arjuna.

10

न द्वेष्ट्यकुशलं कर्म
कुशले नानुषज्जते।
त्यागी सत्त्वसमाविष्टो
मेधावी छिन्नसंशयः।।

na dveṣṭyakuśalaṁ karma
kuśale nānuṣajjate
tyāgī sattva-samāviṣṭo
medhāvī chinna-saṁśayaḥ ||

na—never; dveṣṭi—hates; akuśalam—inauspicious; karma—work; kuśale —inauspicious; na—nor; anuṣajjate—becomes attached; tyāgī—the renouncer; sattva—goodness; samāviṣṭaḥ—absorbed in; medhāvī—intelligent; chinna—cut up; saṁśayaḥ—all doubts.

Meaning: The renouncer who is seated in the mode of goodness is full of wisdom and free of all doubt about work. He does not dislike action when he is in an uncomfortable position to perform it and neither does he like it when he is in a comfortable position to perform it.

11

न हि देहभृता शक्यं
त्यक्तुं कर्माण्यशेषतः।
यस्तु कर्मफलत्यागी
स त्यागीत्यभिधीयते॥

na hi deha-bhṛtā śakyaṁ
tyaktuṁkarmāṇyaśeṣataḥ
yas tu karma-phala-tyāgī
sa tyāgīty-abhidhīyate||

na—never; hi—certainly; deha-bhṛtā—of the embodied; śakyam—possible; tyaktum—to renounce; karmāṇi—activities of; aśeṣataḥ—altogether; yaḥ tu—anyone who; karma—work; phala—result; tyāgī—renouncer; saḥ—he; tyāgī—the renouncer; iti—thus; abhidhīyate—it is said.

Meaning: Indeed, it is not possible for an embodied one to renounce all actions completely, but it is said that one who renounces the fruits of action instead of the actions themselves, is the one who has truly attained renunciation.

12

अनिष्टमिष्टं मिश्रं च
त्रिविधं कर्मणः फलम्।
भवत्यत्यागिनां प्रेत्य
न तु सन्न्यासिनां क्वचित्॥

aniṣṭamiṣṭaṁ miśraṁ ca
tri-vidhaṁ karmaṇaḥ phalam
bhavaty-atyāgināṁ pretya
na tu sannyāsināṁ kvacit ||

aniṣṭam—leading to hell; iṣṭam—leading to heaven; miśram ca—or mixture; tri-vidham—three kinds; karmaṇaḥ—work; phalam—result; bhavati—becomes; atyāginām—of the renouncer; pretya—after death; natu—but not; sannyāsinām—of the renounced order; kvacit—at any time.

Meaning: The triple fruit of action- desirable, undesirable, and mixed is for the non-renouncer after death. But, for the one who has reached the renounced order of life, he does not have such results to suffer or enjoy.

13-14

पञ्चैतानि महाबाहो
कारणानि निबोध मे।
साङ्ख्ये कृतान्ते प्रोक्तानि
सिद्धये सर्वकर्मणाम्॥

अधिष्ठानं तथा कर्ता
करणं च पृथग्विधम्।
विविधाश्च पृथक्चेष्टा
दैवं चैवात्र पंचमम्॥

pañcaitāni mahā-bāho
kāraṇāninibodhame
sāṅkhye kṛtānte proktāni
siddhayesarva-karmaṇām||

adhiṣṭhānaṁ tathā kartā
karaṇaṁ ca pṛthag-vidham
vividhāśca pṛthakceṣṭā
daivaṁ caivātra pañcamam||

pañca—five; etāni—all these; mahā-bāho—O mighty-armed one; kāraṇāni —cause; nibodha—just understand; me—from Me; sāṅkhye—in the Vedas; kṛtānte—after performance; proktāni—said; siddhaye—perfection; sarva—all; karmaṇām—actuated; adhiṣṭhānam—place; tathā—also; kartā—worker; karaṇam ca—and instruments; pṛthak-vidham—different kinds; vividhāḥsca—varieties; pṛthak—separately; ceṣṭāḥ—endeavor; daivam—the Supreme; ca—also; eva—certainly; atra—here; pañcamam—five.

Meaning: Learn from Me the five causes that produce results in all actions, O mighty-armed Arjuna, which are mentioned in the Sankhya action-theory to be the place of action, the performer of action, the sense various organs, the endeavour, and ultimately the divine Supersoul.

15

शरीरवाङ्मनोभि-
र्यत्कर्म प्रारभते नरः।
न्याय्यं वा विपरीतं वा
पञ्चैते तस्य हेतवः॥

śarīra-vāṅmanobhir-
yat karma prārabhate naraḥ
nyāyyaṁ vā viparītaṁ vā
pañcaite tasya hetavaḥ ||

śarīra—body; vāk—speech; manobhiḥ—by the mind; yat—anything; karma—work; prārabhate—begins; naraḥ—a person; nyāyyam—right; vā—or; viparītam—the opposite; vā—or; pañca—five; ete—all these; tasya—its; hetavaḥ—causes.

Meaning: Whatever the action, right or wrong, undertaken or performed by a man with body, mind, or speech, these five factors are the causes.

16

तत्रैवं सति कर्तारमा-
त्मानं केवलं तु यः।
पश्यत्यकृतबुद्धित्वान्न
स पश्यति दुर्मतिः॥

tatraivaṁ sati kartāram
ātmānaṁ kevalaṁ tu yaḥ
paśyaty akṛta-buddhitvānna
sa paśyati durmatiḥ||

tatra—there; evam—certainly; sati—being thus; kartāram—of the worker; ātmānam—the soul; kevalam—only; tu—but; yaḥ—anyone; paśyati—sees; akṛta-buddhitvāt—due to unintelligence; na—never; saḥ—he; paśyati—sees; durmatiḥ—foolish.

Meaning: Therefore, whoever by reason or lack of understanding thinks himself to be the only actor, he is wrong-notioned and sees not things as they are.

17

यस्य नाहङ्कृतो भावो
बुद्धिर्यस्य न लिप्यते।
हत्वापि स इमाँल्लोकान्न
हन्ति न निबध्यते॥

yasya nāhaṅkṛto bhāvo
buddhiryasya na lipyate
hatvāpi sa imām̐llokānna
hantina nibadhyate ||

yasya—of one who; na—never; ahaṅkṛtaḥ—false ego; bhāvaḥ—nature; buddhiḥ—intelligence; yasya—one who; na—never; lipyate—is attached; hatvā api—even killing; saḥ—he; imān—this; lokān—world; na—never; hanti —kills; na—never; nibadhyate—becomes entangled.

Meaning: He whose nature is not driven by self-ego, whose understanding is not contaminated, he is not the killer even if he has killed men in this world and neither is he bound by his actions.

18

ज्ञानं ज्ञेयं परिज्ञाता
त्रिविधा कर्मचोदना।
करणं कर्म कर्तेति
त्रिविधः कर्मसङ्ग्रहः।।

jñānaṁ jñeyaṁ parijñātā
tri-vidhākarma-codanā
karaṇaṁ karma karteti
tri-vidhaḥkarma saṅgrahaḥ ||

jñānam—knowledge; jñeyam—objective; parijñātā—the knower; tri- vidhā— three kinds; karma—work; codanā—impetus; karaṇam—the senses; karma —work; kartā—the doer; iti—thus; tri-vidhaḥ—three kinds; karma—work; saṅgrahaḥ—accumulation.

Meaning: Knowledge, the object of knowledge, and the knower are the three factors which are the motivators of action in a man. The appliance, the act, and the actor make up the threefold basis of action.

19

ज्ञानं कर्म च कर्ता च
त्रिधैव गुणभेदतः।
प्रोच्यते गुणसङ्ख्याने
यथावच्छृणु तान्यपि॥

jñānaṁ karma ca kartā ca
tridhaivaguṇa-bhedataḥ
procyate guṇa-saṅkhyāne
yathāvacchṛṇu tānyapi||

jñānam—knowledge; karma—work; ca—also; kartā—worker; ca—also; tridhā—three kinds; eva—certainly; guṇa-bhedataḥ—in terms of different modes of material nature; procyate—is said; guṇa-saṅkhyāne—in terms of different modes; yathāvat—as they act; śṛṇu—hear; tāni—all of them; api —also.

Meaning: Knowledge, action, and the performers of action is derived from the three modes of material nature and is three-fold as well. Listen to Me as I describe all of them to you.

20

सर्वभूतेषु येनैकं
भावमव्ययमीक्षते।
अविभक्तं विभक्तेषु
तज्ज्ञानं विद्धि सात्त्विकम्॥

sarva-bhūteṣu yenaikaṁ
bhāvam-avyayamīkṣate
avibhaktaṁ vibhakteṣu
tajjñānaṁ viddhi sāttvikam||

sarva-bhūteṣu—in all living entities; yena—by whom; ekam—one; bhāvam—situation; avyayam—imperishable; īkṣate—does see; avibhaktam—undivided; vibhakteṣu—in the numberless divided; tat—that; jñānam— knowledge; viddhi—knows; sāttvikam—in the mode of goodness.

Meaning: The knowledge by which one sees one unperishing spiritual nature is observed in all creatures in existence, the undivided in the several divided, know that knowledge to be in the attribute of goodness.

21

पृथक्त्वेन तु यज्ज्ञानं
नानाभावान्पृथग्विधान्।
वेत्ति सर्वेषु भूतेषु
तज्ज्ञानं विद्धि राजसम्॥

pṛthaktvena tu yajjñānaṁ
nānā-bhāvānpṛthag-vidhān
vetti sarveṣu bhūteṣu
tajjñānaṁ viddhi rājasam||

pṛthaktvena—because of division; tu—but; yat jñānam—which knowledge; nānā-bhāvān—multifarious situations; pṛthak-vidhān—differently; vetti—one who knows; sarveṣu—in all; bhūteṣu—living entities; tatjñānam—that knowledge; viddhi—must be known; rājasam—in terms of passion.

Meaning: But the knowledge that perceives a different type of living entity in the bodies of different creatures, know that knowledge to be in the mode of passion.

22

यत्तु कृत्स्नवदेकस्मि-
न्कार्ये सक्तमहैतुकम्।
अतत्त्वार्थवदल्पंच
तत्तामसमुदाहृतम्।।

yat tu kṛtsnavad ekasmin
kārye saktama-haitukam
atattvārthavad alpaṁ ca
tattāma-samudāhṛtam||

yat—that which; tu—but; kṛtsnavat—all in all; ekasmin—in one; kārye—work; saktam—attached; ahaitukam—without cause; atattva-arthavat—without reality; alpam ca—and very meager; tat—that; tāmasam—in the mode of darkness; udāhṛtam—is spoken.

Meaning: However, that knowledge by which one is associated with a single effect as if it were the whole, and is without foundation and knowledge of the truth, aimless and narrow, that kind of dark knowledge is declared to be derived from Darkness.

23

नियतं सङ्गरहितम-
रागद्वेषतः कृतम्।
अफलप्रेप्सुना कर्म
यत्तत्सात्त्विकमुच्यते॥

niyataṁsaṅga-rahitam
arāga-dveṣataḥkṛtam
aphala-prepsunā karma
yattatsāttvikam-ucyate||

niyatam—regulative; saṅga-rahitam—without attachment; arāga- dveṣataḥ—without love or hatred; kṛtam—done; aphala-prepsunā—without fruitive result; karma—acts; yat—that which; tat—that; sāttvikam—in the mode of goodness; ucyate—is called.

Meaning: As for actions, the action performed in a regulated manner without any attachment and in accordance with duty, performed without liking or hatred by the seeker who has renounced the fruits of actions, is called good.

24

यत्तु कामेप्सुना कर्म
साहङ्कारेण वा पुनः।
क्रियते बहुलायासं
तद्राजसमुदाहृतम्॥

yat tu kāmepsunā karma
sāhaṅkāreṇavāpunaḥ
kriyate bahulāyāsaṁ
tadrāja-samudāhṛtam||

yat—that which; tu—but; kāma-īpsunā—with fruitive result; karma— work; sāhaṅkāreṇa—with ego; vā—or; punaḥ—again; kriyate—performed; bahula-āyāsam—with great labor; tat—that; rājasam—in the mode of passion; udāhṛtam—is said to be.

Meaning: But that action which is performed with great effort by a seeker who wishes the gratification of his desires, or done from a false sense of ego is called action in the modes of passion.

25

अनुबन्धं क्षयं हिंसाम-
नवेक्ष्य च पौरुषम्।
मोहादारभ्यते कर्म
यत्तत्तामसमुच्यते॥

anubandhaṁ kṣayaṁ hiṁsām
anapekṣya ca pauruṣam
mohād ārabhyate karma
yattattāma-samucyate ||

anubandham—future bondage; kṣayam—distracted; hiṁsām—violence; anapekṣya—without consideration of consequences; ca—also; pauruṣam—distressing to others; mohāt—by illusion; ārabhyate—begun; karma—work; yat—that; tat—which; tāmasam—in the mode of ignorance; ucyate—is said to be.

Meaning: The impractical action that is undertaken in ignorance and delusion without thinking about consequences like loss, injury, and ability, is termed as action in the mode of ignorance or darkness.

26

मुक्तसङ्गोऽनहंवादी
धृत्युत्साहसमन्वितः।
सिद्ध्यसिद्ध्योर्निर्विकारः
कर्ता सात्त्विक उच्यते॥

mukta-saṅgo 'nahaṁvādī
dhṛty-utsāha-samanvitaḥ
siddhy-asiddhyornirvikāraḥ
kartā sāttvika ucyate||

mukta-saṅgaḥ—liberated from all material association; anaham-vādī—without false ego; dhṛti-utsāha—with great enthusiasm; samanvitaḥ—qualified in that way; siddhi—perfection; asiddhyoḥ—failure; nirvikāraḥ—without change; kartā—worker; sāttvikaḥ—in the mode of goodness; ucyate—is said to be.

Meaning: The worker who is liberated from material attachment and false ego, who is resolute and enthusiastic and unaffected by success or failure, possesses the attribute of goodness.

27

राणी कर्मफलप्रेप्सु-
लुब्धो हिंसात्मकोऽशुचिः।
हर्षशोकान्वितः कर्ता
राजसः परिकीर्तितः॥

rāgī karma-phala-prepsur
lubdhohiṁsātmako'śuciḥ
harṣa-śokānvitaḥ kartā
rājasaḥ parikīrtitaḥ||

rāgī—very much attached; karma-phala—to the fruit of the work; prepsuḥ—desiring; lubdhaḥ—greedy; hiṁsā-ātmakaḥ—and always envious; aśuciḥ—unclean; harṣa-śoka-anvitaḥ—complicated, with joy and sorrow; kartā—such a worker; rājasaḥ—in the mode of passion; parikīrtitaḥ— is declared.

Meaning: The worker who is attached to the fruits of his actions with the intention of enjoying them passionately, and who is greedy, harmful, impure, envious and moved by exultation and grief is called passionate.

28

आयुक्तः प्राकृतः स्तब्धः
शठोनैष्कृतिकोऽलसः।
विषादी दीर्घसूत्री च
कर्ता तामस उच्यते॥

ayuktaḥ prākṛtaḥ stabdhaḥ
śaṭho-naiṣkṛtiko'lasaḥ
viṣādī dīrgha-sūtrī ca
kartā tāmasa ucyate||

ayuktaḥ—without reference to the scriptural injunctions; prākṛtaḥ—materialistic; stabdhaḥ—obstinate; śaṭhaḥ—deceitful; naiṣkṛtikaḥ—expert in insulting others; alasaḥ—lazy; viṣādī—morose; dīrgha-sūtrī—procrastinating; ca—also; kartā—worker; tāmasaḥ—in the mode of ignorance; ucyate—is said to be.

Meaning: The one who is always engaged in work not recommended by the scriptures, and who is inattentive, uncultured, materialistic, stubborn, despondent, lazy, deceitful, misdoing, and procrastinating is a worker in the mode of ignorance or darkness.

29

बुद्धेर्भेदं धृतेश्चैव
गुणतस्त्रिविधं शृणु।
प्रोच्यमानमशेषेण
पृथक्त्वेन धनंजय॥

buddherbhedaṁ dhṛteścaiva
guṇatas tri-vidhaṁ śṛṇu
procyamānam aśeṣeṇa
pṛthaktvena dhanañjaya||

buddheḥ—of intelligence; bhedam—differences; dhṛteḥ—of steadiness; ca—also; eva—certainly; guṇataḥ—by the modes of material nature; tri-vidham—the three kinds of; śṛṇu—just hear; procyamānam—as described by Me; aśeṣeṇa—in detail; pṛthaktvena—differently; dhanañjaya—O winner of wealth.

Meaning: Now, O Dhananjaya, listen as I declare to you the division of the three kinds of understanding and determination according to the three attributes of nature along with their distinguishing features.

30

प्रवृत्तिं च निवृत्तिं च
कार्याकार्ये भयाभये।
बन्धं मोक्षं च या वेत्ति
बुद्धिः सा पार्थ सात्त्विकी॥

pravṛttiṁ ca nivṛttiṁ ca
kāryākārye bhayābhaye
bandhaṁ mokṣaṁ ca yā vetti
buddhiḥ sā pārtha sāttvikī||

pravṛttim—deserving; ca—also; nivṛttim—not deserving; kārya—work; akārye—reaction; bhaya—fearful; abhaye—fearlessness; bandham—obligation; mokṣam ca—and liberation; yā—that which; vetti—knows; buddhiḥ—understanding; sā—that; pārtha—O son of Pṛthā; sāttvikī—in the mode of goodness.

Meaning: That understanding is considered good, O Partha, by which one knows what should be done in terms of right action and what should not be done in terms of restraint, what is to be feared and what is not to be feared, what is bondage and what is liberation.

31

यया धर्ममधर्मं च
कार्यं चाकार्यमेव च।
अयथावत्प्रजानाति
बुद्धिः सा पार्थ राजसी।।

yayā dharmam-adharmaṁ ca
kāryaṁ cākāryameva ca
ayathāvat-prajānāti
buddhiḥ sā pārtha rājasī||

yayā—by which; dharmam—principles of religion; adharmam ca—and irreligion; kāryam—work; ca—also; akāryam—what ought not to be done; eva—certainly; ca—also; ayathāvat—not perfectly; prajānati—knows; buddhiḥ—intelligence; sā—that; pārtha—O son of Pṛthā; rājasī—in the mode of passion.

Meaning: That imperfection of understanding which cannot distinguish between right and wrong, the religious way of the life and the irreligious, between action that should be performed and action that should not be performed, is called passionate, O son of Kunti.

32

अधर्मं धर्ममिति या
मन्यते तमसावृता।
सर्वार्थान्विपरीतांश्च
बुद्धिः सा पार्थ तामसी॥

adharmaṁ dharmamiti yā
manyate tamasāvṛtā
sarvārthān viparītāṁś ca
buddhiḥ sā pārtha tāmasī||

adharmam—irreligion; dharmam—religion; iti—thus; yā—which; manyate—thinks; tamasā—by illusion; āvṛtā—covered; sarva-arthān—all things; viparītān—the wrong direction; ca—also; buddhiḥ—intelligence; sa—that; pārtha—O son of Pṛthā; tāmasī—the mode of ignorance.

Meaning: That clouded understanding which perceives wrong to be right, and irreligion to be religion, under the dark spell of illusion, and always leads one in the wrong path, O Partha, is the mode of ignorance or darkness.

33

धृत्या यया धारयते
मनःप्राणेन्द्रियक्रियाः।
योगेनाव्यभिचारिण्या धृतिः
सा पार्थ सात्त्विकी।

dhṛtyāyayā dhārayate
manaḥprāṇendriya-kriyāḥ
yogenāvyabhicāriṇyā dhṛtiḥ
sā pārtha sāttvikī||

dhṛtyā—determination; yayā—by which; dhārayate—is sustained; manaḥ—mind; prāṇa—life; indriya—senses; kriyāḥ—activities; yogena—by yoga practice; avyabhicāriṇyā—without any break; dhṛtiḥ—such determination; sā—that; pārtha—O son of Pṛthā; sāttvikī—in the mode of goodness.

Meaning: That determination that is unbreakable by the practice of Yoga and controls the functions of the mind, life, and the acts of the senses, is in the mode of goodness, O Partha.

34

यया तु धर्मकामार्था
-न्धृत्या धारयतेऽर्जुन।
प्रसङ्गेन फलाकाङ्क्षी
धृतिः सा पार्थ राजसी॥

yayā tu dharma-kāmārthān
dhṛtyā dhārayate'rjuna
prasaṅgena phalākāṅkṣī
dhṛtiḥ sā pārtha rājasī||

yayā—by which; tu—but; dharma-kāma-arthān—for religiosity and economic development; dhṛtyā—by determination; dhārayate—in such terms; arjuna—O Arjuna; prasaṅgena—for that; phala-ākāṅkṣī—desiring fruitive result; dhṛtiḥ—determination; sā—that; pārtha—O son of Pṛthā; rājasī—in the mode of passion.

Meaning: But, O Arjuna, that determination by which one holds dear to fruitive result through attachment in religion, development, and the gratification of the senses, is in the mode of passion.

35

यया स्वप्नं भयं शोकं
विषादं मदमेव च।
न विमुञ्चति दुर्मेधा
धृतिः सा पार्थ तामसी॥

yayā svapnaṁ bhayaṁ śokaṁ
viṣādaṁ madam eva ca
na vimuñcati durmedhā
dhṛtiḥ sā pārtha tāmasī||

yayā—by which; svapnam—dream; bhayam—fearfulness; śokam—lamentation; viṣādam—moroseness; madam—illusion; eva—certainly; ca—also; na—never; vimuñcati—is liberated; durmedhāḥ—unintelligent; dhṛtiḥ—determination; sā—that; pārtha—O son of Pṛthā; tāmasī—in the mode of ignorance.

Meaning: The determination by which a dull-witted one cannot shake off sleep, fear, grief, moroseness, illusion as well as recklessness, is thought to be in the mode of darkness.

36-37

सुखं त्विदानीं त्रिविधं
शृणु मे भरतर्षभ।
अभ्यासाद्रमते यत्र
दुःखान्तं च निगच्छति।।

यत्तदग्रे विषमिव
परिणामेऽमृतोपमम्।
तत्सुखं सात्त्विकं
प्रोक्तमात्मबुद्धिप्रसादजम्।।

sukhaṁtvidānīṁtri-vidhaṁ
śṛṇu me bharatarṣabha
abhyāsād ramate yatra
duḥkhāntaṁ ca nigacchati ||
yat tad agre viṣam iva
pariṇāme'mṛtopamam
tat sukhaṁ sāttvikaṁ
proktamātma-buddhi-prasāda-jam ||

sukham—happiness; tu—but; idānīm—now; tri-vidham—three kinds; śṛṇu—hear; me—from Me; bharatarṣabha—O best amongst the Bhāratas; abhyāsāt—by practice; ramate—enjoyer; yatra—where; duḥkha—distress; antam—end; ca—also; nigacchati—gains; yat—that which; tat—that; agre—in the beginning; viṣam iva—like poison; pariṇāme—at the end; amṛta—nectar; upamam—compared to; tat—that; sukham—happiness; sāttvikam—in the mode of goodness; proktam—is said; ātma—self; buddhi—intelligence; prasāda-jam—satisfactory.

Meaning: O mighty Bharata, now hear from Me of the three kinds of pleasures enjoyed by the conditioned soul and which sometimes helps to end all his distress. In the beginning, however, it might seem like poison but in the sequel it is just like the nectar of immortality. That pleasure which awakens one to self-realisation because of the health of his understanding is said to reside in the mode of goodness.

38

विषयेन्द्रियसंयोगाद्य-
त्तदग्रेऽमृतोपमम्।
परिणामे विषमिव
तत्सुखं राजसं स्मृतम्॥

viṣayendriya-saṁyogād
yattadagre'mṛtopamam
pariṇāme viṣam iva
tatsukhaṁ rājasaṁ smṛtam||

viṣaya—objects of sense; indriya—senses; saṁyogāt—combination; yat—that; tat—which; agre—in the beginning; amṛta-upamam—just like nectar; pariṇāme—at the end; viṣam iva—like poison; tat—that; sukham—happiness; rājasam—in the mode of passion; smṛtam—is considered.

Meaning: That happiness which springs from the contact of sense and their objects feels like the nectar of immortality in the beginning, but is revealed to be poison in the sequel. That happiness or pleasure is known to be of passionate nature.

39

यदग्रे चानुबन्धे च
सुखं मोहनमात्मनः।
निद्रालस्यप्रमादोत्थं
तत्तामसमुदाहृतम्॥

yadagre cānubandhe ca
sukhaṁ mohanamātmanaḥ
nidrālasya-pramādotthaṁ
tattāma-samudāhṛtam ||

yat—that which; agre—in the beginning; ca—also; anubandhe—by binding; ca—also; sukham—happiness; mohanam—illusion; ātmanaḥ—of the self; nidrā—sleeping; ālasya—laziness; pramāda—illusion; uttham—produced of; tat—that; tāmasam—in the mode of ignorance; udāhṛtam—is said to be.

Meaning: That happiness which is oblivious to self-realisation, which is delusion in the beginning as well as the sequel, that pleasure springing from sleep, sloth, and illusion is said to be of the nature of ignorance or darkness.

40

न तदस्ति पृथिव्यां वा
दिवि देवेषु वा पुनः।
सत्त्वं प्रकृतिजैर्मुक्तं
यदेभिःस्यात्त्रिभिर्गुणैः॥

na tad asti pṛthivyāṁ vā
divideveṣuvāpunaḥ
sattvaṁprakṛti-jairmuktaṁ
yadebhiḥ syāttribhir guṇaiḥ ||

na—not; tat—that; asti—there is; pṛthivyām—within the universe; vā—or; divi—in the higher planetary system; deveṣu—amongst the demigods; vā—or; punaḥ—again; sattvam—existence; prakṛti-jaiḥ—under the influence of material nature; muktam—liberated; yat—that; ebhiḥ—by this; syāt—so becomes; tribhiḥ—by three; guṇaiḥ—modes of material nature.

Meaning: There is no being in existence, either on earth or among the demigods in heaven, that is free from these three attributes of material nature, O Arjuna.

41

ब्राह्मणक्षत्रियविशां
शूद्राणां च परन्तप।
कर्माणि प्रविभक्तानि
स्वभावप्रभवैर्गुणैः॥

brāhmaṇa-kṣatriya-viśāṁ
śūdrāṇāṁca parantapa
karmāṇi pravibhaktāni
svabhāva-prabhavairguṇaiḥ ||

brāhmaṇa—the brāhmaṇas; kṣatriya—the kṣatriyas; viśām—the vaiśyas; śūdrāṇām—the śūdras; ca—and; parantapa—O subduer of the enemies; karmāṇi—activities; pravibhaktāni—are divided; svabhāva—own nature; prabhavaiḥ—born of; guṇaiḥ—by the modes of material nature.

Meaning: The duties are divided among Brahmanas, Kshatriyas, Vaishyas, and Shudras according to the attributes that spring from their respective natures, O dismayer of foes.

42

शमो दमस्तपः शौचं
क्षान्तिरार्जवमेव च।
ज्ञानं विज्ञानमास्तिक्यं
ब्रह्मकर्म स्वभावजम्॥

śamo damas tapaḥ śaucaṁ
kṣāntir ārjavam eva ca
jñānaṁ vijñānamāstikyaṁ
brahma-karmasvabhāva-jam||

śamaḥ—peacefulness; damaḥ—self-control; tapaḥ—austerity; śaucam—purity; kṣāntiḥ—tolerance; ārjavam—honesty; eva—certainly; ca—and; jñānam—wisdom; vijñānam—knowledge; āstikyam—religiousness; brahma—of a brāhmaṇa; karma—duty; svabhāva-jam—born of his own nature.

Meaning: Harmonising of the internal and the external faculties, peacefulness, self-control, austerity, purity, tolerance, honesty, forgiveness, simplicity, wisdom, knowledge, and religiousness are the nature-born functions and qualities of the Brahmana.

43

शौर्यं तेजो धृतिर्दाक्ष्यं
युद्धे चाप्यपलायनम्।
दानमीश्वरभावश्च
क्षात्रं कर्म स्वभावजम्॥

śauryaṁ tejo dhṛtir dākṣyaṁ
yuddhe cāpyapalāyanam
dānamīśvara-bhāvaś ca
kṣātraṁ karma svabhāva-jam||

śauryam—heroism; tejaḥ—power; dhṛtiḥ—determination; dākṣyam—resourcefulness; yuddhe—in battle; ca—and; api—also; apalāyanam—not fleeing; dānam—generosity; īśvara—leadership; bhāvaḥ—nature; ca—and kṣātram-kṣatriya; karma—duty; svabhāva-jam—born of his own nature.

Meaning: The nature-born qualities and functions of the Kshatriya include heroism, power, energy, determination, resourcefulness, dexterity, courage in battle, generosity, charity, and leadership.

44

कृषिगौरक्ष्यवाणिज्यं
वैश्यकर्म स्वभावजम्।
परिचर्यात्मकं कर्म
शूद्रस्यापि स्वभावजम्।।

kṛṣi-go-rakṣya-vāṇijyaṁ
vaiśya-karmasvabhāva-jam
paricaryātmakaṁ karma
śūdrasyāpi svabhāva-jam||

kṛṣi—ploughing; go—cows; rakṣya—protection; vāṇijyam—trade; vaiśya—vaiśya; karma—duty; svabhāva-jam—born of his own nature; paricaryā service; ātmakam—nature; karma—duty; śūdrasya—of the śūdra; api —also; svabhāva-jam—born of his own nature.

Meaning: Farming, trade, business, and cattle-breeding are the nature-born functions of the Vaishya. The Shudras do the services of labour and service to the other groups.

45

स्वे स्वे कर्मण्यभिरतः
संसिद्धिं लभते नरः।
स्वकर्मनिरतः सिद्धिं
यथा विन्दति तच्छृणु॥

sve sve karmaṇy abhirataḥ
saṁsiddhiṁ labhate naraḥ
sva-karma-nirataḥ siddhiṁ
yathā vindati tacchṛṇu||

sve—own; sve—own; karmaṇi—in work; abhirataḥ—following; saṁsiddhim —perfection; labhate—achieves; naraḥ—a man; svakarma— by his own duty; nirataḥ—engaged; siddhim—perfection; yathā—as; vindati—attains, tat—that; śṛṇu—listen.

Meaning: By following and engaging in his characteristic function of work, each man gains success and perfection. Now, hear from Me how this can be achieved.

46

यतः प्रवृत्तिर्भूतानां
येन सर्वमिदं ततम्।
स्वकर्मणा तमभ्यर्च्य
सिद्धिं विन्दति मानवः॥

yataḥ pravṛttir bhūtānāṁ
yena sarvamidaṁ tatam
sva-karmaṇā tam abhyarcya
siddhiṁ vindati mānavaḥ||

yataḥ—from whom; pravṛttiḥ—emanation; bhūtānām—of all living entities; yena—by whom; sarvam—all; idam—this; tatam—is pervaded; svakarmaṇā—in his own duties; tam—Him; abhyarcya—by worshiping; siddhim—perfection; vindati—achieves; mānavaḥ—a man.

Meaning: Man can achieve success and attain perfection in the performance of his own duty by worshipping the Lord, who is the source of all things created and is all-pervading.

47

श्रेयान्स्वधर्मो विगुणः
परधर्मात्स्वनुष्ठितात्।
स्वभावनियतं कर्म
कुर्वन्नाप्नोति किल्बिषम्॥

śreyān sva-dharmo viguṇaḥ
para-dharmātsv-anuṣṭhitāt
svabhāva-niyataṁ karma
kurvannāpnoti kilbiṣam||

sreyān—better; sva-dharmaḥ—one's own occupation; viguṇaḥ—imperfectly performed; para-dharmāt—another's occupation; svanuṣṭhitāt perfectly done; svabhāva-niyatam—prescribed duties according to one's nature; karma—work; kurvan—performing; na—never; āpnoti—achieve; kilbiṣam—sinful reactions.

Meaning: It is better to engage in one's own characteristic duty or occupation, even though it is performed with imperfection rather than take up another's occupation and perform it perfectly. The performance of the prescribed duties which are nature-ordained incurs no sin.

48

सहजं कर्म कौन्तेय
सदोषमपि न त्यजेत्।
सर्वारम्भा हि दोषेण
धूमेनाग्निरिवावृताः॥

saha-jaṁ karma kaunteya
sa-doṣamapi natyajet
sarvārambhā hi doṣeṇa
dhūmenāgnirivā-vṛtāḥ||

saha-jam—born simultaneously; karma—work; kaunteya—O son of Kuntī; sa-doṣam—with fault; api—although; na—never; tyajet—to be given up; sarva-ārambhāḥ—any venture; hi—is certainly; doṣeṇa—with fault; dhūmena—with smoke; agniḥ—fire; iva—as; āvṛtāḥ—covered.

Meaning: O son of Kunti, every undertaking is enveloped by fault just like fire is enveloped by smoke. So, one should not renounce the prescribed duty or function which is born of his nature even though it may be faulty.

49

असक्तबुद्धिः सर्वत्र
जितात्मा विगतस्पृहः।
नैष्कर्म्यसिद्धिं परमां
सन्न्यासेनाधिगच्छति॥

asakta-buddhiḥ sarvatra
jitātmāvigata-spṛhaḥ
naiṣkarmya-siddhiṁ paramāṁ
sannyāsenādhigacchati ||

asakta-buddhiḥ—unattached intelligence; sarvatra—everywhere; jita- ātmā —control of the mind, vigata-spṛhaḥ—without material desires; naiṣkarmya- siddhim—perfection of non-reaction; paramām—supreme; sannyāsena—by the renounced order of life; adhigacchati—attains.

Meaning: One can achieve the results of renunciation by remaining unattached to material things, by being self-subdued, and without longings for material enjoyments. By doing this, he transcends to the highest perfection in renunciation.

50

सिद्धिं प्राप्तो यथा ब्रह्म
तथाप्नोति निबोध मे।
समासेनैव कौन्तेय
निष्ठा ज्ञानस्य या परा।।

siddhiṁ prāpto yathā brahma
tathāpnoti nibodha me
samāsenaiva kaunteya
niṣṭhā jñānasya yā parā ||

siddhim—perfection; prāptaḥ—achieving; yathā—as; brahma—the Supreme; tathā—so; āpnoti—achieves; nibodha—try to understand; me—from Me; samāsena—summarily; eva—certainly; kaunteya—O son of Kuntī; niṣṭhā—stage; jñānasya—of knowledge; yā—which; parā— transcendental.

Meaning: O son of Kunti, learn from me, briefly of course, how one can attain to the supreme stage of perfection and wisdom known as Brahman by acting in the way which I shall now summarise.

51-53

बुद्ध्या विशुद्धया युक्तो
धृत्यात्मानं नियम्य च।
शब्दादीन्विषयांस्त्यक्त्वा
रागद्वेषौ व्युदस्य च॥
विविक्तसेवी लघ्वाशी
यतवाक्कायमानसः।
ध्यानयोगपरो नित्यं
वैराग्यं समुपाश्रितः॥
अहङ्कारं बलं दर्पं
कामं क्रोधं परिग्रहम्।
विमुच्य निर्ममः शान्तो
ब्रह्मभूयाय कल्पते॥

buddhyā viśuddhayā yukto
dhṛtyātmānaṁ niyamyaca
śabdādīn viṣayāṁs tyaktvā
rāga-dveṣauvyudasyaca ||
vivikta-sevīlaghv-āśī
yata-vāk-kāya-mānasaḥ
dhyāna-yoga-paro nityaṁ
vairāgyaṁ samupāśritaḥ ||

ahaṅkāraṁ balaṁ darpaṁ
kāmaṁ krodhaṁ parigraham
vimucya nirmamaḥ śānto
brahma-bhūyāya kalpate||

buddhyā—by the intelligence; viśuddhayā—fully purified; yuktaḥ—such engagement; dhṛtyā—determination; ātmānam—self; niyamya—regulated; ca—also; śabdādīn—the sense objects, such as sound, etc.; viṣayān—sense objects; tyaktvā—giving up;rāga—attachments; dveṣau—hatred; vyudasya—having laid aside; ca—also; vivikta-sevī—living in a secluded place; laghu-āśī—eating a small quantity; yata-vāk—control of speech; kāya—body; mānasaḥ—control of the mind; dhyāna-yoga-paraḥ—always absorbed in trance; nityam—twenty-four hours a day; vairāgyam—detachment; samupāśritaḥ—taken shelter of; ahaṅkāram—false ego; balam—false strength; darpam—false pride; kāmam—lust; krodham—anger; parigraham—acceptance of material things; vimucya—being delivered; nirmamaḥ—without proprietorship; śāntaḥ—peaceful; brahma- bhūyāya—to become self-realised; kalpate—is understood.

Meaning: Purified with refined understanding, regulating the mind with determination, giving up sound and other sense-objects, growing free of attachment and hatred, living in an isolated place, eating little, and controlling the body, speech and mind, living in detachment and in a state of perpetual trance, without false ego, violence, false strength, arrogance, desire, anger, and lust, and one who does not accept material things, such a tranquil man is most certainly elevated to attain the position of Brahma-nature.

54

ब्रह्मभूतः प्रसन्नात्मा न
शोचति न काङ्क्षति।
समः सर्वेषु भूतेषु
मद्भक्तिं लभते पराम्।।

brahma-bhūtaḥ prasannātmā na
śocati na kāṅkṣati
samaḥ sarveṣu bhūteṣu
mad-bhaktiṁlabhateparām ||

brahma-bhūtaḥ—being one with the Absolute; prasanna-ātmā—fully joyful; na—never; śocati—laments; na—never; kāṅkṣati—desires; samaḥ—equally disposed; sarveṣu—all; bhūteṣu—living entity; mat-bhaktim—My devotional service; labhate—gains; parām—transcendental.

Meaning: The one who is thus transcendentally located instantly realises the Supreme Brahman. He does not grieve nor desires for anything ever again. He is equal in his behaviour to all creatures and attains supreme devotion in that state to Me.

55

भक्त्या मामभिजानाति
यावान्यश्चास्मि तत्त्वतः।
ततो मां तत्त्वतो ज्ञात्वा
विशते तदनन्तरम्॥

bhaktyā mām abhijānāti
yāvānyaścāsmitattvataḥ
tato māṁ tattvato jñātvā
viśatetad-anantaram||

bhaktyā—by pure devotional service; mām—Me; abhijānāti — one can know; yāvān—as much as; yaḥcaasmi — as I am; tattvataḥ—in truth; tataḥ —thereafter; mām — Me; tattvataḥ — by truth; jñātvā —knowing; viśate—enters; tat—thereafter; anantaram —after.

Meaning: He is instructed about Me in the course of his devotional service and understands the Supreme

Peronality in Me and when such devotion leads him to a state of full consciousness, he enters into My kingdom forever.

56

सर्वकर्माण्यपि सदा
कुर्वाणो मद्व्यपाश्रयः।
मत्प्रसादादवाप्नोति
शाश्वतं पदमव्ययम्।।

sarva-karmāṇy api sadā
kurvāṇomad-vyapāśrayaḥ
mat-prasādād avāpnoti
śāśvataṁ padamavyayam ||

sarva—all; karmāṇi—activities; api—although; sadā—always; kurvāṇaḥ —performing; mat—under My; vyapāśrayah—protection; mat—My; prasādāt —mercy; avāpnoti—achieves; sāśvatam—eternal; padam—abode; avyayam—imperishable.

Meaning: Even if My devotee is constantly performing all kinds of activities, if he is resigned to Me, he attains the gates of My eternal and imperishable kingdom because of My grace.

57

चेतसा सर्वकर्माणि मयि
सन्न्यस्य मत्परः।
बुद्धियोगमुपाश्रित्य
मच्चित्तः सततं भवः।।

cetasāsarva-karmāṇi mayi
sannyasyamat-paraḥ
buddhi-yogam upāśritya
mac-cittaḥ satataṁ bhava||

cetasā—by intelligence; sarva-karmāni—all kinds of activities; mayi
—unto Me; sannyasya—giving up; mat-paraḥ—My protection; buddhi-yogam—devotional activities; upāśritya—taking shelter of; mat-cittaḥ—consciousness; satatam—twenty-four hours a day; bhava—just become.

Meaning: Surrender all actions unto Me always, working under My protection, regarding Me as the Supreme One, and always fixing your mind on Me.

58

मच्चित्तः सर्वदुर्गाणि
मत्प्रसादात्तरिष्यसि।
अथ चेत्वमहाङ्कारान्न
श्रोष्यसि विनङ्क्ष्यसि॥

mac-cittaḥ sarva-durgāṇi
mat-prasādāttariṣyasi
atha cettvam-ahaṅkārānna
śroṣyasi vinaṅkṣyasi ||

mat—My; cittaḥ—consciousness; sarva—all; durgāṇi—impediments; mat—My; prasādāt—My mercy; tariṣyasi—you will overcome; atha—therefore; cet—if; tvam—you; ahaṅkārāt—by false ego; na—not; śroṣyasi—do not hear; vinaṅkṣyasi—then lose yourself.

Meaning: If you have your mind settled on Me always, you will cross all the difficult paths of conditional life that you traverse thanks to My grace. But, if you choose not to work in such divine consciousness, acting instead with false ego, without listening to Me, that will bring about your ruin.

59

यदहङ्कारमाश्रित्य न
योत्स्य इति मन्यसे ।
मिथ्यैष व्यवसायस्ते
प्रकृतिस्त्वां नियोक्ष्यति॥

yad ahaṅkāram āśritya na
yotsya iti manyase
mithyaiṣa vyavasāyas te
prakṛtistvāṁ niyokṣyati ||

yat—therefore; ahaṅkāram—false ego; āśritya—taking shelter; na—not; yotsya—shall fight; iti—thus; manyase—think; mithyāeṣaḥ—this is all false; vyavasāyahte—your determination; prakṛtiḥ—material nature; tvām—you; niyokṣyati—will engage you.

Meaning: If you choose not to fight, being sheltered in egoism and do not act according to My direction, your belief is false. It is your nature to fight and your nature will impel you to do so, O Arjuna.

60

स्वभावजेन कौन्तेय
निबद्धः स्वेन कर्मणा।
कर्तुं नेच्छसि यन्मोहा-
त्करिष्यस्यवशोऽपि तत्॥

svabhāva-jena kaunteya
nibaddhaḥ svenakarmaṇā
kartuṁ necchasi yanmohāt
kariṣyasy avaśo 'pi tat||

sva-bhāva-jena—by one's own nature; kaunteya—O son of Kuntī; nibaddhaḥ—conditioned; svena—by one's own; karmaṇā—activities; kartum—to do; na—not; icchasi—like; yat—that; mohāt—by illusion; kariṣyasi—you will act; avaśaḥ—imperceptibly; api—even; tat—that.

Meaning: As you are tied to your own nature-born function, O son of Kunti, you are powerless to perform the action which under the spell of illusion you do not wish to perform.

61

ईश्वरः सर्वभूतानां
हृद्देशेऽर्जुन तिष्ठति।
भ्रामयन्सर्वभूतानि
यन्त्रारुढानि मायया॥

īśvaraḥ sarva-bhūtānāṁ
hṛd-deśe›rjunatiṣṭhati
bhrāmayan sarva-bhūtāni
yantrārūḍhāni māyayā||

īśvaraḥ—the Supreme Lord; sarva-bhūtānām—of all living entities; hṛd- deśe—in the location of the heart; arjuna—O Arjuna; tiṣṭhati—resides; bhrāmayan—causing to travel; sarva-bhūtāni—all living entities; yantra—machine; ārūḍhāni—being so placed; māyayā—under the spell of material energy.

Meaning: O Arjuna, the Lord of all creatures dwells in everyone's heart, causing all the living creatures to wander with His Divine Power as if they are seated on a machine composed of the material energy.

62

तमेव शरणं गच्छ
सर्वभावेन भारत।
तत्प्रसादात्परां शान्तिं
स्थानं प्राप्स्यसि शाश्वतम्॥

tam eva śaraṇaṁ gaccha
sarva-bhāvenabhārata
tat-prasādāt parāṁ śāntiṁ
sthānaṁ prāpsyasi śāśvatam||

tam—unto Him; eva—certainly; śaraṇam—surrender; gaccha—go; sarva-bhāvena—in all respects; bhārata—O son of Bharata; tat-prasādāt—by His grace; parām—transcendental; śāntim—peace; sthānam—abode; prāpsyasi— you will get; śāśvatam—eternal.

Meaning: O son of Bharata, surrender to Him totally with all your nature. By His grace, you shall attain supreme peace and the eternal resting place.

63

इति ते ज्ञानमाख्यातं
गुह्याद्गुह्यतरं मया।
विमृश्यैतदशेषेण
यथेच्छसि तथा कुरु॥

iti te jñānam ākhyātaṁ
guhyādguhyataraṁ mayā
vimṛśyaitad aśeṣeṇa
yathecchasi tathā kuru||

iti—thus; te—unto you; jñānam—knowledge; ākhyātam—described; guhyāt—confidential; guhyataram—still more confidential; mayā—by Me; vimṛśya—by deliberation; etat—that; aśeṣeṇa—fully; yathā—as you; icchasi—you like; tathā—that; kuru—perform.

Meaning: Thus I have explained to you the wisdom which is the most confidential. Consider this knowledge fully, and then decide on your course of action.

64

सर्वगुह्यतमं भूतः
शृणु मे परमं वचः।
इष्टोऽसि मे दृढमिति
ततो वक्ष्यामि ते हितम्॥

sarva-guhyatamaṁ bhūyaḥ
śṛṇu me paramaṁ vacaḥ
iṣṭo'si me dṛḍhamiti
tato vakṣyāmi te hitam||

sarva-guhyatamam—the most confidential; bhūyaḥ—again; śṛṇu—just hear;me—from Me; paramam—the supreme; vacaḥ—instruction; istaḥasi—you are very dear to Me; dṛḍham—very; iti—thus; tataḥ—therefore; vakṣyāmi—speaking; te—for your; hitam—benefit.

Meaning: Listen to Me again as I share the greatest of all secrets, My last word. Because you are extremely dear to Me, therefore I speak for your own good.

65

मन्मना भव मद्भक्तो
मद्याजी मां नमस्कुरु।
मामेवैष्यसि सत्यं ते
प्रतिजाने प्रियोऽसि मे।।

man-manā bhava mad-bhakto
mad-yājī māṁ namaskuru
mām evaiṣyasi satyaṁ te
pratijāne priyo'sime||

man-manāḥ—thinking of Me; bhava—just become; mat-bhaktaḥ—My devotee; mat-yājī—My worshiper; mām—unto Me; namaskuru—offer your obeisances; mām—unto Me; eva—certainly; eṣyasi—come; satyam—truly; te—to you; pratijāne—I promise; prijaḥ—dear; asi—you are; me—My.

Meaning: Always fix your mind on Me, and devote yourself to Me, offer sacrifices to Me, make yourself humble before Me, and you shall come to Me without fail. I vow to you that you are very dear to Me.

66

सर्वधर्मान्परित्यज्य
मामेकं शरणं व्रज।
अहं त्वा सर्वपापेभ्यो
मोक्षयिष्यामि मा शुचः॥

sarva-dharmān parityajya
māmekaṁ śaraṇaṁ vraja
ahaṁ tvāṁ sarva-pāpebhyo
mokṣayiṣyāmi mā śucaḥ||

sarva-dharmān—all varieties of religion; parityajya—abandoning; mām—unto Me; ekam—only; śaraṇam—surrender;vraja—go; aham—I; tvām—you; sarva—all; pāpebhyaḥ—from sinful reactions; mokṣayiṣyāmi—deliver; mā—not; śucaḥ—worry.

Meaning: Renounce all duties and come to Me, the Sole Refuge. I shall release you from all sins. Fear not.

67

इदं ते नातपस्काय
नाभक्ताय कदाचन।
न चाशुश्रूषवे वाच्यं न
च मां योऽभ्यसूयति।।

idaṁ te nātapaskāya
nābhaktāya kadācana
nacāśuśrūṣave vācyaṁ
na ca māṁ yo'bhyasūyati ||

idam—this; te—you; na—never; atapaskāya—one who is not austere; na—never; abhaktāya—one who is not a devotee; kadācana—at any time; na—never; ca—also; aśuśrūṣave—one who is not engaged in devotional service; vācyam—to be spoken ; na—never; ca—also; mām—unto Me; yaḥ—anyone; abhyasūyati—envious.

Meaning: This confidential knowledge is for you and cannot be declared to the ones who are not austere, devoted, who do not engage in devotional service, or to someone who is envious of Me or dislikes Me.

68

य इदं परमं गुह्यं
मद्भक्तेष्वभिधास्यति।
भक्तिं मयि परां कृत्वा
मामेवैष्यत्यसंशयः॥

ya idaṁ paramaṁ guhyaṁ
mad-bhakteṣv-abhidhāsyati
bhaktiṁ mayi parāṁ kṛtvā
māmevaiṣyatya-saṁśayaḥ||

yaḥ—anyone; idam—this; paramam—most; guhyam—confidential; mat Mine; bhakteṣu—amongst devotees of; abhidhāsyati—explains; bhaktim devotional service; mayi—unto Me; parām—transcendental; kṛtvā —having done; mām—unto Me; eva—certainly; eṣyati—comes; asaṁśayaḥ —without doubt.

Meaning: The one that preaches this supreme secret among My devotees is guaranteed to be performing the highest devotion to Me and shall return to Me undoubtedly at the end.

69

न च तस्मान्मनुष्येषु
कश्चिन्मे प्रियकृत्तमः।
भविता न च मे तस्मा-
दन्यः प्रियतरो भुवि॥

na ca tasmān manuṣyeṣu
kaścinme priya-kṛttamaḥ
bhavitā na ca me tasmād
anyaḥ priyatarobhuvi ||

na—never; ca—and; tasmāt—therefore; manuṣyeṣu—among mankind; kaścit—anyone; me—My; priya-kṛttamaḥ—more dear; bhavitā—will become; na—no; ca—and; me—My; tasmāt—than him; anyaḥ—other; priyataraḥ— dearer; bhuvi—in this world.

Meaning: There will be no one in the world of men who will be doing a greater service to Me than him, and he shall be held dearer to Me than any other on earth.

70

अध्येष्यते च य इमं
धर्म्यं संवादमावयोः।
ज्ञानयज्ञेन तेनाहमिष्टः
स्यामिति मे मतिः॥

adhyeṣyate ca ya imaṁ
dharmyaṁ saṁvādam-āvayoḥ
jñāna-yajñena tenāham iṣṭaḥ
syāmiti me matiḥ||

adhyeṣyate—will study; ca—also; yaḥ—he; imam—this; dharmyaṁ—sacred; saṁvādam—conversation; āvayoḥ—of ours; jñāna—knowledge; yajñena—by sacrifice; tena—by him; aham—I; iṣṭaḥ—worshipped; syām—shall be; iti—thus; me—My; matiḥ—opinion.

Meaning: The one who will study this righteous discourse of ours shall be deemed to be worshipping Me with wisdom-sacrifice. That is My decree.

71

श्रद्धावाननसूयश्च
शृणुयादपि यो नरः।
सोऽपि मुक्तः शुभाँल्लोका-
न्प्राप्नुयात्पुण्य कर्मणाम्।।

śraddhāvān anasūyaś ca
śṛṇuyādapiyo naraḥ
so 'pi muktaḥ śubhāl lokān
prāpnuyātpuṇya-karmaṇām||

sraddhāvan—faithful; anasūyaḥ ca—and not envious; śṛṇuyāt—does hear; api—certainly; yaḥ—who; naraḥ—man; saḥapi—he also; muktaḥ—being liberated; śubhān—auspicious; lokān—planets; prāpnuyāt—attains; puṇya- karmaṇām—of the past.

Meaning: The one who merely listens to this sacred conversation of ours with faith and without dislike or envy, even he will become free from sinful reaction to attain the good worlds where the pious and virtuous dwell.

72

कच्चिदेतच्छ्रुतं पार्थ
त्वयैकाग्रेण चेतसा।
कच्चिदज्ञानसम्मोहः
प्रनष्टस्ते धनंजय।।

kaccidetacchrutaṁ pārtha
tvayaikāgreṇa cetasā
kaccid ajñāna-sammohaḥ
praṇaṣṭaste dhanañjaya||

kaccit—whether; etat—this; śrutam—heard; pārtha—O son of Pṛthā; tvayā—by you; ekāgreṇa—with full attention; cetasā—by the mind; kaccit—whether; ajñāna—ignorant; saṁmohaḥ—illusion; praṇaṣṭaḥ—dispelled; te—of you; dhanañjaya—O conqueror of wealth (Arjuna).

Meaning: O Partha, have you listened to my words with single-pointed attention? Are your illusions and ignorance now dispelled, O conquerer of wealth?

73

अर्जुन उवाच
नष्टो मोहः स्मृतिर्लब्धा
त्वत्प्रसादान्मयाच्युत।
स्थितोऽस्मि गतसंदेहः
करिष्ये वचनं तव।।

arjunauvāca
naṣṭo mohaḥ smṛtir labdhā
tvat-prasādānmayācyuta
sthito 'smi gata-sandehaḥ
kariṣye vacanaṁ tava||

arjunaḥuvāca—Arjuna said; naṣṭaḥ—dispelled; mohaḥ—illusion; smṛtiḥ —memory; labdhā—regained; tvat-prasādāt—by Your mercy; mayā—by me; acyuta—O infallible Kṛṣṇa; sthitaḥ—situated; asmi—I am; gata—removed; sandehaḥ—all doubts; kariṣye—I shall execute; vacanam—order; tava—Your.

Meaning: Arjuna said: My illusion is now destroyed, O Unfallen One. Thanks to Your grace and mercy, I have managed to recollect myself. I am now resolute and free from all doubts. I am prepared to do Your bidding.

74

संजय उवाच
इत्यहं वासुदेवस्य
पार्थस्य च महात्मनः।
संवादमिममश्रौष-
मद्भुतं रोमहर्षणम्॥

sañjaya uvāca
ity ahaṁ vāsudevasya
pārthasyacamahātmanaḥ
saṁvādam imam aśrauṣam
adbhutaṁroma-harṣaṇam

sañjayaḥ uvāca—Sañjaya said; iti—thus; aham—I; vāsudevasya—of Kṛṣṇa; pārthasya—of Arjuna; ca—also; mahātmanaḥ—two great souls; saṁvādam—discussing; imam—this; aśrauṣam—heard; adbhutam—wonder; romaharṣaṇam—hair standing on end.

Meaning: Sanjaya said: Thus, have I heard the conversation between the two great souls, Lord Krishna and the great-souled Arjuna. This marvellous discourse has such a wonderful message that my hair stands on end after listening to it.

75

व्यासप्रसादाच्छ्रुत-
वानेतद्गुह्यमहं परम्।
योगं योगेश्वरात्कृष्णा-
त्साक्षात्कथयतः स्वयम्।।

vyāsa-prasādāc chruta
vānetadguhy-amahaṁ param
yogaṁ yogeśvarāt kṛṣṇāt
sākṣātkathayataḥs vayam||

vyāsa-prasādāt—by the mercy of Vyāsadeva; śrutavān—heard; etat—this; guhyam—confidential; aham—I; param—the supreme; yogam—mysticism; yogeśvarāt—from the master of all mysticism; kṛṣṇāt—from Kṛṣṇa; sākṣāt— directly; kathayataḥ—speaking; svayam—personally.

Meaning: Through the grace of Vyasa I have heard this highest secret, the Yoga, directly from the Lord of Yoga, the master of all mysticism when he Himself taught Arjuna personally in my presence.

76

राजन्संस्मृत्य संस्मृत्य
संवादमिममद्भुतम्।
केशवार्जुनयोः पुण्यं
हृष्यामि च मुहुर्मुहुः॥

rājan saṁsmṛtya saṁsmṛtya
saṁvādamimam-adbhutam
keśavārjunayoḥ puṇyaṁ
hṛṣyāmi ca muhurmuhuḥ||

rājan—O King; saṁsmṛtya—remembering; saṁsmṛtya—remembering; saṁvādam—message; imam—this; adbhutam—wonderful; keśava—Lord Kṛṣṇa; arjunayoḥ—and Arjuna; puṇyam—pious; hṛṣyāmi—taking pleasure; ca—also; muhuḥ muhuḥ—always, repeatedly.

Meaning: O King, recalling this wondrous and holy dialogue between Lord Krishna and Arjuna repeatedly, I rejoice again and again.

77

तच्च संस्मृत्य संस्मृत्य
रूपमत्यद्भुतं हरेः।
विस्मयो मे महान् राज-
न्हृष्यामि च पुनः पुनः॥

tac ca saṁsmṛtya saṁsmṛtya
rūpamaty-adbhutaṁhareḥ
vismayo me mahān rājan
hṛṣyāmi ca punaḥ punaḥ ||

tat—that; ca—also; saṁsmṛtya—remembering; saṁsmṛtya—remembering; rūpam—form; ati—great; adbhutam—wonderful; hareḥ— of Lord Kṛṣṇa; vismayaḥ—wonder; me—my; mahān—great; rājan—O King, hṛṣyāmi—enjoying; ca—also; punaḥ punaḥ—repeatedly.

Meaning: O King, repeatedly remembering the most marvellous and wonderful Form of Lord Krishna, I am struck with even greater wonder, and I rejoice again and again.

78

यत्र योगेश्वरः कृष्णो
यत्र पार्थो धनुर्धरः।
तत्र श्रीर्विजयो भूति-
र्ध्रुवा नीतिर्मतिर्मम।।

yatra yogeśvaraḥ kṛṣṇo
yatra pārtho dhanur-dharaḥ
tatra śrīr vijayo bhūtir
dhruvā nītir-matirmama||

yatra—where; yogeśvaraḥ—the master of mysticism; kṛṣṇaḥ—Lord Krṣna; yatra—where; pārthaḥ—the son of Pṛthā; dhanur-dharaḥ—the carrier of the bow and arrow; tatra—there; śrīḥ—opulence; vijayaḥ—victory; bhūtiḥ— exceptional power; dhruvā—certainly; nītiḥ—morality; matiḥ mama—is my opinion.

Meaning: Wherever there is Lord Krishna, the master of all mystics and combinations, and wherever there is Arjuna, the supreme wielder of the bow, there, I am convinced, would be victory, glory, extraordinary power, opulence, and firm morality.

ॐ तत्सदिति श्रीमद्भगवद्गीतासूपनिषत्सु ब्रह्मविद्यायां योगशास्त्रे

श्रीकृष्णार्जुनसंवादे मोक्षसन्न्यासयोगो नामाष्टादशोऽध्यायः।

Thus, in the Upanishad of the Glorious Divine Lay, the Science of Brahma, the Ordinance of Yoga, the Discourse between the Glorious Lord Krishna and Arjuna, the Eighteenth Chapter entitled 'Moksha Sannyasa Yoga' (The Yoga of Liberation Through Renunciation).

78

यत्र योगेश्वरः कृष्णो
यत्र पार्थो धनुर्धरः।
तत्र श्रीर्विजयो भूति-
र्ध्रुवा नीतिर्मतिर्मम॥

yatra yogeśvaraḥ kṛṣṇo
yatra pārtho dhanur-dharaḥ
tatra śrīr vijayo bhūtir
dhruvā nītir-matirmama||

yatra—where; yogeśvaraḥ—the master of mysticism; kṛṣṇaḥ—Lord Krṣna; yatra—where; pārthaḥ—the son of Pṛthā; dhanur-dharaḥ—the carrier of the bow and arrow; tatra—there; śrīḥ—opulence; vijayaḥ—victory; bhūtiḥ— exceptional power; dhruvā—certainly; nītiḥ—morality; matiḥ mama—is my opinion.

Meaning: Wherever there is Lord Krishna, the master of all mystics and combinations, and wherever there is Arjuna, the supreme wielder of the bow, there, I am convinced, would be victory, glory, extraordinary power, opulence, and firm morality.

ॐ तत्सदिति श्रीमद्भगवद्गीतासूपनिषत्सु ब्रह्मविद्यायां योगशास्त्रे

श्रीकृष्णार्जुनसंवादे मोक्षसन्न्यासयोगो नामाष्टादशोऽध्यायः।

Thus, in the Upanishad of the Glorious Divine Lay, the Science of Brahma, the Ordinance of Yoga, the Discourse between the Glorious Lord Krishna and Arjuna, the Eighteenth Chapter entitled 'Moksha Sannyasa Yoga' (The Yoga of Liberation Through Renunciation).